ANGLO-SAXON
ARCHITECTURE

ANGLO-SAXON ARCHITECTURE

BY

H. M. TAYLOR

formerly Vice-Chancellor, University of Keele, and
Honorary Fellow of Clare College, Cambridge

AND

JOAN TAYLOR

formerly of Girton College, Cambridge

VOLUME II

CAMBRIDGE UNIVERSITY PRESS

Cambridge

London   New York   New Rochelle
Melbourne   Sydney

Published by the Press Syndicate of the University of Cambridge
The Pitt Building, Trumpington Street, Cambridge CB2 1RP
32 East 57th Street, New York, NY 10022, USA
296 Beaconsfield Parade, Middle Park, Melbourne 3206, Australia

First published 1965
First paperback edition 1980

Printed in Great Britain at the
University Press, Cambridge

British Library Cataloguing in Publication Data
Anglo-Saxon architecture.
    1. Church architecture – England
    2. Architecture, Anglo-Saxon
    I. Taylor, Harold McCarter
    II. Taylor, Joan
    726'.5'0942   NA5463   65-3244

ISBN 0 521 29914 4 paperback set of Volumes I and II
The volumes are also issued in hard covers
ISBN 0 521 06611 5 Volumes I and II
ISBN 0 521 21692 3 Volume III

DETAILED DESCRIPTIONS OF
INDIVIDUAL CHURCHES
CONTINUED

PADDLESWORTH

Kent

Map sheet 173, reference TR 195397

ST OSWALD

Main fabric: Saxo-Norman

A church at Paddlesworth is mentioned in Domesday Book; its dedication to St Oswald is unusual in southern England; but it is close to Lyminge, where a nunnery was founded in the seventh century by St Ethelburg, widow of King Edwin of Northumbria, St Oswald's predecessor in that Kingdom.

The present church, picturesquely standing in the midst of open fields on the Downs, about 3 miles north-west of Folkestone, is almost certainly a post-Conquest structure, but nevertheless has strong Anglo-Saxon affinities. These may be seen in the monolithic jambs and pseudo-arched, monolithic, round heads of the three small original windows of the nave. By contrast, the south doorway of the nave and the chancel-arch show marked and well-developed Norman technique, while the north doorway is of the type so common in the Saxo-Norman churches of the Cotswolds, with a flat lintel above which a semi-circular tympanum is enclosed beneath a semi-circular arched head.

DIMENSIONS

The nave is 34 ft long by 17 ft wide internally, and the chancel about 13 ft by 10 ft with walls 2 ft 8 in. thick. The chancel-arch is 6 ft 6 in. wide and 11 ft high.

PATTISHALL

Northamptonshire

Map sheet 146, reference SP 671542

HOLY CROSS

Nave: period C

About 4 miles north-west of Towcester, and less than a mile east of Watling Street, the small church of the Holy Cross at Pattishall has retained parts of the main fabric of its aisleless Anglo-Saxon nave within a later church which now consists of an aisled nave and chancel, with a west tower. The principal evidence of the pre-Conquest date of the nave is provided by the well-defined north-west quoin, whose original long-and-short construction remains beyond doubt even although three of the short stones have been disturbed from their original position and used to bond the medieval aisle wall into the Anglo-Saxon nave. There are vestiges of similar quoining at the north-east angle of the nave, above the roof of the aisle. The lower part of this quoin is inside a north chapel, now used as the vestry, but its character is wholly concealed beneath plaster. At the south-east of the nave, the quoin appears to have been rebuilt, but the walling seems to be largely original, and stands on a plain square plinth. A short section of the original walling of the chancel has also survived at this point.

A blocked, round-headed doorway in the north wall of the north aisle is clearly much earlier than the wall in which it stands; but, although it is clear that it has been re-erected here after removal from an earlier position, its detail does not settle its date with certainty as between Anglo-Saxon or early Norman. Its jambs have some suggestions of 'Escomb technique' but have been chamfered on their exterior angles, perhaps at a later date; the imposts are chamfered, and have a lightly incised ornament on their vertical faces; the round head is arched in ten well-laid voussoirs; and the head is outlined by a hood-moulding of half-round section.

In the interior, the chief feature of interest is the

483

chancel-arch, a round-headed opening of two square orders enclosed beneath a simple chamfered hood-moulding. The inner order is recessed about $\frac{1}{2}$ in. behind the outer order, and three or four of its stones are through-stones. Moreover, the whole of the soffit of the arch and jambs is lined with dressed stone. The imposts are returned along the faces of the wall far enough to stop the hood-moulding. They are different in section on the two sides of the arch, and are enriched with incised ornament which on the chamfered lower faces takes the form of upright and inverted triangles. The north impost has no other incised ornament but that on the south has on its vertical face a series of arcs of circles so arranged as to form an arcade of *pointed* arches. The jambs are of plain square section with chamfered bases, which project only on the soffit.

A tall, narrow, round-headed doorway opening westward from the nave into the tower seems to be early in character, but has been so much modified in later times as to give no reliable indication of date.

DIMENSIONS

The nave is 45 ft long internally and varies in width from 17 ft 7 in. at the west to 18 ft at the east. Its side walls are 3 ft 1 in. thick and are now 25 ft high.

The chancel-arch is 8 ft 10 in. wide and 14 ft 9 in. high, in a wall 2 ft 11½ in. thick. The doorway in the north wall of the aisle is 2 ft 9 in. wide externally and 7 ft 6 in. high, while the corresponding rear-arch internally is 3 ft 5 in. wide and 9 ft 4 in. tall.

REFERENCE

R. P. BRERETON, 'Notes on some unrecorded Saxon work in and near Northamptonshire', *A.A.S.R.* **27** (1903–4), 397–400. Pattishall, 399.

PAXTON, GREAT

Huntingdonshire

Map sheet 134, reference TL 210642

Figures 547–9

HOLY TRINITY

Nave and crossing of a formerly cruciform aisled church with clear-storey: period C3

The transeptal, aisled church of the Holy Trinity at Great Paxton, about 3 miles north of St Neots and 5 south of Huntingdon, possesses many features of outstanding interest which have not in the past received as much attention as they deserve. The most prominent feature is the fifteenth-century tower; and at first sight the aisled nave and aisleless chancel may appear to be of the same date, but a good indication of the earlier date of the main walls of the nave is given by the round-headed, double-splayed windows of the clear-storey. The fabric is mainly of stone rubble, with some large blocks of undressed stone in the walls, and dressed stone for quoins and facings. In each of the north and south walls of the nave, two complete clear-storey windows remain, with the blocked outline of half a similar window against the tower to show that the original nave was at least one bay longer to the west. From the north side of the churchyard the old height and alignment of the north transept is made clear by the gabled roof, which now covers the eastern bay of the north aisle. The Royal Commission on Historical Monuments reported that probing to the north of the church indicated that the transept originally extended about 10 ft further to the north.[1]

Domesday Book records a church and a priest at Great Paxton; it also records that Edward the Confessor held the manor before the Conquest, and that it was at the time of the survey in the hands of Countess Judith, widow of Earl Waltheof. The character of the church is consistent with its having been erected by Edward. To visualize the church as it then existed, one must imagine the west tower removed, and the nave continued west so as to cover much the same area of ground; the transepts would be roofed with gables like that still existing on the north side, but extending wider from the nave; and the aisles would be narrower than at present. It is not now possible to say with certainty whether the central crossing carried a stone tower as at Norton, County Durham, or whether there was a wooden

[1] *R.C.H.M., Huntingdonshire* (London, 1926), 198.

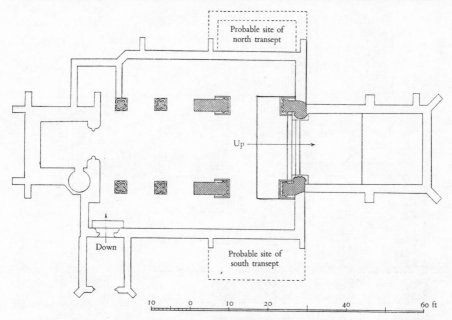

FIG. 236. GREAT PAXTON, HUNTINGDONSHIRE

Plan showing the arcades of the Anglo-Saxon nave in relation to the much later church as it stands at present. The outer walls of the Anglo-Saxon aisled nave have disappeared, but the main walls still stand over the original arcades. Only two arches remain in each of the arcades, but fragments of a third are preserved at the west, and it seems likely that the later medieval tower stands on the ground originally occupied by the western part of the nave. If this is so, there would originally have been four arches on each side of the nave.

superstructure such as may now be seen at Breamore, Hampshire. We think that the latter is much more likely.

Returning now to the present building, it will be noted that the clear-storey windows are unusually wide and high, with heads carefully turned in blocks of brownish ironstone, a substance which is used elsewhere in the walls, more particularly towards the top. A horizontal string-course which runs along the south wall about the level of the middle of the windows must be a later insertion, as is shown by its crossing the blocked western window. Parts of an original string-course, however, remain on both north and south walls, lower down, below the sills of the windows, and now not visible from the ground. This original string-course is of the same simple chamfered section as the string-course which remains within the nave. The eastern quoins of the nave are possibly original, although they

present no Anglo-Saxon characteristics except perhaps the large stones that are used, particularly in the upper part of the north-east angle. Of the original walls of the aisles and chancel nothing seems to remain; the present walls of the aisles appear to date from the fifteenth century or later, when the transepts were destroyed; while the western part of the chancel was apparently rebuilt late in the thirteenth century, and an eastward extension was built in the fifteenth century.

The interior of the church is most attractive, quite apart from its interest as a unique pre-Conquest monument. The very high walls of the nave, 3 ft in thickness, are carried on an arcade of round arches of two square orders, themselves carried on a line of delicately moulded piers each of which is fundamentally of square outline, but is formed of four half-round attached shafts separated by fillets. The four shafts of each pier are provided with individual, annular, moulded

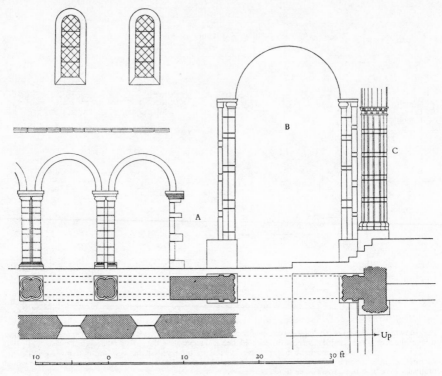

FIG. 237. GREAT PAXTON, HUNTINGDONSHIRE

Elevation of the north wall of the nave, with plans at the levels of the arcade and of the double-splayed windows. Note the massive pier (A) at the east of the arcade, to separate it from the great arch (B) which led to the north transept. Of the three (or possibly four) arches at the crossing only this one has survived. Note also that the jambs (C) of the chancel-arch have survived and are of through-stones, as are the jambs of the arches leading to the transepts.

bases, resting on a single square plinth; while at the top they have individual, bulbous capitals, which support a single abacus, in the form of two superimposed overlapping square blocks.

The plain square responds at the east of each arcade are built of large slabs of stone extending through the full thickness of the wall and laid alternately upright and flat in 'Escomb fashion'. Each respond carries a boldly projecting impost about 1 ft in depth, square in section above, and with its chamfered lower part carrying a series of recessed mouldings, all of which are returned about 2 ft along both faces of the wall.

A little above the heads of the arches of the arcade, a chamfered string-course runs along the walls from the west, to points roughly above the eastern responds, where the Royal Commission suggest that it was stopped by a return wall which carried a western arch of the crossing. This wall and arch no longer exist, but the stopping of the string-course and a roughness of the inner walls of the nave give some evidence in support of their former existence. To complete the description of the walls it should be added that the clear-storey windows, with sills about 24 ft above the floor, are aligned above the arches of the arcade in accordance with Norman and medieval practice. At Brixworth and Lydd, on the other hand, the only other Anglo-Saxon aisled churches whose clear-storey windows are still visible, the upper windows are aligned above the piers.

The crossing has retained much of its original

486

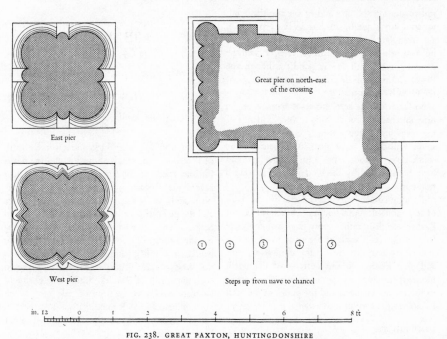

East pier

West pier

Great pier on north-east
of the crossing

Steps up from nave to chancel

in. 12   0   1   2   4   6   8 ft

FIG. 238. GREAT PAXTON, HUNTINGDONSHIRE

Plans of the east and west piers of the arcades of the nave, and plan of one of the great piers of the crossing.

grandeur, although of its original arches all but the northern one have been altered or removed. This northern round arch of a single square order is unfortunately now plastered so that its construction is hidden, but its noble scale makes it an impressive feature. Its jambs, like the responds of the arcades, are built of massive stones, spanning the full thickness of the wall and laid in 'Escomb fashion'; but here they are ornamentally moulded to represent four vertical half-round shafts separated by three roll-mouldings. The shafts, springing from a common, square, very tall base, have separate bulbous capitals, which support a single square impost for the arch. On the return walls of the nave and the aisle, a square pilaster-strip was originally carried up the whole height from the base to the impost; but on the north face it has now been largely cut away. A similar arch must originally have opened to the south transept; but this has been removed, and its jambs, otherwise similar to those on the north, have been lowered several feet to

carry a pointed medieval arch of three chamfered orders.

The chancel is approached from the level of the nave by a flight of no less than five steps, one of which is within the body of the crossing and four at the chancel-arch. This arrangement appears to be original, because the bases of the eastern jambs of the arches of the transepts are higher than their fellows to the west by the amount of the one step; while the bases of the jambs of the chancel-arch are higher again by the amount of the further four steps. The chancel-arch itself has been replaced in medieval times by an arch similar to that opening to the south transept; but the jambs are original, and of great elaboration, consisting of six flattish shafts separated by fillets and arranged in plan on a convex curve. These ornamental mouldings are, like those of the other jambs, cut on massive stones running through the full thickness of the wall and in general laid alternately upright and flat. The shafts have individual moulded bases, standing on a common square massive plinth; and at the top they end, without any capitals, on curious imposts, which are irregularly carved with something akin to billet ornament. These imposts might well be contemporary with the responds, although the Royal Commission describe them as probably of the twelfth century.

So far as can be seen, no trace remains of the original chancel, but there is further evidence of the transepts in the irregular outer face of the south wall of the nave, near its east end, in the south aisle, at about the point where it would have been joined by the west wall of the south transept.

To summarize, therefore, the structural remains of the mid-eleventh-century church at Great Paxton comprise rather more than two complete bays of the main walls of the nave, with arcades and clear-storey windows; the complete jambs and arch leading to the remains of the north transept; the steps and jambs of the arch leading to the former chancel; and the jambs of the arch leading to the former south transept.

DIMENSIONS

The nave of two and a half bays is about 30 ft long and 18 ft broad, with walls 3 ft thick and 38 ft high. The crossing is about 18 ft square, and the arch to the north transept is about 14 ft in span and about 30 ft high to the crown. The piers of the arcade are spaced at roughly 10 ft between centres, with arches about 14 ft 6 in. to the crown; and the clear-storey windows have apertures 2 ft 4 in. broad and about 8 ft high, with their sills about 24 ft above the floor. The surviving jambs of the chancel-arch define an opening 15 ft wide. Their imposts are 20 ft 6 in. above the floor of the nave.

REFERENCES

A. G. CANE, 'Great Paxton'. *T. Cambs. Hunts. Arch. Soc.* **2** (1904–7), 33–45. General descriptive account, in which the church is described as Saxon of not very early date.

L. COBBETT and C. FOX 'The Saxon church of Great Paxton', *P. Camb. Ant. Soc.* **25** (1922–3), 50–77. This is by far the most complete published account of Great Paxton church. The account which we have given above owes much to it.

R.C.H.M., *Huntingdonshire* (London, 1926), 198–200. Plan, 199.

PEAKIRK

Northamptonshire

Map sheet 123, reference TF 168067

ST PEGA

Nave walls, cut through by later arcades: period C

The small village of Peakirk, about 5 miles north of Peterborough, stands about a mile east of the Lincoln road, within a wide sweep of the Car Dyke, the Roman canal which connected the Nene and the Witham. The name of the village and the dedication of its church both derive from St Pega who, after burying her brother St Guthlac, the founder of Crowland Abbey, is reputed to have lived a solitary life in a cell four leagues to the west of Crowland, traditionally associated with the village of Peakirk. Little reliance should be placed on a late Crowland tale that, when on a pilgrimage to Rome, St Pega died there in 716 and was buried in a church dedicated in her honour.

The church now consists of an aisled nave and an aisleless chancel, with a small north chapel which continues the north aisle of the nave eastward for one bay. The north arcade of the nave is of well-developed Norman work, the south arcade is Early English, and the chancel-arch is of an intermediate transitional style. It is, however, abundantly clear that the fabric of the nave through which these arches have been cut is of late-Saxon date. In the angle between the south aisle and the chancel, the south-east quoin of the nave may be seen outside the church to be a good example of long-and-short technique, with four pairs of stones of which the longs average 2 ft 9 in. and the shorts about 7 in. A similar quoin, somewhat obscured by plaster, may be seen at the north-east angle of the nave, within the north-east chapel.

The fabric of the nave is everywhere covered by plaster, except for the two quoins already mentioned and the external face of the west wall, which is of roughly squared stones. But the north-west quoin is completely covered by a later buttress and the south-west quoin appears to be of side-alternate construction, so that it is not apparent that the west wall is necessarily of the same date as the eastern part of the nave. Nevertheless, the long narrow proportions of the nave and its very thin walls confirm the evidence of Anglo-Saxon date given by its eastern quoins.

Other features of interest are the fine medieval mural paintings on the north walls of the nave and the north aisle, and the Norman south door with delicately carved arch and tympanum.

DIMENSIONS

The nave is 37 ft 2 in. long internally, and its width varies from 13 ft 2 in. at the west to 14 ft at the east. The chancel is about a foot narrower than the nave, and substantial sections of the side walls of both nave and chancel remain as responds beside the northern jamb of the chancel-arch. These walls are 2 ft 4 in. in thickness, and those of the nave are about 14 ft high to the top of the original quoining.

REFERENCES

G. PATRICK, 'Some account of Peakirk, Northamptonshire', *J.B.A.A.* **55** (1899), 215–21.

E. C. ROUSE 'Wall paintings in the church of St Pega, Peakirk, Northamptonshire', *Arch. J.* **110** (1953), 135–49. Very full account of the wall paintings. Plan, 136. Saxon nature of south–east quoin questioned, 137.

PECKHAM, WEST
Kent
Map sheet 171, reference TQ 644525

ST DUNSTAN

West tower, and west wall of nave: possibly period C

The small village of West Peckham, about 5 miles north-east of Tonbridge, has two interesting manors of which one is of Georgian red brick while the other is probably Tudor, with half-timbered walls and pargeted gables. The church, at the west of the village, now consists of a low west tower, a nave with north aisle and south porch, and a chancel with a north aisle which contains an upper-level chamber beautifully furnished as a squire's pew, with very fine renaissance woodwork.

The earliest part of the church is the west tower and the adjoining west wall of the nave. The fabric is of rough rubble of greyish brown hue, with larger pieces of the same stone used for the quoining, in which the stones are not dressed but are laid on their faces. The tower is square and unbuttressed, with early windows in the north and south faces on the ground floor, and in the north, west, and south faces in the upper floor. The upper windows are round-headed, single-splayed openings, with the splay carried through the full thickness of the wall to the outer face. Their jambs and arched heads are wholly formed of the same rough rubble as the walls themselves. The lower windows, by contrast, are double-splayed; that on the north has been much modified in later times, but that on the south seems to be in its original form, wholly constructed of the same rough rubble as the walling.

The west face of the tower has a much later medieval west doorway, and the tower-arch seems to be of quite modern construction, perhaps widened when the tower was brought into use as a baptistry.

DIMENSIONS

The tower is roughly 14 ft square internally, with walls 3 ft 7 in. thick. The double-splayed south window has an aperture 1 ft 2 in. wide and 6 ft tall, splayed to 3 ft 3 in. by nearly 8 ft, with its interior sill 5 ft above the floor. The upper windows are about 3 ft wide externally and about 5 ft tall, with their sills about 20 ft above the ground.

PENTLOW
Essex
Map sheet 149, reference TL 812461
Figure 550

ST GEORGE AND ST GREGORY
Nave and apsidal chancel: Saxo-Norman

The adjoining villages of Cavendish, in Suffolk, and Pentlow, in Essex, are separated by the River Stour, which here forms the boundary between the two counties, about 5 miles north-west of Sudbury. The church, mainly built of uncut

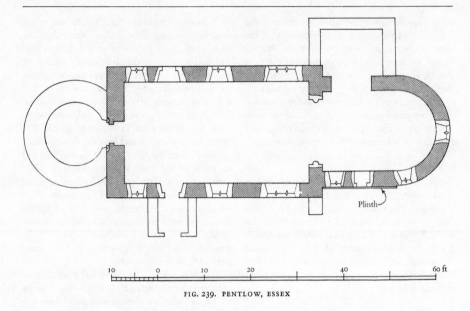

FIG. 239. PENTLOW, ESSEX

in. 12   0   1   2   3   4   5 ft

FIG. 240. PENTLOW, ESSEX

Elevation and plan of the west doorway. The left-hand part of the plan is at the level of the jambs, and the right-hand part is at the level of the springing of the arch. The diagrams show how the doorway is partially obscured by the west tower and how the Norman cushion capitals are not correctly integrated into the composition.

flints, consists of a round west tower, an aisleless nave with south porch, and an aisleless, apsidal chancel with large north chapel. The earliest parts of the church are the nave and the chancel, for it is clear that the tower has been built later against the west wall of the nave, where it partially obscures the pleasant mouldings of the round head of the Norman outer facing of the original west doorway.

The history of the west wall of the nave is complicated and interesting. The original west doorway is tall and narrow, with a later outer face built to the west of it, showing a straight vertical joint where the two meet. Both openings are round-headed, and the western one is both wider and taller, so as to outline the original and simpler one to the east. The western opening has free-standing angle-shafts with mitred cushion capitals; these in turn carry tall chamfered imposts which are enriched with diaper ornament and which themselves support the arch, orna-mented with an angle-roll on its western arris. The earlier eastern arch is of plain square section, with simple chamfered imposts and plain square jambs. The round tower which obscures the outer mouldings of the doorway seems itself to be of Norman date, with later work in its upper stages. The outer arch of the west doorway is clearly Norman, but presumably therefore not of late-Norman date; and the original eastern part of the doorway must therefore be either early Norman or pre-Norman.

An Anglo-Saxon or Saxo-Norman date for the nave and chancel is supported by the plain flint quoins at the western angles of the nave and at the south-eastern angle of the straight south wall of the chancel, where the wall is set back slightly at the springing of the curve of the apse.

DIMENSIONS

The nave is 39 ft 9 in. long internally, and its width varies from 21 ft 2 in. at the east to 20 ft 8 in. at the west. Its side walls are 3 ft thick and about 16 ft tall. The chancel is 16 ft 8 in. wide and 26 ft long internally. The west tower is 13 ft 3 in. in internal diameter, with walls about 4 ft 6 in. thick.

The clear opening of the original west doorway is 3 ft 7 in. wide and 9 ft 2 in. tall. It is rebated on the east for the hanging of the door.

PETERBOROUGH

Northamptonshire

Map sheet 134, reference TL 194986

CATHEDRAL CHURCH OF ST PETER, ST PAUL AND ST ANDREW

Foundations and lower courses of walls of earlier transepts and chancel, beneath floor of present cathedral: period C1, possibly with remains of period A2

HISTORY

In attempting to reconstruct the history of the Anglo-Saxon monastery of *Medeshamstede*, at Peterborough, it is important to distinguish between the early records, such as those of Bede, which represent almost first-hand information, and the much later and more elaborate accounts, which were correspondingly less reliable. An important review of the evidence which is provided by charters has been given by Sir Frank Stenton, and reference should be made to it for a more detailed account than is given below.[1]

Bede (*H.E.* IV, 6) records that not long after the synod which was held at Hertford in 673 Archbishop Theodore appointed as bishop of the Mercians Sexwulf, who was the founder and abbot of the monastery in the region of the *Gyrwe* which is called *Medeshamstede*. Bede does not give a precise date for the foundation, but it must have been after the Middle Angles received Christianity in 653, and it must have been some time before Sexwulf was made bishop of the Mercians.[2]

Under the year 870, the early texts of the *Anglo-Saxon Chronicle* record that the Danes took up winter quarters at Thetford, that King Edmund fought against them, and that the Danes had the victory and killed the king and conquered all the land. The Peterborough additions to the *Chronicle* include the statement that the Danes came to the monastery at *Medeshamstede* and burned and destroyed it, and killed the abbot and the monks and all they found there.[3] A reliable contemporary account of the refoundation by Ethelwold is given in Aelfric's *Life* of that bishop;[4] and a less reliable account in much greater detail is given in the Peterborough additions to the *Chronicle* under the year 963.

In 1070 the *Chronicle* records a disastrous raiding of the monastery by Hereward and his men, who came to plunder it because they had heard that the king had given the abbacy to a Frenchman called Turold. The account includes a detail which is of particular interest in connexion with architectural history, namely, the statement that the raiders climbed up the tower and brought down the altar-frontal of gold and silver that was hidden there.

---

[1] F. M. Stenton, 'Medeshamstede and its Colonies', *Historical Essays in honour of James Tait*, ed. J. G. Edwards, V. H. Galbraith, and E. F. Jacob (Manchester, 1933), 313–26.

[2] F. M. Stenton, *loc. cit.* 313, gives reasons for believing that the foundation must have been some considerable time before Sexwulf was made a bishop. The Peter-

borough insertions in the *Anglo-Saxon Chronicle* boldly claim foundation in the year 654 by Peada; they also claim support and enrichment by Wulfhere after Peada's death.

[3] D. Whitelock, *E.H.D.* (1955), 177.

[4] D. Whitelock, *loc. cit.* 836.

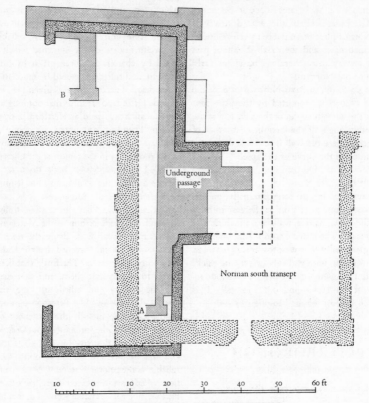

B

Underground
passage

Norman south transept

A

|10 0 10 20 30 40 50 60 ft|

FIG. 241. PETERBOROUGH, NORTHAMPTONSHIRE

Plan of the Anglo-Saxon foundations and of the Norman south transept. The underground passage was constructed during the repairs of 1883 in order to give permanent access to the Anglo-Saxon remains. It is entered at A and the exit is at B.

The final reference in the *Chronicle* to the Anglo-Saxon abbey is the account of its destruction by fire in 1116, when all the buildings except the chapter-house and the dormitory, and in addition most of the town, were burned down on Friday, 4 August. On the ruins, the Normans began the erection of the much more ambitious abbey which forms the core of the present cathedral; and, until repairs to the cathedral necessitated excavations under the central tower in 1883, it was not known that any part of the pre-Conquest fabric had survived.

DESCRIPTION OF THE RUINS

The earlier walls and flooring discovered under the present church in 1883 were interpreted by Irvine as the transepts and chancel of Ethelwold's tenth-century abbey.[1] Butterick later gave reasons for believing that the tenth-century walls incorporated earlier fabric and were in part built upon remains of Sexwulf's seventh-century church.[2] These interesting remains are preserved in vaults beneath the present floor of the nave and transept, where they are accessible to visitors on

[1] J. T. Irvine, *J.B.A.A.* **47** (1891), 184; and *ibid.* **50** (1894), 45–54.

[2] T. C. Butterick, *Builder* (14 March 1903), 269.

application to the cathedral authorities. The entry is by way of a stair which, from a point close to the south wall of the present south transept, leads to the east wall of the Anglo-Saxon south transept. The south wall is no longer accessible; but it was discovered and recorded by Irvine, just outside the south wall of the present transept. The passage leads along the whole extent of the Anglo-Saxon transepts, from south to north, a distance of over 80 ft; and, towards the middle, the side walls of the chancel are to be seen running away to the east, until they are lost beneath the sleeper wall built by the Normans to support the eastern arcade of their transept. Under Irvine's direction excavations were made to the east of this sleeper wall; but, as no further trace was found of Anglo-Saxon walling, Irvine deduced that the east end of the early chancel had been square and was wholly buried beneath the sleeper wall. Having reached the north wall of the north transept, the passage crosses it and then turns west to run along the entire extent of this wall, a distance of about 35 ft, at the end of which the wall may be seen to turn south. Close to this point a second stair leads up from the vaults into the church, between the two eastern piers of the south arcade of the nave.

It is thus possible to obtain a clear picture of the extent and general construction of the early abbey, the whole of whose width is included in less than half that of its Norman successor. The walls, as they are now visible in the vaults, stand to a height of several courses of roughly squared stones. Indications of foundations for an altar may be seen against the east wall in the south transept; and a stone bench runs along the entire length of the corresponding wall in the north transept. Outside the north wall, near its eastern angle, a projecting stone appears to have been a base for a double pilaster-strip; and in the masonry of this wall it is possible to distinguish larger, more regularly laid, and much more carefully dressed stones in the western part and in the lower courses of the eastern part, by contrast with the smaller and less carefully laid stones in the upper eastern courses. This is the most obvious evidence

for Butterick's theory that the walls are of two periods, of which the earlier is represented by the well laid, larger blocks, while the smaller more irregular stones represent Ethelwold's rebuilding.[1]

DIMENSIONS

The chancel is about 22 ft wide internally; and, if Irvine's theory about its square east end is correct, it must have been about the same length from east to west. The extreme distance from north to south across the transepts was about 82 ft, and they were about 35 ft wide from east to west. The surviving walls are about 2 ft 6 in. in thickness.

CARVED STONES

In recent years, largely as the result of Sir Alfred Clapham's masterly reappraisal of the carved stones at Breedon-on-the-Hill,[2] it has come to be appreciated that in eighth-century Mercia there must have been an outstanding school of figure-sculpture from which there were produced works such as the great collection at Breedon and the isolated fragments of the same character at Fletton, Castor, and Peterborough. Since Fletton and Castor are both neighbours of Peterborough, and since Peterborough was the centre from which a great group of monasteries took their foundation, it is possible that this school of carving was centred on Peterborough. However this may be, the antiquity of the site as a place of Christian worship and burial is confirmed by the considerable number of carved stones, which were discovered under the Norman flooring during the nineteenth-century restorations, and which are now preserved, some in the cathedral itself and some in the vaults beside the walls of the early church. These stones include several grave-slabs and cross-shafts, as well as a number of pieces of architectural sculpture to which reference is made below, but the most remarkable carvings are the two stones carved with figures standing in recesses beneath an arcade. These two important pieces of figure-sculpture are preserved in the church, and there is no record of the time or place of their discovery. The first and by far the greater of these relics is the Hedda stone or monks' stone, now

---

[1] The immense size of the stones of the foundations greatly impressed the twelfth-century writer Hugh Candidus when he saw them after the fire (W. T. Mellows, *The Chronicle of Hugh Candidus* (Oxford, 1949), 8).

[2] A. W. Clapham, *Arch.* 77 (1927), 219–40.

standing near the south-east of the chancel; while the other is a slab 2 ft tall by 1½ ft wide, now to be seen inside the south transept, built into its west wall beside a door to a vestry.

The Hedda stone is fully described and illustrated in a number of articles to which reference is given in the bibliography. It is a stone 3 ft 6 in. long, 2 ft 4 in. high, and 1 ft wide, with a sloping ridged roof; both gabled ends are quite plain, as though it had been one stone of a longer structure; the sloping roofs are ornamentally carved with interlace and similar patterns; and both sides bear arcades of six round arches in each of which there stands a delicately carved nimbed figure in fairly high relief.

It is difficult to suggest the form of the structure of which the Hedda stone originally formed a part. The plain ends suggest that the pattern of arches was continued on neighbouring stones, perhaps forming some kind of screen or shrine. The form of the arches and of the figures beneath them is very similar to that on a panel found in 1935 at Castor, only 4 miles from Peterborough, and thought to be part of the shrine of St Kyneburga. Convincing arguments have recently been given for believing that the stone was a shrine, to be placed above relics beside the altar.[1]

The stone in the south transept contains two figures under somewhat similar arches; but the figures seem to be of martial rather than clerical aspect. Unlike the Hedda stone this slab appears to be carved on one face only, like those at Breedon, Castor, and Fletton.

The discoveries at Peterborough also included a number of wrought stones which had formed part of the structure of the pre-Conquest church. These were described and illustrated by Irvine in 1884; but they seem to have received very little subsequent attention.[2] They are perhaps unequalled as examples of carved structural stonework, except by the great collection at Hexham. They include several pieces of jambs of arches, of complicated section like the chancel-arch at Wittering, two pieces of imposts or string-courses with horizontal mouldings, one piece of string-course with interlace-ornament, several pieces of plain

vertical pilaster-strip, two pieces of the stone midwall frame of a double-splayed window, and a large section of a lintel of a doorway, carved so as to show a semicircular, perfectly plain tympanum recessed behind an outline of raised strip-work.

In connexion with the account by Symeon of Durham of the crosses which stood at the head and foot of Acca's grave at Hexham it is of interest to record that one of the grave-slabs found in situ at Peterborough during the works of restoration had a foot-stone erect and in situ beside it.[3]

REFERENCES

J. T. IRVINE, 'Account of the pre-Norman remains discovered at Peterborough cathedral in 1884', A.A.S.R. 17 (1883–4), 277–83. Important description of the discoveries, with plan and sections. Also description and illustration of the structural stonework found beside the ruins or re-used in later work.

J. T. IRVINE, 'Fragment of Saxon stonework', J.B.A.A. 47, (1891), 184–5.

J. T. IRVINE, 'Account of the discovery of part of the Saxon abbey church of Peterborough', ibid. 50 (1894), 45–54. Full account of the discoveries and their interpretation, with plan.

T. C. BUTTERICK, 'Church at North Elmham', Builder (14 March 1903), 269. Arguments for two periods of building, as shown in the surviving fabric at Peterborough.

J. R. ALLEN, 'Early Christian sculpture in Northamptonshire', A.A.S.R. 19 (1887–8), 398–423. Peterborough, 416–21.

C. A. R. RADFORD, 'Two Scottish shrines: Jedburgh and St Andrews', Arch. J. 112 (1955), 43–60. Hedda Stone, 58–9.

PETERSTOW

Herefordshire

Map sheet 142, reference SO 574249

ST PETER

Part of north wall of a pre-Conquest church, now overlaid by a longer early Norman wall: period doubtful

The simple, aisleless, early Norman nave at Peterstow, about 2 miles west of Ross-on-Wye, incorporates in its north wall part of the wall of an

---

[1] C. A. R. Radford, Arch. J. 112 (1955), 58.
[2] J. T. Irvine, A.A.S.R. 17 (1883–4), 277–83.

[3] J. R. Allen, A.A.S.R. 19 (1887–8), 418–19.

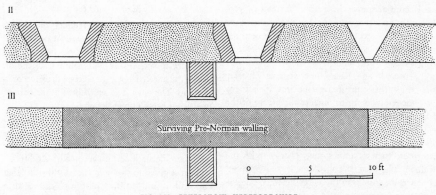

FIG. 242. PETERSTOW, HEREFORDSHIRE

Elevation and plans of the north wall of the nave. I, elevation; II, plan at level A; III, plan at level B. Note the massive stones of the early walling and note particularly the well-defined west quoin below the later small Norman window.

earlier building, which seems to have been shorter than the present nave. The earlier wall is of exceptionally large irregularly shaped stones; but, about 15 ft from the present western quoin, the large stones end, and the western edge of the last of the large stones has been neatly dressed, as if to form the north-west quoin of the early wall. This quoin is vertically below the early Norman north window of the present nave, thereby proving that the early Norman fabric is a later adaptation of an even earlier building.

No features have survived in the early wall to give any indication of its date.

DIMENSIONS

The surviving section of early wall is about 24 ft in length, and about 3 ft 1 in. in thickness. It is about 3 ft 6 in. in height and it comprises six large stones, with a number of smaller stones filling the irregular spaces between.

REFERENCE

R.C.H.M., *Herefordshire*, I (London, 1931), 217. Plan.

PITTINGTON

County Durham

Map sheet 85, reference NZ 328436

ST LAWRENCE

Side walls of nave, over later arcades:
possibly Saxo-Norman

About 4 miles north-east of Durham, and formerly one of the residences of the bishop, Pittington has

495

a church of more than usual interest. It now consists of a west tower, an aisled nave with south porch, and an aisleless chancel with south organ-chamber and north vestry. The chancel dates from the nineteenth century, though in the Early English style. Only the walls of the western part of the nave, above the elaborate Norman arches, have any claim to inclusion in this book, and we cannot agree with Pevsner in regarding them as 'clearly Saxon' or their windows as being comparable with those at Jarrow, Escomb or Seaham.[1]

Bishop Pudsey's late-twelfth-century arcades cut away parts of windows in the walls above. The walls must therefore be earlier Norman or pre-Norman, and there is little but the character of these windows to guide us in the choice between these possibilities. Four windows have survived, round-headed and single-splayed. Internally they are plastered, and with some vestiges of early frescoes, so that one cannot hope for the plaster to be removed in order to disclose the nature of the fabric beneath. Externally the round heads are cut in the lower faces of single stones, which are also cut to a semicircular shape above, while the jambs are each of four stones, coursed with the walling. The general impression, in our opinion, is of workmanship on the verge between Anglo-Saxon and Norman, and probably nearer the latter. On the other hand, the walls are thin, and we have accordingly included the church in the Saxo-Norman category.

DIMENSIONS

The original nave seems to have been about 42 ft long internally; and it is 18 ft wide, with walls 2 ft 8 in. thick and about 20 ft high, excluding the later clear-storey. The windows have apertures 4 ft 3 in. tall and 1 ft 3 in. wide at the sills, narrowing about 1 in. towards the top. Externally their sills are 14 ft above the floor. Internally they are splayed to become 4 ft wide and 7 ft tall.

REFERENCES

J. BARMBY, 'Pittington and its church', *T. Durham Northd. A.A.S.* **3** (1880–9), 1–32. Plan, interior and exterior views. Details of the fabric, and suggested building dates, all post-Conquest.

J. F. HODGSON, 'Architectural notes on the parish church of Pittington', *ibid.* **7** (1934–6), 13–24. Detailed argument for interpretation of the complicated architectural history of the nave. Original fabric dated to a period close before the Conquest.

POLING

Sussex

Map sheet 182, reference TQ 046046

ST NICHOLAS

Nave: period C3

About 2 miles south-east of Arundel, the church of St Nicholas, pleasantly situated in open fields south of the small village of Poling, now consists of a west tower, a nave with south aisle, and an aisleless chancel, mostly of Perpendicular workmanship. The nave, however, contains the core of an aisleless pre-Conquest church.

The piers and the arches between the nave and its south aisle are of late-Norman or Transitional form, and it is fairly clear that the openings have been cut through an earlier wall. Additional support is given to this deduction by the fact that the wall is only 2 ft 5 in. thick, and is thus unusually thin for a wall erected from the beginning in the twelfth century. The corresponding north wall of the original aisleless nave is of the same thin construction. It is now in line with the north wall of the chancel; but vestiges of a long-and-short quoin have remained to show that the wall of the nave is earlier than the north wall of the enlarged chancel, which is now built up against the quoin, with a straight vertical joint between the flint fabric of the later wall and the rubble fabric of the original nave.

The early north wall contains further evidence of its pre-Conquest fabric in the form of a double-splayed, round-headed window, high up in the wall, between two Perpendicular windows. Its actual aperture is cut in a stone slab, which is placed a little nearer the outer than the inner face of the wall. Both internally and externally, the salient angle of each jamb is formed of two dressed stones set upright to line the jamb, while

[1] N. Pevsner, *County Durham, The Buildings of England* (London, 1953), 192.

the roughly shaped head appears to be formed of rubble, like the fabric of the wall, but lightly covered with plaster. Apparently the stone slab is a modern insertion in the wall, since Johnston's account of the discovery of the window in 1917–18 records that a large part of the original wooden shutter-board remained in the groove and was got out entire.

DIMENSIONS

The original nave seems to have been 27 ft 2 in. long internally, by 13 ft 4 in. wide, with walls 2 ft 5 in. thick, and about 17 ft high.

The actual aperture of the double-splayed window is 1 ft wide at the bottom, narrowing slightly towards the top, and 2 ft 9 in. tall. In the outer face of the wall, the window is 1 ft 8 in. wide, and 3 ft 6 in. tall, with its sill 10 ft above the ground.

REFERENCE

P. M. JOHNSTON, 'An early window and wall-paintings in Witley Church, Surrey', *Surrey Arch. C.* **31** (1918), 28–44. Poling, 34 n.; footnote describing how the hitherto unsuspected double-splayed window was opened out by the writer within the last year.

POTTERNE

Wiltshire

(See page 734)

PRESTEIGNE

Radnorshire

Map sheet 129, reference SO 314645

ST ANDREW

North wall of north aisle. Mainly early Norman, but incorporating some earlier work in the lower part of the eastern section of the wall. Possibly pre-Norman.

The fascinating and problematical church of St Andrew stands beside a pleasant green, between Presteigne's busy main street and the banks of the River Lugg.

The church now consists of an aisleless chancel partly flanked on the south by a wide Lady Chapel, and an aisled nave with a south-western tower and porch of entry. No part of the church can at present be said with certainty to be earlier than Norman but part of the north wall may be, and we have described its development in some detail in the hope that further study will lead to a more precise dating.

The earliest part of the church is clearly the north wall of the narrow north aisle, which originally formed the north wall of an earlier aisleless church. It is unusual for a church to be widened in this way by moving southward, but there can be no doubt about this interpretation of the fabric, because the northern half of the original chancel-arch is still to be seen in the east wall of the present north aisle, now blocked and in line with the north arcade. Moreover, the round-headed, blocked, west doorway of the narrow earlier nave has survived in the present west wall, where it is partially obscured internally by the western respond of the north arcade and externally by the great buttress that has been added to resist the lateral thrust of the arcade.

The enlargement of an aisleless church in this unusual fashion is easier to understand if it be assumed that the original church was partially destroyed and that only its northern half was considered worth retaining in the new fabric. There would have been ample opportunity for such destruction in the border wars between the English and Welsh; for the district was ravaged in 1052 by Gruffydd ap Llwellyn, in 1213 by Llwellyn the Great, and in 1402 by Owen Glyndwr.

Enough remains of the early chancel-arch and of the west doorway to fix the centre-line of the early nave and thereby to settle that it was about 19 ft wide internally although it is about 82 ft long. This is an exceptionally long, narrow plan; and it is reassuring to find evidence from the fabric of the north wall that the early church was originally only about half as long.

The exterior of the north wall shows evidence of three separate building dates. A marked change of fabric and a slight change of alignment near the centre indicate that the eastern and western halves were built at separate times, and another very marked change of fabric suggests that the eastern half is itself of two separate periods. The lower part, about 4 or 5 ft in height, is of coursed grey ragstone, while the upper part is of courses

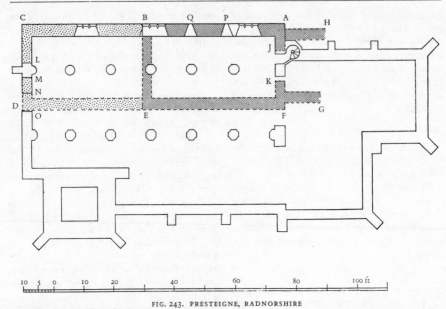

FIG. 243. PRESTEIGNE, RADNORSHIRE

Plan of surviving and conjectural earlier buildings. A, B, E, F, original pre-conquest aisleless nave; G, H, conjectural alignment of pre-Conquest chancel walls; J, K, pre-Conquest chancel-arch, of which jamb J survives with sufficient part of the arch to determine the former position of the vanished jamb K; A, C, D, F, lengthened aisleless nave, probably Norman; L, M, partially surviving jambs of western doorway of lengthened aisleless nave; N, O, jambs of present west doorway; P, Q, early Norman round-headed single-splayed windows in later upper part of wall erected on earlier lower wall.

of roughly squared brown stone separated by courses of thin stones almost of the shape of tiles. In this upper part of the eastern half of the wall are two blocked, round-headed, single-splayed windows, whose jambs and heads are formed of tufa. Although neither window is complete, enough remains to settle the external and internal character with certainty, and to fix them as of early Norman date. A similar date would also be consistent with the appearance of the simple, round-headed chancel-arch, which is also of tufa. The blocked west doorway, however, has facings of stone and is therefore probably of a later Norman date.

Since the upper part of the eastern section of the north wall is fixed as early Norman by its windows, and since the lower part is so different in character, there is an indication that the grey ragstone lower part is of pre-Conquest date, but there is no confirmatory evidence such as would be provided by a surviving door, or window, or quoining.

The architectural history which we tentatively

give for the early part of Presteigne church is therefore as follows. Soon after the Norman Conquest, the small aisleless nave was built, possibly incorporating part of a pre-Conquest church that was of grey ragstone. This early Norman church was 19 ft wide internally and about 40 ft long. Its chancel-arch and its north windows serve to define its date. Later in the Norman era, the nave was extended westward to about twice its former length, as is shown by the surviving, blocked west doorway. At the end of the Norman period and at the time of transition to the Early English style, the new aisled nave was built, as is indicated by the survival of two Transitional piers in the western part of the arcade.

Such a history could be given a reasonable, even if quite conjectural, association with the known record of border raids. The fragment of grey ragstone walling beneath the early-Norman church could be a survival from a pre-Conquest church that was left derelict after the raid of 1052.

The early Norman church and its westward extension could then have followed in the period before the next raid of 1213, and the rebuilding and southward extension could have followed that raid.

This account of Presteigne church is highly conjectural and should not be accepted, without further investigation, as clear proof that any part dates from before the Norman Conquest. In conclusion it should be noted that the north wall is 3 ft 4 in. thick and therefore receives no support for pre-Conquest date on grounds of thinness. The remains of the chancel-arch determine an opening 15 ft 9 in. tall and about 10 ft wide.

PRITTLEWELL

Essex

Map sheet 162, reference TQ 876868

ST MARY

West part of north wall of chancel: possibly period A

Prittlewell is now a northern suburb of the large but relatively modern town of Southend, of which the church of St Mary was the parish church until last century. This fine church, mentioned in Domesday Book, stands just to the east of the busy main road which runs north from the two railway stations, beside Priory Park, to Rayleigh. The present fabric consists of an aisleless chancel with south chapel, a nave with south aisle, two-storeyed south porch, and north vestry, and a fine Perpendicular west tower.

The western part of the north wall of the chancel may clearly be seen to incorporate a section of earlier walling, about 12 ft in length and 15 ft in height. This is slightly thicker than the wall which adjoins it and is continued on top of it; and the junction is effected by a chamfered course of dressed stone, which runs vertically and horizontally along the straight junctions. It seems likely that the present chancel replaces a fabric which for some reason had become ruinous and that this part, alone, of the old fabric was fit to preserve.

At the east of this section of earlier walling part of a blocked, round-headed doorway has been preserved, roughly half the original opening. Its western jamb is of the same rubble construction as the wall in which it stands, and its head is arched

partly with Roman tiles and partly with thin pieces of stone. The workmanship is rough, and the tiles next the springing are fairly steeply tilted by the interposition of wedge-shaped stones. The head, too, is somewhat ovoid in shape, rather taller than would be the case with a semicircular opening. The arched head and square jambs seem, from measurement outside and within the church, to have been cut straight through the wall, without any rebate for a door. On the outer face of the wall there are some indications of a second row of tiles to form an outer arch, but internally there is only a single arch, wholly of tiles, without any use of stones. The true proportions of this doorway have been somewhat masked by the rising of the ground in the centuries since the wall was first built. The existing remains seem to define an opening of quite reasonable proportions, about 4 ft in width and 7 ft in height. But excavations within the church have established the former existence of three earlier floor-levels beneath the present floor of the chancel; and the sill of the doorway, at the lowest of these levels, 2 ft 6 in. beneath the present floor, defined an opening 9 ft 6 in. tall.

All this workmanship is quite different from that which is to be seen in the Norman nave. The early wall of the chancel is only 2 ft 6 in. thick, whereas the walls of the nave are 3 ft to 3 ft 3 in. The early wall of the chancel and the jambs of the doorway are of rubble, whereas the walls of the nave are of carefully dressed stone, and its windows are faced with ashlar and are neatly arched.

The surviving work is hardly sufficient to justify a precise dating, but the fabric is not inconsistent with what would have been expected in the seventh century when the Kentish group of churches, and St Peter-on-the-Wall at Bradwell-on-Sea, were being erected, with aisleless naves and chancels flanked by *porticus*. The north *porticus* was most often entered by a doorway near the western end of the chancel; and it would therefore be of great interest if excavations could be made to see whether any evidence has survived of walls running north from the north wall of the church.

DIMENSIONS

The surviving early wall is 12 ft in length, 15 ft in height, and 2 ft 6 in. thick. The opening

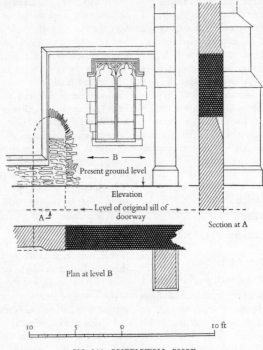

B

Present ground level

Elevation

Level of original sill of
doorway

A

Section at A

Plan at level B

10   5   0   10 ft

FIG. 244. PRITTLEWELL, ESSEX

Elevation, section and plan of a surviving early fragment of wall, now incorporated into the north wall of the chancel. Our drawing does not show the faint indications of a second row of tiles round the head of the arch, to which we refer on p. 499.

defined by the vestiges of doorway must have been about 4 ft wide and 9 ft 6 in. tall, with its sill about 2 ft 6 in. below the present floor of the chancel.

REFERENCES

P. M. JOHNSTON, 'An early pre-Conquest doorway in Prittlewell Church', *T. Essex A.S.*, n.s., **20** (1930–3), 328–30.

J. C. COX, 'The church of Prittlewell', *Builder* (10 September 1904), 263–5.

E. N. GOWING, *The Story of Prittlewell Church* (Prittlewell, 1958).

QUARLEY

Hampshire

Map sheet 167, reference SU 273440

Figures 551, 552

ST MICHAEL

Nave: Saxo-Norman

This church, pleasantly situated in rolling, wooded country, about 6 miles west of Andover, a little south of the main road to Amesbury, is one of the many which have certain features of Anglo-Saxon character alongside others of Norman. It now consists of an aisleless nave and chancel to which a south porch and north vestry have been added in later times.

The eastern quoins of the nave are of plain flint construction, in a way which indicates pre-Norman work. Similarly, the single-splayed, round-headed windows that are still visible, although blocked, high up in the north and south walls of the nave, have jambs constructed of thin, flat pieces of stone like tiles; and their heads are turned in thin pieces of stone, laid with complete dis-

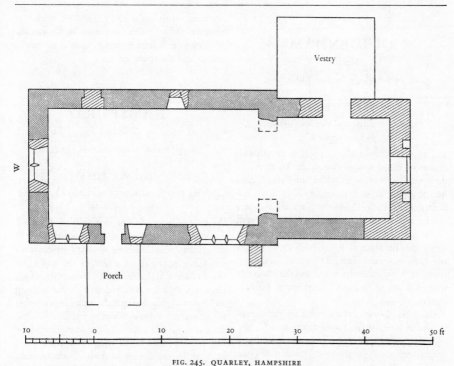

Vestry

W

Porch

10   0   10   20   30   40   50 ft

FIG. 245. QUARLEY, HAMPSHIRE

The west window W is of two lights, but an earlier single-splayed round-headed
window has survived above it in the gable of the west wall.

regard for the principle of radial setting of voussoirs. The blocked north doorway of the nave, although rebated in Norman fashion for the hanging of a door, is very tall, and narrow, and therefore suggestive of Anglo-Saxon influence. In the western gable of the nave a round-headed, single-splayed window has one of its jambs laid in something approaching 'Escomb fashion', while the other jamb has one upright stone followed by three smaller ones. Its head is cut from a single stone, which is shaped to a semi-circle both above and below.

DIMENSIONS

The nave is 31 ft long internally by 16 ft 4 in. wide, with side walls 2 ft 9 in. thick and now 15 ft high, but certainly originally higher, since the

tops of the side windows have been partly cut away.

The side windows have apertures 1 ft 3 in. wide and 3 ft tall, splayed to become 2 ft 9 in. wide and about 6 ft tall. Their sills externally are 12 ft above the ground. The west window has an aperture 1 ft 8 in. wide and 4 ft 2 in. tall, splayed to become 3 ft 6 in. by about 8 ft. Its external sill is 13 ft 8 in. above the ground. The blocked north doorway is 2 ft 10 in. wide and 10 ft high externally.

REFERENCES

A. R. and P. M. GREEN, *Saxon Architecture and Sculpture in Hampshire* (Winchester, 1951), 28.

V.C.H., *Hampshire and the I.o.W.* **4** (London, 1911), 385–6. Dated not later than twelfth century. Plan. Mentioned in Domesday Book.

QUIDENHAM
Norfolk
Map sheet 136, reference TM 028876

ST MARY THE VIRGIN
*Round west tower, and west wall of nave:
possibly period C*

The church at Quidenham is pleasantly situated, about 10 miles east-north-east of Thetford, in the extensive grounds of Quidenham Park. It consists of a circular west tower, with an octagonal Perpendicular belfry; a nave with a south aisle and porch; and an aisleless chancel. The north wall of the nave contains a fine early Norman doorway; and the south wall has been pierced by a tall Early English arcade. The north wall is of cut flints, but the circular tower and the adjoining west wall are of uncut flints, of quite different texture.

The most obvious feature which suggests a pre-Conquest date for the round tower and for the adjoining west wall is the presence, in the re-entrant angles, of quarter-round pilasters of plain flint fabric. This impression receives confirmation from the blocked circular windows which are to be seen, about 20 ft above the ground, in the south, west, and north faces of the tower. These have heads which are very roughly arched in rectangular pieces of brown carstone, laid with their longer sides along the radii. The blocking makes it impossible to be certain that these windows are double-splayed, but this is likely from their general appearance.

Internally, there are no features which give strong support to a pre-Conquest date; although the tower-arch is of tall and narrow proportions and the walls are tall and thin. The tower-arch is constructed of dressed stone, and its imposts are chamfered. Its fabric is so finely dressed as to suggest that it has been resurfaced in a modern restoration.

DIMENSIONS

The nave is 53 ft 6 in. long and 19 ft 5 in. wide, internally; with side walls 2 ft 5 in. thick and 19 ft high. The tower is about 11 ft in internal diameter, with walls about 4 ft 6 in. thick and about 45 ft high. The outer faces of the circular windows are 2 ft in diameter, with their centres about 22 ft above the ground.

RAMSBURY
Wiltshire
Map sheet 157, reference SU 274716

HOLY CROSS
*Possibly some foundations of pre-Conquest cathedral
church of 909–1045*

About 5 miles east of Marlborough, on the north bank of the River Kennet, the pleasant village of Ramsbury now has little outward evidence of having been for about a century the seat of an Anglo-Saxon bishopric. Until restorations of the church in 1891 it was indeed thought that nothing had survived; but during the restorations a number of important carved stones were found, some built into the foundations of the south pier of the chancel-arch, and some lying buried close by, near the line of the foundations of what seemed to be the wall of an earlier church. This earlier foundation may still be seen, running parallel to the south wall of the chancel, a few feet further to the south.

The carved stones now stand in the north-west corner of the church. They comprise three large sections of a big cross-shaft, and two unusual grave-slabs of domed cross-section, with rounded ends. These lie outside the scope of our book but their importance is such that they cannot be passed without mention or without reference to the usual dating of them in the tenth century, during the location of the bishopric at Ramsbury. By contrast, Kendrick boldly dates the carvings to the period 860–80, with the entirely logical argument that the carvings could well have belonged to an earlier church and should be dated on their merits.

REFERENCES

E. H. GODDARD, 'Notes on pre-Norman sculptured stones in Wilts.', *Wilts. A.N.H. Mag.* **27** (1893–4), 43–9. Ramsbury, 44–5.

T. D. KENDRICK, *Anglo-Saxon Art to A.D. 900* (London, 1938), 211–15, and pls. XCIX and C. Particularly also footnote on p. 211.

D. T. RICE, *English Art, 871–1100* (Oxford, 1952) 127 and 137.

RECULVER

Kent

Map sheet 173, reference TR 228694

ST MARY

Ruins of complete church: nave, apsidal chancel, and flanking 'porticus'; period A2. Later 'porticus' enclosing nave and forming west porch; period A3

HISTORY

The wanton demolition in 1805 of St Mary's church at Reculver, on the north coast of Kent between Herne Bay and Margate, was an act of vandalism for which there can be few parallels even in the blackest records of the nineteenth century. It is remarkable that in spite of this demolition, and of the inroads of the sea that were used to excuse and explain it, there should still remain on the site enough of the original fabric to establish the complete plan of the early church, to enable parts of it to be accepted with confidence as the church which is known to have been erected towards the end of the seventh century, and to show that other parts should be regarded as later additions, probably in the eighth century. The *Anglo-Saxon Chronicle* records that in the year 669 King Egbert of Kent gave Reculver to Bassa the priest to build a minster there. The history of the monastery at Reculver can be inferred in outline from a series of charters which give references to it as an independent establishment.[1] The monks of Christ Church Canterbury, claimed that it was granted to them by King Eadred in 949.

The church is mentioned in Domesday Book, and a record of taxations in 1281 shows that it had outlying chapels at Hoathe, St Nicholas, All Saints, and Herne.

A new piece of architectural history appears in a decree of Archbishop Winchelsey, dated at Reculver in A.D. 1296, with regard to an agreement between the vicar and parishioners concerning 'oblations and alms in a certain chest near the great stone cross between the church and the chancel'. Leland visited the church about 1540 and wrote the following detailed description of the cross:

Yn the enteryng of the quyer ys one of the fayrest, and the most auncyent crosse that ever I saw, a ix footes, as I ges, yn highte. It standeth like a fayr columne. The base greate stone ys not wrought. The second stone being rownd hath curiously wrought and paynted the images of Christ, Peter, Paul, John and James as I remember. Christ sayeth *Ego sum Alpha et Omega*. Peter sayith *Tu es Christus filius Dei vivi*. The saying of the other iii. wher painted *majusculis literis Ro.* but now obliterated. The second stone is of the Passion. The iii. conteineth the xii Apostles, The iv. hath the image of Christ hanging and fastened with iiii nayles, and *sub pedibus sustentaculum*. The hiest part of the pyller hath the figure of a crosse.

Leland also noticed the remains of the monastery. He said that the whole of its precincts could be determined from the walls, that the vicarage was made of the ruins, and that a neglected chapel outside the churchyard was said by some to have been a parish church before the abbey was suppressed and given to the Archbishop. He also recorded that the sea was a quarter of a mile or more to the north of the village.

The history is next continued by three maps, the first drawn by James Castell about 1600, the second by Thomas Hill, surveyor, in 1685, and the third by William Boys, M.A., in 1781.[2] In Castell's map the church and three houses stand within the square Roman fort, a village street runs parallel to the west side of the fort and the sea-shore lies about a hundred yards away

---

[1] A convenient summary of the charters is given in C. R. Smith's *Antiquities of Richborough, Reculver, and Lymne* (London, 1850), 221–6. In A.D. 679, King Lothari granted land at Westney to Abbot Berhtwald, who in 693 was consecrated Archbishop of Canterbury. In 747 King Eadbert granted the church the toll and customs of one ship at Fordwich. Grants of land were made by King Ealhmund in 784 and by Archbishop Wulfred in 811. In

825 Archbishop Wulfred recovered his rights in this monastery after a dispute with Abbess Cwoenthryth, daughter and heir of Coenwulf of Mercia (Birch, *C.S.*, no. 384).

[2] Castell's map was published in *Arch. Cant.* 12 (1878), facing p. 8. Hill's map faces p. 193 of Smith's *Antiquities of Richborough, Reculver, and Lymne*. For the map by W. Boys see J. Nichols, *Bibliotheca Topographica Britannica*, 1 (London, 1780–90), pls. IV and XI.

from its north side. Hill's map shows the same arrangement of church and houses within the fort, but indicates an appreciably greater village consisting of two roads crossing at right angles, and each lined with houses or cottages. In the 85 years between the two maps the sea is shown as having advanced to within about twenty yards of the north wall of the Roman fort. The further hundred years to the map of William Boys (reproduced with additions as Fig. 246) saw the disappearance into the sea of three-quarters of the north wall of the fort by 1781 and the whole north wall by 1785. The house marked G was damaged in 1771 and taken down before 1783. In 1784 the Rev. J. Duncombe, writing in *Bibliotheca Topographica Britannica*, recorded that Capt. Sir T. H. Page, who had lately arranged the supply of fresh water to Sheerness, had undertaken the protection of the village, church, and Roman fort of Reculver by a series of works consisting of fascines, jetties, and sea-walls. These works were apparently to some extent successful, but the church was demolished in 1805 in circumstances which are set out very clearly in the following notes which were recorded by Mr Brett, parish clerk.[1]

October 13th 1802. The chapel house[2] fell down.

Mr C. C. Nailor been Vicar of the parish, his mother fancied that the church was kept for a poppet show, and she persuaded her son to take it down, so he took it in consideration and named it to the farmers in the parish about taking it down; sum was for it and sum was against it, then Mr Nailor wrote to the Bishop to know if he might have the church took down, and is answer was it must be dun by a majority of the people in the parish, so hafter a long time he got the majority of one, so down come the church. for it Mr Nailor, vicker, Mr Tom Denne, Reculver, Mr W. Staines, Brooke, Mr Tom Fox, Hilbrow. against it Mr Wm. Brown, Reculver, Mr Step Sayer, Bishopstone, Mr Brett, clerk to the old church 40 years.

1805. Reculver church and village stood in safety.

1806. The sea began to make a little incroach on the village.

1807. The farmers begun to take up the seaside stonework and sold it to the Margate Pier Company for a foundation for the new pier, and the timber by action as it was good oak fit for their home use, and then the village became a total rack to the mercy of the sea.

In 1809 the Trinity Board purchased the ruins of the church as a navigation mark and took steps to secure its preservation from further encroachment by the sea, with an efficiency that may be judged by the present line of the sea-front as marked in Fig. 246.

In 1850 C. R. Smith published his *Antiquities of Richborough, Reculver, and Lymne*, with pictures of the columns and arches which had separated the nave and chancel of the ancient church, and which he described as Roman. By a singular piece of good fortune some of the stones of these columns were seen in an orchard near Canterbury in 1860 by a Mr Sheppard, who had read Mr Smith's book, and who at once recognized the stones as being parts of the columns from Reculver; a thorough search then produced the complete fabric of both columns with the exception of one capital, which Mr Sheppard later found in a farmyard at Reculver, thus providing further evidence of their true identity.[3] By arrangement between the Kent Archaeological Society and the Dean and Chapter of Canterbury Cathedral the columns are now preserved in safety in the crypt of the cathedral.

The remaining history of the church can be briefly told. In 1878 Dowker published a full description of the ruins of the church and of his reasons for attributing the earliest part of them to Bassa's original foundation in A.D. 669.[4] Dowker also recorded that he had found a number of stones from the early church built into the fabric of the new structure at Hillborough. In 1928 Peers published the results of a more detailed investigation of the ruins, fully confirming the earliest work as being that of Bassa's seventh-century church, with additions probably of the eighth century. Moreover, having described in detail five pieces of carved stone then preserved in the new church at Hillborough and two recently discovered in the old church at Reculver, Peers gave a closely reasoned argument for accepting them as parts of the fair and ancient cross seen by Leland, and also for believing that the cross itself was probably contemporary with Bassa's original church.[5]

[1] G. Dowker, *Arch. Cant.* **12** (1878), 255.

[2] This is the house marked H on the plan in Fig. 246.

[3] Editorial note, *Arch. Cant.* **3** (1860), 135-6.

[4] G. Dowker, *Arch. Cant.* **12** (1878), 248-68.

[5] C. R. Peers, *Arch.* **77** (1927), 241-56. [These fragments of the cross-shaft are now also preserved in the crypt of Canterbury Cathedral. See p. 508 for details and for a note about dating.]

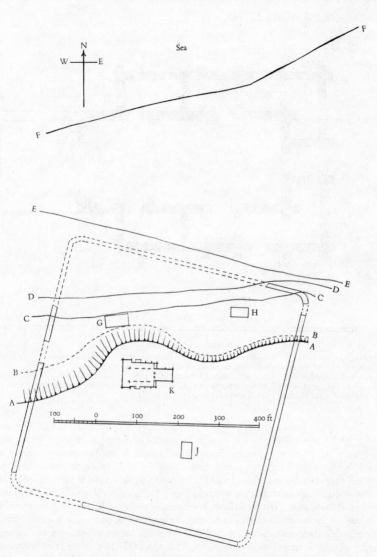

FIG. 246. RECULVER, KENT

Map showing the inroads of the sea. A, A, cliff top as shown on Ordnance Survey 1:2,500 map in 1939; B, B, high-water mark at mean tide 1939; C, C, cliff top in 1785 as shown in *Bibliotheca Topographica Britannica*; D, D, cliff top in 1780 as shown in *Bibliotheca Topographica Britannica*; E, E, cliff top in 1685 as shown in C. R. Smith's *Richborough, Reculver, and Lymne*; F, F, cliff top about 1600 as shown in *Archaeologia Cantiana*, **12** (1878), 8; G, house standing in 1780 but demolished about 1781; H, remains of chapel, used as a cottage in 1780; J, vicarage in 1780; K, Reculver church, standing complete in 1780 and until demolished in 1805. The Roman wall is shown as it stood in 1780, following plate IV of *Bibliotheca Topographica Britannica*. In 1685 the wall was complete round the whole fort.

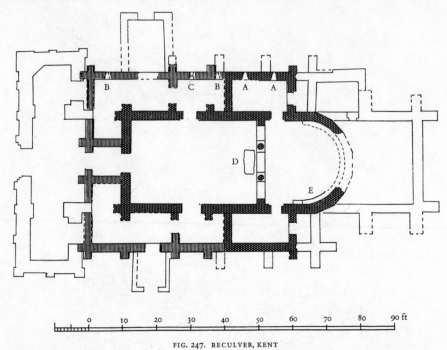

FIG. 247. RECULVER, KENT

Plan, showing the results of the excavations conducted by Peers in 1927. A, A, single-splayed windows of the seventh-century *porticus*; B, B, single-splayed windows of the eighth-century additions; C, double-splayed window inserted later in the eighth-century north wall below a window of type B; D, outline of rectangular base for the great cross; E, remains of stone seat inside the apsidal east end. The twelfth-century towers and the thirteenth-century and later additions to the chancel are shown in outline only.

DESCRIPTION OF THE RUINS

The Transitional Norman west towers still stand to their full height, but now with flat tops in place of their former graceful spires. The greater part of the remainder of the church appears only as lines of foundations, or low walling; but the outer wall on the north still stands to a height of 5 or 6 ft, while the thirteenth-century walls of the lengthened square chancel stand considerably higher.

The careful investigation made by Peers in 1927 established that the original church consisted of a rectangular nave and an apsidal chancel from which doorways led to small rectangular north and south *porticus*. The similarity of plan and of workmanship to that of other early Kentish churches convinced Peers that this was indeed the

church erected by Bassa in 669. The nave had external doorways in its west, north, and south walls; and, as was known from the picture published by C. R. Smith, it was divided from the chancel by an arcade of three round arches. The two tall sturdy columns which supported this arcade may now be seen in the crypt of Canterbury cathedral; their shafts are each built of nine cylindrical stones which taper in diameter from 2 ft 3 in. at the base to 1 ft 11 in. at the top; their bases are ornamented with boldly projecting rings of cable moulding; and their remarkable capitals each consist of a triple fillet beneath three superimposed bevelled members, which serve to transform the circular plan of the fillet into the square plan of the springing of the arch. Peers confirmed Dowker's earlier report of the sleeper wall which supported these columns and of the

506

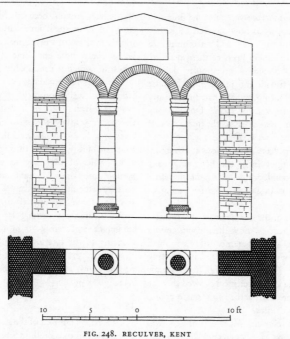

FIG. 248. RECULVER, KENT

Elevation and plan of the triple chancel-arch before its destruction in 1805. The elevation is from C. R. Smith's *Antiquities of Richborough, Reculver, and Lymne*, and the plan is from the excavations by Peers.

square responds of walling which carried the outer ends of the arches. He also excavated the whole line of the early apse and established that, while its foundation was semicircular as reported by Dowker, its main walling was externally polygonal, of seven sides, and internally semicircular, the inner face having a low stone bench running along most of its length. The walls of the original church are all thin, and are built of flint and stone rubble, with bonding courses of Roman bricks or tiles. At the western angles of the nave, and on either side of its lateral doorways, the original building had typical early Kentish buttresses, with a projection of about 2 ft, the remains of which can still clearly be seen.

The north and south *porticus* opened to the outside by doorways in their east walls, and into the chancel by doorways in its north and south walls, close to the east side of the triple arcade. Both these doorways into the chancel are thought to have had their jambs lined with upright stone slabs, because the stone threshold of the north door still bears on its upper face two pairs of stone fillets close to the two jambs, as though to fit into grooves in the lower faces of the lining slabs; both doorways are also rebated on their inner faces as though to bear inset vertical facing strips of stone. Similar rebates as if for inset stone facing strips may be seen in the inner face of the north door of the nave and the outer face of the east door of the north *porticus*. These rebates may be compared with the similar treatment of the external face of the west doorway of St Mary's chapel in St Augustine's abbey at Canterbury; while the device of lining the jambs with slabs of stone may be compared with the existing work at Britford in Wiltshire.

Peers reported that much of the original flooring remained in the nave and the *porticus*, and a little in the apse. As had been recorded by eighteenth-century writers, he confirmed that it was very strong and about 10 in. thick, made of mortar set on a foundation of rough flints, and covered

507

with a red polished surface of cement and pounded brick; all this flooring is now covered by lawns. At the east end of the nave, and set centrally in front of the triple arcade, Peers confirmed Dowker's earlier report that a rectangular slab of masonry about 7 ft wide and 3 ft deep had been set in the original flooring, which had been neatly finished against its vertical faces. Dowker had suggested that this was originally the foundation of an altar, which later carried the great cross referred to by Leland; but Peers gave reasons for thinking that the cross might from the beginning have stood on this foundation, and might therefore have been part of Bassa's original furnishing of the monastery.

The north wall of the north *porticus* still remains to a height sufficient to show the inward-sloping sills and inward-splayed jambs of two small windows faced with brick or tile. The drawing published by C. R. Smith of the triple arcade between the nave and the chancel showed that the round arches were each turned in a single course of similar bricks or tiles.

The original church described above was enlarged fairly soon after its erection by carrying the outer walls of the *porticus* westward, beyond the west wall of the nave, and by returning them so as to enclose the nave on the north, south, and west within a line of flanking chambers, while at the same time forming a porch over the west door. Peers reported that his excavations showed that no new openings were made in the original walls of the church at this date; so that the new flanking chambers were entered only through what had originally been the north and south external doors of the nave; while the nave itself at this stage had only one doorway leading outside, through the new west porch. The fabric of these later additions differs from the original work by being of coursed blocks of stone; but the flooring is of the same kind as before, and the general style of the work, with buttresses of low projection and walls of the same thickness as before, is so similar to that of the original church that Peers assigned a date not more than a century after Bassa's original foundation. In the north wall

of the later *porticus* there still remain the sills and jambs of three small internally splayed windows similar to those of the original north *porticus*; but below the middle one there is a double-splayed window, which is presumably a later insertion.

The church received its next substantial addition late in the twelfth century when the Transitional western towers were built at its west end. In the thirteenth century the chancel was lengthened eastward. It also seems likely that at or before this time arcades were cut through the north and south walls of the nave so as to convert the *porticus* into aisles; at any rate the eighteenth-century account given by William Boys[1] described a nave separated from aisles by pointed arches resting on rectangular pillars 3 ft 10 in. in length and 1 ft 3 in. in thickness; while a drawing of the interior made by the Rev. John Pridden in 1787 showed arcades of four arches on the south and five on the north carried on rectangular pillars.[2]

THE CROSS

The cross is not part of the structure and should, therefore, fall outside the scope of this book, but for completeness it is convenient to summarize very briefly the argument advanced by Peers for identifying the seven surviving stones as parts of the cross seen by Leland, and for assigning a seventh-century date to them.[3]

Leland's description gives a picture of a cross standing on a large plain base of unknown shape, the carved shaft itself being built of four cylindrical stones, on top of which came the head of the cross. Of the seven surviving stones described by Peers, four represent parts of cylindrical drums, carved with scrolls and with full-length draped figures; while one represents part of a slightly thinner cylinder, carved with interlacing knot-work and with vine-scroll which contains human busts where the Northumbrian crosses would have had birds or animals. Each of the first four is part of a cylinder 18 in. in diameter, while the fifth represents a diameter of 15 in. No fragment has more than half the circumference, and none is more than 1 ft 2 in. in height; but each has one

---

[1] *Bibliotheca Topographica Britannica*, I, 85.
[2] *Ibid.* pl. x, facing p. 165.

[3] But Talbot Rice (*English Art, 871–1100*, 96–8 and pl. 9b) argues for a tenth-century date.

plane end with a dowel-hole in the centre; and the figures on each indicate that it might be about one-half the height of a whole section with full-length figures. The sixth stone is a fragment containing vine-scroll like that on the fifth; while the seventh is part of the cross-head, with ornament consisting of a beaded edge and a concave disc, which has a small hole drilled in its centre.

No two fragments fit together, and the surviving pieces are clearly insufficient to confirm a reconstruction of the cross, but they are not incompatible with Leland's shaft of four superimposed cylinders carved with figures. In style and execution the fragments indicate a reasonably close similarity to the seventh-century Ruthwell and Bewcastle crosses, whose principal decorative elements are figure sculpture, vine-scroll with animals, and knot-work; the principal difference at Reculver being the substitution of human busts for animals in the vine-scroll. Cross-shafts of the Anglo-Saxon period are usually monolithic in construction; and, since this one is a notable exception, it is not unreasonable to note the similarity of its construction to that of the columns which supported the triple arcade, and to suggest that this similarity is one more feature confirming the likelihood of its having been part of Bassa's original work.

DIMENSIONS

The original nave measured 37 ft by 24 ft internally; the chancel was the same width and 23 ft 6 in. in depth; while the *porticus* were each 17 ft from east to west and 9 ft wide. The enlarged church of the eighth century differed only in that the flanking chambers, 9 ft in width, were continued westward and returned round the west wall of the nave. The walls were of a uniform thickness of 2 ft 4 in. and the doorways were 3 ft 2 in. wide. The arches of the triple arcade between the nave and the chancel were 14 ft 9 in. in height overall, and had tapering shafts 12 ft 4 in. high, with a diameter of 2 ft 3 in. at the bottom and 1 ft 11 in. at the top.

REFERENCES

J. NICHOLS, *Bibliotheca Topographica Britannica*, 1 (London, 1780–90), no. XVIII, 65–161, and no. XLV, 163–99.

E. W. BRAYLEY, *Deliniations of the Isle of Thanet and the Cinque Ports* (London, 1817), 138–47. Engravings by W. Deeble, showing the church after the demolition, but with the chancel-arch still standing, although its southern column had been removed.

C. R. SMITH, *Antiquities of Richborough, Reculver, and Lymne* (London, 1850), 175–230. Drawings and notes by the late Mr J. Gandy; plan, 196; chancel-arch, 197; details of columns, caps, and bases, 198. Leland's account of Reculver, in full, 194–5. Charters relating to Reculver, 221–30.

Editorial, 'The columns of Reculver church', *Arch. Cant.* 3 (1860), 135–6.

G. DOWKER, 'Reculver church', *ibid.* 12 (1878), 248–68. Very valuable account of the church, its destruction, and its surviving remains. First reasoned interpretation of the remains as those of Bassa's church.

J. T. MICKLETHWAITE, 'Something about Saxon church building', *Arch. J.* 53 (1896), 293–351. Reculver, 298–9.

C. R. PEERS, 'Reculver, its Saxon church and cross', *Arch.* 77 (1927), 241–56. Detailed account of the church, with excellent pictures and dated plan.

REED

Hertfordshire

Map sheet 148, reference TL 361356

Figure 553

ST MARY

Nave: period C3

About 3 miles south of Royston and beside the Roman Ermine Street, the Anglo-Saxon aisleless nave of the church at Reed has survived intact between a fourteenth-century chancel and a fifteenth-century west tower. Both the early work and the later additions are built of flints, with dressed-stone facings.

The character of the nave is clearly attested by long-and-short quoins at all four angles, and its lateness in the period is indicated by the fine blocked north doorway, which has advanced features similar to some in the late-Saxon church at Langford in Oxfordshire.

The long-and-short quoins of the nave are unusually complete, perhaps because they are so carefully built of neatly dressed stone with closely fitted joints. An interesting feature is the rectangular rather than square plan of the upright stones, which are placed with their longer horizontal sides alternately along adjoining wall faces.

All four quoins rise from projecting square bases, and a peculiarity of the west wall is that an off-set runs across it about 2 ft above the ground, the quoining below the off-set consisting of one 'long' stone supporting a short which is chamfered on its western face by the width of the off-set. A similar off-set carried round the tower makes it a matter of some doubt whether the medieval builders copied an unusual Anglo-Saxon form of ornament, or whether they devised the off-set as an ornament, and changed the lower courses of the earlier wall to match their tower. On balance we favour the first alternative, not only because the western quoins and wall show no sign of having been disturbed, but also because the eastern quoins show a similar but not identical off-set near their bases. In all four quoins the long stones are mostly about 2 ft in height, but a few are as short as 1 ft 4 in. and several are as long as 3 ft. The shorts are of a fairly uniform height of about 6 in.

A feature of special interest is the blocked north doorway. Internally, all detail of its construction is hidden by plaster, and the doorway appears simply as a round-headed recess cut straight into the wall. Externally, however, the original details are all well preserved and none of them is hidden by the blocking wall, which is fortunately set well back in the doorway. The original opening seems to have been rectangular, beneath a plain stone tympanum, which fills the whole of the round head. Although both the jambs and the round-arched head of the doorway are of two orders, the tentative Anglo-Saxon approach to the use of separate orders is well illustrated by the way in which the whole structure is almost flush with the main face of the wall, whereas in a Norman doorway the inner order would normally have been boldly recessed behind the outer.

In both arch and jambs the outer order is of plain square section, and in the jambs a small section of rubble walling intervenes rather oddly between this outer order and the dressed stones of the inner order. The inner order of the arch is very slightly recessed behind the outer and is ornamented on its archivolt face with a roll-moulding reminiscent of those on the belfry windows at

Langford, Oxfordshire. The inner order of each jamb is in the same plane as the outer, and is fundamentally square in section, but is enriched by the carving of its salient angle to represent an attached angle-shaft with a conical base and a rudimentary capital. These capitals are square above, with lightly incised volutes on the angles; they taper in somewhat bell-shaped form to meet the circular shafts; and the transition from square to circular section is helped by the provision of a simple upright leaf on each angle. The lowest section of each jamb is of the nature of a shallow plinth, rounded on the salient angle, and placed so as to support the conical base of the angle-shaft. Finally, the doorway as a whole has a separate sill or plinth which projects a few inches from the wall-face.

No original windows have survived, and the original chancel-arch has been replaced, by what appears to be a modern imitation of fifteenth-century Gothic workmanship.

DIMENSIONS

The nave is 34 ft 6 in. long by 19 ft wide, internally; with walls 2 ft 11 in.[1] thick and about 20 ft high. The doorway is 2 ft 10 in. wide and 6 ft 4 in. tall, to the lower face of the stone tympanum; or 7 ft 9 in. to the soffit of the arched head.

REFERENCES
R.C.H.M., Hertfordshire (London, 1910), 169–70.
V.C.H., Hertfordshire, 3 (London, 1912), 252–3. Plan.

REPTON
Derbyshire
Map sheet 121, reference SK 303272
Figures 554–8

ST WYSTAN

Chancel with crypt; central crossing; and transepts: periods A to C

The important and interesting church of St Wystan at Repton, probably belonged to an abbey which was founded for men and women in the second

---

[1] G. Baldwin Brown (1925), 476, says about 2 ft 6 in.

half of the seventh century. It immediately adjoins the Norman priory which succeeded the earlier abbey, and which, having fallen into decay after the Dissolution, later served to provide a site and buildings for Repton School.

Evidence of the existence of the abbey at Repton at the close of the seventh century as a house for men and women under the rule of an abbess is given in the eighth-century *Life of St Guthlac*, which records that after the twenty-fourth year of his age the saint renounced the pomps of this world and came to the monastery of Repton, in which he received the tonsure of St Peter under an abbess whose name was Ælfthryth.[1] It is reasonable to suppose that the church at Repton continued to be one of importance, for the *Anglo-Saxon Chronicle* records that the murdered King Ethelbald was buried there in 757. Repton next appears in the *Chronicle* under the years 873 and 874 when the Danish host wintered there.

EXTERIOR (FIGS. 249, 556 AND 557)

The church now consists of a later medieval west tower and spire, an aisled nave of various medieval dates, and a square-ended aisleless chancel almost wholly pre-Conquest in fabric. The walls of the chancel and of the remarkable crypt beneath it show clear evidence of at least two separate building periods. Between the chancel and the nave there intervened a square central space or tower, wider than the chancel, and perhaps than the nave, with narrow transepts opening from it to north and south. Parts of the north transept still remain, and form the east wall of the present north aisle as well as the lowest three courses of the eastern part of its north wall. The north-east angle of the central space also remains intact, forming a salient angle between the chancel and the north aisle; while the east wall of the similar south-east angle likewise remains, with the medieval east wall of the south aisle built up to it, showing a straight vertical joint against the early quoining. In both the eastern walls of the central space a string-course, hollow-chamfered above (*e* in Fig. 249), is carried across the whole extent of the wall. Higher up in

these same walls, just a little below the eaves, a moulded feature is carried across the outer half of the width of the wall. Its profile is square above and half-round below, these two mouldings being cut on separate stones (*d, d* in Fig. 249).

Although there does not seem to be any simple and reliable recorded history of the pre-Conquest abbey at Repton, or any easy interpretation of the buildings that now remain, yet it is clear that the earliest part is the lowest few courses of the walling of the crypt beneath the chancel, and it seems not unreasonable on stylistic grounds to associate this part with the seventh-century church of the monastery which received St Guthlac about 698. The fine quality of the walling, and the use of large stones, may be compared with work of similar excellence in Wilfrid's crypts in Northumbria. The walls may now be seen, outside the church, within a trench about 4 ft deep, which has been excavated round the whole east end. The lower part of the walling is built of long blocks of well-dressed stone each 2 ft or more in length and about 1 ft in height. The lowest course projects about 6 in. from the course above, forming a well-defined plinth, while each successive course is set back about 1 in. from the course next below. Internally the walls slope inward as they rise, just as many early Saxon windows narrow towards the top.

In each of the side walls, and in the east wall, there is a rectangular recess, possibly for a tomb or shrine. Those to the north and east have later been adapted for use as stairways leading to the crypt, but the recess to the south appears to be in something like its original condition. Within the trench on the south of the chancel, two large blocks of stone project horizontally from the walling to provide bases for a triangular stone gable over this southern recess. This gable has now disappeared but its outline may be clearly traced on the south wall, as may the outlines of similar gables on the east and north walls, above the corresponding openings.

Above these earliest walls, an intermediate section of the main walling of the crypt and

---

[1] B. Colgrave, *Felix's Life of St Guthlac* (Cambridge, 1956), 83 and 85. On p. 2 it is recorded that Guthlac was probably born in 674, and on p. 4 that it was probably in the year 699 that he began his solitary life at Crowland after his stay at Repton.

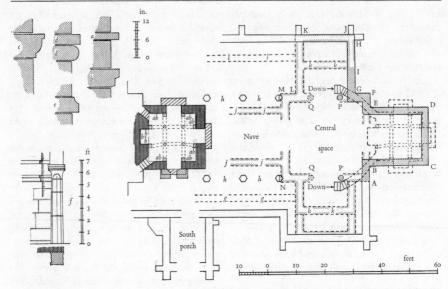

FIG. 249. REPTON, DERBYSHIRE

The main plan at the right shows the church above-ground, with certain details of the crypt in dotted outline. The insets at the left show the full plan of the crypt, at the same scale, together with details of one of the pilasters and of various mouldings, at larger scales.

A, F, M, N, inferred area of the central space; B, C, D, E, walls of chancel still standing to the eaves; E, F, G, north-east angle of central space, also standing to much the same level; G, H, east wall of north *porticus* pierced by medieval three-light window, but standing to the eaves in its southern portion G, I, and to the level of the sill of the window in its northern part I, H; J, K, north wall of north *porticus* standing only four courses high, on a square plinth of large stones; K, L, inferred position of west wall as indicated by foundations reported by Irvine and by ending of north wall at K; P, P, bases of Anglo-Saxon columns *in situ*; Q, Q, inferred positions of companion columns; g, g, and l, l, destroyed outer walls of earlier aisles as reported by Irvine; h, h, present pointed arcades; j, j, inferred position of original walls of pre-Norman aisleless nave.

In the larger-scale insets, *a* and *b* are the two members of the double cornice of the crypt; *c* is the surviving string-course in the central space; *d, d* is the curious moulded feature near the eaves of each of the eastern faces of the central space; *e* is the hollow-moulded string-course on the lower part of each of these faces; and *f* is an elevation and plan of one of the pilasters of the crypt. In the drawing *f* it should particularly be noted how the jointing of the stonework of the pilaster is quite unrelated to that of the wall against which it is placed, and how the position of the capital is unrelated to either of the levels of the double cornice on the wall.

In the plan of the crypt, the letters *ab* denote the parts of the wall which carry the two mouldings *a* and *b* of the double cornice; the letters *b* in the western recess indicate how its three walls carry only the one moulding, *b*, of double-stepped pattern.

chancel is of rather different construction, being built of roughly squared blocks of brown stone, laid in courses. The angles of this section are treated in a form peculiar to Repton, with quoin-stones of massive flat blocks which are almost square in plan. The walls of the central space seem to be of the same date as this intermediate section of the chancel, for they are of the same roughly squared blocks of brown stone, and they have the same distinctive type of quoining.

A further change in character of stone and workmanship occurs at about the level of the sill

of the medieval four-light east window. Below this level the stone is brown in colour and is in large blocks, many of which are almost square; above this level the stone is white or grey in colour, and is in smaller, flatter, rectangular blocks, while the wall is ornamented with vertical pilaster-strips. These pilasters rise from a square-sectioned string-course and run up the whole upper part of the side walls, to stop on curious caps placed just below the present eaves. Two pilaster-strips run up each side wall of the chancel and there are vestiges of two on the east face, in the part of the wall above the medieval window and below the restored gable. There is an Early English lancet in the north wall of the chancel; and a window of similar design was inserted in the south wall after 1937, cutting through the Anglo-Saxon string-course, which is shown intact in our photograph of 1937 (Fig. 556). No original windows have survived in this upper walling to help to determine its date, but from the evidence of the pilaster-strips it may reasonably be dated to period C. This date would be consistent with the evidence provided by a monolithic window-head of later Anglo-Saxon form, which is now preserved in the south porch. It serves to define a single-splayed window whose aperture, 7 in. wide externally, was outlined by a shallow rebate as if for a shutter.

THE CRYPT (FIGS. 249 AND 558)

Two flights of steps lead from the two transepts into the crypt.[1] This is a chamber, about 16 ft. square, vaulted in nine roughly square bays. These are covered by simple almost domical vaults borne on the outside walls and on two sets of transverse arches, which spring from two pilasters on each outer wall and which rest on four columns in the interior of the crypt. These four remarkable monolithic columns are each ornamentally carved with two encircling fillets, which run spirally round and up the column as though to bind and support it. The columns rest on rude annular bases and support equally rude square chamfered capitals, whose vertical faces are enriched with characteristically Anglo-Saxon ornament in the form of lightly incised horizontal grooves. The capitals are of remarkably irregular thickness and make no serious attempt to change the square plan of the vaulting ribs into the circular plan of the supporting columns.

The side and east walls of the crypt are each divided into three sections, of which that in the middle is a deep recess, which now serves as a form of basement window, but which no doubt originally housed a tomb or shrine. All three sections of the wall are built of smooth-faced, long,

flat stones, similar to those visible externally; and a double cornice is carried along the tops of the sections of the main wall, but not into the recesses. The double cornice consists of two quite separate string-courses (a and b in Fig. 249), divided by an area of plain wall 10 in. in height. The upper string-course is of simple rectangular section and the lower is of double-stepped profile, with two vertical faces which are separated from each other and from the wall below by *oblique* steps. It will be seen from the plan of the crypt in Fig. 249 how the double cornice is carried round the north, east, and south sides of the original rectangular area of the crypt, but not into the recesses, which therefore appear to be later modifications.[2] Moreover, it will be seen that there is no cornice at all on the west wall, but a single cornice (identical with the lower member b) round all three sides of the western recess. It was for this reason that Irvine regarded the west wall and western recess as later insertions into a crypt which had been polygonal in this region.

At the salient angles, where the main walls turn into the recesses, pilasters have been set against the walling, but not in bond with it. They carry capitals roughly similar to those of the columns and, like them, they serve to support the transverse ribs of the vaulting. The pilasters are about 1 ft. square in plan at the base, narrowing slightly as they rise, to about 10 in. square at the top (see f in Fig. 249). Each of their three exposed faces is enriched by a recessed round-headed panel, about 8 in. wide and sunk at the edges about ½ in. behind the face of the pilaster. The faces of these recesses are not plane but are V-shaped in plan so as to show an arris which runs vertically up the centre of each recessed panel. On the north, west, and south walls, the capitals of these pilasters project both forward and laterally; but on the east wall neither capital has any projection on the side that adjoins the central space. It seems clear that this peculiar arrangement was planned from the start and is not merely a subsequent cutting back, because the ornamentation on the vertical faces of each capital is carried without change round all its three faces.

---

[1] The existence of the crypt had been forgotten in the middle ages; it was rediscovered in 1779 (J. C. Cox, *Churches of Derbyshire*, III (London, 1877), 434).

[2] In Fig. 249 the double cornice a, b should be shown with the same early date-shading as the lower walls.

The west wall of the crypt also has a recess; but, unlike the other three, its walls have a single cornice which is the same as the lower member of the double cornice that runs round the main walls of the crypt. In its west wall there is a small triangular cavity immediately above the cornice. It is difficult to interpret this small cavity, which might have been a lamp socket, a relic-container, or even part of a long squint, formerly opening through the chancel steps into the nave. The north and south main walls of the crypt each rest on a plinth which is about 1 ft. in width and which is formed of large flat stones. These are laid only slightly above the level of the present rather uneven floor of the crypt. The west wall rests on a similar plinth which, however, is about 1 ft above the level of the floor.

INTERIOR OF THE MAIN CHURCH (FIG. 249)

Close beside the upper ends of the passages leading to and from the crypt, small areas of the original flooring of the nave are exposed, about 2 ft below the present floor-level. On this flooring there rest the bases and the lowest courses of circular columns which formerly carried the eastern ends of arches opening from the central space into the transepts. The remaining sections of these columns, and their capitals, strongly reminiscent of the capitals of the columns in the crypt, are preserved in the south porch, where they were placed some time after the original arches were most unfortunately replaced in 1854 by pointed arches copied from those of the main arcade. Above these nineteenth-century arches the Anglo-Saxon walling of the central space may still be seen, in clear contrast to the medieval walling over the western arches. A drawing made by G. M. Gorham in 1847 when he was a boy at Repton School shows the east end of the nave as it was before the restoration of 1854.[1] The drawing shows the north and south walls each pierced by two rather stilted round arches, each of a single plain square order. The outer ends of the arches rested on round responds with simple square capitals, and a single circular column with a similar square capital stood in the centre of each

side. By itself the drawing could scarcely be accepted as reliable evidence for so unusual an arrangement, but by very good fortune the arches were seen and described by Father D. H. Haigh before their destruction. It therefore seems clear beyond doubt that until 1854 the early side walls of the central space were each pierced by two round-headed arches, each of which was of a plain square order. It is still, however, not certain that one should accept this fact as proving that the pre-Conquest church at Repton had the unique arrangement of twin arches opening from the central space to each of the transepts; for it is possible that the eastern arch on each side was the original Anglo-Saxon arch which opened from the central space to the transept, and that the western arch on each side was a later insertion, from a date when the nave was given aisles. Indeed, this interpretation receives support from Father Haigh's description, since he noted that the western arch of each pair was higher and wider than its eastern companion. His words are of sufficient importance to justify our quoting them in full:[2]

In the interior, the two eastern responds to the piers of the nave have abaci of the same sort as those of the crypt, thus proving that the crypt and the church above it are of the same date. The arches which spring from them are semi-circular, of square soffits; the piers next them are cased in wood; the next arch in each side is also single sofitted, but higher and of wider span than the first. At a considerable height above these arches there is a cornice moulding extending over both, and terminating where the Early English work of the nave begins.

That the side walls of the original central space have indeed remained above the pointed arcades of 1854 is attested not only by the character of the fabric, in striking contrast to the much smoother masonry above the medieval arcade of the nave, but also by the fact that in these walls at a height of 23 ft above the floor the string-course (or cornice moulding) mentioned by Haigh has survived, 25 ft in length, and of a characteristically Anglo-Saxon profile (c in Fig. 249).

No trace now remains of a west wall to this central space, nor of side walls of the nave,

---

[1] A copy of this drawing may be seen in the School's Undercroft Museum beside the entrance to the Masters' Common Room. It was published by F. C. Hipkins in a booklet of local pictures Repton and its Neighbourhood

(Repton, 1899). See Fig. 555. Note that the drawing also shows the surviving string-course mentioned by Haigh.
[2] D. H. Haigh, 'Ancient Saxon monastery at Repton', Trans. Arch. Ass., Winchester, 1845 (London, 1846), 448–51.

whether along the line of the present arcades or on some narrower alignment, but there are reasons for thinking that the original nave, like the chancel and transepts, may have been narrower than the central space. In the first place, it is likely that if (as at Dover and Breamore) the nave had been of the same width as the central space then its walls would have been suffered to remain, above the medieval arcades, just as the walls of the central space were retained when the two pointed arches were inserted in place of the earlier round arches in 1854. Secondly, it should be noted how Irvine's plan of 1894 gives evidence of an earlier outer wall for the south aisle on a narrower alignment (*gg* in Fig. 249). If at the time of that outer wall *gg* the main wall of the nave had been in its present position *hh*, the aisle could not have been much more than 5 ft in width. While this is not an impossible arrangement, it seems much more likely that at that time the main walls of the nave were on a narrower alignment *j, j*.

Irvine reported that the floor of the Anglo-Saxon nave had been traced westward about half the length of the present nave. At the west of the church, externally and close beside the south of the tower, there are visible at the foot of the west wall some courses of brown stone walling like that of the chancel. These are sometimes regarded as evidence that the Anglo-Saxon church extended thus far, but we doubt whether this argument can be accepted.

The chancel has no original openings to fix its date, but over the medieval pointed chancel-arch is a square-headed doorway whose south jamb, in clearly defined 'Escomb technique', appears to have been one side of an opening which was originally more than twice its present width. The former north jamb, of equally clear 'Escomb technique', still remains in the walling, but the opening has been blocked; and it was originally of such width that it must have been spanned by a multiple arch on intermediate baluster shafts like the opening in the west wall at Brixworth. This would be consistent with the date in period C which we have suggested for the chancel in Fig. 249.

DIMENSIONS

The chancel is 14 ft 8 in. wide internally and 20 ft 3 in. long, if measured from the angle of the central space. Its walls are 2 ft 6 in. thick, and they stand to a height of over 28 ft above the ground, or over 38 ft from the floor of the crypt.

The transepts were about 16 ft wide internally from east to west. Their internal width from north to south, as determined by the surviving north wall of the north transept, was about 18 ft; but the foundations (*k, k*) reported in 1894 by Irvine and in 1951 by Fletcher indicated that earlier transepts or *porticus* were only 8 ft in width from north to south.

The central space is 24 ft wide internally from north to south, and its surviving string-course indicates that it was about 25 ft in length from east to west.

As has been mentioned above, there is no conclusive evidence for the original length or width of the Anglo-Saxon nave.

The crypt is about 16½ ft square internally; at the level of the floor the measurements are 16 ft 7 in. east–west by 16 ft. 5 in. north–south, but the walls slope inward so that at the level of the double cornice each of these dimensions is reduced by about 3 in. The floor of the crypt is 12½ ft below the floor of the present chancel or about 10 ft below the floor of the Anglo-Saxon nave.

The interior width of the chancel (14 ft 8 in.) is appreciably less than the width of the crypt at the level of the springing of its vault (*c.* 16 ft 2 in.). This seems to constitute good reason for believing that the walls of the chancel (as distinct from the main walls of the crypt) are no earlier than the vaulting of the crypt.

The columns from the openings to the transepts are 1 ft 4 in. in diameter. They each consist of a bulbous base and one cylindrical drum *in situ*, together with eight cylindrical drums and a capital which are now preserved in the south porch. The total height when *in situ* must have been about 10½ ft. If, as seems probable from the width of the transepts and the position of the bases *in situ*, the openings were about 10 ft wide, the arches would have been about 15½ ft in total height.

REFERENCES

J. RICKMAN, 'Ecclesiastical architecture of France and England', *Arch.* **26** (1836), 26–46. Repton, 34.

D. H. HAIGH, 'The ancient Saxon monastery at Repton, Derbyshire', *Trans. Arch. Ass., Winchester, 1845* (London, 1846), 448–51.

A. Ashpitel, 'Repton church and priory', *J.B.A.A.* **7** (1852), 263–83. Picture and plan of crypt, and of chancel from north-east. Compared with drawings of Saxon churches in early manuscripts.

R. Bigsby, *Historical and Topographical Description of Repton* (London, 1854). Chapter on the church by Father Haigh, containing much the same information as his 1845 article, but with some pictures.

J. T. Irvine, 'On the crypt beneath Repton church', *J. Derby. A.N.H.S.* **5** (1883), 165–72. Detailed description of crypt with many useful plans, elevations, and sections. In his text (p. 166) Irvine described, and in his pl. XII he illustrated (figs. 5 and 6), two narrow single-splayed windows whose outer faces (about 6 in. wide and 2 ft tall) he showed at 7 ft and 14 ft from the south-east quoin of the chancel. The inner faces he showed rising from the level of the present floor of the chancel to a level about 4½ ft higher. Baldwin Brown (p. 317) described these windows as 'among the hardest of the little nuts the elucidator of Repton will have to crack'. He incorporated them in his plan (his fig. 142). We have not incorporated them in our plan (Fig. 249) because we have not been able to trace conclusive evidence of their existence either internally or externally. When we first visited the church in 1937 it was plastered internally. The plaster had been removed (and the new south window inserted) before our next visit in 1956, but the area where the faces of Irvine's windows would lie had been covered by oak panelling fixed in position. Externally we can trace what could possibly be one jamb of each window and a flat stone for a head, but the evidence is slight.

If these windows could be shown to have existed, they would suggest to us that the lower parts of the present walls of the chancel (from the string-course downward, and including the present crypt) originally served to define an open rectangular chapel, which these windows then lit. It would have been natural for the windows to be blocked when the insertion of the vault rendered them useless. But for reasons stated under 'Dimensions' we think it likely that the upper walls of the chancel did not precede the vault, from which it would seem unlikely that the windows have a real existence.

J. C. Cox, 'Note on the restoration of Repton church', *ibid.* **8** (1886), 231–6.

J. T. Irvine, 'Notes on discoveries made in the nave and aisles of Repton church during the recent restoration', *ibid.* **14** (1892), 158–60.

J. T. Irvine, 'Plans of discoveries lately made in the nave of Repton church', *J.B.A.A.* **50** (1894), 248–50. General and useful account of what is to be seen and how it developed, but some of the later Anglo-Saxon work wrongly described as Norman.

F. C. Hipkins, *Repton: Village, Abbey, Church, Priory and School* (Derby and London, 1894). The church de-

scribed, 12–15. Account of the destruction of the eastern arches, 18–19.

F. C. Hipkins, *Repton and its Neighbourhood* (Repton, 1899). Booklet of pictures, including Mr Gorham's drawing of the nave in 1847.

F. C. Hipkins, 'A note on discoveries at Repton priory and church', *J. Derby. A.N.H.S.* **23** (1901), 105–7.

J. C. Cox, 'A note on discoveries at Repton priory and church', *ibid.* **35** (1913), 245–6.

T. L. Tudor, 'Repton, Northworthy, and Wirksworth', *ibid.* **44** (1922), 44–57.

A. Macdonald, *A Short History of Repton* (London, 1929).

A. W. Fletcher, 'The south transept of Repton church', *J. Derby. A.N.H.S.*, n.s., **24** (1951), 82–3. Carved stone found in later east wall of transept, 82. Saxon east wall of south transept found in line with corresponding wall of north transept, 82. Base of column for south arcade found *in situ* opposite corresponding base of column for north arcade, 83.

C. A. R. Radford, 'Repton, the church of St Wystan', *Arch. J.* **118** (1961), 241–3.

RIPON

Yorkshire, West Riding

Map sheet 91, reference SE 313711

ST PETER

Crypt beneath nave of present cathedral: period A 2

Bede (*H.E.* v, 19) records how Alchfrith, sub-king of Deira, befriended Wilfrid when he first returned from Rome. Alchfrith first gave Wilfrid an estate of ten hides at *Stanford*, a place which has not been located with certainty; and, not long afterward, he installed Wilfrid as abbot at Ripon, where the Scottish monks whom the king had lately established there had quitted the place rather than adopt the Roman method of determining Easter. After outlining Wilfrid's adventurous life Bede also records how, after his death at Oundle in 709, his body was carried to his first monastery at Ripon and there buried in the church of St Peter the Apostle close by the south of the altar. A more detailed account of the building and consecration of the church at Ripon between 671 and 678 is given in Eddius's *Life of Bishop Wilfrid*,[1] where chapter XVII records how Wilfrid

---

[1] Text, translation, and notes, ed. B. Colgrave (Cambridge, 1927).

'built and completed from the foundations in the earth up to the roof, a church of dressed stone, supported by various columns and side aisles or porches'. Although there now remains of this

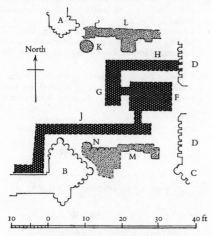

FIG. 250. RIPON, YORKSHIRE (W.R.)

Plan of St Wilfrid's crypt, showing its position in relation to the present cathedral and showing also the pre-Norman masonry discovered in 1932. A, north-west pier of central tower; B, south-west pier; C, south-east pier; D, D, screen at entrance to choir; F, main chamber of crypt; G, vestibule to main chamber; H, north passage, now blocked at its eastern end; J, south passage, now serving as the only entry; K, cylindrical drum found in 1932, not *in situ*, and now standing at western end of north aisle of nave; L, M, foundations discovered in 1932 and thought to belong to a tenth-century church; N, cylindrical drum found in 1932, and left *in situ*.

(946–55) is said to have 'harried all Northumbria because they had taken Eric for their king; and on this raid the glorious minster at Ripon which St Wilfrid built was burnt down'.

With the possible exception of some foundations under the crossing and a massive stepped base of a circular column preserved at the west end of the north aisle of the present cathedral, the crypt under the nave is the sole surviving part of St Wilfrid's

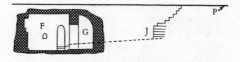

Transverse section of crypt, looking west

Longitudinal section of crypt, looking south

FIG. 251. RIPON, YORKSHIRE, (W.R.)

Sections of crypt. F, main chamber; G, vestibule at west; J, south passage, now serving as only entry; K, cylindrical drum found in 1932 and removed to north aisle; L, M, foundations discovered in 1932 and thought to belong to a tenth-century church; N, cylindrical drum found in 1932 and left *in situ*; P, floor of present cathedral church.

church only a crypt of similar form to that of Wilfrid's other church at Hexham, yet the workmanship is of a quality which well justifies the use by Eddius of the description 'dressed stone'. The importance of the monastery is indicated by Eddius in his description of its consecration in the presence of kings, abbots, reeves, sub-kings, and dignitaries of every kind; the altar vested in purple woven with gold; and Wilfrid reading aloud a list of the lands which the kings had dedicated to it. The end of the history of Wilfrid's church is given in the 'D' text of the *Anglo-Saxon Chronicle* under the year 948 where King Eadred

noble monastery. It is similar to the crypt at Wilfrid's other monastery at Hexham; but has only two passages, one leading to the ante-chamber and one to the crypt itself, whereas the more ambitious arrangement at Hexham had three passages. The crypt at Ripon consists of an ante-chamber oriented from north to south, and a main chamber oriented from east to west and covered by a barrel vault about 9 ft high from the floor to the crown of the arch. It has recently been shown[1] that the vault is formed of flagstones wedged between vaulting ribs, which cross the chamber from north to south, and are about

[1] C. R. Peers, *Ant. J.* **11** (1931), 116, fig. 3, and pl. XII; or W. T. Jones, *Yorks. Arch. J.* **31** (1932–4), 74.

15 in. deep, tapering from a width of about 8 in. on the inner face to about 5 in. above. The walls of the chamber are built of carefully dressed large blocks of stone and contain four small recesses presumably designed to hold lamps. There is also a large recess or passage in the east wall, perhaps to receive large relics.

The main chamber is entered from a western ante-chamber, or vestibule as at Hexham, but unlike Hexham this vestibule is covered by a quadrant-shaped half vault instead of a semi-circular barrel vault; and it has only one passage of access so that pilgrims must either have been allowed into the crypt itself or must have returned to the church by the single narrow passage.

DIMENSIONS

The ante-chamber is about 12 ft 6 in. long from north to south and about 4 ft 6 in. wide. The main chamber is about 11 ft 6 in. long from east to west and about 7 ft 6 in. wide and 9 ft high.

If certain foundations which were found under the crossing in 1931 were those of Wilfrid's church, it must have been about 30 ft in width internally. The great columns found in these foundations in 1931 were 3 ft 6 in. in diameter. The one now standing at the west of the north aisle is about 1½ ft high; it was not *in situ* and was therefore removed for exhibition. Its companion on the south side was *in situ* and was not disturbed.

REFERENCES

R. J. WALBRAN, 'On a crypt at Ripon cathedral', *Proc. Arch. Ass., Winchester, 1845* (London, 1846), 339–54. Crypt attributed to Wilfrid.

R. J. WALBRAN, 'St Wilfrid and the Saxon church of Ripon', *A.A.S.R.* 5 (1859–60), 63–96.

J. T. MICKLETHWAITE, 'On the crypts at Hexham and Ripon', *Arch. J.* 39 (1882), 347–54. Plans, history, difficulties associated with Leland's remarks about Ripon, and somewhat fanciful theories about western apses.

J. T. MICKLETHWAITE, 'The Saxon crypt of Ripon minster', *P. Soc. Ant.* 14 (1892), 191–6. Account of excavations.

J. T. MICKLETHWAITE, 'Something about Saxon church building', *Arch. J.* 53 (1896), 293–351. Ripon, 344. West passage interpreted as a burial chamber.

W. G. COLLINGWOOD, 'Anglian and Anglo-Danish sculpture in the West Riding', *Yorks. Arch. J.* 23 (1915), 129–299. Ripon, 233–5. Stones on buttress on west of north transept, with interlacing ornament. Clearly part of an early string-course or impost.

C. R. PEERS, 'Recent discoveries in the minsters of Ripon and York', *Ant. J.* 11 (1931), 113–22. Discovery of foundations of side walls; of the two sections of columns; and of the nature of the vaulting. Plans and sections, and photograph of the upper surface of the vaulting, showing the vaulting-ribs and the flat flagstones between.

W. T. JONES, 'Recent discoveries at Ripon cathedral', *Yorks. Arch. J.* 31 (1932–4), 74–6. Much the same material about Ripon as in the previous reference.

ROCHESTER
Kent

Map sheet 172, reference TQ 742684

ST ANDREW
Foundations of nave and apsidal chancel: period A1

Bede records that in 604 Augustine consecrated Mellitus bishop of London and Justus bishop of Rochester; he also records that the latter place possessed a church dedicated to St Andrew and built by King Ethelbert.[1]

The remains of an early church were uncovered here in 1889 and their plan is preserved by markings on the floor of the nave of the present cathedral near its west doors. The plan conforms so closely to those of the early churches at Canterbury that little doubt can be left that this is indeed King Ethelbert's church of St Andrew. Further remains were reported by Sir W. St J. Hope, perhaps those of the apse of a second and larger church, in the angle between the nave and south transept of the cathedral. By analogy with Canterbury it would be quite in accordance with custom for there to have been two early churches close together in this way.

DIMENSIONS

The foundations by the west of the cathedral indicate a simple rectangular nave which appears

[1] *H.E.* II, 3.

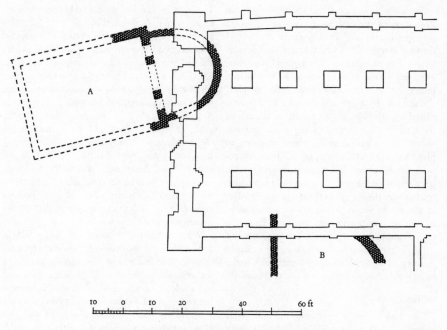

FIG. 252. ROCHESTER, KENT

Plan to show the two sets of early remains in relation to the Norman and later cathedral. A, church attributed to the time of Ethelbert; B, remains, possibly those of another early church.

to have been 28 ft 6 in. broad internally, by about 42 ft long, with a chancel consisting of a stilted apse 24 ft 6 in. in width and 19 ft in depth. The walls appear to have been little over 2 ft in thickness.

REFERENCES

G. M. LIVETT, 'Foundations of the Saxon cathedral church at Rochester', *Arch. Cant.* **18** (1889), 261–78. Full description of the remains discovered at the west of the cathedral. Plan and sections. Details of carved stones.

W. H. ST J. HOPE, 'The architectural history of the cathedral church and monastery of St Andrew at Rochester', *ibid.* **23** (1898), 194–328. Second Saxon church, 214–15; and plan facing p. 215.

C. R. PEERS, 'On Saxon churches of the St Pancras type', *Arch. J.* **58** (1901), 402–34. Rochester, 418–19.

F. H. FAIRWEATHER, 'Gundulf's cathedral and priory church of St Andrew, Rochester; some critical remarks on the hitherto accepted plan', *ibid.* **86** (1929), 187–212. Plan showing two Saxon churches, facing p. 187. Reference to the two churches, 192.

ROCKLAND

Norfolk

Map sheet 136, reference TL 994960

Figure 559

ALL SAINTS

Nave: period C3

Neither of Rockland's two churches is close to the centre of the present village: St Peter has a few houses nearby; but All Saints stands in open country south of the village, beside a by-road to Great Ellingham, about 3¼ miles west of Attleborough.

The church is built of flints with stone dressings; and it now consists of a west tower, an aisleless nave with south porch, and an aisleless chancel. The walls of the nave are tall in proportion to its size, and the impression of unusual height is further emphasized by the absence of aisles.

No early openings have survived, but the assignment of the nave to the late-Saxon period may be taken as fairly certain on the evidence of the four quoins, all of which are of well-defined long-and-short technique. The upright long stones, averaging about 20 in. in height, are not square pillars but are markedly rectangular in plan, about 12 in. by 5 in.; and they are in the main placed with the longer side parallel to the axis of the church. The short bonding stones average about 5 in. in height and are mainly square in plan, with sides of about 15 in. All these dimensions are rather small by comparison with the usual run of long-and-short quoining, a fact which led Baldwin Brown (p. 477) to suggest a date late in the Anglo-Saxon period. A confirmation of lateness in date might also be taken from the unusual thickness of the walls, but indications of dating by the thickness of the walls must necessarily be accepted with caution by reason of the existence of early churches with thick walls, as at Brixworth.

DIMENSIONS

The nave is about 34 ft long and 19 ft wide internally, with walls 3 ft 5 in. thick and about 18 ft tall.

REFERENCE

V.C.H., Norfolk, 2 (London, 1906), 555. Discovery in 1860 of a carved grave-slab like that at Cringleford; part was found in the porch and part in a heap of earth against the church. Stone now preserved in chancel. Illustration, 556.

ROMSEY

Hampshire

Map sheet 168, reference SU 350212

ST MARY AND ST ELFLAEDA

No structural remains have survived from before the Conquest, but evidence is summarized below to indicate that a transeptal pre-Conquest church survived for about a century after the Conquest.

The certain history of the abbey at Romsey begins with its foundation by Edgar in 967, under an abbess named Merwynn, though it is possible that there had been an earlier foundation as was claimed by a spurious charter attributed to Edgar. St Elflaeda is likely to have been a later abbess than Merwynn, though a fourteenth-century writer seems to have identified her with a daughter of Edward the Elder.[1] It was here that Christina, grand-daughter of Edmund Ironside and sister of Queen Margaret of Scotland, took the veil; and Margaret's daughters Matilda (later wife of Henry I) and Mary were educated.[2] Additions seem to have been made to the abbey shortly after the Norman Conquest; while still later, perhaps between 1120 and 1160, the greater part of the present Norman abbey was built.

When wood-block floors were being laid in 1900 in the nave and crossing, some early foundations were found beneath the existing floor.[3] On the evidence provided by those foundations and by a close examination of minor differences between parts of the existing walls, Peers was able to build up the following picture of the pre-Conquest church which existed at the time of the Conquest and of the way in which it was enlarged in the Saxo-Norman style and subsequently replaced by the present Norman abbey.

The foundations discovered beneath the crossing, and a single course of ashlar masonry above them, clearly defined a short apsidal chancel rather narrower than the present nave, and with walls 4 ft 9 in. thick. The ashlar masonry and the thick walls argued a Norman date for this short chancel, which must nevertheless be earlier than the present Norman chancel dating from 1120 to 1160. Changes in the masonry of the outer wall of the Norman south aisle of the nave enabled Peers to see that the bay at the west of the south door was appreciably earlier than the adjoining walling either to the west or to the east. He was thus led to suggest that the Anglo-Saxon abbey which survived the Conquest was cruciform in plan, with an aisleless nave, small square transepts or *porticus*, and a small chancel; the additions made soon

---

[1] See Birch, *C.S.*, no. 1187; *Liber Monasterii de Hyda*, ed. E. Edwards (Rolls series, 45) (London, 1866), 112; and *Liber Vitae of the New Minster and Hyde Abbey*, ed. W. de G. Birch (London, 1892), 58.

[2] *Anglo-Saxon Chronicle*, 1085 (for 1086); and Ordericus Vitalis, *Ecclesiastical History of England and France*, ed. T. Forrester, II (London, 1854), 12–13.

[3] C. R. Peers, *Arch.* 57 (1901), 317–20.

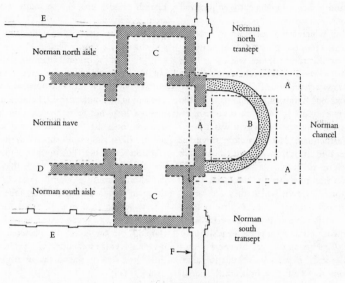

FIG. 253. ROMSEY, HAMPSHIRE

Plan showing the apse discovered in 1900 in relation to the existing Norman abbey and the conjectural Anglo-Saxon transeptal church. A, A, A, ground-plan of present Norman central tower; B, the apsidal wall discovered in 1900; C, C, conjectural walls of Anglo-Saxon transepts or *porticus*; D, D, conjectural side wall of aisleless Anglo-Saxon nave; E, E, present side walls of aisles of Norman nave; F, present position of great Rood. The central space was about 34 ft square, and the transepts about 25 ft by 16 ft.

after the Conquest consisted of the short apsidal chancel and the north and south aisles of the nave, the side walls of these aisles being carried westward in the alignment of the north and south outer walls of the Anglo-Saxon transepts. Peers dated these additions about 1090 to 1100, and of the work of that period he thought there remained only the foundations of the apse, the early bay of the outer wall of the south aisle, and two vaulting shafts on the interior of the north wall of the north aisle. The rebuilding of the abbey in the fully developed Norman style between 1100 and 1160 swept away the whole of the Anglo-Saxon nave and transepts, but the former existence of the Anglo-Saxon south transept seemed to Peers to be proved by the fact that the Norman walling of the bay containing the present south doorway is appreciably later in style than that to the west, which he assigned to the early work of about 1100, or that to the east which he dated about 1120. The reason why this one bay was appreciably later, about 1160, was that until then the Normans

had left the Anglo-Saxon transept in place, and that only when all the other work was completed did they remove the last of the Anglo-Saxon walls.

This evidence for a substantial church of stone on the site from before the Conquest is of interest in connexion with the important stone Rood, which is built into the west wall of the south transept, close to the south door of the nave. This is a more naturalistic carving than the great Langford Rood, but the figure of Christ is represented without any of the agonized distortion of the Rood at Breamore or the small Rood in the gable of the south porch at Langford. As in the great Rood at Langford, the intention seems to have been to represent divine majesty standing above human suffering even when on the cross. Above the head of Christ, but carved on the same massive stone, is the hand of God appearing from a cloud, as at Breamore and Headbourne Worthy. The importance of this feature in settling a pre-Conquest date for the carving was first pointed out by Casson and was subsequently emphasized by Clapham.[1]

The wall in which this Rood is set is dated by Peers to about 1160, but the run of the masonry makes it clear that the sculpture was re-set here, no doubt when the time came to demolish the earlier wall in which it stood. Talbot Rice dates the Rood *c.* 1010, but Kendrick excludes it from the Anglo-Saxon period.[2] If the work is not Anglo-Saxon it is hard to understand why it was inserted in this wall rather than placed in a more important position prepared for it from the outset. Another point which is in favour of an Anglo-Saxon rather than a Norman date for the major Langford and Romsey Roods is that they are carved upon enormous stones; since Norman technique was much more likely to have favoured ashlar stonework rather than these great slabs.

A further Crucifixion of great interest, but on a much smaller scale, is preserved beside the altar. This is a stone about 2 ft 6 in. in height.[3]

ROPSLEY
Lincolnshire

Map sheets 113 and 123, reference SK 992342

ST PETER
Nave walls: period C

About 5 miles east of Grantham and half that distance from the Roman Ermine Street, Ropsley is one of the many Lincolnshire Anglo-Saxon villages which were situated close to but not immediately beside a Roman road. The village streets enclose a large square of sloping meadow, which rises to the south, where several paths converge on the parish church.

In its present form, the church consists of a west tower with Perpendicular broach spire, an aisled nave with Perpendicular clear-storey windows, and an aisleless chancel partly flanked on the south by a chapel. The main fabric of the Anglo-Saxon nave has remained, with a Norman arcade cut through its north wall and an Early English arcade through the south. The chancel-arch and main fabric of the chancel are Early English, while most of the windows of the aisles and chancel are Perpendicular.

All trace of the original chancel has disappeared, but all four quoins of the nave remain, three visible externally and the fourth at the south-east within the south chapel. These quoins are all of massive long-and-short construction with well-dressed stones carefully jointed, and set forward slightly from the main wall-face as though to act as a stop for plaster. The upright or 'long' stones are of fairly uniform width, while the faces of the flat 'short' stones are carefully cut back level with the main wall-face along the line of the uprights so that when the wall was plastered the quoining would show as a stone facing of uniform width clasping the angle of the plastered wall. The uprights average something like 3 ft in height and the lowest one on the south-east angle is no less than 5 ft tall.

DIMENSIONS

The nave measures 45 ft by 15 ft 3 in. internally, with walls 2 ft 6 in. in thickness.

REFERENCE

E. TROLLOPE, 'St Peter's, Ropsley', *A.A.S.R.* 13 (1875), 3–4. Church claimed as Saxon on the strength of the long-and-short quoins.

ROTHWELL
Lincolnshire

Map sheets 104 and 105, reference TF 149993

Figures 560, 561

ST MARY MAGDALENE
West tower and nave walls: period C 3

The pleasantly situated church at Rothwell stands beside meadows, in the extensive park of one of the large houses of the village, and serves a small but prosperous community in a steep-sided valley of the Lincolnshire wolds, about 2 miles south-

---

[1] S. Casson, *Burl. Mag.* **61** (1932), 274. A. W. Clapham, *Ant.* **25** (1951), 192. Roods that show the Hand of God survive *in situ* at Breamore and Headbourne Worthy.

[2] D. T. Rice, *English Art 871–1100*, 98, and pl. 13. T. D. Kendrick, *Late Saxon and Viking Art*, 48–51.
[3] D. T. Rice, *loc. cit.* 118, and pl. 18 *b*.

east of Caistor. It now consists of a late-Saxon west tower; an aisled nave, which has been formed by cutting fine Norman arcades of two bays through each of the side walls of the original aisleless nave; and an aisleless chancel of later date, rather heavily restored at the end of the nineteenth century.

The fabric of the tower and of the early walls of the nave is of roughly squared blocks of brown ironstone laid in courses, with side-alternate quoins of much larger stones. The south-west quoin of the nave shows clearly, like a buttress, in the angle between the tower and the south aisle; and, although Baldwin Brown refers to it as showing long-and-short technique, it is in fact a good example of megalithic side-alternate quoining. The north-west quoin of the nave does not project in this way; but its position may nevertheless be clearly traced, as a straight joint, against the later west wall of the north aisle.

The tower, standing on a bold plinth of two chamfered orders, is of the usual Lincolnshire type, with two unequal stages separated by an off-set above a square string-course. The original capping has been lost, but the tower is now quite pleasantly topped by a simple medieval moulded string-course, and a plain parapet, with vestiges of finials at its four corners.

The belfry has the usual Lincolnshire form of tall double windows in each face, resting on the intermediate string-course as a sill, and with square jambs built of very roughly dressed stones rather larger than the normal run of those in the walling. Each window has slightly projecting rectangular imposts and through-stone slabs; the latter are supported by mid-wall shafts of circular section, with conical bases, square plinths, and cushion capitals which are classed by Baldwin Brown as of a matured post-Conquest type. The head of each double window, except that to the west, is formed of two rectangular stones, each of which is shaped below to form the round head of an individual window of the pair; by contrast, the heads of the two individual windows to the west are cut in two whiter stones whose upper faces have been left quite unusually rough in outline.

At about the middle height of each of the three external faces of the lower stage of the tower,

small round-headed internally splayed windows, about 9 in. wide and 20 in. high, serve to light the upper floor of the tower. These have their round heads cut from single stones and their jambs formed of rectangular stones which bond deeply into the wall. Beside the north and south of these windows small horizontal sections of string-course seem to suggest that flanking annexes were at some stage built against the tower. The north face has no other opening, but to light the ground floor of the tower the south face has a second window, narrower and taller than those above, about 8 in. by 34 in., with a single stone for its head, but with its slightly sloping jambs formed of tall monoliths. All these windows are widely splayed internally, with flat heads formed by placing lintel-stones across the splayed jambs.

The tower may still be entered from the west by the fine original doorway, whose round-arched head of a single square order is outlined by a slightly projecting square hood-mould, which is stopped at each side on sturdy, square imposts. The round-arched head is filled by a plain stone tympanum, which is set back about an inch behind the arch to leave a rectangular doorway 2 ft 9 in. wide and 7 ft 6 in. high. The square jambs are built of large stones with a strong flavour of 'Escomb technique'. They are cut straight through the wall, and the chamfered plinth of the tower is not returned into the doorway. Internally, the imposts and the tympanum are carried only so far as to meet the face of the door; and thereafter the doorway appears as a round-headed opening, whose arched head is set back about 2 in. behind the vertical lines of its jambs.

The floor of the nave is three steps lower than that of the tower, which is itself two steps below the sill of the west doorway. The round-headed tower-arch is of a single square order, with bold square imposts returned as a string-course along the whole width of the west wall of the nave, but not along the interior of the tower. Within the arch the imposts are chamfered below; but, by contrast, the string-course returned into the nave is of plain square section. The arch is not of through-stones, and the construction of the square jambs is hidden by plaster; the jambs, however, have a double chamfered plinth in the actual opening of the arch; but this plinth is not returned along the nave wall. There is no sign of a doorway above the tower-arch to give access from the nave to the upper chamber of the tower.

DIMENSIONS

The tower-arch is 5 ft 5 in. wide, in a wall 3 ft 9 in. thick; and from the floor of the nave the arch is about 14 ft high to the crown. The tower is 10 ft square internally and the nave is 36 ft long by 16 ft 5 in. wide, with fine Norman arcades of two bays cut through its side walls, which are 2 ft 8 in. thick on the south and 2 ft 6 in. on the north. The outer faces of these walls are aligned with the western quoins already noted, and there appears therefore every reason to regard the walls as part of the original Anglo-Saxon fabric.

REFERENCES

Editorial, 'Saxon churches', *Ecclesiologist*, **3** (1843–4), 138–9. Rothwell noted as Saxon, 139. Engraving of west doorway.

A. SUTTON, 'Churches visited from Grimsby', *A.A.S.R.* **29** (1907–8), 71–90. Rothwell, 87–8. Record of blocking of the aisles in the seventeenth or eighteenth century. Brief architectural description.

A. H. THOMPSON, 'Pre-Conquest church-towers in North Lincolnshire', *ibid.* **29** (1907–8), 43–70. Rothwell, 67–8.

ROUGHTON

Norfolk

Map sheet 126, reference TG 220364

ST MARY

Round west tower, and west wall of nave: period C3

The interesting church at Roughton, about 4 miles south of Cromer, now consists of a circular west tower with later battlements, an aisled nave with north and south porches, and an aisleless chancel.

Only the west wall of the nave and the round west tower have survived from the original church, which has been enlarged at various later dates by the addition of the aisles, by the raising of the side walls for the clear-storey, and probably by considerable extension eastward.

The otherwise awkward re-entrant angle in each of the junctions between the tower and the nave is, as at several other pre-Conquest churches in Norfolk, filled by a quarter-round pilaster or column, which extends from the ground roughly to the height of the original side walls of the nave, at which level it dies away with a conical taper. The lateral extent and height of the original west wall of the nave are shown by the quoins of brown carstone against which the flanking aisles abut with straight vertical joints. The quoins are of fairly large blocks of this characteristic brown stone, about 7 in. in height and up to 2 ft in length along the wall. Apart from the quoins, the main fabric of the west wall is of flints; while by contrast the tower is built of varied strata of different composition. The lowest and shortest stage is of brown carstone, in undressed blocks, which seem to have been laid for decoration sometimes horizontally coursed and sometimes in diagonally laid or herring-bone courses. The much taller second stage, mainly of flints, extends to about the level of the ridge of the present roof of the nave; and it would seem of itself to have been amply high in proportion to the small original church. Finally, the shorter belfry stage containing four double windows, is mainly of small car-stone rubble, with an appreciable admixture of flint.

At about 11 ft above the ground is a group of three windows. Of these windows, one, facing west, is a later insertion or pointed adaptation; while the others, facing north and south, are original, small, circular, double-splayed openings, roughly formed of the same flint fabric as the wall itself.

A further group of three windows is placed near the top of the flint stage, again facing north, west, and south. But these windows are in the form of tall, narrow slits, with their jambs and triangular heads formed of small, brick-like pieces of carstone.

The four double belfry windows, with twin triangular heads, are of unusual construction in that they do not have a monolithic mid-wall shaft, but a central pier of carstone rubble instead, carried through the full thickness of the wall and rounded on the outer face. The triangular heads of the individual windows are formed in the usual way, of pairs of flat stones sloped together; but, apart from the flat stones laid on the central piers as imposts, these are the only large stones used in the belfry windows, all the remainder being small rubble of about the size of bricks.

The interior of the church is plastered, but a few interesting details may be seen. Short sections of wall, 26 in. in thickness, forming the western responds of the north and south arcades, are probably parts of the original side walls of the nave. In the west wall, with its sill about 16 ft above the floor, is a round-headed doorway about 6 ft tall, with jambs sloping slightly inwards so that the opening narrows from 2 ft 2 in. at the sill to 2 ft at the shoulders. The tower-arch below, of a single square order, is of unusual shape as if it had been built over the inverted hull of a boat or by using a cruck-frame of bent tree-trunks.

DIMENSIONS

The internal breadth of the nave as defined by the surviving western responds is 16 ft 3 in., with walls 2 ft 2 in. thick and originally about 15 ft tall. The tower is 8 ft in internal diameter, with walls about 4 ft thick. The circular double-splayed windows in the tower have apertures about 9 in. in diameter, splayed to just over 2 ft in the wall-surfaces; their glass-line is about 30 in. from the interior.

RUMBOLDSWHYKE

Sussex

Map sheet 181, reference SU 870041

ST MARY (formerly ST RUMBOLD)

Main fabric: probably period C

The parish of Rumboldswhyke is now a southern suburb of Chichester, and the church stands beside the road leading from the city to Hunston and Selsey.

Baldwin Brown (p. 456) places Rumboldswhyke in his list of south coast churches which have no characteristic features sufficiently clear to justify inclusion in the pre-Conquest category. We think, however, that its inclusion is justified by the cumulative evidence of the following features:

the fabric of flint, tile, and rubble; the thin walls, all within 1 in. below or above 2 ft; the quoins, all of side-alternate construction of large stones, some of which are very large; and the chancel-arch which, although not thoroughly Anglo-Saxon in detail, yet seems to be much more so than Norman both in form and in detail.

The church was originally a two-cell structure, all of which still remains except that in the nineteenth century an arcade was cut through the north wall of the nave to a north aisle, and a vestry was added near the east of the north wall of the chancel.

The original megalithic side-alternate quoins remain at both eastern angles of the chancel, and at both southern angles of the nave. The original north-west angle of the nave is clearly marked by a few similar surviving quoin-stones, but the remainder of these and the whole of the north-east quoin appear to have been removed for the better bonding of the aisle; and many of the original stones seem to have been worked into the nineteenth-century north quoins of the aisle.

The chancel-arch is an excellent example of its type: the jambs are of plain square section, and the round arch is of a single square order, resting on projecting square imposts 9 in. in total height, with a 3 in. chamfer below. The opening is 7 ft 6 in. wide and about 13 ft 6 in. in height to the crown of the arch. Although neither the jambs nor the arch are of through-stones, yet the full thickness of the 25 in. wall is in every case spanned by two stones, with no rubble or other infilling between them.

DIMENSIONS

The internal dimensions of the original nave are about 38 ft by 19 ft, and of the chancel about 18 ft by 12 ft, with walls between 23 and 25 in. thick and about 18 ft high.

REFERENCES

G. M. HILLS, 'The church of Westhampnett, Sussex', *Sussex Arch. C.* **21** (1869), 33–43. Rumboldswhyke briefly described, with plan, and claimed as late-Saxon, 40.

H. L. JESSEP, *Anglo-Saxon Church Architecture in Sussex* (Winchester, undated), 33–4.

RUSHBURY

Shropshire

Map sheet 129, reference SO 513918

Figure 562

ST PETER

Side walls of nave: possibly Saxo-Norman

Rushbury is pleasantly situated in rolling country, 8 miles south-west of Much Wenlock, with the striking outcrop of Wenlock Edge not far away to the south-east. The church has a square Early English west tower, an earlier aisleless nave and an Early English chancel of the same width as the nave. The pleasant Transitional south doorway is protected by a timber porch, but the simpler and earlier north doorway has no protection.

Both north and south walls of the nave are of herring-bone masonry in their lower courses, with plain coursed rubble above. There seems no doubt that the simple, round-headed, early Norman north doorway is a later insertion in the lower herring-bone walling, since the fabric is disturbed on either side of the doorway instead of being neatly fitted to it. We are, therefore, inclined to regard the lower parts of the side walls of the nave as survivals from a pre-Conquest church, later incorporated in the early Norman nave, of which the north doorway and the coursed rubble walls still survive.

DIMENSIONS

The nave is 42 ft long internally and 18 ft wide. The north wall is 2 ft 11 in. thick and the south wall 2 ft 8 in.; and they are both about 16 ft tall.

RYBURGH, GREAT

Norfolk

Map sheet 125, reference TF 962272

ST ANDREW

Round west tower, and west wall of nave: possibly period C 3

Great Ryburgh stands on the south of the River Wensum, about 3 miles south-east of Fakenham.

Its large church now consists of a round west tower with later octagonal belfry, an aisleless nave with south porch, very large north and south transepts, and an aisleless chancel.

The indications of pre-Conquest workmanship are far from conclusive. The clearest is the triangular-headed doorway which opens from the nave to the upper chamber in the tower. Other confirming indications are the extensive use of brown carstone in the lowest stage of the tower; and the large side-alternate quoin-stones, also of carstone, in the north-west quoin of the nave. It is of interest to note that the level of the ground must have risen appreciably at the west of the church, since the original walls of the tower and the nave continue downward about 3 ft into a modern heating chamber in the north-west angle between the tower and the nave.

Within the church the principal feature of interest is the tower-arch, a fine round-headed opening of two orders, each of plain square section. The jambs are also of two plain square orders, with chamfered imposts and bases.

RYTHER

Yorkshire, West Riding

Map sheet 97, reference SE 555394

Figure 563

ALL SAINTS

Chancel-arch: period uncertain

About 6 miles north-west of Selby, Ryther church stands beside the Wharfe about a mile upstream from its junction with the Ouse. The church, now consisting of a nave with south aisle and south porch, and an aisleless chancel, stands in open fields about a quarter of a mile east of the village.

From outside, there is little to prove the former presence of a pre-Conquest church; massive side-alternate quoins at the east of the chancel may be re-used material; three monolithic window-heads used as building-stone in the north wall of the nave are certainly relics of a pre-Conquest church; and a plain square plinth beneath the

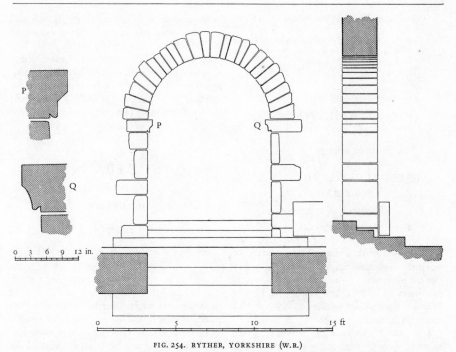

0 3 6 9 12 in.

0 5 10 15 ft

FIG. 254. RYTHER, YORKSHIRE (W.R.)

Elevation, section, and plan of the chancel-arch, showing its construction wholly of through-stones. Detailed sections at larger scale are given to show the unusual profiles of the two imposts P and Q.

greater part of the chancel walls may denote the line of the original walls. The south-east quoin of the aisleless nave may be seen beside the chancel, on the south, with the east wall of the south aisle built up against it; but the quoin is not of a distinctive type that would serve to settle a date for the nave.

Internally, however, the chancel-arch, although of Norman proportions, is unquestionably of Anglo-Saxon workmanship, with jambs in 'Escomb fashion', and both jambs and arch wholly constructed of through-stones. Moreover the lower voussoirs on each side are much more wedge-shaped than would be necessary to give radial joints, while the succeeding few voussoirs on each side are scarcely wedge-shaped at all. The imposts, also, are of rough and early character, projecting on the soffit only; and each is of different section from the other. That on the north has two vertical faces separated by a simple chamfer, while that on the south has a single vertical face

above a hollow chamfer. Both imposts are undercut below, like sections of a string-course designed to throw water clear of the wall beneath.

The church has an interesting survival from much later times in the form of five stone altar-slabs.

DIMENSIONS

The nave is about 54 ft long internally, by 19 ft 6 in. wide, with side walls 2 ft 6 in. thick. The chancel is 30 ft long by 15 ft wide, with side walls less than 2 ft thick, probably rebuilt in the fifteenth century.

The chancel-arch is 7 ft 10 in. wide, and 11 ft 8 in. tall as measured from the floor of the nave, or 10 ft 2 in. from the floor of the chancel. The wall in which it stands is 2 ft 3 in. thick.

REFERENCE

J. E. MORRIS, *The West Riding of Yorkshire*, Methuen's Little Guides, 3rd ed. (London, 1932), 46 and 433–5.

Morris draws attention to the chancel-arch. He also describes the jambs of the priest's door on the south of the chancel as having 'something that at any rate resembles the familiar long-and-short work'. We regard this doorway as Norman.

ST ALBANS

Hertfordshire

Map sheet 160, reference TL 145070

CATHEDRAL OR ABBEY CHURCH OF ST ALBAN

Baluster-shafts: date doubtful

After recording the martyrdom of St Alban, Bede (*H.E.* 1, 7) tells how, at the end of the Diocletian persecutions, a church was erected, of wonderful workmanship, suitable to commemorate his martyrdom. But nothing is known of this church or of the abbey which Offa, king of Mercia, is traditionally supposed to have founded about 793 on the same site.[1]

There are, however, in the triforium of the transepts of the Norman abbey church a series of eight lathe-turned baluster-shafts of Barnack stone which have all the appearance of Anglo-Saxon rather than Norman workmanship. The Royal Commission on Historical Monuments[2] recorded their opinion that these might 'perhaps be assigned to the end of the eighth century', but Baldwin Brown claimed (p. 265) that they resemble the later group of turned baluster-shafts at Dover and Canterbury rather than the early ones at Monkwearmouth and Jarrow. The Anglo-Saxon abbots of St Albans cannot be reliably dated, but two of them, Ealdred and Eadmer, are described as having collected materials for a rebuilding of the abbey and it may therefore be that these shafts represent their work rather than that of Offa's eighth-century workmen.[3]

In any event it is important to note that, as now assembled, the shafts are composite units, each of which consists of two or more pieces of Anglo-Saxon shafting and a splayed Anglo-Saxon base. These stand on square bases or plinths and support Norman cushion capitals. Baldwin Brown also records that in some instances the turned mouldings are defective and are made up with plaster in a makeshift manner consistent with the theory that they were re-used material from an older building or a store. This theory is further supported by the fact that not all the shafts have this turned form; the remainder being perfectly plain cylinders.

ST ALBANS

Hertfordshire

Map sheet 160, reference TL 135073

ST MICHAEL

Side walls of nave and chancel: period doubtful; but possibly C1

In spite of an unfortunate extension and restoration in the nineteenth century, the church of St Michael, standing in the centre of the site of the ruined Roman city of Verulamium, within half a mile of the cathedral of St Albans, is of more than usual architectural interest. It has apparently been lengthened both eastward and westward, so that only the side walls remain from the original aisleless nave and chancel. The chancel remains aisleless, but the early doorway in its north wall now opens into a twentieth-century flat-roofed vestry. The nave, lengthened westward in the nineteenth century by incorporating the area formerly occupied by a western tower, now has flanking buildings along its whole length on both sides. On the north, an arcade of four Norman arches opens to an aisle whose outer walls and windows are mainly of the thirteenth to fifteenth centuries; while the tower at the west of the aisle was added by Lord Grimthorpe in 1896. On the south, a somewhat different arcade of four Norman arches has subsequently been much altered; the two at the east now open to a thirteenth-century Lady Chapel almost as wide as the nave itself; the third arch now contains the main entrance doorway to the church; and the fourth frames a modern doorway which opens to Lord

---

[1] *Gesta Abbatum Monasterii S. Albani*, ed. H. T. Riley (Rolls series, 28, IV, i) (London, 1867), 4.

[2] *R.C.H.M.*, *Hertfordshire* (London, 1910), 10.
[3] *Gesta Abbatum*, *loc. cit.* 24 and 28.

Grimthorpe's south vestry. The main fabric of the church is of flints and Roman tiles, with stone for the medieval window-facings; and at the east end of the nave its originally aisleless form is indicated externally by the remains of north and south quoins constructed in Roman tiles, in a manner similar to those of the neighbouring church of St Stephen.

The architectural history of the church is as complex and difficult as its present plan; and in our opinion Baldwin Brown too lightly dismissed its claims to contain to this day the main fabric of the church which is recorded in the history of St Albans Abbey as having been built here in honour of St Michael by Abbot Ulsinus, or Wulsin.[1] Baldwin Brown's argument is that the walls are 'of the very un-Saxon thickness of nearly 4 ft and the proportions of the nave are quite Norman'.[2] We prefer to accept the conclusions of the Royal Commission on Historical Monuments[3] who asserted in 1910 that 'the chancel and nave both contain detail which is evidently of pre-Conquest date although the walls are unusually thick for the period'.

We are indebted to Dr R. Vaughan for information that it is impossible to give reliable dates to Abbot Wulsin, but that he probably lived about the middle of the ninth century. Too much reliance should not be put on the attribution of the work to Wulsin, but the record of the work in the history of the abbey may be accepted as good evidence of the belief in early medieval times that a church on this site had been built by one of the pre-Conquest abbots.

Apart from the quoins already mentioned, none of the early work is visible from outside, but internally the early, round-headed, single-splayed windows of the original nave are visible on both sides, above and partly cut away by the Norman arches. The early nave evidently had, on each side, four of these large windows, of which there are now (1957) three exposed on the north side and one on the south. The eastern window on the north is now open to the aisle and the nave,

showing the whole of its arched head and one splayed jamb, both faced internally and externally with Roman tiles, and both constructed in a fashion which is Anglo-Saxon rather than Norman, namely, that the splay is continued straight through the full thickness of the wall without any rebate on the outer face or any groove for housing glass or a window-frame. This north wall is of somewhat varying thickness but on average is about 3 ft 5 in., while the south wall is about 3 ft 10 in. The Norman arcades are both of simple round arches of a single square order; but that on the north appears to have been cut at an earlier date, for it is of a somewhat tentative form, with irregularly spaced arches of varying size, separated by wide piers of solid masonry; while by contrast the south arcade is of regularly spaced arches, between which much narrower piers of masonry have been left. These facts indicate that the building of these arcades extended over a considerable period of time, thus suggesting that they are more likely to be fairly early Norman arches cut through an Anglo-Saxon wall, rather than, as Baldwin Brown suggested, late-Norman arches cut through the walls of a Norman church which was consecrated at the beginning of the twelfth century.

There is nothing to indicate the form of the original chancel-arch, but the wall in which it stood still remains; and in the north wall of the chancel an early round-headed doorway, 3 ft 6 in. wide and 8 ft 1 in. tall, has been reopened in recent years to give access to the modern vestry. The eastern jamb of this doorway has apparently been destroyed at some time, but its west jamb and arched round head of a single square order, both faced with Roman tiles, appear to be original, and are both cut straight through the wall in thoroughly Anglo-Saxon fashion.

The fabric of this church, the detail of construction of the early openings, and the detail of the Norman arches, all agree so closely with the corresponding features at the neighbouring church of St Stephen, except in the size of the windows

---

[1] *Gesta Abbatum, loc. cit.* 22.

[2] G. Baldwin Brown (1925), 440. But the walls of the undoubtedly Anglo-Saxon church at Brixworth are 4 ft thick, and the dimensions of the nave of St Michael's do not differ appreciably from those of several Anglo-Saxon

churches whose plans are shown by Baldwin Brown on his page 21. The record of Wulsin's helping in the building of the three churches of St Michael, St Peter, and St Stephen is given in *Gesta Abbatum, loc. cit.* 22.

[3] *R.C.H.M., Hertfordshire* (London, 1910), 191.

and the thickness of the walls, that one is bound to regard the two churches as having originally been built about the same time, and to think that when later they were altered in Norman times a single person organized the cutting of the arches through their walls. If this be accepted, the Anglo-Saxon date for the early work is called less into doubt by the thicker walls of St Michael's, since the walls of St Stephen's are only 3 ft in thickness, and as is mentioned under St Stephen's, its window has a very close parallel in the late-Saxon south window of the first-floor chamber in the west tower at Brixworth.

In conclusion, then, we think that the side walls of the nave and chancel of St Michael's should be accepted as the work of an Anglo-Saxon abbot of St Albans, possibly Abbot Wulsin.

DIMENSIONS

It is not now possible to determine the original lengths of the nave and chancel with certainty, but their widths were the same as at present. The nave is 21 ft 2 in. wide internally and was probably about 58 ft long. The chancel is 14 ft 6 in. wide and was probably about 16 ft long. The walls vary in thickness from 3 ft 5 in. to 3 ft 10 in.

The early windows in the nave appear to have had apertures 2 ft wide and 4 ft high, splayed to a width of about 4 ft 6 in. and a somewhat uncertain height, perhaps about 6 ft. Their sills were externally about 10 ft 6 in. above the ground.

REFERENCE

There is available in the church an excellent group of coloured plans indicating the development of the structure through the centuries, and copies may be obtained in the church of an illustrated guide prepared by the late Mr J. C. Rogers who was responsible for interpreting much of its history while supervising repairs in recent years: *The Parish Church of St Michael, St Albans* (St Albans, 1956).

ST ALBANS
Hertfordshire

Map sheet 160, reference TL 141061

Figures 564, 565

ST STEPHEN
North and west walls of nave: period doubtful;
but possibly C1

The church of St Stephen stands immediately beside the Roman Watling Street, on the Hill of St Stephen, about a mile south-west of the centre of St Albans, close beside the southern boundary of Roman Verulamium. Although the records of St Albans Abbey describe the founding of churches by Abbot Ulsinus or Wulsin in honour of St Michael, St Peter, and St Stephen, it was thought until recently that all traces of his work had disappeared except in St Michael's. An account of the finding of clear evidence of Anglo-Saxon work in St Stephen's church was given in 1934 by Mr H. O. Cavalier,[1] and this evidence is of double importance by reason of the support which it gives to the acceptance of the early work in the neighbouring church of St Michael as being also the work of one of the pre-Conquest abbots. Like St Michael's, the church of St Stephen is built of flints and Roman tiles; but at St Stephen's the western quoins of the original aisleless nave are clearly defined by their bonding courses of tiles.

The church now consists of a medieval chancel with a south aisle, and a nave of about twice its original length, with a south aisle, a small north-west annexe, and a tall, square, shingled bell-cote and spire. In the north wall of the nave the blocked remains of two Early English arches are visible, beside a blocked Norman arch, which contains a blocked Decorated doorway. Beside the eastern jamb of the Norman arch, and close to the foot of a later buttress, two dressed stones in the wall indicate the former position of the eastern quoin of the nave, as is confirmed internally by a long vertical crack in the plaster at the junction of the later wall with the original one. Close beside the eastern curve of the Norman arch, and partly cut away by it, there is now to be seen a tall, narrow, round-headed window, whose presence was not suspected until it was discovered and opened out by Mr Cavalier. The tile sill and the tile facings of the head and western jamb are restorations of 1934; but otherwise, both externally

---

[1] *T. St Albans Herts. A.A.S.* (1934), 188–95.

and internally, the window is exactly as it was when blocked by the Normans in the twelfth century. It is of particular interest that the eastern jamb, partly in tiles and partly in clunch, was so perfectly preserved that it was possible to say without doubt that the internally splayed jamb continued in a single straight line through the wall from its inner face to its outer, without any rebate or groove for glass, shutter, or window-frame. In this respect the window differs fundamentally from the two, smaller, Norman round-headed internally splayed windows, which have been inserted in the west wall of the nave, for these have the outer 2 in. of their jambs and heads cut square through the wall, with a rebate for the glass.

The full extent of this recent discovery is even more apparent within the church, for the whole of the eastern splayed jamb has remained intact; as well as the whole of the arched head, and great parts of the sill and western jamb. Moreover, a further feature of particular interest is displayed by the arched head, which shows with great clarity the marks of the wooden frame round which the mortar was set. This is a feature which is precisely reproduced in the late-Saxon south window of the first-floor chamber of the tower at Brixworth, a window whose jambs also continue their splay in a single straight line right through to the outer face of the wall. On this evidence, taken in conjunction with the general similarity of the flint walling and tile quoining to that at the church of St Peter at Iver, it seems reasonable to accept the west and north walls of St Stephen's church as being those of the church built by one of the pre-Conquest abbots of St Albans, possibly Abbot Wulsin.

DIMENSIONS

A few feet east of the window the eastern extent of the original nave is marked by a long crack, already referred to, running vertically up the plaster of the wall. On this evidence, the internal length of the nave must have been about 36 ft. Its north wall is about 3 ft thick and its west wall, measured between the tile quoins, is about 30 ft wide externally so that the original nave must have been about 24 ft wide internally. The single remaining early window is 4 ft high and 8 in. wide externally, splayed to a height of 8 ft and a width of 4 ft 6 in. internally. Its outer sill is about 9 ft 6 in. from the present ground level and its inner sill 7 ft above the floor.

ST MARGARET'S-AT-CLIFFE
Kent

Map sheet 173, reference TR 358447

ST MARGARET
North-east quoin of nave: period unknown

Mr Loftus Brock first drew attention in 1895 to the pre-Conquest nature of a plain flint quoin which survives in the angle between the north wall of the Norman chancel and the east wall of the north aisle of the interesting Norman church at St Margaret's-at-Cliffe, about 4 miles north of Dover. The following description amplifies Brock's brief note, from our personal observation, but nevertheless follows it closely.[1]

The chancel is of well-defined Norman work, and the nave of equally well-defined later Norman, the work of building having begun, as was usual, at the east, and having ended at the west. But on the north side there are remains of an earlier building, at the junction of the nave and chancel, where an angle of plain irregular stonework still exists, quite different from the later work to its right and left. This part of an earlier church, having been incorporated into the first part of its Norman successor, was clearly left standing when the second part of the Norman church was built, and still stands to this day, in marked contrast to the work of both the periods of Norman re-building, and as a happy piece of evidence of the existence of a church on this site before the Conquest.

The early fabric projects rather less than 1 ft from the face of the chancel wall, and can be seen to extend about 2 ft along the nave, after which, if it extends any further, it is obscured by the east wall of the north aisle. It is about 6 ft in height and then slopes back to die into the Norman wall at

---

[1] E. P. L. Brock, 'The Saxon church at Whitfield', *Arch. Cant.* **21** (1895), 301–7; St Margaret's, 302.

the level of a Norman string-course. This early fragment, clearly containing the north-east quoin of the original nave, is wholly of flints, with larger flints to form the actual angle. There is no evidence available on which to assign this quoin to any particular part of the pre-Conquest period.

SCARTHO

Lincolnshire

Map sheet 105, reference TA 267063

ST GILES

West tower and parts of nave walls: period C3

The ancient village of Scartho has now been almost swallowed up by the rapidly spreading joint borough of Grimsby with Cleethorpes, which has also absorbed the adjoining pre-Conquest village of Clee. The church of St Giles still has open fields towards Cleethorpes and is separated from the modern part of its own village by a district of older houses; but ribbon development along the main road is continuous from Scartho to Grimsby.

The medieval church, consisting of a west tower, an aisled nave and an aisleless chancel, has recently been enlarged by the addition of a wide northern annexe, beside both nave and chancel, in a modern style which is sufficiently restrained to be accepted as a genuine piece of twentieth-century workmanship standing on its own merits and not clashing unduly with its much earlier neighbours.

The Anglo-Saxon tower is of more slender proportions than its neighbour at Clee, but resembles it in having two unequal stages separated by a square string-course and an off-set. The lower stage is of stone rubble, roughly coursed, with some admixture of flint. By contrast, the upper stage is of larger squared blocks, almost like rough ashlar. Both stages have side-alternate quoins of stones of about the same size, so that in the lower stage the quoin-stones are appreciably larger than the rubble of the walling, while in the upper stage the courses are continuous across the whole of the wall-face, including the quoins.

The tall lower stage stands on a double plinth, consisting of a square order below a chamfered one. Its east and north faces have no openings save a small, modern, pointed north window to light the ground floor. In the west face, an original doorway has been blocked to carry a modern window, while above it a keyhole window which formerly served to light the ground floor now lights an upper chamber that has been formed by the insertion of an extra floor. The blocked doorway has a much-restored round head of a single square order framed in a hood-mould of square section. The imposts, much weathered but apparently square in section, extend along the wall-face beyond the hood-mould but neither they nor the plinths of the tower are returned into the soffit of the doorway. The internally splayed keyhole window above the doorway is also much weathered and somewhat restored; its round head is cut in a single stone, shaped to a curve both below and above; while its jambs are each formed of two stones.

The south face is now very complicated; at about mid-height an internally splayed keyhole window clearly served to light the original first-floor chamber, now the second floor. This window has at some time apparently been partly covered by some form of medieval annexe, the drip course of whose roof has been carried right across the window and still remains there. At ground level the Early English south doorway, which now serves as the entry to the church, is covered by a pointed arch of somewhat earlier date, springing from square imposts of much earlier type. On each side of this pointed arch the two lowest voussoirs look as if they might originally have formed part of a round arch associated with the early imposts.

Each face of the belfry stage has a double window of rather tall proportions. These windows have steeply sloping sills from which the cylindrical mid-wall shafts rise, without any form of base. The square jambs, coursed with the wall like the quoining, carry thin, rectangular, slightly projecting imposts, and the mid-wall shafts carry similar through-stones, to support round window-heads which are each cut from a single stone, carefully shaped below, but left irregular above. The eastern mid-wall shaft is corbelled out above into a rectangular shape which supports the

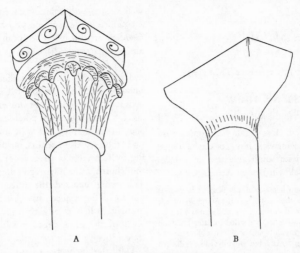

FIG. 255. SCARTHO, LINCOLNSHIRE

The capitals of the double belfry windows. The windows on the north and south faces have foliated capitals of type A. The window on the west was probably similar but its capital is now so severely weathered that its original form is uncertain. In the east face the window has a simple elongated capital of type B which should be compared with those at Sompting, Sussex, and at Heapham, Lincolnshire.

greater part of the length of the through-stone. The shafts on the north and south faces carry elaborately carved capitals whose square upper corners are treated with well-formed volutes, while the conical lower part of each capital is ornamented with a circlet of upright leaves turned over outward at the top. The western face may have been similarly treated but is now too weathered to be interpreted.

The tower ends above in a plain medieval parapet, with finials at the four corners and a flat lead roof.

Internally, the tower-arch has a round head of two square orders, of which the outer is in the wall-face, while the inner is recessed about 1 in. behind it. The arch rests on square chamfered imposts, which are returned along the face of the wall only so far as to carry the inner order; and the square jambs, of well-dressed stone, rest on a simple chamfered plinth. About 20 ft above the floor a rectangular doorway gives access to what was originally the first floor of the tower. The modern first floor is clearly a later insertion, for it cuts across the jambs of the tower-arch at a height of about 8 ft above the floor.

DIMENSIONS

The tower is about 9 ft 3 in. square internally, with walls about 3 ft 6 in. thick and almost 60 ft high, to the top of the later parapet.

The tower-arch is 6 ft wide and 14 ft 3 in. tall, and the blocked doorway in the west face of the tower is 3 ft 6 in. wide and 7 ft 10 in. tall.

The nave is about 16 ft wide internally, with side walls about 2 ft 6 in. thick. The south wall seems to be part of the original church, for it is aligned with the side-alternate quoin which projects about 3 ft southward from the tower.

REFERENCES

Editorial, 'Saxon churches', *Ecclesiologist*, **3** (1843–4), 138–9. Scartho noted as Anglo-Saxon, 138.

A. H. THOMPSON, 'Pre-Conquest church-towers in North Lincolnshire', *A.A.S.R.* **29** (1907–8), 43–70. Scartho, 68–9.

SCOLE

Norfolk

Map sheet 137, reference TM 151790

ST ANDREW

No reliable Anglo-Saxon evidence

This small church, close beside the Roman road from Ipswich to Norwich, now consists of a west tower, a nave with south aisle and an aisleless chancel. Of it Baldwin Brown writes (p. 477):

The only Saxon sign here remaining is some long-and-short work at the top of the south-east quoin of the original nave, the wall of which on the south is 2 ft 3 in. thick. The other quoins are concealed by later building, such as the recent organ chamber which obliterates the north-east quoin, or by ivy, but what is visible is distinct and quite significant.

When we visited the church in 1955 there was no longer any ivy to conceal the other quoins, but no evidence of long-and-short technique had come to light, and we were inclined to feel very doubtful of the south-east quoin which, although it had five stones in something like a long-and-short arrangement, yet did not give the impression of Anglo-Saxon work.

SEAHAM

County Durham

Map sheet 78, reference NZ 422505

Figure 566

ST MARY (said formerly to have been ST ANDREW)

Complete nave; with foundations of chancel and western annexe: period A 2

Although the church of St Mary at Seaham was not suspected of pre-Conquest date until 1913, the picturesque site beside the North Sea was known to have ancient associations with other well-known early foundations, for example, it is mentioned by the tenth-century *Historia de Sancto Cuthberto* in connexion with South Weremouth among estates said to have been granted to St Cuthbert by King Athelstan.[1]

The church, standing within a couple of hundred yards of cliffs that fall to the sea, now consists of a square west tower, a long, tall, aisleless nave with south porch and north vestry, and an aisleless chancel. In 1913 the patron undertook extensive repairs, including the lowering by some feet of the level of the soil around the church, and the repointing of its walls. This work exposed the three quite different plinths of the chancel, nave, and tower, and it brought to light three early windows in the side walls of the nave, together with vestiges of a fourth.[2]

Until the discoveries of 1913, the chancel had been regarded as the earliest part of the church; its tall, narrow, round-headed windows are at first sight Transitional in character, dating perhaps from near the end of the twelfth century; but, on closer inspection, they are seen to be fundamentally of quite early Norman character, with later modifications. This is made particularly clear by comparison of the simple round-headed east windows of the chancel with the later form of those in the side walls, where the inner arch of the heads is slightly pointed.

The workmanship of the nave is quite different from that of the Norman chancel, both in the nature of the fabric and the character of the quoins and windows. The walling of the chancel is of Norman ashlar, with side-alternate quoins in the same courses as the walling; by contrast, the nave is built of stone that has been very roughly squared, with side-alternate quoins of appreciably larger size. The north wall is of somewhat smaller stones, and it has a band of herring-bone masonry along its whole length, a few feet above the ground. All this serves only to define the nave as of different date from the chancel; but a positive indication of early Saxon date is given by the three surviving windows, high up in the side walls.

[1] Symeon of Durham, *Hist. Dunelm. Ecclesiae*, ed. T. Arnold (Rolls Series, 75, 1) (London, 1882), 211.
[2] R. A. Aird, *Proc. Soc. Ant. Newcastle*, 3rd ser., 6 (1913), 23 and 59–71. The same material was also published in *Antiquities of Sunderland*, 15 (1914).

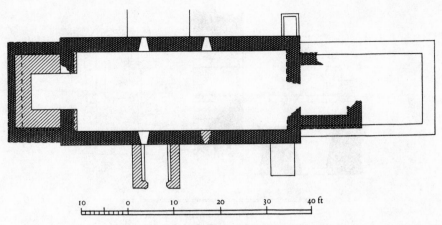

FIG. 256. SEAHAM, COUNTY DURHAM

The plans shows the surviving nave and the evidence which Aird found by excavation for a square chancel and a rectangular western annexe. It also shows the three surviving early windows and the position of the blocked fourth window of which only one jamb survives.

These are round-headed, single-splayed openings which in size, in general form, and in details of construction are very like the side windows of the nave at Escomb. Externally, their jambs (save where they have later been modified) are each of one upright stone and one laid flat, to bond into the wall; and their round heads are cut out of single stone lintels. Internally, also, the heads are cut from single lintels, and the upper parts of the jambs are of large stones laid upright and flat; the lower parts of the internal jambs are of stones coursed with the walling; but the sills are much more sharply splayed than the jambs or the heads, and it may be that the downward splays of the sills have been increased at a later date.

The proportions of the nave and the character of the internal walling are also reminiscent of those of the nave at Escomb, although the walls are not now quite as high. The excavations in 1913 revealed the foundations of the original chancel, about 10 ft 6 in. square internally, also closely resembling the dimensions of that at Escomb.

In addition to the foundations of the chancel, Aird's excavations showed early foundations westward of the nave, outside the present walls of the

tower. He suggested that these might have been for a narthex or a baptistry.

In spite of Aird's closely reasoned statement of the case for Seaham, its claims for inclusion in the list of Anglo-Saxon churches seem to have been almost completely ignored.[1] We believe it has claims similar to those of Escomb for inclusion in the early group of Northumbrian churches.

Like those at Escomb, the windows are not widely splayed; and there is no external splay or rebate for glass, but a groove is cut in the jambs for a wooden shutter, roughly in the middle of the thickness of the wall. By contrast with Escomb, the windows are enriched with simple carving both externally and internally. The vertical exterior wall-faces of the window-heads are ornamented by the carving of two shallow grooves which outline the curve of the head, and are concentric with it; this is reminiscent of the ornament of the doorways at St Patrick's chapel, Heysham, and at the church at Somerford Keynes, but is much more tentative. Internally, the eastern window on the north is also ornamented with bands of lightly incised wheat-ear or cable ornament carved on the soffit of the window-head.

[1] N. Pevsner accepts the church as late-Saxon or earliest Norman, County Durham, The Buildings of England (London, 1953), 204–5. Otherwise the only notice of Aird's work that we have been able to find is in Methuen's Little Guides, J. E. Hodgkin, Durham, 2nd ed. (London, 1926), 222.

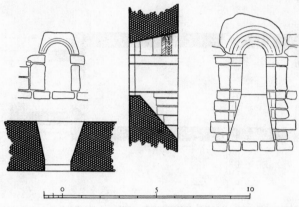

FIG. 257. SEAHAM, COUNTY DURHAM

Details of the western window in the north wall of the nave. The interior and exterior elevations show how the vertical face of each lintel is decorated by the incision of two semicircles concentric with the round head of the window. The section shows how the soffit face is enriched by a band of ornament like wheat-ear. (This ornament is in fact on the eastern window, not on its western counterpart.)

DIMENSIONS

The nave, still standing complete, with all four quoins, is 46 ft 9 in. long internally, and 16 ft 6 in. wide, with walls 2 ft 7 in. thick and about 19 ft high. The foundations of the chancel determined a building about 10¼ ft square internally. By comparison, the nave at Escomb is 43 ft 6 in. long by 14 ft 6 in., with walls 2 ft 4 in. thick and about 23 ft high, while the chancel is 10 ft square.

The windows have slightly sloping jambs, so that their apertures, which are 2 ft 8 in. high, narrow from 1 ft 4½ in. at the sill to 1 ft 3½ in. at the shoulders. Internally they are splayed to openings 2 ft 6 in. wide and 5 ft high. Externally their sills are about 14 ft above the ground.

REFERENCE

Aird's excellent accounts of the church have been noted in the text. They give dimensioned drawings and plans, and a very fully reasoned architectural history.

SELHAM
Sussex

Map sheet 181, reference SU 933206

Figures 567–9

ST JAMES
Nave and chancel: period C 3

About mid-way between Petworth and Midhurst, and about a mile south of the main road between the two, the little church of St James at Selham is a particularly interesting example of the small, simple parish church which originally consisted of a rectangular nave and an almost square chancel. In later times a small chapel has been added to the south of the nave; and a porch protects its only doorway, on the north. The west wall of the nave has been rebuilt in recent times, and none of the original windows has survived, but the main fabric of the church has suffered little change in its many centuries of life. Of the many other small, late-Saxon churches in the Rother Valley, at Chithurst, Elsted, Hardham, Stopham, and Woolbeding, none has such elaboration of detail as is here lavished on the chancel-arch, in a church which is otherwise so plain and simple.

The fabric of the church is of rubble, with very great use of herring-bone technique, which appears throughout the north and east walls of the chancel and the surviving west part of the south wall of the nave. The north walls of the nave and chancel are more heavily plastered, and much of their surface is therefore obscured, but there is no reason to doubt the use of herring-bone there also, particularly as traces are visible on the only part of the north wall of the nave where the fabric may be seen. The quoins are laid in careful side-alternate fashion, using large stones. The west wall of the nave, and its quoins, are of different character from the remainder of the fabric, as a result of rebuilding in the nineteenth century.

The north doorway gives very clear indications of Anglo-Saxon workmanship. It is a tall, narrow

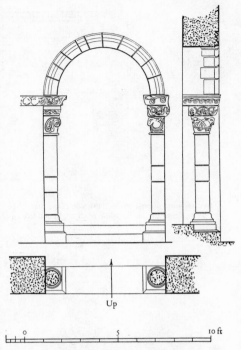

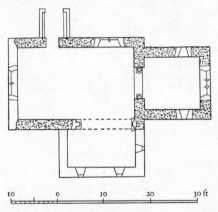

FIG. 258. SELHAM, SUSSEX

The plan shows how the church has been modified by the insertion of later windows, by the addition of a chapel on the south of the nave and by the rebuilding of the west wall.

FIG. 259. SELHAM, SUSSEX

Elevation, section, and plan of the chancel-arch. Details of the carvings on the capitals and imposts are given in Figs. 260 and 261.

opening, cut straight through the wall, with plain square jambs, simple imposts, and a round-arched head of a single plain square order. No stones of the jambs or of the head pass through the full thickness of the wall, but the imposts appear to be through-stones. They are square in plan, with no projection except on the soffit face, where the profile consists of an upper vertical face, followed by a quirk, a roll-moulding, and a hollow-chamfer.

The most elaborate feature of the church is the chancel-arch, and particularly the imposts and capitals upon which it rests. The arch itself is of semicircular shape and fundamentally plain square section; but it is enriched on its western archivolt face by three concentric roll-mouldings. The jambs are also fundamentally of plain square section, but set back about 8 in. behind the line of the arched head, and provided on their soffit

faces with detached three-quarter-round shafts which bear the elaborate capitals and imposts that support the arch. The circular section of these soffit-shafts has no counterpart in the arch itself, and the transition from the comparatively small circular shape of the shafts to the broad square section of the arch is effected by means of a triple feature which may be described as consisting of a capital, an abacus, and an impost.

While the principle of construction is the same on both sides of the arch, the detailed treatment is different from side to side, in a way which gives a strong impression that the work was executed without a comprehensive design and using such materials as were to hand from some earlier building. In particular, the northern impost seems to be a section of a re-used Roman string-course or architrave, still bearing its original classical mouldings on the soffit face but carved with a

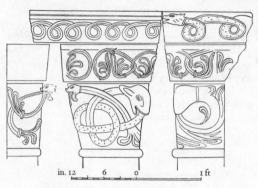

FIG. 260. SELHAM, SUSSEX

The capital and impost on the south side of the chancel-arch. The central part of the figure shows the soffit face as seen from the north, while to the right and left are shown the faces toward the nave and the chancel.

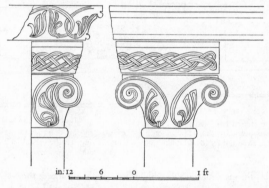

FIG. 261. SELHAM, SUSSEX

The capital and impost on the north side of the chancel-arch. The right-hand part of the figure shows the soffit face as seen from the south, while the left-hand part shows the face toward the nave.

simple pattern of foliage on the western vertical face which was no doubt originally plain.

On each side of the arch, the imposts are rect-angular in plan, to support the whole width of the arch. They project boldly from the soffit of the arch, but hardly at all on the east and west. The abaci which intervene between the imposts and the capitals are square in plan and are not set cen-trally beneath the imposts, but are displaced west-ward so that their western carved faces continue the alignment of the western carved faces of the imposts. This westward displacement of the abaci has the curious effect that the eastward part of the imposts, amounting to about one-third

of their width, is left unsupported. The abaci, although square in plan, taper from above to below so as to reduce the bold projection of the imposts to the smaller scale of the capitals and of the shafts on which they rest. The capitals are square in plan above and circular in plan below, so as to conform to their supporting shafts. In the northern capital, the transition from the square to the circle is effected by the traditional artifice of volutes at the angles, but in the southern capital, a typically Anglo-Saxon device is used, whereby heads of monsters occupy the upper corners, while their interlaced bodies cover the curved lower parts. The soffit-shafts are about 10 in. in diameter and are placed about 5 in. from the western face of the wall and 10 in. from its eastern face. They are separated from the capitals by a fillet of semicircular section, and each shaft is built of three separate sections.

The ornament on the imposts, abaci, and capitals is of sufficient importance to merit description and illustration. The west face of the north impost is carved in low relief to show linked acanthus or palmette leaves; the south face, as already mentioned, still bears a classical series of mouldings. The abacus beneath has a triple, interlacing, two-strand pattern which is carved in high relief and is carried round the west and south faces in a continuous pattern. The capital has well-developed volutes at each corner; the stems of these volutes run down almost to the fillet which separates the capital from the shaft; and then the stems turn outward and upward in typically Anglo-Saxon palmette leaves. The south impost is carved to show a continuous pattern of simple loops on its north and west faces; on the north face these loops are represented in a two-strand rope; and on the west face in the body of a long serpent. The abacus beneath has a pattern of palmette leaves with interlocking stems, in a manner somewhat reminiscent of some of the Sompting carvings. The interesting animal pattern on the capital beneath has already been described.

To complete the description of the chancel-arch, it should be noted that the floor rises by two steps from the nave to the chancel. The first step is flush with the west face of the wall, and the second is within the thickness of the wall. Each of the soffit-shafts has a square plinth which stands on the lower step and rises to the level of the next. On these plinths, each shaft has a moulded base of circular plan and bell-like profile.

DIMENSIONS

The nave is 25 ft long internally and 14 ft 10 in. wide, with walls 1 ft 11½ in. thick and about 16 ft high. The chancel is 11 ft 10 in. (east–west) by 10 ft 11 in. (north–south), with walls only 1 ft 9 in. thick.

The north doorway is 2 ft 10 in. wide and 8 ft 5 in. tall, and the chancel-arch is 5 ft wide in clear between the soffit-shafts and 10 ft 3 in. tall.

REFERENCES

H. L. JESSEP, *Anglo-Saxon Church Architecture in Sussex* (Winchester, undated), 55–6. Dated to the overlap, with some preference for Norman.

H. POOLE, 'The Domesday Book churches of Sussex', *Sussex Arch. C.* **87** (1948), 29–76. Selham, 49. Dated post-Conquest, largely on the ground of herring-bone fabric.[1] Good pictures of the capitals.

V.C.H. Sussex, **4** (London, 1953), 81. St James a modern invocation, formerly St Mary. There was at one time a west tower, and the west wall of the nave was rebuilt in the nineteenth century.

SHELFORD, LITTLE

Cambridgeshire

Map sheet 148, reference TL 453516

ALL SAINTS

*Double-splayed window in south wall of chancel:
period C3*

The villages of Great and Little Shelford stand on opposite sides of the upper waters of the Cam, about 5 miles south of Cambridge, with their churches less than half a mile apart. The church of All Saints at Little Shelford is a veritable museum of antiquities, for several pre-Conquest carved stones are built into its south wall and south porch, and the walls also contain many carved stones of later medieval dates.

The church consists of an aisleless nave and chancel, with a later south porch and west tower. The fabric is of uncut flints, with dressed stone for quoins and facings. The nave is indicated as Norman by the blocked round-headed north doorway of simple character, and by the round-headed single-splayed window above it. But the character of the work also has Anglo-Saxon affinities in the megalithic upright jambs of the window, and in its monolithic head which has been

---

[1] Baldwin Brown rejected the claims of a number of late-Saxon churches of Sussex (his p. 456), perhaps in part influenced by the appearance of herring-bone work. We believe that herring-bone work does not discrimi-nate between Anglo-Saxon and Norman date (see particularly pp. 212–13) and we accordingly accept at their face-value the Anglo-Saxon indications enumerated above.

carved with radial lines to indicate the joints of voussoirs.

The double-splayed window high up in the south wall of the chancel is, however, clearly pre-Conquest in character. It is now blocked and visible only on the exterior; and it is difficult to say whether it is *in situ* unless it can be opened out and inspected internally. Its jambs are carved with interlacing patterns, and its head is a single stone hollowed out to form a rather elliptical bonnet-

REFERENCE

C. Fox, 'Anglo-Saxon monumental sculpture in the Cambridge district', *P. Camb. A.S.* **23** (1920–1), 15–45. Little Shelford, 22, 33–4, and pl. 5. Careful argument for dating the grave-slabs to about the end of the tenth century, and for believing that the stones in the window were re-used in a pre-Conquest church that was built after destruction of an earlier church in the Viking raids of the time of Ethelred the Unready, perhaps when the *Anglo-Saxon Chronicle* records the harrying and burning of East Anglia, including Cambridge and Thetford in 1010.

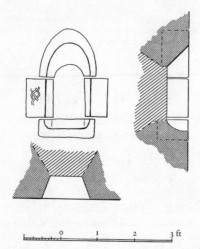

0   1   2   3 ft

FIG. 262. LITTLE SHELFORD, CAMBRIDGESHIRE
The bonnet-shaped outer face of the blocked double-splayed window in the south wall of the chancel. Its sill is 12 ft 6 in. above the footing of the wall.

shaped opening. The carved stones in the jambs are probably of tenth-century date, and their re-use as part of the fabric suggests that the window was built quite late in period C.

DIMENSIONS

The blocked aperture of the window is 11 in. wide and 1 ft 4 in. tall, splayed to become an opening 1 ft 2 in. by 2 ft 2 in. in the outer face of the wall, where its sill is 12 ft 6 in. above the original level of the ground. The south wall of the chancel is 3 ft thick and about 16 ft tall. By contrast, the north wall of the nave is 3 ft 10 in. thick.

SHERBORNE
Dorset

Map sheet 178, reference ST 637166

ST MARY THE VIRGIN
North bay of west wall, with doorway: period C2

The importance of Sherborne's medieval abbey of St Mary is well attested by the size and architectural excellence of the church which has survived the Dissolution, and which has served since about 1540 as the parish church. The first impression of this fine building is of a church almost wholly of the Perpendicular style, with fan vaulting of unusual elaboration; but on closer inspection the Perpendicular work is seen to be largely a veneer applied to a structure that seems to be fundamentally Norman. Still closer inspection leads to the conclusion that the plan is that of an even earlier building of which it is now impossible to say how much still survives beneath the later coverings.

In common with the neighbouring churches at Wimborne and Milborne Port, Sherborne has the peculiarity that the tower is wider in plan than any of the four arms of the building attached to it, so that the four angles of the tower stand free as salient angles, projecting beyond the walls of the adjoining nave, chancel, and transepts. This is not a feature normally found in Anglo-Norman churches, whereas it is found in exactly this form in a number of cruciform pre-Conquest churches; for example at Norton, in County Durham, and Stow, in Lincolnshire. There is, therefore, a strong presumption that the existing building at Sherborne either stands on the Anglo-Saxon

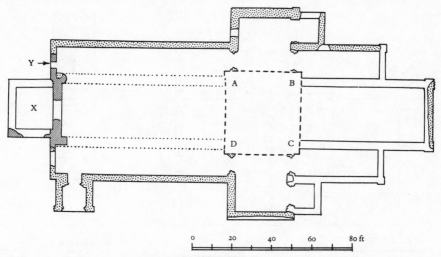

FIG. 263. SHERBORNE, DORSET

Plan showing the relation of the surviving Anglo-Saxon fabric to the Norman and later abbey church. The square A, B, C, D, represents the ground plan of the central tower, which is markedly wider than any of the four arms of the church. The alignment of the arcades of the nave has been shown by dotted lines in order to facilitate comparison of widths. The western projection X is the foundation of the porch or tower first discovered by R. H. Carpenter. The surviving doorway is at Y.

foundations or, more probably, incorporates part of the original fabric. Further support for the latter alternative is given by the unusual shortness of the nave by comparison with other Norman churches and by the irregular spacing of the columns of the nave arcade.

Indirect evidence for the former existence of a pre-Conquest church of the same length as the present church was provided by the discovery about 1840 of a coffin of Purbeck marble below the flooring of the ambulatory near the east end. This is believed to be the coffin of King Ethelbert, brother and predecessor of King Alfred the Great; Leland recorded that both Ethelbert and his brother Ethelbald were buried in the Anglo-Saxon cathedral of Sherborne by Bishop Ealhstan, behind the high altar, though at Leland's time there was no knowledge of the precise position of the tombs. The burial of the two brothers at Sherborne is recorded in the 'A' version of the *Anglo-Saxon Chronicle* under the year 860, when Ethelbald died.[1]

The former existence of a west tower (as well as a central tower) as part of the pre-Conquest church was postulated by R. H. Carpenter[2] on the evidence of foundations discovered by his father in the course of repairs in 1849. These foundations were in the form of a massive plinth or base-course of a building 29 ft wide, running westward from the west face of the present nave. Carpenter argued that these must have been of pre-Conquest date because the mouldings were of an unusual, almost Roman, form; and because they were embedded in the west wall of the present abbey, a wall which is Norman on the south and pre-Norman on the north. That they represented the base of a western tower he deduced from the former existence, higher up in the west wall, of 'a double row of small pillars and arches of early date' which had been destroyed by his father in order to increase the size of the Perpendicular west window by lowering its sill. Carpenter deduced that these arches had opened from an upper floor of the tower towards the nave in

[1] D. Whitelock, *E.H.D.* (1955), 175.
[2] R. H. Carpenter, 'On the Benedictine Abbey of St Mary, Sherborne', *Royal Institute of British Architects Transactions* (1876–77), 137–51.

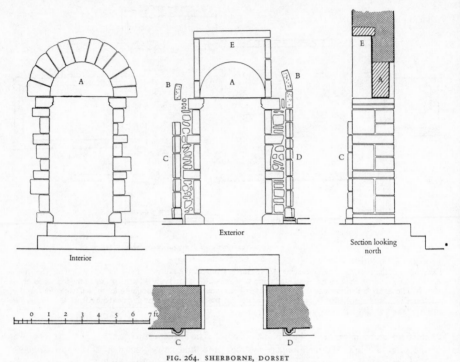

Interior

Exterior

Section looking
north

0 1 2 3 4 5 6 7 ft

C   D

FIG. 264. SHERBORNE, DORSET

Details of the west doorway of the north aisle. A, later tympanum; B, vestiges of original hood-moulding now cut back flush with west wall; C, pilaster-strip beside north jamb; D, pilaster-strip beside south jamb; E, square-headed recess cut above doorway in later medieval period.

much the same way as does the present triple opening at Brixworth. Carpenter's deductions have recently been given firm support by excavations which have traced the extent of the early foundations and have established that they represented a solid platform covering the whole area.[1]

A picture thus emerges of a tenth-century monastic cathedral church with square western and central towers; a church of a total length not less than that of the present church excluding its Lady Chapel, and with transepts and an aisled nave. The Royal Commission (loc. cit.) give further evidence for this picture of the pre-Conquest church, namely the existence to this day of a common seal which, by reason of the existence of four square Cs in its inscription can with some

certainty be dated from before the building of the Norman abbey. This seal shows what is evidently a picture of the abbey, confirming the general description given above, and showing a chancel, a central tower, a nave, and a western tower with a porch to the west of it.

The visible remains, apart from the coffin attributed to King Ethelbert, consist of the west doorway of the north aisle. The outer face of this doorway has now very wisely been protected from the weather by a small porch, so that the remains must be approached from within the church. The inner face of the doorway is complete; the sill is two steps above the floor of the nave; and the square jambs are cut straight through the wall, and rest on chamfered bases,

[1] R.C.H.M., Dorset, West (London, 1952), xlvii.

with quirked and chamfered imposts to support the stilted round head. It is no longer possible to say whether the eleven stones forming the arch were originally through-stones, because the whole outer face of the head has been cut away at some subsequent date to form a square head; but the inner face appears to be original, with markedly non-radial jointing. The arched head is now filled with a semicircular stone tympanum but this is almost certainly a later insertion.[1] The jambs are built in 'Escomb fashion', with large stones set alternately upright and flat. The flat bonding stones are without exception through-stones, but each of the characteristically tall upright stones extends only about half-way through the wall and the remaining half is filled with two stones of smaller size.

The external wall-face is of flat rubble fabric on either side of the doorway, and the opening is flanked by vertical pilaster-strips of half-round section, about 4 in. in diameter, with a small square-sectioned moulding 1½ in. wide on the side remote from the door. These pilasters, formed of stones about 10 in. in length, rest on bases which are separately shaped to match the main roll-moulding and its square-sectioned outer component. The bases themselves stand on a plain square plinth, which extends along the whole face of the early walling.

From above the level of the imposts, the outer face of the doorway has been cut away; but enough remains of the surrounding strip-work to show that it continued round the head of the doorway as a semicircular hood-moulding.

The doorway is 3 ft 9 in. wide and 9 ft 6 in. tall to the top of the interior arched head, this height being measured from the sill of the doorway, not from the floor of the nave which is two steps lower. The rubble wall in which the doorway stands is 2 ft 7 in. in thickness.

The general character of the doorway would fit a date at the end of the tenth century, and, as the Benedictine rule was introduced at Sherborne in 998 by Bishop Wulfsige, it is not improbable that it dates from a rebuilding of the church at that time.

SHEREFORD
Norfolk

Map sheet 125, reference TF 886295

ST NICHOLAS

South wall of nave, and possibly lower part of tower: period C3

The church at Shereford, standing close to the right bank of the River Wensum, about 2 miles west of Fakenham, is a small aisleless building with a round west tower and a pleasant, simple, Norman south doorway, which is sheltered by an unusually shallow open porch. The present chancel, slightly wider than the nave, was no doubt built outside the original smaller and narrower chancel. The fabric of the tower and of the nave is of flint mixed with brown carstone, and the western quoins are of large blocks of this brown stone laid side-alternately. At about the level of the eaves of the nave, the tower contracts, or batters, perhaps an arrangement designed to simplify the junction between the tower and the roof of the nave.

No original openings have survived in the tower, but there is some slight evidence of an original, western, triangular-headed doorway, framed in blocks of carstone, but now blocked and carrying an inserted window of two lights. Above this doorway there are also traces of the carstone jambs of an early window which has also been blocked and has lost its head. The tower-arch as seen from the nave is Norman, no doubt contemporary with the south doorway, but what seems to be an earlier and taller arch is visible within the tower, with rough undressed stones forming its round-arched head. The evidence for a pre-Conquest date for the tower is somewhat inconclusive, even although it rests on a number of items.

The assignment of a pre-Conquest date to the south wall of the nave hangs quite straightforwardly on the survival in it of a double-splayed round-headed window. This is formed wholly

---

[1] The Royal Commission's photograph (their pl. 210), taken before modern restoration, shows the present opening of the doorway wholly blocked by a rubble wall.

without the use of dressed stone and without any true arching of its head, beside which the flints may be seen to lie in the ordinary coursing of the wall. The lower courses of the south wall, beneath this window, are laid in well-defined herring-bone fashion.

The church is entered, through the Norman south doorway, down two steps, and the inner face of the doorway has a tall narrow arch which may be a survival from the original opening.

DIMENSIONS

The nave is 42 ft long internally by 18 ft wide, with side walls a little over 3 ft thick and 20 ft high.

The double-splayed window has an aperture 9 in. wide and 2 ft tall, splayed to become 3 ft wide and 6 ft tall in the inner face of the wall, where its sill is 10 ft above the floor. The glazing is carried in an oak mid-wall frame which is placed 2 ft from the inner face of the wall and 1 ft from the outer.

The tower is 11 ft 4 in. in internal diameter, with walls 4 ft 6 in. thick.

SHOREHAM, OLD

Sussex

Map sheet 182, reference TQ 208060

ST NICHOLAS

Parts of nave walls: period C

The cruciform, aisleless, Norman church of St Nicholas, close beside the east bank of the River Adur at Old Shoreham, has retained in the north and west walls of its nave some parts of an earlier church, almost certainly dating from before the Conquest. The north wall, about 50 ft in length, is in two sections, both built of flints, but with a break in the alignment about the middle, so that the western section, which is slightly over 3 ft in thickness, is set back a few inches to the south of the eastern section, which is only 2 ft 2 in. thick. Neither the north-west quoin of the nave

nor the quoining which faces the set-back in the wall now shows any distinctive Anglo-Saxon workmanship, although Jessep[1] stated that the lowest four quoin-stones in the north-west angle were built in long-and-short fashion. This quoin had recently been repaired when we first visited the church in 1956, and it is possible that the early work was destroyed in the course of the repairs.

In the western and thicker part of the north wall there are visible, externally, scattered remains of the stone facings of a blocked round-headed doorway which Jessep regarded as closely similar to the interesting doorway preserved in the otherwise modern church of St John-sub-Castro at Lewes. We could see no ground for this comparison because the remains at Shoreham, although so fragmentary as to indicate little more than the outline of a doorway, nevertheless indicate an opening framed by two orders, both of plain square section; whereas the doorway at Lewes is of a single order which is rather elaborately worked to show concentric mouldings round the head and pilasters beside the jambs.

In the south wall, beneath the central pseudo-Norman window, a different type of doorway has a square head and a round arch enclosing a solid tympanum. This doorway might be late-Saxon, of the same period as its many analogues in the Cotswolds; but since it differs so fundamentally from the north doorway we are inclined to agree with Baldwin Brown in regarding it as of early Norman date.[2] In any event, it gives a clear indication that the vestiges of the north doorway are of pre-Norman character.

There seems little doubt that the thicker-walled western part of the nave was formerly an Anglo-Saxon west tower and that the church then consisted of that tower, a nave occupying the remainder of the space of the present nave, and a chancel occupying the space of the present central tower. Its also seems reasonable to assume that the Normans lengthened the nave by absorbing the Anglo-Saxon west tower into it, and that they erected a new tower over the Anglo-Saxon chancel, and then built a new chancel further to the east. This interpretation of the history would

---

[1] H. L. Jessep, *Anglo-Saxon Church Architecture in Sussex*, 34–5.

[2] Baldwin Brown, 478.

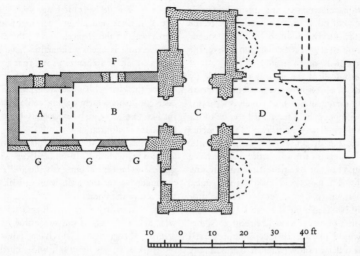

FIG. 265. OLD SHOREHAM, SUSSEX

Plan showing the Anglo-Saxon fabric in relation to the Norman and later additions. A, Anglo-Saxon western porch or tower; B, Anglo-Saxon nave partially refaced and used by the Normans after enlargement by incorporating the western porch or tower; C, Norman tower probably replacing or incorporating the Anglo-Saxon chancel; D, destroyed Norman apsidal chancel and later enlarged chancel; E, Anglo-Saxon doorway blocked by Normans; F, Norman doorway inserted in Anglo-Saxon wall; G, modern windows of pseudo-Norman form. The central pseudo-Norman window partially cuts away the head of an early-Norman south doorway.

account for the very irregular ground-plan of the Norman tower, a feature which would otherwise be difficult to explain.

DIMENSIONS

The blocked north doorway in the wall of the former west tower is 2 ft 10 in. wide and 7 ft 6 in. tall. The wall in which it stands is 3 ft thick, whereas the north wall of the Anglo-Saxon nave further east is only 2 ft 2 in. thick. If our interpretation, as given above, is correct, the tower would have been about 15 ft square, internally, the nave would have been about 28 ft by 18 ft, and the chancel about 15 ft square, but all are so irregularly laid out that these dimensions are only approximate.

REFERENCES

H. L. JESSEP, loc. cit.

P. M. JOHNSTON, 'Low side windows in Sussex churches', Sussex Arch. C. 42 (1899), 117–79. Old Shoreham, 153.

F. S. W. SIMPSON, The Churches of Shoreham, Sussex, 2nd ed. (Gloucester, 1950), 21–31. Plan, 20.

W. E. GODFREY, 'Old Shoreham church', Arch. J. 116 (1959), 245. Brief account, with dated plan.

SHORNE

Kent

Map sheet 171, reference TQ 690710

Figure 570

ST PETER AND ST PAUL

Nave: period C

The small village of Shorne, pleasantly situated in rolling wooded country midway between Gravesend and Rochester, has a lofty and spacious church of very considerable interest, which would well repay further detailed study. The church now consists of a west tower, an aisled nave with north porch, and a chancel flanked by a medieval chapel on the north and a modern chapel on the south. It seems probable that the original Anglo-Saxon church occupied the space of the present nave and the western bay of the present chancel, and that it perhaps had *porticus* opening to the north and south from the eastern part of the nave.

The side walls of the nave and the north wall of the chancel are indicated as possibly pre-Norman

545

by their thin construction, and this indication is proved beyond doubt for the north wall of the nave by the survival in it of a small, round-headed, double-splayed window, high up over the middle arch of the north arcade.

The north wall of the nave is remarkable by virtue of its arcade of three arches, all of which are of different design and each of which is separated from its neighbours by a substantial section of the original walling. The western two of these arches are pointed, but of considerably different dates. The eastern arch is of much earlier date; it has a simple round head of a single square order, resting on chamfered imposts and plain square jambs. Baldwin Brown (p. 478) dates this arch as 'probably early Norman'; but the arch leaves us with an impression of earlier date, like those at Wing, and we would like to see the plaster removed from it in order to show whether there are any features which would settle its age beyond reasonable doubt. There is a local tradition of the discovery of old foundations beneath the north aisle in a position which would indicate the former presence of a north *porticus* opening from the nave through this arch. A north aisle was formed at quite an early date, as is indicated by the lancet window in the west wall of the aisle. A confirmation of the former existence of a north *porticus* is provided by the existence of a Norman or Transitional respond on the north face of the main wall of the nave, indicating that at one time the aisle was spanned by an arch; such an arch would ordinarily be difficult to understand, but its presence would at once become intelligible if the north aisle had originated by the westward extension of a *porticus* and by the subsequent cutting of an arch through its west wall.

The double-splayed window, now wholly covered in plaster, is so placed that its downward-sloping sill has just escaped destruction by the pointed middle arch of the arcade, on whose apex it rests, at a height of about 18 ft above the floor. The aperture is not in the centre of the wall but at a distance of less than 1 ft from its outer face.

DIMENSIONS

No details of the construction of the walls of the nave and chancel can now be seen, since everything is covered with plaster; but the nave is a rectangle

about 21 ft wide by 54 ft long, with walls only 2 ft 6 in. thick and about 30 ft high; while the north wall of the chancel, also of the same thin construction, is suitably aligned to have been the original wall of a chancel about 15 ft square. In this connexion it is worth noting that the first bay of the chancel has the appearance of having been cut through early walling while the two bays further east are clearly extensions built *ab initio* in the thirteenth century.

The aperture of the double-splayed window is about 8 in. wide by 2 ft tall, and the window is splayed to become about 3 ft wide and 4 ft tall in the inner face of the wall, where its sill is about 18 ft above the floor.

The eastern arch of the north arcade is 8 ft 6 in. wide and 15 ft tall. If our suggestion of a north *porticus* is correct, the surviving fabric would suggest that it was about 9 ft wide (north–south) and about 10 ft long (east–west).

REFERENCE

Anonymous, 'Shorne church and Master John Shorne', *Arch. Cant.* 11 (1877), lxi–lxiv. Plan, and reference to double-splayed window as an indication of pre-Conquest date.

SHREWSBURY

Shropshire

Map sheet 118, reference SJ 493126

ST MARY THE VIRGIN

Foundations seen in 1864: possibly two dates, period C1 and earlier

During the course of works in the nave of St Mary's church in 1864, earlier foundations were discovered beneath the floor, extending from the eastern face of the present west tower, running roughly along the line of the present arcades, and ending at the east in an apse to the east of the present chancel-arch.

According to Archdeacon Lloyd, who examined these foundations, those of the apse consisted of stones which had been used once only, whereas those of the nave had been used on a previous occasion. He came to the conclusion that the apse belonged to the original Anglo-Saxon church and that the nave represented an enlargement which he attributed to a rebuilding in the tenth century. The nave was about 70 ft in length and about 27 ft in breadth, internally.

REFERENCES

LLOYD, 'St Mary's Church, Shrewsbury', *T. Shropshire A.N.H.S.*, 2nd ser., **6** (1894), 358–71. Also *ibid.* **4** (1892), vii–xiii.

J. E. HUNT, *The Collegiate and Parish Church of St Mary the Virgin, Shrewsbury* (London, 1947), 5–7. Details of the finding of the Anglo-Saxon foundations of two dates.

D. H. S. CRANAGE, *An Architectural Account of the Churches of Shropshire*, **2** (Wellington, 1912). Shrewsbury, St Mary, 923.

SHREWSBURY
Shropshire

DESTROYED EARLY CHURCHES OF ST ALKMUND, ST CHAD, AND ST JULIAN

In addition to the remains of early foundations at St Mary's, there are traditions of early fabric at three other churches, all of which were, unfortunately, destroyed or rebuilt towards the end of the eighteenth century. We know of no early basis for local claims that St Chad's was founded by King Offa about 780, or St Alkmund's by Æthelfleda, daughter of Alfred the Great, about 912. St Julian's is claimed locally as the earliest of all, on the very doubtful evidence of its dedication, which is said to have been to St Juliana, an early fourth-century martyr, to whom the notes in the church suggest that a dedication would have been unlikely as late as Offa's reign.[1]

It seems likely that substantial parts of the early fabric remained at St Alkmund's and St Julian's until both churches were almost completely rebuilt at the close of the eighteenth century. Notes in St Julian's church record that foundations of two earlier churches were seen during repairs to the church in 1883, but no record seems to have been kept of the nature of the discoveries.

At Old St Chad's, an early crypt, originally beneath the north transept, is still visible, although

unroofed and in an advanced state of decay. The greater part of the church collapsed in the eighteenth century, and a new church has been built on a quite different site.

REFERENCES

H. OWEN and J. B. BLAKEWAY, *History of Shrewsbury* (London, 1825).

J. NURSE, *T. Shropshire A.N.H.S.*, 2nd ser., **2** (1890), 359–66.

W. A. LEIGHTON, *ibid.* **6** (1883), 268.

D. H. S. CRANAGE, *Churches of Shropshire*, **2** (Wellington, 1912). Shrewsbury, St Alkmund, 893; St Chad, 899.

SIDBURY
Devon

Map sheet 176, reference SY 139917

ST GILES
Remains of crypt

The small village of Sidbury, picturesquely situated between the River Sid and the ancient earthwork known as Sidbury Castle, has a church with an early Norman chancel below which was discovered a square crypt. This had been filled in when the chancel was built, thus giving good evidence of its pre-Norman date. It is a roughly square chamber with sides about 10 ft in length; and it is now accessible by lifting trap-doors in the chancel floor. Only a few courses of its walls can be seen, but these are sufficient to show three or four steps up from the crypt on the north side. It has been suggested that the crypt was open to the west, and that the space of the chancel-arch contained two flights of steps, those on the north leading down to the crypt while those on the south led up to the chancel. It has, however, been suggested more recently that the crypt was part of a shrine which was not originally within the fabric of the church.[2]

Baldwin Brown (p. 323) says that the chancel must have had a wooden floor because there are no signs of a vault. This conclusion may well be

---

[1] The poet Cynewulf celebrated St Juliana about the end of the eighth century, and her cult survived after the Norman Conquest.

[2] C. A. R. Radford, *Arch. J.* **114** (1957), 166–7.

correct; but it is difficult to follow the argument, since the destruction of the upper walls of the crypt must have involved the destruction of any vault, and there is no reason to assume that any parts of the destroyed vault would necessarily have come to light on the site, or would have been distinguishable from other common building stone in the existing fabric.

DIMENSIONS

The crypt is about 10 ft square internally and its floor was recorded by Reed as 6 ft 6 in. beneath the present floor of the chancel.

REFERENCES

W. CAVE, 'Notes on the Saxon crypt, Sidbury church, Devon', *Arch. J.* **56** (1899), 74–6. Plan, and brief description of the discovery of the crypt. Anglo-Saxon walls surviving for a height of about 4 ft with Anglo-Saxon plaster on the walls and floor.

H. REED, 'Architectural notes on some churches visited during the congress', *J.B.A.A.*, 2nd ser., **33** (1927), 166–82. St Giles, Sidbury, 181–2. Claim that the manor of Sidbury, and others, were given to Exeter Cathedral in 925 was confirmed by Bishop Leofric in 1050. Dimensions given, and a reference to a fragment of Anglo-Saxon carved stone in the south transept.

C. A. R. RADFORD, 'Sidbury', *Arch. J.* **114** (1957), 166–7. The crypt was probably part of a free-standing shrine or memorial of the founder of the church. It most likely did not form part of the church.

SINGLETON
Sussex

Map sheet 181, reference SU 878130

ST JOHN THE EVANGELIST
Lowest stage of west tower: period C

The small village of Singleton, in the South Downs, about 6 miles north of Chichester, has a church now consisting of a west tower, an aisled nave and an aisleless chancel, in which at least the lower part of the large square tower certainly dates from late-Saxon times. The tower is of flint rubble construction, thinly plastered, and with massive side-alternate quoining; it stands on a chamfered plinth and has a square string-course

above the lower stage at about 20 ft from the ground. The church has clearly suffered somewhat severely in the course of nineteenth-century restorations, and the string-course, as now visible from outside, is of chamfered section, but a small part which has most fortunately been preserved, at A, within the south-west angle of the north aisle shows that it was originally of plain square section and has either weathered externally or been cut to its present chamfered form. Above the level of the string-course the tower is set back a few inches and has no further clear indications

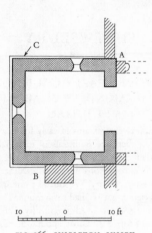

FIG. 266. SINGLETON, SUSSEX

A, original north-east quoin, now visible within later north aisle; B, later buttress; C, original plinth.

of Anglo-Saxon date, although there is no real reason to doubt that the upper part is contemporary with the lower.

Three round-headed, double-splayed windows in the lower stage of the tower serve to date it with reasonable certainty to the late-Saxon period, even though their faces seem to have been seriously modified in later times, probably with the intention of enlarging the area of glass. The interior splays of these windows are plastered, and their exterior faces are formed of well-dressed stone, but their peculiar character is that instead of the interior and exterior splays meeting about the middle of the wall, there is an intermediate section which is cut straight through about one-third of the thickness of the wall. The windows in the north and south walls are set fairly low, with their sills only about 6 ft above the floor, while the west window is placed much higher, near the top of the lower stage, but still lighting the ground-floor chamber.

The south and west faces of the tower have no other openings, but the north face has a double window of two round-headed lights a few feet above the string-course, and a single round-headed window in the belfry stage above the modern clock-face. At about the same level, the east face has a single square-headed window; but none of these windows has any feature which would serve to define their date with certainty.

In the interior of the church a feature of special interest is the north-east quoin of the tower, which may be seen in the north aisle, running down past the string-course to which reference has already been made and continuing the whole way to the floor. This therefore shows either that the tower originally stood free or else that any building to the east of it was narrower than the tower. We believe that the second is the correct inference, and that the tower formed part of a church like those at Broughton, in Lincolnshire, and Earls Barton, in Northamptonshire, with a small chancel to the east of a substantial tower.

The original tower-arch has been replaced by one of pointed form, but high above it an original doorway shows where the upper chamber of the tower opened towards the eastern compartment of the church. The doorway has plain square jambs, cut straight through the wall, but not formed of through-stones. The jambs rest on chamfered bases and support a simple triangular head.

DIMENSIONS

The tower is almost exactly 17 ft square internally, with walls about 2 ft 8 in. thick and roughly 50 ft high.

The high doorway in the east face is about 1 ft 9 in. wide and 5 ft 6 in. tall, with its sill about 20 ft above the floor.

The double-splayed windows now have apertures 1 ft 6 in. wide and 3 ft 8 in. tall, splayed to about 2 ft 6 in. by 5 ft in the faces of the walls.

The present nave is about 36 ft long and 16 ft 3 in. wide internally, with side walls about 2 ft thick and about 25 ft high.

REFERENCES

P. M. JOHNSTON, 'Low side windows of Sussex churches', *Sussex Arch. C.* **42** (1899), 117–79. Singleton, 145–6.

H. L. JESSEP, *Anglo-Saxon Church Architecture in Sussex* (Winchester, undated), 35–6.

W. H. GODFREY, 'St John the Evangelist, Singleton', *Sussex N.Q.* **3** (1930–1), 81. Brief description and plan.

V.C.H., Sussex, **4** (London, 1953), 118–20. Detailed description and plan.

SKILLINGTON
Lincolnshire

Map sheet 122, reference SK 895259

ST JAMES
Nave: period C

The small village of Skillington, situated in pleasantly rolling and wooded country about 6 miles south of Grantham, and about a mile west of the Great North Road, has an interesting church consisting of a west tower and spire, an aisled nave, and an aisleless chancel, with a south chapel. The fabric of the Anglo-Saxon walling of the nave is stone rubble, with well-dressed neatly jointed stone quoining.

The Anglo-Saxon date of the side walls of the nave, which are only 2 ft 6 in. in thickness, is confirmed by their eastern quoins. The south-east quoin, although heavily plastered, may be seen in the south chapel to have a pair of long-and-short quoins where the plaster has peeled away. The north-east quoin, visible from outside, presents about 2 ft of its east face and 4 in. of its north, and shows three good long-and-short pairs. These stand above eight courses of rather random quoining which, however, is also indicated as of the same pre-Conquest date by the cutting back of part of the outer surface of each stone so as to present a straight vertical joint as a stop for the original plaster covering of the wall face.

DIMENSIONS

The nave is 29 ft 3 in. by 18 ft internally, with walls 2 ft 6 in. thick and about 18 ft high to the top of the off-set which marks the junction of the original walls with the later clear-storey.

REFERENCE

E. TROLLOPE, 'Churches visited from Grantham', *A.A.S.R.* **13** (1875), 1-28. Skillington, 25-7. Brief description and notice of Anglo-Saxon character.

SKIPWITH

Yorkshire, East Riding

Map sheets 97 and 98, reference SE 657384

Figures 571-3

ST HELEN

Lower part of tower, and western part of nave: period A or B

Upper chamber of tower: period C2

The quiet village of Skipwith, about 5 miles north-east of Selby and remote from any main roads, has a most interesting church, whose Anglo-Saxon character was noticed as long ago as 1853 by John Phillips.[1] It stands beside Skipwith Common, only 2 miles from Ricall, where the Northmen under Harold Hardrada and Tosti landed in 1066 before their victory at Fulford and their subsequent disastrous defeat by King Harold at Stamford Bridge five days later. The greater part of the church of those days is still preserved in the present building, although its tower has been raised by the addition of a Perpendicular belfry and the walls of its nave have been pierced by arcades of two bays in the late twelfth and early thirteenth century. In the fourteenth century its chancel was swept away to allow the nave and aisles to be extended a third bay eastward, and a most attractive new Decorated chancel was added at the east. Finally, in late Perpendicular or Tudor times, a clear-storey was added to the nave above its earlier walls.

The tower is built of roughly squared stone, which is of large blocks in the lower storey but of small rubble in the upper. It stands on a double plinth of one square and one chamfered order, above which the first stage rises sheer for a height of about 36 ft to a simple square string-course. Above this a second, but much shorter, Anglo-Saxon stage is separated from the Perpendicular belfry by a chamfered string-course.

The short upper Anglo-Saxon stage now has in each face a small square window which has all the appearance of being a later insertion, an impression which is strengthened by signs, in the north face, of the jambs of an early window; and by definite indications in the stonework of the west and south faces of the outlines of blocked round-headed windows that have lost their dressed stone facings. It seems likely therefore that this second stage is all that remains of an Anglo-Saxon belfry, whose windows have been blocked to strengthen the walls, in order to carry the heavy fifteenth-century belfry. The blocked windows may also be faintly seen within the upper chamber of the tower, in a form which suggests that they were originally wide openings of simple round-headed form. The vestiges are, however, insufficiently well defined to justify a confident assertion that these early belfry windows were single openings rather than the usual double windows, with mid-wall shafts.[2]

Near the south edge of the west face a boldly projecting corbel or *prokrossos* may be seen, just below the square Anglo-Saxon string-course; and, about 10 ft lower, the tower is surrounded by what appears to have been a decorative panel consisting of two courses of stones which project slightly from the face of the wall and are separated by a band of stones of slightly different texture. Below this level, the tower has six windows, three of which light the ground floor and three light the upper chamber.

The western window at ground-floor level is a modern insertion and, unlike the others, has no outward splay. The two original windows lighting the ground floor are set high in the north

[1] J. Phillips, *Rivers, Mountains, and Sea Coast of Yorkshire* (London, 1853), 84 and 202.

[2] By contrast, Baldwin Brown (p. 479) suggested that the present belfry probably replaced the upper part of the Anglo-Saxon tower, in which he thought there could be assumed to have been double windows with mid-wall shafts. We think that this suggestion can no longer be accepted.

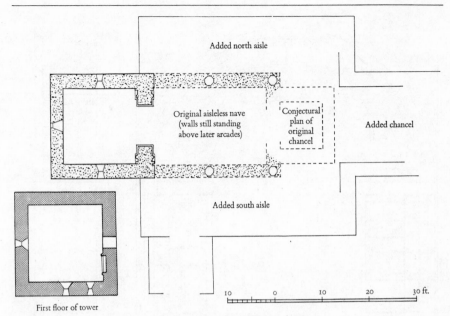

Added north aisle

Original aisleless nave
(walls still standing
above later arcades)

Conjectural
plan of
original
chancel

Added chancel

Added south aisle

First floor of tower

10   0   10   20   30 ft.

FIG. 267. SKIPWITH, YORKSHIRE (E.R.)

The main plan shows the tower and the original nave in relation to the present church which arises from several subsequent enlargements. The extent of the original aisleless nave is known with certainty, as is described in the text. The layout of the original chancel is conjectural, but might be determined by excavation beneath the present floor. The first-floor plan of the tower shows the unusual arrangement of windows and the unique recess in the east wall south of the doorway. The walls of this upper part of the tower are of very different fabric from that of the lower chamber, and a later date has accordingly been shown on the plan. The post-Conquest additions are shown diagrammatically in outline only, and are not drawn accurately to scale.

and south walls and are of tall and narrow shape. They are splayed both internally and externally and are abnormal among double-splayed windows in that their heads are covered on the exterior face of the wall by rectangular blocks of stone that are cut away below to the shape of the window-heads. Internally, their heads are arched with neatly laid voussoirs, and the exterior arrangement is so unusual as to give a considerable suggestion that these windows may originally have been single-splayed and may have been adapted to their present form when the double-splayed windows of the upper storey were constructed.

The arrangement of the three windows of the upper floor is also of considerable interest. There is no window in the north face. The two principal windows are big double-splayed openings in the centres of the west and south faces, and the third window is a smaller one, also double-splayed, but set higher in the south face and near to its eastern angle. The arrangement clearly suggests that the main windows were intended to provide the basic lighting of the upper chamber and that the third window was specially provided to light some particular part of the chamber. This interpretation is confirmed by the arrangements within the upper chamber, as will be noted below. For the present it should be noticed that the fabric in this upper part of the tower is of smaller stones than in the ground-floor walls, and that the two principal windows are constructed of these smaller stones, with their heads roughly arched. The small additional window in the south face, by contrast, has a monolithic head which is now badly weathered. Apart from the first-floor windows in the tower at Jarrow in County Durham these windows at Skipwith are the most northerly examples of the use of double splays.

551

FIG. 268. SKIPWITH, YORKSHIRE (E.R.)

Details of the tower-arch. This figure shows how each face of the tower-arch is outlined by double strip-work of which the inner strip is of half-round section and the outer square. It also shows the unusual jointing of the arch and the unique arrangement whereby horizontally coursed walling is interposed between the arch and its surrounding strip-work.

Within the nave it is possible to confirm the history that has been outlined of its development by noting how the side walls, below the clearstorey, are in bond with the tower at the west, and how above the second pier from the tower they show a straight joint in the masonry where the fourteenth-century walls of the third bay were joined to the early side walls of the Anglo-Saxon nave. Within the aisles it is possible to obtain further confirmation by noting the same vertical joints; it should also be noted that the eastern part of the north wall is appreciably thinner than the earlier wall over the two western bays.

The principal feature of the nave is, however, the round-headed tower-arch, of a single square order, outlined on both faces by pilaster-strips and

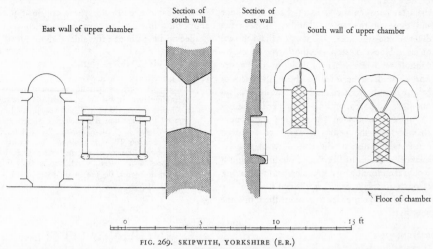

East wall of upper chamber

Section of south wall

Section of east wall

South wall of upper chamber

Floor of chamber

0   5   10   15 ft

FIG. 269. SKIPWITH, YORKSHIRE (E.R.)

Details of the upper chamber in the tower. The left-hand figure shows the doorway and recess in the east wall of the chamber, with a section through the eastern window in the south wall. The right-hand figure shows the two windows in the south wall, with a section through the recess in the east wall. The floor of the chamber is 19 ft above the floor of the nave.

hood-moulds which consist of an inner half-round strip and an outer square one. A particularly interesting and peculiar feature of this arch and its surrounding hood-moulds is that a section of normal walling with horizontal and vertical joints intervenes between the radially jointed arch and its radially jointed hood-moulds. Although only a few of the stones of the square jambs and of the arch pass through the full thickness of the wall, the Anglo-Saxon character indicated by the strip-work is further confirmed by the megalithic construction of the jambs and by their simple square plinths and imposts, all of which are returned along the full width of both wall-faces.

Above the tower-arch, access to the first-floor chamber was formerly given through a doorway which is now blocked, but which is still visible as a recess with square jambs resting on chamfered bases and carrying chamfered imposts. Towards the nave the round head of this blocked doorway is now obscured by a roof-truss, but within the first-floor chamber it is seen to be of six voussoirs of very varied size laid with joints which, even by Anglo-Saxon standards, are remarkably far from radial.

Towards the ground floor of the tower all the

features of the tower-arch are similar to those seen from the nave. The inner faces of the early windows set high in the side walls should be noted, with particular reference to the way in which their heads are arched with well-laid voussoirs, in sharp contrast to the monolithic and rather roughly cut heads on the exterior.

A fixed ladder now gives access to the first-floor chamber whose special feature is the interesting recessed panel described and illustrated by Baldwin Brown (p. 333). This shallow rectangular recess is more or less centrally placed in the section of wall to the south of the blocked doorway which formerly led out into the space above the nave. As is mentioned by Baldwin Brown, it appears to have formed an important part in the design of the chamber since the additional small window in the south wall seems to have been designed so as to provide good lighting for the recess throughout the day. Although it will probably never be possible to settle without doubt the purpose of this recess it seems reasonable to suggest that it was designed to support or contain an enriched back for an altar placed against the east wall.

In describing the exterior of the tower we have called attention to two marked differences in character between the walls of the ground floor and those of the upper chamber, namely the different construction of the windows and the use of large blocks of stone in the lower storey by contrast with the small rubble in the upper storey. We have been led by these differences to believe that the western chamber was originally a one-storeyed porch, with single-splayed windows of quite early character. The addition of the upper chamber and the belfry would have followed considerably later, in the period when double-splayed windows had become fashionable; and it would therefore be easy to understand the cutting of outward splays on the heads and jambs of the lower windows in order to convert them into the new style.

DIMENSIONS

The original internal dimensions of the nave must have been about 25 ft in length and 16 ft in width, with walls 2 ft 10 in. in thickness and about 20 ft in height. The ground floor of the tower is 15 ft 10 in. square internally, with walls 2 ft 11 in. in thickness. Externally the tower is about 21 ft 8 in. square and about 44 ft high to the top of the Anglo-Saxon second stage.

The tower-arch is 8 ft 6 in. wide and 13 ft tall, and the side windows of the ground-floor chamber have apertures 1 ft wide and 4 ft 6 in. tall, splayed to become about 1 ft 6 in. wide and 5 ft 6 in. tall in the exterior face of the wall, where their sills are about 11 ft above the ground.

In the first-floor chamber, the blocked eastern doorway is 2 ft 5 in. wide and 7 ft 3 in. tall, with its sill on the floor and 19 ft above the level of the floor of the nave. The recess in the east wall is 3 ft 6 in. wide, 2 ft 6 in. tall, and is recessed to a depth of 7 in. into the wall; its sill is 2 ft 2 in. above the floor. The principal windows, in the south and west walls, have apertures between 10 in. and 1 ft in width and between 3 ft and 4 ft tall. They are splayed to become about 3 ft by 5 ft in the wall-face, and their sills are about 1 ft above the floor. The smaller eastern window in the south wall is placed with its sill about 4 ft above the floor.

The short Anglo-Saxon belfry stage represents the part of the tower from 36 ft to 44 ft above the ground. The blocked windows in its four faces seem to have rested on the string-course at 36 ft above the ground and to have been simple round-headed openings about 3 ft wide and about 6 ft tall.

REFERENCES

In spite of its unusual interest, Skipwith church seems to have escaped other than passing mention in archaeological literature. It was mentioned as Anglo-Saxon by Phillips (*loc. cit.*) in 1853. It was visited on 6 July 1899 by the Yorkshire Archaeological Society and is briefly described in the *Excursion Notice* published for that occasion. The only mention which we have found in the Reports of the Associated Architectural Societies has reference to the remarkably fine wrought-iron-work on the south door (*A.A.S.R.* **14** (1877–8), 75).

SNORING, LITTLE
Norfolk
Map sheet 125, reference TF 953325

ST ANDREW
Detached round tower: possibly Saxo-Norman

The interesting church at Little Snoring now stands in open fields at the north-west of its small village, and about 3 miles north-east from Fakenham. The present church is a rectangular building, which seems to be principally of the period of the transition from the Norman to the Early English style. It seems clear, however, that this church replaced an earlier one, for the detached belfry-tower which stands a few yards to the south-west has a wide, blocked, early-Norman or Saxo-Norman tower-arch in its east face, where there are also rough areas which represent the tearing away of the walls of a small, narrow nave.

The tower contains no original windows or doorways to determine its date with precision. Its fabric is of flint, with some admixture of car-stone, in the way that seems in Norfolk to give an indication of Anglo-Saxon or Saxo-Norman workmanship. The blocked tower-arch is of two plain square orders, wholly constructed of car-stone. The present church is unlikely to have been built much later than 1200 and its predecessor must have been appreciably earlier to have warranted demolition by that time. The present church may, however, incorporate material re-used from its predecessor and its date may therefore be later than would be indicated simply by study of its component parts.

On these rather inadequate grounds we have included this church in the hope that others may be encouraged to work out its history in more detail.

REFERENCES

J. H. PARKER, 'Churches in the neighbourhood of Norwich', *Trans. Brit. Arch. Ass. Norwich, 1847* (London, 1851), 184. Brief description. Church noted as mainly transitional Norman, and detached tower as Norman.

C. J.W. MESSENT, *Parish Churches of Norfolk and Norwich* (Norwich, 1936), 220. Tower noted as Saxo-Norman.

C. J.W. MESSENT, *The Round Towers to English Parish Churches* (Norwich, 1958), 188. Tower noted as pre-Conquest.

H. M. CAUTLEY, *Norfolk Churches* (Ipswich, 1949), 245. Tower noted as pre-Conquest.

SOCKBURN

County Durham

Map sheet 85, reference NZ 349070

ALL SAINTS

Ruins of nave: possibly period A

After possibly more than a thousand years of use, the little church of All Saints at Sockburn was unroofed and deliberately allowed to fall into ruin early in the nineteenth century, when a new church was built in 1838 across the river at Girsby. There is no recorded early history of the church itself, but the place is mentioned by Symeon of Durham under the name Sochasburg in connexion with the consecration of Archbishop Eanbald II in 796; and later, in the time of Bishop Aldhun of Durham (990–1018), Symeon records the gift of Socceburg to the church of St Cuthbert at Durham by Snaculf son of Cytel.[1] The great antiquity of the church, then a ruin, was first noticed by Hodges[2] in 1891, since when the fifteenth-century north aisle known as the Conyers porch has been made weatherproof

and used to house memorials of that family as well as a large number of pre-Conquest stones which formerly stood neglected among the ruins.

The church has a most romantic setting at the south end of a long narrow loop of the Tees about 6 miles south-east of Darlington in the private grounds of Sockburn Hall, where permission should be sought to visit the ruin. The remains of the Anglo-Saxon church consist of a nave measuring internally only 24 ft 4 in. by 15 ft 11 in., with walls varying between 2 ft 3 in. and 2 ft 5 in. in thickness and of no less than 25 ft in height. Through the south wall an arcade of two tall pointed arches was pierced in the thirteenth century, and a wide low arch was opened to a north chapel in the fifteenth century. There are no remains of early doors or windows, nor any trace of the original chancel, which was replaced in the thirteenth century by a long chancel of the same width as the nave.

The proportions of the ruined nave are reminiscent of the small church at Escomb, though on an even smaller scale, and this similarity is further supported by the massive side-alternate quoins which can be seen at the south-east and north-west angles of the nave.[3] Baldwin Brown (pp. 191 and 479) placed this church in the very small group which he assigned to period B I, but the analogy with Escomb suggests the greater probability of the date in period A originally claimed by Hodges.

The importance of Sockburn during the pre-Conquest period is well attested by the remarkable collection of carved stones which has survived on the site and is now preserved in the Conyers chapel. There are twenty-five of these stones, which constitute one of the most important collections on a single site anywhere in England. They are fully described and illustrated in the two places mentioned under References.

REFERENCES (additional to those given in the footnotes)

W. H. KNOWLES 'Sockburn church', *T. Durham Northd. A.A.S.* 5 (1896–1905), 99–120. Important account of

---

[1] Symeon of Durham, ed. T. Arnold (Rolls Series, 75, I) (London, 1882), 83; and (75, II) (London, 1885), 58.
[2] C. C. Hodges, 'Pre-Conquest churches of Northumbria', *Reliquary*, n.s., **8** (1894), 65–83. Sockburn described, with plan and history, 69–71.

[3] Hodges said that the Anglo-Saxon quoins were visible at all four angles. We believe that the north-eastern one was destroyed by the building of the Conyers chapel and that the south-western one was masked by the addition of a thirteenth-century buttress.

restoration carried out at the end of the century. Full details of the church and of the carved stones. Plans, elevations, and photographs.

V.C.H., *County of Durham*, 1 (London, 1905), 235–8. Sculptured stones described and illustrated.

SOMBORNE, LITTLE

Hampshire

Map sheet 168, reference SU 382326

ALL SAINTS

Nave: period C

In a pleasant wooded setting, about 2 miles south-west of Stockbridge, the church at Little Somborne now consists of a single rectangular building with a blocked twelfth-century chancel-arch to indicate the former existence of a chancel of that date. The walls are of plastered rubble with long-and-short western quoins. A complete pilaster-strip has survived on the western part of the north wall; and the lower part of a similar pilaster-strip may be seen on the south wall, between the western quoin and the doorway.

It is therefore clear that the west end and at least the western parts of the side walls are of Anglo-Saxon date, and it is possible that the building may represent the original Anglo-Saxon nave.

DIMENSIONS

The interior measurements are 44 ft 8 in. by 14 ft; and the walls are 2 ft 5 in. thick and about 15 ft in height.

The pilaster-strips project between 2 in. and 4 in. from the face of the wall and are about 6 in. in width. They are placed about 11 ft from the western angles.

REFERENCES

J. H. PARKER, 'Churches in the neighbourhood of Winchester', *Proc. Arch. Inst.,Winchester 1845* (London, 1846), 24. Pilaster-strips noted as similar to those at HeadbourneWorthy and Corhampton.

V.C.H., *Hampshire and the I.o.W.*, 4 (London, 1911), 482.

SOMERFORD KEYNES

Gloucestershire (Wiltshire until 1897)

Map sheet 157, reference SU 016955

Figure 574

ALL SAINTS

Blocked north doorway: period A2 or 3

The small stone-built village of Somerford Keynes, near the source of the Thames, about 4 miles south of Cirencester, first appears in history in the year 685 in a grant of land comprising forty hides, by Berhtwald, nephew of King Aethelred of Mercia (675–704), to Abbot Aldhelm, later St Aldhelm, for the support of the monks of Malmesbury.[1] The Anglo-Saxon doorway surviving in the church is dated by Baldwin Brown somewhat conjecturally to the eighth century,[2] but there is nothing in its general form or detail inconsistent with Stenton's suggestion, which we have adopted, that it is a survival from a church of Aldhelm's time, possibly one built at his orders for the peasants living on his new estate.

The church has an attractive setting amid trees and beside an ancient stone manor house. It now consists of an aisleless chancel with a modern organ-chamber on the north, a nave with a short Early English arcade cut through the eastern part of its north wall, a south porch, and a Perpendicular west tower. The ancient doorway which has survived in the aisleless part of the north wall of the nave, between a Gothic window and the west wall of the north aisle, stands in a short section of original walling of undressed flat blocks of stone rubble, which are still lightly covered with a thin coat of what appears to be the original plaster facing. The square jambs are each built of three massive roughly dressed blocks of stone, standing on a square plinth of undressed stones, and laid in 'Escomb fashion', upright-flat-upright. The imposts are in the form of bonding stones and their boldly projecting soffit faces are cut in a characteristically Anglo-Saxon pattern of three steps. The curiously stilted arch of the head is cut in the

[1] F. M. Stenton, *Anglo-Saxon England*, 2nd ed. (Oxford, 1947), 151.

[2] G. Baldwin Brown (1925), 191 and 479.

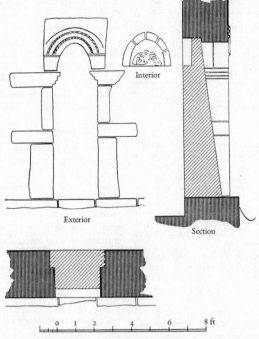

Interior

Exterior

Section

0 1 2   4   6   8 ft

FIG. 270. SOMERFORD KEYNES, GLOUCESTERSHIRE

Details of the blocked doorway. On the interior of the wall the doorway is concealed beneath modern plaster except for the shallow recess, which represents its elliptical head, and which contains the piece of sculpture of which a sketch is shown in the figure. It is impossible at present to be certain that the jambs of the doorway are recessed as is shown in the plan. The head of the doorway is slightly taller internally as is shown in the section. In order to settle the nature of the jambs it would be desirable to remove some of the plaster. It should particularly be noted both in Fig. 270 and in Fig. 574 how the steps of the imposts are cut with obtuse angles.

lower face of a single square stone whose outer face is enriched by the shallow recessing of a semicircular area, within which two concentric bands of cable-moulding have been left standing in relief, with small horizontal fillets to stop the cable-mouldings about 8 in. above the main imposts.

The doorway is blocked by a wall of rubble, which slopes inward to leave a recess that increases in depth from 5 in. at the sill to 1 ft 6 in. at the head. Within the church, the lower part of the doorway is completely obscured by plaster, but the oval head appears as a recess about 5 in. in depth. This recess is 2 ft in width by comparison with a width of 1 ft 9 in. externally; and it would be of great interest if the lower part of the doorway could be opened out in order to see whether the jambs are rebated for the hanging of a door, like

the jambs of the three somewhat similar early doorways at Heysham.

By contrast with the monolithic exterior head of the doorway, the head of the recess within the church is arched by five voussoirs of very unequal length along its circumference.

Within this recess there is preserved an unusual and interesting carved stone dated by Clapham to the first half of the eleventh century. It shows the heads of two fierce monsters facing each other, with open jaws, and both biting a ball. The head of one monster is practically complete; the other has been broken away close to the jaws.

DIMENSIONS

The doorway is 8 ft 4 in. in height; and a very distinctive feature, which supports the early date

557

suggested above, is the inward slope of its jambs, by which the opening narrows from 2 ft 6 in. at the plinth to 2 ft 4 in. at the level of the imposts. The effect of narrowing to the top is further emphasized by the narrow and elliptical form of the pseudo-arched head. This is only 21 in. wide and no less than 18 in. high. The early north wall is 2 ft 4 in. in thickness, about 15 ft in height, and about 18 ft in surviving length.

REFERENCES

Anonymous, 'Saxon doorway at Somerford Keynes', *Illustrated Archaeologist*, **1** (1893–4), 46–9. Perspective drawing and measured elevation of doorway. Carved stone illustrated and described. Suggestion that the stone might have been a headstone, in conjunction with a recumbent grave-slab.

J. R. ALLEN, 'Notes on the ornamentation of the early Christian monuments of Wiltshire', *Wilts. A.N.H. Mag.* **27** (1893–4), 50–65. Carved stone and doorway described and illustrated, 65.

A. W. CLAPHAM, 'Three carved stones in the collection of the Society', *Ant. J.* **11** (1931), 133–5. The three stones compared with those at Somerford Keynes and Bibury, and dated to the first half of the eleventh century.

R. A. SMITH, 'Sculpture of the Viking period', *P. Soc. Ant.* **26** (1913–14), 60–72. Carved stone illustrated and similar stones listed.

SOMPTING

Sussex

Map sheet 182, reference TQ 161056

ST MARY THE VIRGIN

West tower, and possibly parts of nave walls: period C3

Although now in considerable danger of being swallowed up as a north-eastern suburb of Worthing, the ancient village of Sompting has so far preserved its rural independence, at the foot of the Downs. Its church, unique in possessing a pre-Conquest form of shingled pyramidal spire, still stands amid fields, with an uninterrupted view to the Channel, which is less than 2 miles away to the south. There is a persistent tradition[1]

that the tower was lowered 25 ft in 1762. It seems clear, however,[2] that the tower is original, and that it was a taller spire or *flèche* that was modified into the present form of a Rhenish helm, of which the only other example known to us in England is on the Victorian tower at Flixton, Suffolk. The fabric is of flint rubble, thinly plastered; with window-facings, long-and-short quoins, and pilaster-strips all in cream-coloured, well-dressed, Selsey limestone.

Externally all four faces of the tower are different, but all have as a common feature that from a square corbel or *prokrossos* at the gable a vertical half-round pilaster-strip runs down the centre of each face, dividing it in two. On the eastern face this pilaster ends at the level of the roof-ridge of the nave; but on all other faces it runs down to a square string-course, which separates the short lower stage of the tower from the much taller upper stage. Just below the level of the belfry windows on each face the pilaster carries a capital, of conical shape, two of which are ornamented with upright leaves, now much weathered, see Figs. 272–3.

On each face there are belfry windows close on either side of the pilaster. On the east and west faces each belfry window is single, and triangular-headed; while on the north and south faces they are double, and round-headed, with mid-wall shafts and through-stone slabs. On the south face, the mid-wall shafts have simple capitals which might be described as cushion capitals drawn out along the thickness of the wall so as to become through-stone slabs. On the north face, the capitals are similar in general form, but they are enriched with long leaves, which are carved in relief on the capitals, turning over at the ends like volutes, see Fig. 273.

On the east and west faces these belfry windows are the only original openings; but the south face has, in addition, a small triangular-headed window, which is placed a few feet above the horizontal string-course. The north face has five further Anglo-Saxon windows. In the lowest stage, a double-splayed, round-headed window in the

---

[1] M. H. Bloxam, *Gothic Ecclesiastic Architecture*, 11th ed. (London, 1882), 44. F. Harrison, *Notes on Sussex Churches*, 4th ed. (Hove, 1920), 187–8.

[2] J. Dallaway and E. Cartwright, *County of Sussex*, **2**, II (London, 1830), 106–7.

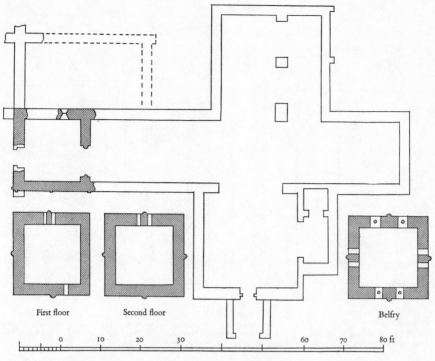

FIG. 271. SOMPTING, SUSSEX
General ground plan, and plan of the upper three levels of the tower.

eastern half of the wall serves to light the ground-floor chamber. There may originally have been a similar window in the western half; but, if so, it has been destroyed in the construction of the medieval north chapel, whose ruins still remain, to the north of the tower. In the second stage, a few feet above the horizontal string-course, a pair of triangular-headed windows are placed, one on either side of the vertical pilaster-strip and close to it, so that it forms their common central jamb. These windows have their jambs cut straight through the wall and enriched on the outer faces with a half-round moulding. Finally, about mid-way between these and the belfry windows, a further pair of windows, rather larger and with round heads, are set a little further away from the vertical pilaster. These also have jambs cut straight through the wall, with half-round mouldings carried up the jambs and round the

heads, but with a small square fillet beside the opening, while above their heads are traces of relieving arches, irregularly turned in tiles.

The ground stage has further distinctive Anglo-Saxon features in the form of square pilaster-strips which are particularly well preserved on the south face. The eastern strip on the south face is at the point of junction of the tower with the south wall of the nave, thus giving a clear indication that at least the western part of the wall of the nave is contemporary with the tower. A second strip runs up the south face close to the centre, but slightly displaced to the east, so as to be about its own width to the east of the upper half-round pilaster-strip. Yet a third runs up the face just a little to the east of its western angle; but only the upper part of this strip is visible, because a medieval buttress has been built to support this angle of the tower. All these pilasters are of long-and-short

559

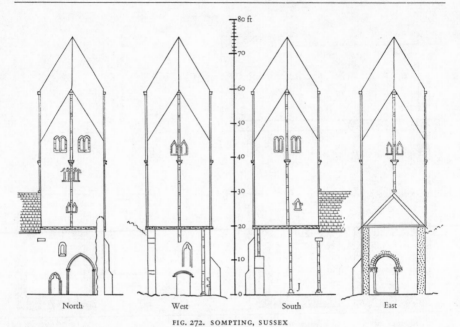

FIG. 272. SOMPTING, SUSSEX

Elevations of the four faces of the tower. The eastern elevation also includes a transverse section through the Norman walls of the nave so as to show the Anglo-Saxon tower-arch. Note how the square pilaster-strip J on the lower stage is not aligned with the half-round pilaster-strip on the upper stage of the south face.

construction, about 9 in. wide, projecting about 2 in. from the wall-face, and with long stones about 2 ft in length and shorts varying from about 4 in. to 7 in. Some of the short stones are appreciably wider than the pilaster, so as to bond into the wall, but their faces are then cut back to the standard width, so that when the wall was plastered they would match the width of the other stones. The pilasters rise from well-defined bases whose lower stones are of simple cubical shape, while those next above are chamfered to meet the pilasters.

On the west face, the pilasters have suffered more damage than on the south, but one is visible near the south corner; and part of the central one has survived over the head of a medieval window. Nothing can be seen of the original work near the north corner, where the wall of the medieval north chapel and a supporting buttress conceal the whole angle; but at the south angle, part of the original long-and-short quoining is visible, and the faces of the stones may clearly be

seen to have been cut back for plaster, so as to present the appearance of a pilaster-strip clasping the corner.

On the north face, no complete pilaster-strips have remained on the lower storey; but it is clear that there were originally three, arranged in the same way as on the south, for vestiges may be seen of the upper ends of the western and central strips and also of the bases of those to the east and west.

The pyramidal shingled roof of the tower has already been mentioned; it is unique among the Anglo-Saxon churches of England, although it has been copied in the nineteenth century at Flixton in Suffolk; and the type is common among churches in the Rhineland.

Another unique feature of the tower is the horizontal string-course above its lower stage. In essence this is square in section; but it is enriched with an ornament, peculiar to Sompting, which has sometimes been inaccurately described as Norman-like billet ornament, and which has

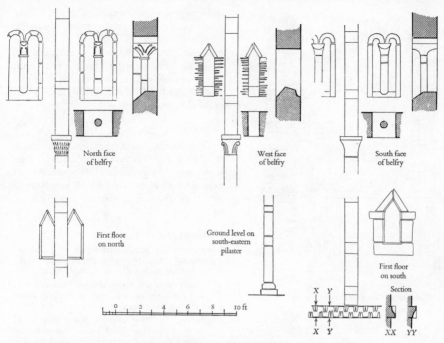

North face
of belfry

West face
of belfry

South face
of belfry

First floor
on north

Ground level on
south-eastern
pilaster

First floor
on south

Section

0   2   4   6   8   10 ft

X Y   X Y

X Y   XX YY

FIG. 273. SOMPTING, SUSSEX

Larger-scale details of the windows and other architectural features of the tower. The elevation and sections of the
string-course at the bottom right-hand corner of the figure show how incorrect it is to regard this feature as an
instance of Norman billet-moulding.

therefore been used as an argument for assigning
a post-Conquest date to the tower.[1] The ornament is now much weathered, but close inspection
will show that it is fundamentally different from
Norman billet ornament and that it can perhaps
best be described by saying that it could be
constructed from a plain square string-course by
gouging out pairs of vertical half-round channels.
The first pair would begin from a little above the
centre and would run downwards to the lower
edge, then alongside these a further pair would
run upwards towards the upper edge, and so on
along the whole string-course, all the channels
beginning as shallow depressions but deepening
towards the edge.

Within the church another interesting late-
Saxon feature is the tower-arch, which is round-
headed and fundamentally square in section, but
with a half-round soffit-shaft carried up the jambs
and round the arch as a soffit-roll. A thin square
impost is recessed in rectangular form to match
the recessed jambs; and, beneath this, the shaft
and the jambs are provided with most curiously
ornamented capitals. On the shaft, the capital is
a simple bell enriched with three superimposed
rows of vertical leaves, turned over outwards at
their tips, like the single row round the belfry
capital at Scartho; on the square jambs, the capital
does not project, but is merely an ornamental frieze
carved in relief to show large voluts or horns,

---

[1] G. Baldwin Brown (1925), 430–1. A good illustration of the string-course, showing clearly that it had no
true resemblance to billet ornament was given by Rick-
man; see, for example, his *English Architecture*, 5th ed.
(London, 1848), Appx. p. xxix, or *Arch.* 26 (1836), 43.

FIG. 274. SOMPTING, SUSSEX
Details of the tower-arch.

arcade of semi-circular arches with reeded mould-ings; secondly, eight lengths of friezes of palmette ornament; thirdly, a fragment of scrolled orna-ment; and finally a figure of a nimbed abbot, which has very generally been ascribed to the twelfth century or later, but which Talbot Rice concurs with Clapham in dating to the early part of the eleventh-century.[2]

DIMENSIONS

The tower is about 15 ft square internally, with walls 2 ft 3 in. thick and about 60 ft high to the tops of the gabled faces. The tower is about 75 ft in total height, to the top of its pyramidal roof. The tower-arch is 6 ft wide and 10 ft 10 in. tall.

REFERENCES

T. RICKMAN, 'Ecclesiastical architecture of France and England', *Arch.* **26** (1836), 26–46. Sompting de-scribed and illustrated, 42–4. String-course, 43.

T. WRIGHT, 'Anglo-Saxon architecture illustrated from illuminated manuscripts', *Arch. J.* **1** (1845), 24–35. Sompting, 26 and 34.

J. L. ANDRÉ, 'Sompting church', *Sussex Arch. C.* **41** (1898), 7–24. Plan, church and carvings described. Carving of abbot dated to twelfth century, 18.

F. A. CROUCH, 'Sompting church, Sussex', *Architectural Association Sketch Book* (1910), pls. 36–9. Plans, elevations, sections and detailed drawings.

A. W. CLAPHAM, 'Sompting church', *Arch. J.* **92** (1935), 405–9. Plan, description, and important reappraisal of the date of the carvings.

P. EDEN, 'Sompting: church of St Mary', *ibid.* **116** (1959), 245–6.

whose scrolls are placed at the top, enclosing cir-cular areas that are filled with representations of bunches of grapes.

Another interesting feature of the tower-arch is the way in which it is displaced southward from the centre of the wall in which it stands, possibly in order that an altar could be placed in the tower at the north of the arch.

Finally, mention should be made of the import-ant series of carved stones which were first critically studied by Clapham, with particular reference to their probable date and original use.[1] He sug-gested that they formed part of the pre-Conquest church, perhaps as an altar-front or reredos. He compared and contrasted them with the earlier work at Breedon-on-the-Hill and Fletton, and gave reasons for assigning them to the same early-eleventh-century date as the main fabric of the tower. He classified the carvings at Sompting into four main types: first, three portions of a wall-

SPRINGFIELD

Essex

Map sheet 162, reference TL 719080

Eastern part of nave: possibly Saxo-Norman

Springfield has now become almost a north-eastern suburb of Chelmsford, straddling the Roman road that runs to Colchester; but the older part of the former village, on the north of the railway, is still pleasantly rural, with the church beside an open green at the south of the extensive

---

[1] A. W. Clapham, 'Sompting church', *Arch. J.* **92** (1935), 405–9. The dating and description of the carvings, 408.

[2] D. T. Rice, *English Art, 871–1100* (Oxford, 1952), 107 and pl. 15 *b*.

grounds of Springfield Place. The church consists of a buttressed western tower, heavily patched in brick in the nineteenth century, a long aisleless nave with south porch, and a Decorated aisleless chancel with northern vestry and organ-chamber.

The somewhat inconclusive evidence of Saxo-Norman workmanship is represented by the use of tile for the quoins and the window-facings, by the use of carstone in the walls and for the voussoirs of the window-heads, and by the very irregular setting of these voussoirs in the way described by Baldwin Brown as 'Tredington fashion'.

The fabric is of flint, with appreciable admixture of tile and carstone in the eastern part of the walls of the nave. The western parts of these walls are practically free from tile or carstone, and it therefore seems reasonable to regard the nave as having been extended westward at a later date. In the earlier eastern part, the eastern quoins are almost wholly of tile; and three single-splayed, round-headed windows have survived: one nearly perfect above the north doorway; another almost opposite, above the south doorway, and a third further east in the north wall, these latter two only in fragmentary condition. The jambs of all three windows are partly of tile and partly of flat pieces of carstone, and their heads are of thin voussoirs of carstone laid without attention to radial setting of the voussoirs. The splays of the jambs are continued through the full thickness of the wall, without any rebate or other provision for glazing.

The indications of Saxo-Norman workmanship are far from conclusive; and, as the walls are 3 ft 4 in. thick, there is some reason for regarding this church as being on the Norman side of the boundary.

DIMENSIONS

The nave is 24 ft wide internally and was originally about 42 ft in length. Its side walls are 3 ft 4 in. thick and about 20 ft high.

The windows are 11 in. wide externally and 3 ft tall, with sills about 10 ft above the original ground-level, as indicated by the level of the sills of the doorways. Internally, the windows are splayed to become 3 ft 10 in. wide by 5 ft 6 in. tall, with their sills 9 ft 6 in. above the floor.

SPRINGTHORPE
Lincolnshire
Map sheet 104, reference SK 875897

ST LAWRENCE AND ST GEORGE
West tower: period C3

The small village of Springthorpe, about 4 miles east of Gainsborough, probably once possessed a late-Saxon church like those which have survived at the two neighbouring villages of Corringham and Heapham, but the drastic 'restorations' to which the church was subjected in 1845 and 1876 have left very little than can now be recognized as Anglo-Saxon workmanship.

The unbuttressed west tower is of small, flattish stone rubble, with side-alternate quoining of larger, well-dressed stones, set slightly forward from the wall-face to serve as a stop for plaster. The tower now rises sheer from a chamfered plinth to a simple modern parapet, but the whole of the belfry with its pseudo-Saxon double windows is modern, and the original fabric seems to end about the level of the ridge of the roof of the nave. Externally, the north and east faces of the original tower have no openings; while in the west face a blocked doorway has apparently been used as a museum, to house a number of salvaged fragments, which have been built into the wall round a small modern window. It is now impossible to be sure whether the doorway originally had a semicircular stone tympanum under its round-arched head, but neither the present tympanum nor the arch surrounding it appears to be original. By contrast, the square jambs and the projecting imposts seem to be original, and their positions correspond with the internal opening, which has a round head about 9 ft high and about 3 ft wide.

A small window high up in the south face is now much weathered, but appears originally to have had tall monolithic jambs, wide horizontal imposts, and a monolithic round head outlined by a semicircular hood-moulding.

The tower is roughly 10 ft 6 in. square internally with walls about 2 ft 9 in. thick.

STAFFORD

Map sheet 119, reference SJ 919234

ST BERTELIN

Foundations of St Bertelin's church and replica of cross, beside St Mary's church: period uncertain, probably period C for the stone church

In the summer of 1954, when the graveyard of St Mary's church at Stafford was laid out as a Garden of Remembrance, the opportunity was taken to investigate the area at the west of the church where it was known that an ancient chapel dedicated to St Bertelin had formerly stood. The excavations yielded the foundations of a simple, two-cell church of stone, with evidence of an earlier wooden building within it. In addition, part of a simple wooden cross was found, buried within the wooden enclosure.[1]

The discoveries suggest that the early burial-ground at first had no church, but only a wooden cross; and that the cross was later buried within the wooden church, which was in turn super-seded by the stone church. It is suggested in the report that the cross was certainly pre-Danish; that the wooden church might also have been pre-. Danish but was most likely of the time of the Anglo-Saxon reconquest of Stafford, early in the tenth century; and that the stone church can reliably be dated in the early part of the eleventh century.

DIMENSIONS

The stone church consisted of a nave 32 ft long internally and 16 ft wide, with a chancel of uncertain length, but about 10 ft wide. The walls were a little less than 3 ft in thickness and of large stones, many of which extended through their full thickness. The wooden enclosure was a little over 20 ft long internally and a little over 10 ft wide, lying wholly within the late nave.

The cross was about 8 ft in length, with shallow,

hooked arms, reminiscent of those of the stone cross which is traditionally associated with Lilla and which is now on the Yorkshire moors near Whitby.

STAINDROP

County Durham

Map sheet 85, reference NZ 131206

Figures 575–7

ST MARY (formerly ST GREGORY)

Eastern part of nave: period A2 or A3

Western part of nave, and lower part of tower: probably period C2

About 11 miles west-north-west of Darlington and on the main road from Barnard Castle to Bishop Auckland, Staindrop was in the past a market town of some importance, particularly in the days when the powerful Neville family had their principal seat nearby at Raby Castle. The history of the village begins with King Canute's pilgrimage to Durham in 1020, when he gave Staindrop and a number of other places to the church of St Cuthbert at Durham.[2] The earliest part of the present church appears, for reasons explained below, to date from before this grant, but the second phase of Anglo-Saxon building, including the lower part of the tower and the western part of the nave, may well date from the eleventh century and may be associated with an increase of importance at that time.

The church now consists of an aisleless chancel, with a two-storeyed priest's residence attached to the eastern part of its north wall; a nave, wholly flanked by aisles and transepts wider than itself; and a west tower, which opens on three sides to the nave and aisles, through broad thirteenth-century arches.

The true nature of the main walls of the nave was first noticed by the Rev. J. F. Hodgson, who was led to suspect their early character by com-

---

[1] A full account of the excavations is given in *The Church of St Bertelin at Stafford and its Cross*, ed. A. Oswald, published by the City of Birmingham Museum and Art Gallery.

[2] Symeon of Durham, *Hist. Dunelm. Ecclesiae*, ed.

T. Arnold (Rolls Series, 75, 1) (London, 1882), 90 and 213. The first of these references is to Symeon's twelfth-century history, but the second is to the earlier *Historia de S. Cuthberto*, a tenth-century document, continued down to the reign of Canute.

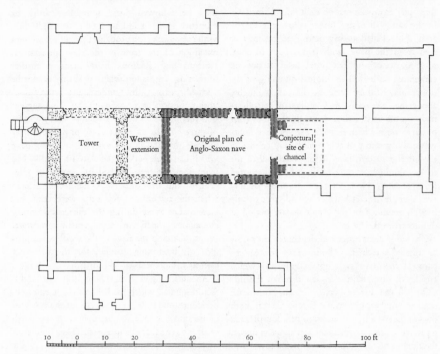

FIG. 275. STAINDROP, COUNTY DURHAM

Plan, showing the early aisleless church in relation to the greatly enlarged present fabric.

parison of the long narrow plan and high walls with those of the Anglo-Saxon church at Escomb.[1]

The chancel of the original Anglo-Saxon church has wholly disappeared; but the upper parts of the walls of its nave remain, over the chancel-arch and above the three eastern arches of the present nave. In each of the side walls parts of an original, round-headed, internally splayed window have survived. That on the south shows on the outer face of the wall the whole of its monolithic round head, and towards the nave it shows its wide inner splay, arched in six or seven well-dressed and carefully jointed voussoirs, a form of construction which is reminiscent of the windows high up in the west wall at Monkwearmouth. The windows show no sign of any groove for glass, nor any rebate for a shutter, so that it seems

unlikely that they were ever glazed. Another survival of the earliest church may be seen about 22 ft above the floor, on the outer faces of the walls towards the aisles, where a hollow-moulded string-course runs along the walls. On the evidence of the similarity of this string-course to that on the west of the nave at Monkwearmouth, as well as the similarity of the windows already mentioned, Romans and Radford have suggested a date in the eighth or early ninth century for this part of the nave at Staindrop, that is a date in period A2 or A3.[2]

Early in the eleventh century, perhaps at the time of Canute's gift to Durham, the church was extended westward about 15 ft, and a tower was built beyond; the old west wall was cut away, and a cross-section of it may still be seen above the

---

[1] J. F. Hodgson, 'Staindrop church', *T. Durham Northd. A.A.S.* **3** (1880–9), 75–110, particularly 81 n.

[2] T. Romans and C. A. R. Radford, 'Staindrop church', *Arch. J.* **III** (1954), 215.

third pier from the east on each side of the nave. In the east wall of the tower, above the tower-arch, a blocked doorway of this period may be seen from the nave, with jambs built of small squared stones and flat lintel head carried on chamfered corbels. The original quoining of the tower may also be seen on the eastern angles, above the aisle roofs; and vestiges of it still remain on the west, although much of the exterior of the tower has been refaced. Two blocked door-ways, also possibly of this period, may be seen in the interior eastern face of the west wall of the tower, although all trace of them has disappeared from outside. None of these features has any very definite character which would serve to date it with certainty in the Anglo-Saxon period as distinct from the Norman.

The subsequent history of the church may now be briefly sketched. About 1180, the eastern parts of the nave were given aisles, to which arcades of three bays were cut through the side walls of the earlier nave. In the thirteenth century, the arcades were completed on both sides of the nave by the addition of a fourth arch, separated from the others by a wide pier; and at the same time the ground floor of the tower was thrown open to the body of the church by cutting broad arches through its north, east, and south walls. In the thirteenth century, also, the Anglo-Saxon chancel disappeared, to make way for the present much larger chancel which was then considered necessary. At this period also a short additional stage was added to the Anglo-Saxon tower, separated from it by a slight off-set. Finally, in the fifteenth century, the walls of the nave were raised to provide a clear-storey, and the present tall belfry stage was added to the tower, curiously corbelled out so as to be wider than the stage below. It is a remarkable tribute to the soundness of the eleventh-century foundations and masonry of the west tower that, in spite of the cutting away of a great part of three of its walls in the thirteenth century, the tower has not only stood into the twentieth century, but has supported one additional stage which was added in the thirteenth century and yet a further and heavier one added about two hundred years later.

Most of the architectural history sketched above may be followed fairly straightforwardly by reference to the building as it now stands; but, with reference to the probable form of the western extension of the nave in the eleventh century, Romans and Radford have made a further interesting suggestion which probably cannot be verified, except by undertaking excavations within the area of the present aisles. They suggest that the limitation of the twelfth-century arcades of three bays to the eastern part of the nave may indicate that the more westerly part of the nave which had been built in the eleventh century had from the first been flanked by *porticus* or side-chapels, and that these were suffered to remain when the twelfth-century aisles were built, but were swept away during the thirteenth-century alterations. Such an arrangement of lateral *porticus* flanking the nave at the west would provide an interesting parallel for the surviving *porticus* at Laughton-en-le-Morthen.

An interesting survival at Staindrop is an Anglo-Saxon sundial, which has been used as a common building stone in the interior face of the east wall of the nave, beside its junction with the north wall, above the chancel-arch. The sundial is built in, upside down, partly obscured by the north wall, but with the hole for the gnomon still distinctly visible, as well as the incised tide-lines which run from the centre to a semicircular outer boundary.

DIMENSIONS

The original aisleless nave was about 35 ft long internally, and 19 ft broad, with walls about 2 ft 8 in. thick and about 24 ft high. After the eleventh-century additions, the nave became about 50 ft long; and now, by the inclusion of the space beneath the tower, the total length has become about 70 ft.

The early windows in the side walls have apertures 1 ft 3 in. wide, splayed internally to 4 ft 6 in. Their exterior heads are about 19 ft 6 in. above the floor; and about 2 ft 6 in. of the height of the exterior face has survived in the south window.

REFERENCES

J. F. HODGSON, 'Staindrop church', *T. Durham Northd. A.A.S.* 3 (1880–9), 75–110. First claiming of an Anglo-Saxon date for the eastern part of the nave.

H. C. LIPSCOMBE, 'Staindrop church', *J.B.A.A.* **43** (1887), 138–44. Note of discovery of the windows when plaster was removed from the walls in 1868.

C. C. HODGES, 'Pre-Conquest churches of Northumbria', *Reliquary*, n.s., **8** (1894), 65–83. Staindrop, 71–2.

T. ROMANS and C. A. R. RADFORD, 'Staindrop church', *Arch. J.* **111** (1954), 214–17. Plan, 215. Very good critical account, with pictures facing p. 203.

STANLEY ST LEONARD
(OR LEONARD STANLEY)

Gloucestershire

Map sheet 156, reference SO 802032

Figure 578

Chapel, formerly parish church of
ST LEONARD

Remains of chapel, now used as barn:
period C

In the village of Leonard Stanley, on the south bank of the River Frome, about 3 miles west of Stroud, the present parish church is a fine Norman cruciform building which was formerly the church of St Leonard's Priory; but only a few yards away to the south-west, in the priory grounds, and for long past used as a barn, there still stands the greater part of an earlier church, which apparently served the needs of the parish until, in the fifteenth century, an arrangement was made for the parish to use part of the nave of the abbey church. The early church was apparently diverted to secular use from that date, or from soon thereafter.

The complete form of the ground-plan of the pre-Conquest church, with an eastern apse, was established by excavations in 1914, but all that is now to be seen is a rectangular farm building with some Gothic windows and one fragment of an earlier door, to which further reference is made below. The fabric was claimed as of pre-Conquest date when the apse was first excavated, but the claim was not accepted by Baldwin Brown, who said (p. 465) that an examination had shown much herring-bone work in the walls and had led him to the conclusion that nothing earlier than Norman work was visible. We believe that herring-

bone work provides no sure discrimination between Anglo-Saxon and Norman workmanship; and, in spite of the fact that the apse is no longer visible and the main building is much obscured by other farm buildings, we believe that the pre-Conquest date of the main fabric may be regarded as established by the fact that the western half of the hood-moulding of a blocked doorway has survived in the north wall. This hood-moulding is of characteristic Anglo-Saxon, plain, square section; and its dating is yet further sup-

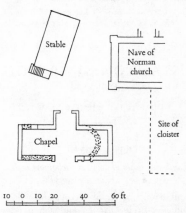

FIG. 276. STANLEY ST LEONARD, GLOUCESTERSHIRE
Plan of the pre-Conquest chapel showing its position at the south-west of the Norman priory. The apsidal foundations were excavated in 1914 but are not now visible. It is difficult to assign a date to these remains, but they have been shown in the plan as of intermediate date in period C.

ported by the way in which the remaining fragment is not built up from a number of stones, but is shaped from a single stone which outlines almost a quadrant of the head of the door, see Fig. 578.

DIMENSIONS

The walls of the existing structure are 2 ft 8 in. thick, and of roughly coursed stone rubble. The excavations showed that the walls of the apse were of the same thickness, but of herring-bone construction. The internal width of the existing structure is 17 ft, and the overall internal length of the nave and apsidal chancel was found to be 49 ft 3 in.

REFERENCES

J. H. MIDDLETON, 'Stanley St Leonard', *T. Bristol Glos. Arch. S.* **5** (1880–1), 119–32. Mainly about the Norman church, but a note on the chapel, with plan, 131–2.

Editorial, 'Proceedings, 8 June 1909', *ibid.* **32** (1909), 1–21. Suggestion that the chapel in the farmyard may be part of the 'earlier Saxon church', 16.

C. SWINNERTON, 'The priory of St Leonard of Stanley', *Arch.* **71** (1920–1), 199–226. Exhaustive account of history, dedication, and architectural history; full account of excavations, with plan. Picture of hoodmoulding, fig. 3; and of excavated apse, fig. 4.

C. SWINNERTON, 'Stanley St Leonard', *T. Bristol Glos. Arch. S.* **44** (1922), 221–69. Historical and documentary evidence.

STANTON-BY-BRIDGE

Derbyshire

Map sheet 121, reference SK 367271

Figure 579

ST MICHAEL

North-east quoin of nave, and adjoining walls of nave and chancel: period C

About 6 miles south of Derby, the village of Stanton-by-Bridge has a commanding position overlooking the wide valley of the Trent from a hill on the south bank. The church consists of an aisleless chancel, and a nave with north aisle and western bell-cote, all built of roughly squared blocks of gritstone except for an area of roughly laid rubble in the centre of the west wall of the nave. The south-east quoin of the nave is of well defined long-and-short construction, with parts of the faces of both long and short stones cut back about ½ in. so as to leave a clearly defined pair of pilaster-strips about 6 in. wide, clasping the angle. The adjoining south wall of the chancel has a group of very large stones set in a somewhat random arrangement of upright and flat stones, as if either to form internal quoining at the re-entrant angle, or else to have been the independent quoining of a chancel which stood on the site before the building of the nave, see Fig. 579.

Baldwin Brown recorded (p. 479) that the quoins were difficult to see because of an overgrowth of ivy but that there appeared to be

definite indications of the use of long-and-short technique in the eastern quoins of the chancel. In 1957 the ivy had long since been cleared away; but, except at the south-east angle of the nave, the church showed no instance of long-and-short quoining, all the other angles being faced with side-alternate quoins of the sort which gives little definite indication of date. The eastern quoins of the chancel are certainly not Anglo-Saxon; and we were inclined to think that they represented the result of a drastic rebuilding in the nineteenth century. The south-west quoin of the nave and an area of walling beside it also represent rebuilding.

Baldwin Brown also recorded that the chancel-arch had been covered with mortar, on which lines of jointing had been drawn so as to indicate that the voussoirs were not through-stones, whereas in his opinion the arch was probably Anglo-Saxon and the voussoirs genuine through-stones. The plaster or mortar covering of the arch is unfortunately still in position, and without its removal we think it is impossible satisfactorily to settle this question of the nature of the voussoirs. We think, however, that it is possible to see at least one true joint that defines a voussoir as being of two stones. Moreover the wide proportions of the arch indicate that it is unlikely to be Anglo-Saxon; while the ashlar jambs and the elaborately moulded imposts look like the work of nineteenth-century restorers.

The single-splayed, round-headed window placed high in the rougher section of walling at the west of the nave is of the type that is almost impossible to date with certainty. Its head is cut in the lower face of a rectangular stone, and its jambs are each built of five rather small stones. Its splayed jambs continue through the full thickness of the wall, with no rebate for the glazing.

In our opinion the only undoubtedly Anglo-Saxon features in this interesting church are the south-east quoin of the nave and the immediately adjoining areas of walling, including the curious 'internal quoin' at the west of the chancel. It is of interest to note that the south-east quoin of the nave stands on a well-defined square plinth; and that, whereas its uppermost five stones are laid in regular long-and-short fashion, the four stones beneath are laid on their faces. As at Skillington, in Lincolnshire, these lower stones are neverthe-

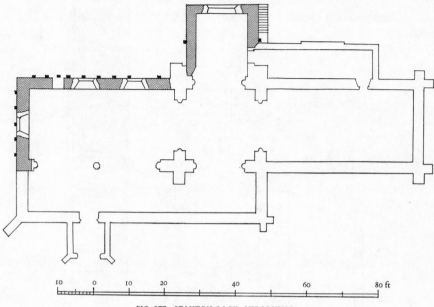

FIG. 277. STANTON LACY, SHROPSHIRE
Plan, showing the surviving sixteen pilaster-strips.

less part of the original design since they are cut to show the same raised pilaster-strip beside the angle.

DIMENSIONS

The chancel is 22 ft 11 in. long internally, and 17 ft 7 in. wide, with side walls 2 ft 5 in. thick and about 10 ft high. The nave is 29 ft 4 in. long internally and 20 ft 5 in. wide, with walls about 2 ft 10 in. thick.

The chancel-arch is 12 ft 5 in. wide and 13 ft 1 in. tall, as measured from the floor of the nave. The wall in which it stands is 3 ft thick.

The aperture of the small west window is 10 in. wide and 3 ft tall, splayed internally to 3 ft 4 in. by 5 ft. The internal sill is 10 ft 6 in. above the floor.

STANTON LACY

Shropshire

Map sheet 129, reference SO 495788

Figure 580

ST PETER

North and west walls of nave; and walls of north transept: period C

The existing plan of the cruciform church of St Peter at Stanton Lacy, about 3 miles north-north-west of Ludlow, indicates that it is only by good fortune that the interesting and extensive Anglo-Saxon remains have been preserved to the present day. It seems clear that in the thirteenth and fourteenth centuries there was an intention to replace the whole of the early church by another, on much the same ground-plan, but in the contemporary style. For some reason, perhaps shortage of funds, this operation was halted after the completion of the new chancel, the central tower, and the south side of the nave with its arcade and south aisle. The remains of the original Anglo-Saxon church are therefore now in two separate parts, of which the first consists of the north and west walls of the nave, while the second is the north transept, except for short pieces cut away by the medieval tower.

The tall Anglo-Saxon walls are built of undressed

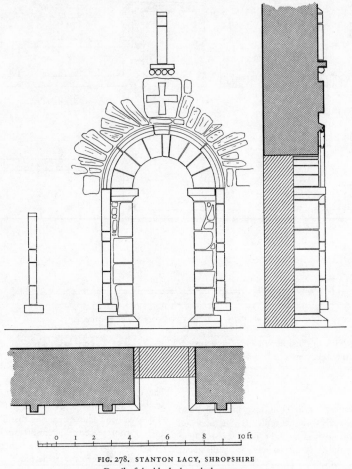

FIG. 278. STANTON LACY, SHROPSHIRE
Detail of the blocked north doorway.

stones of varying but fairly large size, irregularly shaped but well fitted together.

The quoins are of roughly dressed large stones laid in regular side-alternate fashion. But the Anglo-Saxon character of the walling is proved beyond doubt by the presence of five pilaster-strips on the west wall of the nave, nine on the north, and one on each of the side walls of the transept. The walls have no plinth; but the pilasters start from boldly projecting square corbels near the ground, and they run up the wall in a series of long-and-short sections. On the transepts,

each pilaster is crossed, about 6 ft below the eaves, by a small horizontal strip about 1 ft 6 in. long. On the north wall of the nave, the pilasters end somewhat inconsequently at irregular heights, rather suggesting that the upper part of the wall has been rebuilt. On the west wall, the pilasters end at a fairly regular height, and thus give some indication that there may have been cross-pieces, similar to those on the transepts, to serve as stops at this level. There appears, however, to be no evidence of the existence (or of the former existence and removal) of a continuous horizontal string-course such as is suggested by Baldwin Brown's statement (p. 360) that 'a horizontal string-course square in section intersects them on the nave and transept walls, and on the west wall, where there are five strips, cuts them off'.

In the north wall, a blocked doorway of some importance has square jambs, a round head of a single square order, and hollow-chamfered imposts. It is flanked by pilaster-strips and its head is outlined by a hood-moulding. Whereas the pilaster-strips are of the same square section as those elsewhere on the walls, and start from similar square corbels, the hood-moulding is more elaborate, for it is chamfered on its extrados and is enriched with a roll-moulding on its lower arris, Fig. 278.

The arched head of the doorway is formed of well-dressed and excellently laid voussoirs, with radial joints; but outside the hood-mould, the adjoining walling has been laid in the form of a rough relieving arch of irregular stones in non-radial setting. The jambs are of well-dressed stones resting on chamfered plinths, and the outer faces of the chamfered imposts are neatly stopped against the pilaster-strips. Careful measurement inside and out has established that the doorway is formed of through-stones and is not rebated for the hanging of a door.

Above the crown of the hood-mould of this doorway a large flat stone set in the wall is carved with a simple cross in relief; and above this again one of the nine pilaster-strips already mentioned springs from an ornamental corbel consisting of a short horizontal cross-piece above a row of pellets.

In the north wall of the transept there are the remains of another blocked doorway which has lost its dressed-stone facings. A little to the east of this, high up in the wall, is a round-headed, internally splayed window of uncertain date.

DIMENSIONS

The nave is 41 ft long internally, and 19 ft 4 in. wide, with walls 3 ft thick and about 28 ft high. The north transept is 14 ft 5 in. from east to west internally and 17 ft 7 in. from north to south, with walls 2 ft 8 in. thick and about the same height as those of the nave.

The pilaster-strips are all about 5 in. wide and about 3 in. in projection from the face of the wall. They are all of long-and-short construction

with longs averaging about 2 ft and the shorts about 8 in.

The blocked north doorway of the nave is cut straight through the wall, without any rebate, and is 9 ft tall and 3 ft 3 in. wide. The jambs and head appear to be built wholly of through-stones since the pattern of the joints is identical both inside and outside.

REFERENCES

J. L. P., 'Stanton Lacy church', Arch. J. 3 (1846), 297–8.

G. M. HILLS, 'Stanton Lacy church, Shropshire, and Saxon architecture in England', J.B.A.A. 24 (1868), 360–82. A valuable collation of the literary and architectural evidence for a number of early church sites; with map. Stanton Lacy, 380–2; with plan and brief description.

D. H. S. CRANAGE, Churches of Shropshire, 1 (Wellington, 1901), 155–60. Good description and plan.

STEVINGTON
Bedfordshire

Map sheet 147, reference SP 991536

ST MARY THE VIRGIN
Lower part of west tower: period C

The pleasant, small, stone-built village of Stevington has an unusually peaceful position, in a wide bend of the River Ouse, about 4 miles west-north-west of Bedford. The church, at the north of the village, is reached only by a narrow lane; and from the church gates a grassy path leads down to the holy well which once brought pilgrims to the site in sufficient number to support a Hospital for their lodging.

The church consists of a west tower, a nave with aisles continued westward to flank the tower, and an aisleless chancel flanked by the ruins of former north and south chapels. Only the lower part of the tower is Anglo-Saxon, and from outside the church only the west face can be seen, the fabric of large undressed stones contrasting with the smaller and more carefully shaped stones of the later work on either side. The long-and-short quoins at both western angles of the tower are built of particularly large stones of which several of the uprights exceed 3 ft in height.

Within the church, the walls of the tower are plastered except where three early openings have been exposed to view. In the south wall, a very tall narrow doorway opens from the tower to the aisle; and high above it is a double-splayed, round-headed window with its jambs and head very roughly constructed of flattish rubble. In the opposite north wall a similar window may be seen, similarly placed, but in a less good state of preservation. The south window still retains in

somewhat decayed, but apparently undressed, and the round head, of a single square order, is formed of rough flattish pieces of stone. These, being of a soft nature, have broken away in places and now present a very irregular surface. The splayed jambs and arched heads of the windows are also in a decayed and irregular state.

DIMENSIONS

The tower is about 12½ ft square internally (12 ft 4 in. east–west by 12 ft 7 in. north–south),

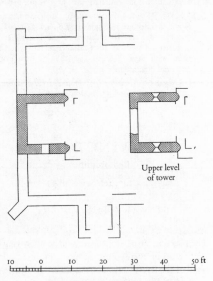

Upper level
of tower

FIG. 279. STEVINGTON, BEDFORDSHIRE
Plan of the west part of the church showing the Anglo-Saxon tower and its south doorway. The inset plan shows the upper level of the tower with its two double-splayed windows.

FIG. 280. STEVINGTON, BEDFORDSHIRE
Elevation and section showing the doorway and double-splayed window in the south wall of the tower.

the middle of the wall the wooden slab through which the tall, narrow, round-headed aperture was cut, in an archaic form narrowing towards the top.

The workmanship of the door and of the windows is of the rudest kind. The square jambs of the door each begin at the foot with a pair of large through-stones laid upright and flat in 'Escomb fashion'; but thereafter the walling is of a random nature, with rubble, large stones, and even an oak beam, all laid in unsystematic fashion. The imposts are flattish pieces of stone now

with walls 2 ft 7 in. thick and 20 ft or more in original height. The south doorway is 2 ft 6 in. wide and 9 ft 4 in. tall; and the window above it has an aperture 2 ft 7 in. tall and narrowing from 10 in. in width at the sill to 7 in. at the shoulders. The window is splayed to become about 3 ft wide and about 4 ft tall, with its sill 14 ft 3 in. above the floor.

REFERENCE

V.C.H., Bedfordshire, 3 (London, 1912), 102–3. Brief architectural description, with plan.

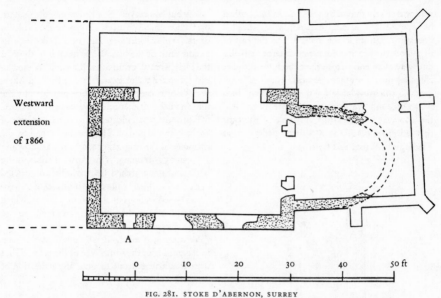

Westward

extension

of 1866

A

| 0 | 10 | 20 | 30 | 40 | 50 ft |

FIG. 281. STOKE D'ABERNON, SURREY

Plan of the church before the extensions of 1866, showing also the original apsidal chancel of which vestiges were discovered by P. M. Johnston after 1909. The doorway at A probably led to a western gallery since its sill is 12 ft above the floor of the nave. In this plan it is wrongly shown rebated for a door, following Johnston's plan of 1909. It is in fact cut straight through the wall.

STOKE D'ABERNON

Surrey

Map sheet 170, reference TQ 129584

ST MARY

South wall of nave, with high side doorway. South wall of chancel, with vestiges of a window. Fragment of north wall of chancel, showing curve of original apsidal east end. Sundial fell from south wall in 1933. Period C3, with earlier remains possibly of period A

Much detail of archaeological interest in this church was destroyed in drastic 'restoration' in 1866; but the surviving features were later ably interpreted and brought to view by P. M. Johnston, who also called attention to important drawings made by William Twopenny before the original chancel-arch and long-and-short quoins were removed.[1]

The main body of the church now consists of a nave and chancel which are flanked on the north by aisles and chapels; a small bell-tower occupies the north-west angle; and the nave has a modern porch over its south doorway. Until the alterations of 1866 the church extended less far to the west and had preserved much of its original fabric. In particular the two western quoins of the nave were of long-and-short construction, as was the upper part of the south-eastern quoin. The original chancel-arch described by Rickman and illustrated by Twopenny had, however, been destroyed in an earlier rebuilding about 1850.[2] The fabric, as now visible, is mainly of uncut flint, with a certain amount of chalk and stone; but in places, particularly in the lower part of the chancel, at the west, there is a considerable quantity of re-used Roman tile, some of which is laid in herring-bone fashion.

The long-and-short quoins have been swept away; but the Anglo-Saxon character of the south

[1] P. M. Johnston, *Surrey Arch. C.* **20** (1907), 1–89; **21** (1908), 127–9; and **26** (1913), 121–33. The latter article contains reproductions of the Twopenny drawings of 1828.

[2] P. M. Johnston, *loc. cit.* **26** (1913), 130, and pl. III.

573

wall was clearly shown by Johnston in 1905, when he opened out a tall, narrow, square-headed doorway, high up in the wall, just to the east of the modern porch. Johnston interpreted this doorway as an entry from the church to an upper chamber over a southern *porticus*. There is, however, no other evidence for the existence of such a *porticus*, and we think it is more likely that the doorway is yet another example of the type that led from outside to a western gallery, as at Tredington, Wing, and Jarrow.

FIG. 282. STOKE D'ABERNON, SURREY

The chancel-arch as it was shown in a drawing by William Twopenny in 1828. Note the consistent use of through-stones in the jambs and in the arch.

A few feet to the east of this doorway a modern circular stone in the outer face of the wall marks the former position of the Anglo-Saxon sundial which fell and was broken in 1933.[1]

Little else of the original fabric is now visible, but Johnston reported in 1913 that in the course of repairs from 1909 onward he had had the opportunity of inspecting the north wall of the chancel, above the fine thirteenth-century vaulting. He made the remarkable discovery that the builders of the rectangular Early English chancel had not destroyed the Anglo-Saxon walling of the earlier chancel where it was concealed from view by their vault, and that the surviving section of earlier wall above the vault was not straight like the wall

below but was curved, clearly defining the western part of an apsidal chancel.[2] It was on the evidence of this apsidal chancel, and of the consequent resemblance of the plan of the church to those of the early Kentish group, that Johnston claimed an early date for the original fabric at Stoke d'Abernon. Confirmatory evidence was provided by the thin and tall character of the walling; by the fabric of flint and Roman tile, set in a very hard mortar of chalk-lime and pounded Roman brick; and by the character of the original chancel-arch as shown in Twopenny's drawing. This shows a tall opening with jambs and arched head wholly constructed of through-stones, while the imposts seem to have been re-used sections of classical mouldings, which projected only on the soffit and were not moulded on the eastern and western faces.

Vestiges of a blocked window may be seen in the outside of the south wall of the chancel, but with insufficient detail to give any indication of date.

DIMENSIONS

The original nave seems to have been about 35 ft long internally and 21 ft broad. It has walls 2 ft 5 in. thick and about 21 ft tall. The apsidal chancel seems to have been of ovoid shape, about 15 to 17 ft in length. It was 15 ft 6 in. broad, internally, with walls only 1 ft 10 in. thick and about the same height as those of the nave.

The surviving high side doorway is cut straight through the wall, 2 ft 2 in. wide and 6 ft 2 in. tall, with its sill 12 ft above the floor. Its jambs rest on plain square bases, which project on the soffit only. Its perfectly plain square head was formed externally by a flat stone lintel and internally by an oak beam which had decayed, and was replaced by Johnston in 1905.

REFERENCES

T. RICKMAN, 'Ecclesiastical architecture of France and England', *Arch.* **26** (1836), 26–46. Stoke church described, with references to its original chancel-arch and quoins, 40.

P. M. JOHNSTON, 'Stoke d'Abernon church', *Surrey Arch. C.* **20** (1907), 1–89. Very detailed account, with

---

[1] A picture of the dial as it existed in 1905 is given by Johnston, *loc. cit.* **20** (1907), 17.

[2] A section of the curved walling may be seen in the

upper part of the north wall of the chancel, from a position within the north chapel.

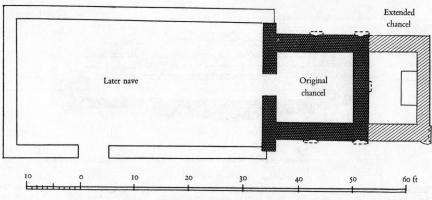

10   0   10   20   30   40   50   60 ft

FIG. 283. STONE-BY-FAVERSHAM, KENT

Plan of the ruined church. The wall at the north-east corner of the later chancel was standing to a height of about 10 ft in 1956. The east wall stood just above the level of the top of the rubble masonry of the altar. The early walling on the north and south of the original chancel varied from 2 to 3 ft in height. The dotted projections and the rough areas behind them on the side walls are based on Irvine's observations that shallow pilasters had been cut away.

plan and many drawings. 'Supplementary notes on Stoke d'Abernon church', *ibid.* **21** (1908), 127–9. 'Stoke d'Abernon: some recent discoveries', *ibid.* **26** (1919), 121–33. Very important record of the character of the chancel; Twopenny's drawings showing the exterior from the south-east and north-west, and the interior, looking through the chancel-arch to the north-west of the nave.

STONE-BY-FAVERSHAM
Kent
Map sheet 172, reference TQ 991613

NO KNOWN DEDICATION
Ruined walls of chancel: probably period A1

A little more than a mile to the west of Faversham, a small copse in the fields between the Roman road and the railway serves to mark the neglected churchyard and ruined chapel which as long ago as 1782 was noted by Hasted as containing remains of unusual interest.[1] The ruins were excavated in 1874 by the Kent Archaeological Society; and

they were then visited by Irvine, who described how the early part of the building, of alternate courses of Roman tile and roughly dressed stone, formed a chancel 14 ft 3 in. long and 13 ft wide internally, which had later been extended eastward in flint walling, probably in the thirteenth century, to about twice its original length.[2] At the west, Irvine found that the junction between the walls of the early chancel and those of the later flint-built nave formed a straight vertical joint, against which the masonry of the early chancel was neatly finished on the west. From this fact he deduced that the early chancel had not been bonded into a contemporary nave of stone, but had been built with a straight joint against an even earlier nave, probably of wood.

The excavations showed that, when the chancel was extended eastward, its early floor had been covered to a depth of 1 ft 6 in., and a new plaster floor had been formed on top. At the same time, the old east wall had been cut down so as to serve as the first of three steps before the new altar. On top of the early side walls, new walling had

[1] E. Hasted, *History of Kent*, **2** (London, 1782), 800, '...in the midst of the south wall of it there is a separate piece of a Roman building, about a rod in length, and near three feet high, composed of two rows of Roman tiles of about fourteen inches square. On them were laid

small stones hewn, but of no regular size or shape, for about a foot high, and then tiles again, and so on alternately'.

[2] J. T. Irvine, *J.B.A.A.* **31** (1875), 249–58.

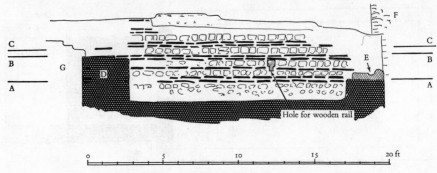

FIG. 284. STONE-BY-FAVERSHAM, KENT

Section through the church, looking south, during the excavations in 1874, based on one of Irvine's drawings. The figure shows the interior elevation of the south wall of the pre-Conquest chancel, and sections through its east and west walls. A, this is the level of the original floor, of red plaster; B, this is the level of the later (post-Conquest) floor, also of red plaster; C, present ground level; D, the old east wall, cut down to form a step into the post-Conquest chancel; E, stone step from the nave down into the pre-Conquest chancel, with a socket for the hinge of a gate or door; F, post-Conquest nave; G, post-Conquest eastern extension of chancel.

been erected, of plain flint construction, with recesses on both sides, in the form of sedilia which had used the tops of the low early side walls as their seats. Irvine did not mention whether this arrangement is to be assumed as implying that at the time of the twelfth-century extension the early chapel had become a ruin, or whether its original masonry walling had perhaps never been more than a few feet in height, possibly surmounted by wooden walls like those of the nave to which he thought it had been joined.

In 1957 the walls of the ruined church still showed most of the features described by Irvine in 1875. The flint walls of the later chancel still stood high in the north-east corner, with some plaster still on their inner faces, and the solid block of masonry for the altar close to the east end. Further west, the recesses in the flint walling were well defined; while below them the early walling could be seen, with its alternate courses of tiles and squared stone in Roman fashion. Finally, the outward-turned shoulders at the west of the chancel clearly showed a short length of the straight vertical joint beside the later flint walling of the nave.

For a complete account of the interesting features discovered during the excavations of 1874, reference should be made to Irvine's excellent and well-illustrated article, but for convenience the principal features are summarized below:

(a) There had apparently been shallow buttresses, or pilasters, at the centre of each face and at the corners. These had been hacked away; but their original width of about 30 in. could be determined from the surviving fragments of bonding tiles. Irvine thought that these pilasters had probably been removed when the eastern extension was built, but he expressed the confident expectation that excavation beside the original east end would show the remains of a complete pilaster.

(b) Both the early floor, and the later one 18 in. above, were of plaster only, without any tiles, but with red colouring.

(c) The early chancel had been entered by steps, which led down from the nave and were hewn in a solid block of stone.

(d) The opening from the nave to the chancel had been 4 ft 4 in. wide from jamb to jamb.

(e) Before the altar in the early chancel there was a raised step, which ran south from the north wall and then turned east, leaving an area at the ordinary floor level beside the south of the altar 'no doubt for a wooden stool for a priest'.

(f) Rough end walls in masonry showed that the altar itself was 3 ft 11 in. wide from north to south, and that it was slightly displaced to the north of the centre of the chancel.

(g) In each of the side walls of the early chancel and below the level of the later floor Irvine saw a cavity which he interpreted as the end support of an oak rail which had run across the chancel. Irvine argued that this built-in rail was necessarily contemporary with the original building because the arrangement of stones in the walling had been made to fit the cavity, one course of tiles had been deflected for it, and the whole assembly had of course been covered up from the time of raising the floor for the eastern extension. He expressed himself as more surprised by this discovery than by any of the others, but he felt convinced that the cavities must have been for an altar-rail, at a height of about 1 ft 3 in. above the early floor, probably kept so low in order that the priest could step across it without needing a central gate.

Having described carefully in words and pictures the remains as he saw them in 1875, Irvine left open the precise date of the early building. Having mentioned that the site passed into the hands of the Archbishop in 1072, he summed up his views about its date as follows:

Mr Parker[1] thinks that the church may be Roman. Sir Gilbert Scott thinks it might probably be Saxon. To this date, perhaps 900 A.D. at earliest, I think it has fair claims, though I should not be at all astonished if it were Norman of A.D.1072.

Baldwin Brown (p. 116) accepts the work as Anglo-Saxon of period A1, apparently by comparing its excellently laid walling of rather Roman character with the somewhat similar work in Roman tiles at the ruined church of St Pancras at Canterbury. Since, in common with most of the early Kentish churches, St Pancras had as one of its special features buttresses or pilasters of low projection it is odd that Baldwin Brown should have failed to see the implications of Irvine's observations, to which he referred in the following curious way:

There is no difficulty on the evidence now available in accepting the work as of early date but it should be said that Mr Irvine proposed at one time to make it Norman. As a proof of this he alleged that there were marks on the north and south exterior walls of the chancel where shallow Norman buttresses had been hacked off. Such a proceeding seems rather improbable and the point cannot now be settled because...ivy renders close inspection impossible. Mr Irvine was always inclined rather to favour Norman dates in cases of chronological difficulty.

It will be clear from the description given above that the ruin presents no single feature which makes an Anglo-Saxon dating straightforward; but the date assigned by Baldwin Brown seems the most reasonable, namely in period A1 when other early Kentish churches were being built with walls of somewhat Roman form and with pilasters of low projection.

DIMENSIONS

The original chancel is 14 ft 3 in. long and 13 ft wide internally, with walls about 3 ft in thickness.

As seen and recorded by Irvine, these walls stood about 4 ft high above the original plaster floor-level, and his drawings show them extending 2 ft beneath the floor.

REFERENCES

Editorial, 'Stone church', *Arch. Cant.* **9** (1874), lxxviii. Brief note of excavations in progress.

J. T. IRVINE, 'On the remains of Saxon or early Norman work in the church of Stone juxta Faversham', *J.B.A.A.* **31** (1875), 249–58.

STONEGRAVE

Yorkshire, North Riding

Map sheet 92, reference SE 655778

HOLY TRINITY

Nave (west wall, and side walls over Norman arcades): possibly Saxo-Norman

West tower: early Norman or Saxo-Norman

About 9 miles west-north-west of Malton, the small village of Stonegrave possesses a fine collection of late-Saxon carved stones, including a wheel-head cross. The church itself has been so heavily restored in the nineteenth century that, with the exception of the tower, there is little visible externally that is not modern. In plan, the church consists of a west tower, an aisled nave with south porch, and an aisleless chancel.

The square, unbuttressed tower of three stages is difficult to date with certainty save to say that it is Norman or earlier. Its walls rest on a chamfered plinth, and are of rough rubble construction, with side-alternate quoin-stones of moderate size. The only surviving original openings are a blocked west doorway whose head has been destroyed by the Decorated west window, and a small, round-headed, internally splayed window in the second stage of the south face. This window is of early Norman or late-Saxon character, with the splay continued through the full thickness of the wall, and with no groove or rebate for the fixing of glass; its jambs are each of two stones which bond deeply sideways into the wall; and its head is cut in the lower face of a single stone.

---

[1] Later Sir J. H. Parker.

The tower has clearly been built against and over the west wall of an earlier nave; for it is at once evident that the side walls of the tower are butted against, but are not in bond with, the west wall of the nave. This is even clearer inside, where a clearly defined straight vertical joint may be seen between the side walls of the tower and the west wall of the nave.

The west doorway of the nave, now opening only to the tower, is a plain round-headed opening 3 ft 3 in. wide by 9 ft 3 in. tall, on the face towards the nave; but it has a separately formed western arch 2 ft 10 in. wide and 10 ft 2 in. high. The doorway is plastered; and its history is, therefore, difficult to disentangle. The narrower western part would naturally be interpreted as the stop for the hanging of a door, but in that case its head ought to be a few inches lower than that of the eastern arch, instead of about a foot higher. It seems at least possible that the original opening was cut straight through the wall, with the door hung on the inner face of the wall, and that the present complicated arrangement arises from later modification, possibly associated with a thickening of this wall. Further support is given to this theory by the fact that the west wall of the nave is 3 ft 8 in. thick; whereas the side walls of the nave are only 2 ft 11 in., and the side walls of the tower 3 ft 2 in.

A Norman arcade of three bays was cut through the north wall of the nave at some date in the twelfth century, and two further Norman arches were subsequently cut at separate times through the south wall. It seems reasonable to assume that the earlier of these two at the east, was made as an entry to a chantry and that the second, which is separated from it by a solid section of the original wall was made at a time when it was decided to extend the chantry westward so as to form an aisle.

No original windows are visible, and we could see no other evidence to help in the dating of the nave; but, as it is clearly earlier than the west tower, there seems good ground for giving it a place in the pre-Conquest category. The existence of a monastery here by about the middle of the eighth century is proved by a letter from Pope Paul I to Eadberht, king of Northumbria, and his brother Egbert, Archbishop of York, reproaching them for taking away the lands of certain monasteries, including Stonegrave.[1]

The nave is about 37 ft long internally and 16¾ ft wide. The chancel is 23 ft by 16¼ ft and the tower 11¾ ft by 11 ft.

REFERENCES

C. C. HODGES, 'Pre-Conquest Churches of Northumbria', *Reliquary*, n.s., **8** (1894), 199–200.
V.C.H., *Yorkshire, North Riding*, **1** (London, 1914), 563–6.

STOPHAM
Sussex

Map sheet 181, reference TQ 026189

Figure 581

ST MARY THE VIRGIN
Nave: period C3

The pleasantly situated and attractive little church of St Mary the Virgin, standing in wooded parkland, about a quarter of a mile north of the Petworth-Shoreham road, has a squat square west tower, a square-ended chancel, and a nave whose south porch is balanced by a small north vestry. The nave walls of coursed brown stone rubble have massive side-alternate quoins.

The most interesting feature of the church is the south doorway, which is of such generous size that the rather mean pointed doorway which now serves as an entry to the church has been inserted in the original opening without cutting any of it away. The original doorway was a simple round-headed opening, with jambs cut straight through the wall but enriched on their outer face by the provision of sturdy detached angle-shafts in simple rectangular rebates. These angle-shafts have curious bulbous bases shaped rather like loaves of farmhouse bread. Their capitals are, however, even more remarkable, each surrounded by three annuli of sharply-pointed section, so that the capital perhaps most nearly resembles a three-ridged section of a Chinese lantern or concertina. These remarkable capitals support imposts of quite

---

[1] D. Whitelock, *E.H.D.* (1955), 764. The letter is assigned to the period 757–8.

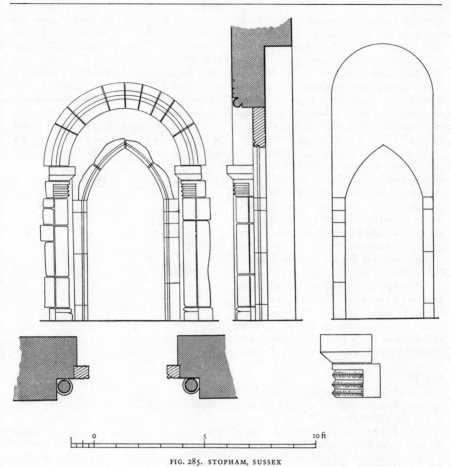

FIG. 285. STOPHAM, SUSSEX

The south doorway of the nave. The figure shows how a pointed doorway has been built within the original opening at a much later date. It also shows the very tall round-headed rear-arch. The inset shows at a larger scale the remarkable construction of the capitals of the original doorway, in the form of three rings of a circular concertina.

ordinary chamfered shape; and the circular head of the doorway is fundamentally of square section, but is moulded on the arris and archivolt to show a three-quarter-round angle-roll, with two shallow concentric grooves above it on the archivolt. The arch is of nine voussoirs, with reasonably radial joints. These voussoirs are not through-stones, and the rear-arch is about 2 ft taller than the outer face.

Baldwin Brown (pp. 398 and 480) inclined to a post-Conquest dating of this doorway, apparently largely on the ground that the angle-shafts were logically placed to support the main arch of the head. We are inclined to give more weight to the peculiar treatment of the bases and capitals, and accordingly to accept the doorway as being of pre-Conquest character. Taking into account both the character of the doorway and also the megalithic quoins and the tall, thin walls, we accept the nave as a work of period C3, probably dating from shortly before the Conquest.

The corresponding north doorway, which now

579

opens into the north vestry, is of a more Norman type with well-formed cushion capitals on its circular angle-shafts. Unlike those of the south doorway, these are attached shafts, formed of the same stones as the jambs themselves. Norman influence would probably be more strongly felt in Sussex than in most other parts of England outside London, and even this doorway does not seem unreasonable as a work of the concluding years of the reign of Edward the Confessor.

The chancel-arch is round-headed, and fundamentally of a single square order; but, like the south doorway, it is enriched on one face (towards the west) to show an arris-roll with a concentric outer groove. The voussoirs are not through-stones but are so cut as to meet along the soffit of the arch and to line it completely with dressed stone. The imposts are chamfered, and the jambs are of plain square section. On the whole, the arch appears likely to be of the same date as the south doorway.

The chancel is of quite different fabric from the nave, and is probably of thirteenth-century date, rectangular in plan externally, but internally consisting of two rectangular cells of which the narrower eastern cell with thicker side walls is covered by a semicircular barrel vault of stone.

DIMENSIONS

The nave is about 33 ft long internally and 18 ft 2 in. wide, with side walls 2 ft 9 in. thick and about 20 ft high. The original south doorway is 4 ft 6 in. wide and 9 ft 3 in. tall, with a rear-arch of the same width but 2 ft taller. The chancel-arch is 10 ft wide and 15 ft tall, in a wall only 2 ft 5 in. thick.

STOTTESDON

Shropshire

Map sheet 129, reference SO 673828

ST MARY

*West wall of nave and west doorway:
possibly Saxo-Norman*

Stottesdon is a somewhat remote village, about 11 miles north-east of Ludlow, but its church has a number of interesting features, including a font of the Herefordshire Norman school.

The west wall of the nave can with some confidence be regarded as a survival from an earlier church, probably dating from before the Conquest. This follows because the early Norman west tower is built against this earlier west wall and is not in bond with it. Moreover, the original west doorway, of elaborately square-headed form, now much mutilated, is enclosed within the tower where it can no longer be properly seen. The head of the doorway is now formed by a rectangular lintel but the upper part of the elaborate carved

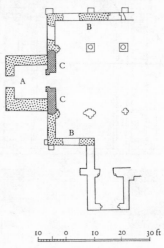

FIG. 286. STOTTESDON, SHROPSHIRE

Plan, showing the early Norman west tower A, the later Norman aisles B, and the pre-Norman west wall C of the nave.

pattern is missing and it seems probable that the lintel was formerly a tympanum, whose upper part has been hacked away. The area above the doorway has clearly been much disturbed, and it is not now possible to say whether the head was semicircular or of triangular shape. It was evidently outlined by strip-work, much of which still exists; on the south, a section of straight strip-work suggests a triangular head, but on the north there is the conflicting evidence of a curved outline.

DIMENSIONS

The west wall is 2 ft 11 in. thick, about 24 ft wide and about 20 ft tall to the eaves. The doorway is 4 ft 10 in. wide and 6 ft 6 in. tall.

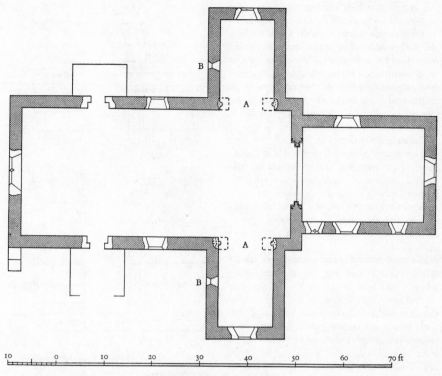

FIG. 287. STOUGHTON, SUSSEX

This ground-plan shows the ambitious scale of the church at Stoughton. The broken lines at A indicate the conjectural original walls pierced by narrower arches to the transepts. A double-splayed original window has survived in each of the transepts at B.

STOUGHTON

Sussex

Map sheet 181, reference SU 801115

Figures 582–4

ST MARY

Main fabric: period C3

This beautifully situated church, standing in a circular churchyard on the north side of a secluded valley of the South Downs, about 6 miles north-west of Chichester, has, in our opinion, not received the attention it deserves. Many of its unusual features have either been overlooked or else have been attributed to a post-Conquest date,

as the result of insufficient attention to the finer detail, which so often alone serves to distinguish between late-Saxon and early-Norman work. The manor was a wealthy one, recorded in Domes-day Book as having been held in the time of King Edward by Earl Godwin; and it is therefore not surprising if some of the features of its Anglo-Saxon church should show the influence of the Norman traditions which were being followed before the Conquest, not only by Edward in his great abbey at Westminster, but by others, perhaps even including Godwin's son Harold in his abbey at Waltham.

The church has a tall, aisleless nave and chancel, with transepts which are placed near to the east of the nave, and which leave its eastern quoins standing free, as distinct architectural features, in the angles between the transepts and the chancel.[1] The fabric is of flint rubble, plastered on the south but bare on the other walls. Massive side-alternate quoining is provided not only on all salient angles but also on all re-entrants, a feature which appears in other pre-Conquest churches in Sussex, notably at Boarhunt and to a certain extent at Bosham. An interesting and peculiar feature is the use of the south transept to form a medieval belfry.

The walls of the church are only 2 ft 5 in. thick and are nearly 30 ft high; the north and south doors of the nave both show vestiges of early internal outlines of characteristically tall proportions, although both are now faced externally with medieval doorways; and in the west walls of both transepts large, double-splayed, round-headed windows have survived in perfect condition.

The most interesting and controversial feature of the church is, however, the tall chancel-arch, whose round head of two orders has the same unusual mouldings as those of the neighbouring church at Bosham, also intimately connected with Earl Godwin and his son Harold. The arch has a soffit-roll on its inner order; and on the outer order it has an angle-roll which is outlined by a half-round hollow. The similarity to Bosham extends even to the number of voussoirs and the width of the arch. But the jambs are totally different from those at Bosham and have generally been described as distinctly Norman. Baldwin Brown (p. 419) is unusually positive in placing the chancel-arch and its capitals in the Norman era, saying that the 'fine chancel arch with volute caps and other characteristics show that it is really a Norman church [although] it has Saxonic features'.

But closer inspection shows that even the jambs and their capitals have many unusual features, which are more akin to the Anglo-Saxon tradition than the Norman. The three attached shafts of the jambs are placed as a soffit-shaft and two angle-shafts, which are separated from one another and from the main wall-surface by substantial rectangular arrises. The lowest stone of each jamb is shaped to form a separate rectangular

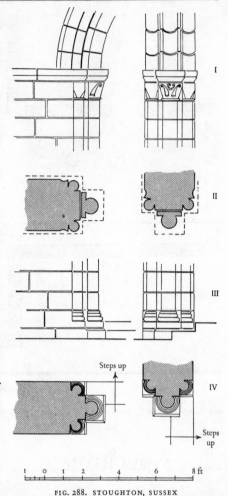

FIG. 288. STOUGHTON, SUSSEX

Details of the chancel-arch and of its jambs. I, elevations of the west face and soffit face of the north springing of the arch and of the capital of the north jamb; II, plan of the mouldings of the arch and of the rectangular outline of the abacus; III, elevations of the west face and soffit face of the bases, showing also their relation to the steps leading to the chancel; IV, plan of the bases.

plinth for each shaft and on this plinth each shaft has a separate simple splayed base, moulded to show three superimposed rings. The angle-shafts have capitals with simple cubical tops, which are

---

[1] This is a distinctly pre-Norman feature which is exactly paralleled at Breamore and at Dover.

reduced to meet the circular shafts by the elementary expedient of chamfering each face and then chamfering each angle, an expedient which has many parallels in Anglo-Saxon work, as at Kirkdale or Kirk Hammerton. The soffit-shafts, however, have the capitals which have generally been cited as Norman, because of their volutes. These, on the other hand, are no ordinary volutes; but are each like a bishop's crozier, or a cornucopia, two of which are placed at each angle, slanting out as the capital widens, with their crooks turned outward. On each face of the capital the V-shaped space between the backs of the croziers is filled by two smaller croziers with their crooks turned inward, to form a shape like an equilateral triangle. Finally, the capitals support quirked and chamfered imposts which are recessed to conform with the recessed form of the jambs and are returned along the full width of the wall towards the nave as a string-course.

The original arches to the transepts have unfortunately been replaced in late-Norman times by pointed arches transitional in form between Norman and Early English. The *Victoria County History* dates the chancel and transepts in the eleventh-century; but, without giving any reasons, it cites the nave as having been built or reconditioned in the thirteenth century. The lancet windows of the nave clearly date from the thirteenth century, but it is hard to account for their high position in the walls unless they are in fact enlargements of eleventh-century windows, as is no doubt also the case with the windows of the chancel. The high walls of the nave and the absence of buttresses would also have been unusual features in the thirteenth century.

DIMENSIONS

The church is on an unusually large and ambitious scale, with a nave 57 ft long by 26 ft wide, a chancel 25 ft by 19 ft, and transepts 12 ft wide from east to west by 16 ft deep. Its walls are 2 ft 5 in. thick, and nearly 30 ft high. The chancel-arch is 11 ft wide and about 20 ft high. The double-splayed windows of the transepts have apertures 1 ft wide and 4 ft tall, splayed internally to become about 2 ft wide and 6 ft tall. The apertures are placed nearer the outer face of the wall than the inner; and the exterior

splays are correspondingly smaller. The sills of these windows, at the glass, are about 12 ft above the floor.

REFERENCES

Editorial, 'Church restorations', *Ecclesiologist*, **4** (1845), 243. Note of particularly unfeeling restoration which cut off the tops of the chancel windows.

V.C.H., *Sussex*, **4** (London, 1953), 124–5. Plan and architectural description.

STOURMOUTH, WEST
Kent
Map sheet 173, reference TR 256629

ALL SAINTS
North wall of nave, and possibly also west wall:
period C3

This church is enclosed by an extensive earthwork, at the north-west of the small and rather scattered village of Stourmouth, roughly mid-way between Canterbury and Ramsgate. Built mainly of flint and clunch, with some Roman tiles, it now consists of an aisleless chancel with Transitional windows, and a nave opening to north and south aisles through late-Norman or Transitional arcades. The western parts of the solid side walls of the originally aisleless nave have been left intact, to carry a square wooden belfry with a pyramidal roof; and heavy brick buttresses have later been added outside the west wall to resist the lateral thrust of the arcades.

The area to the west of the north aisle now forms a vestry, approached through a doorway from the aisle; but it is said formerly to have been an anchorite's cell, completely cut off from the church. In the early wall between this cell and the nave there is now to be seen a blocked, double-splayed, round-headed window with its sill 9 ft above the floor. The indication of pre-Conquest date given by this window is confirmed by the thinness of the side walls of the nave, only 2 ft 1 in. thick, both in the solid sections at the west and also over the later arcades. It would be unusual to find Norman or Transitional arches supporting walls so much less than 3 ft in thickness, unless the arches had been cut through pre-Conquest walls.

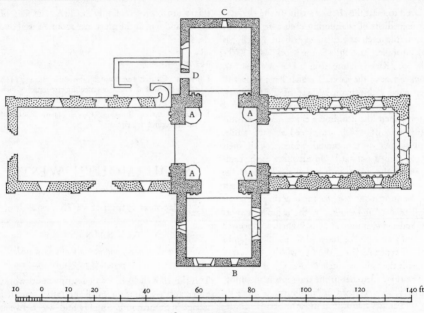

FIG. 289. STOW, LINCOLNSHIRE

A, later medieval piers supporting present belfry wholly within the ground-plan of the Anglo-Saxon central space; B, original south window (see Fig. 290); C, north window with original jambs but modified head (see Fig. 291); D, original doorway (see Fig. 293). The plan shows clearly how the Anglo-Saxon central space was wider than any of the four arms of the church. The floor of the central space is now at its original Anglo-Saxon level, and the plan shows how there is a step up from this central area into each of the arms of the church.

STOW

Lincolnshire

Map sheet 104, reference SK 882819

Figures 585–8

ST MARY

Central crossing, up to the level of the eaves; and transepts

Lower parts of walls: period C1 or earlier

Upper parts of walls: period C2 or 3

INTRODUCTION

The Roman road now known as Tillbridge Lane, which runs north-west from Lincoln to Doncaster, crossing the Trent near Marton, passes close to the village of Stow, with its important and interesting church of St Mary. Local tradition claims the church as the original cathedral church of the diocese of Lindsey, founded in 674 by King Egfrid of Northumbria.[1] The church is still commonly called 'the mother of Lincoln cathedral'; but it is impossible to say on what facts this tradition is founded, or how ancient it is. Apart, however, from any special interest which it may derive from this tradition, the church is of the utmost importance in the study of Anglo-Saxon architecture, for it is one of the few surviving examples of major churches of the pre-Conquest period.

Although it is unusually large in scale, the church at Stow is a particularly simple example of the cruciform plan; for it consists of a square tower, placed between four aisleless rectangular

---

[1] Bede, *H.E.* IV, 12. For the date of the foundation of a diocese of Lindsey see F. M. Stenton, *Anglo-Saxon England*, 2nd ed. (Oxford, 1947), 85 and 134.

arms which constitute the transepts, the nave, and the chancel. The complete simplicity of this plan is broken only by a small modern vestry in the angle between the nave and the north transept, and by the modern stair-turret which rises up, in the same angle, above the roof of the vestry, to give access to the upper part of the tower.

At first sight, the church would be accepted as fundamentally Norman, but with the upper part of the tower rebuilt in the fourteenth or fifteenth century. On closer inspection, however, a number of features will be seen to indicate that the transepts and the lower part of the tower are certainly pre-Norman. In the first place, the plan is not in accordance with Norman custom, since the central crossing, or base of the tower, is a square of larger size than the width of any of the four buildings which are joined to it. Therefore, the four corners of the central crossing are to be seen, rising from the ground to the eaves of the roofs, as salient angles, which stand free from the walls of the transepts, and even from the walls of the nave and chancel. Secondly, although the rubble walls of the nave and chancel are divided into compartments by characteristically Norman buttresses, neatly constructed of ashlar masonry, with similar buttresses clasping the angles, the transepts have no such buttresses, and the angles of the transepts and crossing are constructed, mainly in side-alternate fashion, using very large stones, which contrast sharply with the small stones of the ashlar masonry of the Norman buttresses. Several detailed arguments will be advanced below in support of the pre-Norman date of the transepts and crossing, but mention should be made here of only one other important feature, which was pointed out by Atkinson when he first claimed a pre-Conquest date for the church over a hundred years ago:[1] namely the fact that the Norman nave

and chancel are at no point bonded into the walls of the crossing, but are simply built against them, with a straight vertical joint, which may be seen running from the ground to the eaves at each of the four points of junction.

OUTLINE OF THE HISTORY OF THE CHURCH

Several important questions concerning the date and character of the church still remain to be settled. These will be referred to later, but for the moment it will be convenient to confine attention to the points for which there is good historical authority or on which there is common agreement. A bishop Eadnoth of Dorchester founded a college of canons at Stow in the first half of the eleventh century.[2] This foundation was further supported by Wulfwig, who succeeded the second Eadnoth and who secured the support of Leofric, Earl of Mercia, and Lady Godiva his wife. A charter of about 1055 recites gifts by Leofric and Godiva for this purpose;[3] and Archbishop Kinsius of York, Chaplain to Edward the Confessor, gave the church a bell.[4] There had been a long-standing dispute between the Archbishops of York and the Bishops of Dorchester about possession of this church, and the Archbishop had possession of it when he made his presents of bells to Stow, Beverley, and Southwell; but in 1061, Wulfwig obtained a papal bull in his favour as Bishop of Dorchester.

Shortly after the Conquest, Wulfwig's successor Remigius moved his seat from Dorchester to Lincoln, and installed Benedictine monks at Stow in place of the secular canons. He found the church in a ruined condition and did much reconstruction.[5] The newly installed monks were not left long in peace; for a subsequent bishop, Robert Bloet, removed them to Eynsham, in Oxfordshire, and annexed much of the endowment at Stow for the bishopric.[6] The nave at Stow is

---

[1] G. Atkinson, 'On the restorations in progress at Stow Church, Lincolnshire', *A.A.S.R.* **1** (1850–1), 315–26, particularly 316.

[2] G. Baldwin Brown (1925), 355, following Dugdale, *Monasticon*, **3** (London, 1821), 1, attributed this foundation to about 1040, in the bishopric of Eadnoth II (Bishop, *c.* 1034–50). A. W. Clapham, *Arch. J.* **103** (1946), 168, cited H. E. Salter, *The Cartulary of Eynsham* (Oxford, 1907), x, as authority for attributing the foundation to Eadnoth I (Bishop, *c.* 1004–16).

[3] J. M. Kemble, *Codex Diplomaticus*, no. 956; or A. J. Robertson, *Anglo-Saxon Charters*, no. cxv. Baldwin Brown seems too lightly to accept these gifts as evidence for dating the building.

[4] *Historians of York*, ed. J. Raine (Rolls Series, 71, II) (London, 1886), 344.

[5] Dugdale, *Monasticon*, **3** (London, 1821), 15 (or **1** (London, 1655), 262).

[6] H. E. Salter, *The Cartulary of Eynsham* (Oxford, 1907), xi.

commonly regarded as the work of Remigius, with the elaborate doorways added later, and the chancel as the work of Bishop Alexander.

There has been general agreement for many years past in assigning the greater part of the transepts and crossing at Stow to the period of Eadnoth and Wulfwig; but there has been disagreement as to detail. For instance, Baldwin Brown (pp. 355–6) regarded the whole of the walls as being of this period, but he referred the arches over the crossing to the period of rebuilding by Remigius. Clapham, however, accepted the arches also as pre-Conquest, and he regarded the whole of the transepts and crossing as a work of the first half of the eleventh century.[1]

As will be mentioned in more detail below, we think that the existing fabric shows that the history is more complicated than is indicated by either of these theories. In this respect we agree with the Rev. G. Atkinson, who was Rector of Stow during the important works of restoration about a century ago, and who recorded in detail many of the important discoveries which were made at that time.[2] It will be best to defer the finer points of the argument until the church has been described in detail; but it seems proper to mention here that, while the whole of the main fabric of the transepts and crossing must be accepted as of pre-Conquest date, Atkinson's observations show that the pre-Conquest fabric is of at least two different periods, between which the building suffered very drastic damage by fire. Atkinson claimed that that destruction must have been the work of the Danish host in 870, when they 'conquered all the land, and destroyed all the monasteries they came to'.[3] We do not accept the evidence as proving that any part of the existing fabric necessarily dates from before 870, but we think it is difficult to resist a claim that the earliest work in the transepts and crossing must date from before the eleventh century and that the work of Eadnoth I and his successors must be represented in the upper part of the fabric. That is to say, we believe that the eleventh-century founders of the college of canons did not build the church from the foundations, but that they

repaired an existing fabric for whose age we have at present no certain evidence.

DETAILED DESCRIPTION OF THE EXTERIOR

Throughout the church, the fabric is mainly of small, roughly squared rubble, laid in courses; but in the upper parts of the walls of the transepts the rubble is more neatly squared and more regularly coursed. The ground-level of the churchyard has risen appreciably through the centuries; but the original plinth is now exposed in a trench beside the walls of the transepts, and it may be seen to be of some elaboration, with two successive chamfered orders standing on a squared foundation or base-course.

By contrast with the small squared stones of the Norman buttresses of the nave and chancel, the quoins of the crossing and of the transepts are of very large stones, laid mainly in regular side-alternate fashion, with close joints. Atkinson pointed out, and it is still clearly visible to this day, that the quoins of the transepts show a marked change, at heights that vary from quoin to quoin but are about 9 ft from the present ground-level. Above this level, the quoins are in good condition, with smooth surfaces and sharp salient angles; while below this level, they are reddened by fire, and their surfaces are cracked and roughened, and their angles are appreciably weathered away. The upper parts of the quoins are, indeed, in such good condition that one might have been tempted, but for Atkinson's evidence, to suspect that they had been replaced in the repairs carried out under Mr Pearson's direction about 1850; but Atkinson makes it quite clear that they are part of the early fabric. It was on the evidence of the change in the quoins, and a corresponding change in the walling itself, that Atkinson based his conclusion that the walls were of two separate building periods, of which the later represented a rebuilding after destruction by a very serious fire. The evidence of damage to the lower part of the quoins by fire is most clearly to be seen on the quoins of the south transept; but it is also clear on the north transept, and on the quoins of the central crossing.

The eastern quoins of the crossing and the

---

[1] A. W. Clapham, *Arch. J.* **103** (1946), 168.
[2] G. Atkinson, *A.A.S.R.* **I** (1850–1), 315–26.
[3] *Anglo-Saxon Chronicle*, 'E' version, s.a.870. D. Whitelock, *E.H.D.* (1955), 177 (especially note 4).

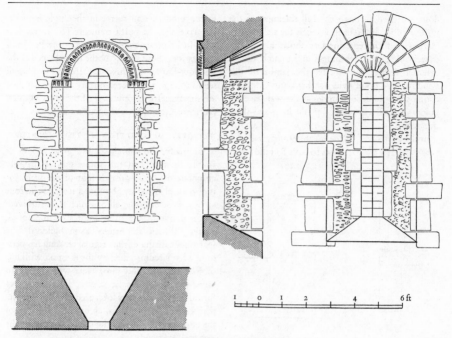

FIG. 290. STOW, LINCOLNSHIRE

Details of the Anglo-Saxon window in the south transept. The dowel-holes mentioned on p. 588 have not been shown here, but they can be seen in Fig. 588.

quoins of the north transept show separate, and perhaps even clearer, evidence of rebuilding, for the stones of the lower parts are shaped so as to show a raised pilaster-strip, about 13 in. wide, running up each face of the quoin beside the salient angle, whereas the upper parts, which represent the later rebuilding, are of stones with plain flat surfaces. Moreover, the burnt and weathered stones below, which have their surfaces worked to show these pilaster-strips, are of smaller average vertical height than the stones above; and, whereas the newer stones above are laid very regularly in side-alternate fashion, those below have a considerable proportion laid in face-alternate fashion. The quoins of the south transept do not show any trace of pilaster-strips on the angles, and it is not now possible to say with certainty whether this is

because there never were any, or whether they were destroyed by the fire.

Several windows have been inserted into the walls of the transepts at later dates; but one complete original window has survived in the south transept, and parts of two others in the north. The south window is a tall, narrow, single-splayed opening, placed at about the middle of the height of the wall, and nearer to the east than the west. Its jambs and arched head are constructed of well-dressed ashlar, neatly jointed; and its head is outlined above with a chamfered hood-moulding, which is enriched on the lower surface with a simple palmette ornament, of a type that is found on several late-Saxon churches in Lincolnshire and nearby.[1] Apart from a small chamfer at the outer wall-face, the interior splay of this win-

[1] It is to be seen, *in situ*, at St Peter at Gowts, Lincoln, and at Coleby and Barholm, all in Lincolnshire. It is also to be seen at Carlton-in-Lindrick, Nottinghamshire, and at Paston, Northamptonshire, but at the latter place not *in situ*. We think there is no doubt about the pre-Conquest character of this ornament, although the case for a post-Conquest date was advanced very forcibly by J. T. Irvine, *J.B.A.A.* **47** (1891), 308–12.

dow is carried through the full thickness of the wall, without any rebate or recess for a shutter or glazing; but the exterior face shows a series of dowel-holes, as if for hinges and a latch for an external shutter. Internally, the jambs of this window give good evidence for a pre-Conquest dating since the salient angles at the wall-face are boldly treated with carefully laid long-and-short quoining.[1]

In the north wall of the north transept, a somewhat similar window seems to have had the upper

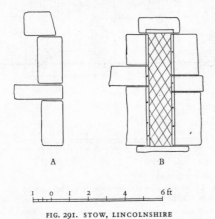

A   B

1   0   1   2   4   6 ft

FIG. 291. STOW, LINCOLNSHIRE

Details of Anglo-Saxon windows in the north transept. A, surviving north jamb of window in west wall; B, window in north wall.

part of its head removed when a large circular window was inserted above it. The outer face of this window is, however, more characteristically pre-Conquest in construction than its southern companion, since its jambs are each of three stones laid successively upright, flat, and upright, in 'Escomb fashion'; and its outer face is surrounded by a small square rebate as if to house a wooden shutter. In the west face of the north transept a single jamb has survived to show the former existence of a third window which has otherwise vanished. This jamb consists of four large stones also laid in 'Escomb fashion'.

The only other early features that should be noted outside are the small stone window-frames in the modern stair-turret in the angle between the nave and the north transept. This turret was built in its present position during Mr Pearson's restoration, about 1850; but the resemblance of the window-frames to those at Hough-on-the-Hill seems to us to make it reasonably certain that they are survivals from some part of the pre-Conquest fabric, re-used in their modern setting.

DETAILED DESCRIPTION OF THE INTERIOR

Internally, the church gives a great feeling of simple dignity, and this impression is strongly emphasized by the great height of the walls. It is also emphasized by the grand scale of the four arches of the crossing, all of which have survived, to form one of the most impressive memorials of the skill of the Anglo-Saxon builders. The spacious character of the original crossing has been somewhat circumscribed by the erection within it of four massive polygonal piers which serve to carry the Perpendicular tower; but these have fortunately in no way obscured the broad vista that may still be obtained along the main axes of the church, either across the transepts or from the east and west ends.

The round arches which carry the walls of the original crossing are by far the tallest and widest that survive in a cruciform pre-Conquest church, and the fact that all four have survived is a wonderful testimonial to the quality of the workmanship. All four arches are of similar construction, fundamentally square in section, with the main body of their soffit faces lined with rubble, and their archivolt faces built of two orders of well-dressed voussoirs, laid more or less in the plane of the face of the wall but moulded to show a series of concentric raised and hollow rolls. Towards the four arms of the church, the faces of these arches are unobscured by any later erections; and all four are similar, except that the western arch facing the nave has a further enrichment in the form of a hood-moulding with a pattern of palmette loop-ornament, like that on the hood-moulding of the south window of the south transept. It was on the basis of this ornament that Clapham postulated a pre-Conquest date for the arches, a dating for which support may be claimed

---

[1] Compare the inner faces of the windows of the tower at St Peter at Gowts, Lincoln.

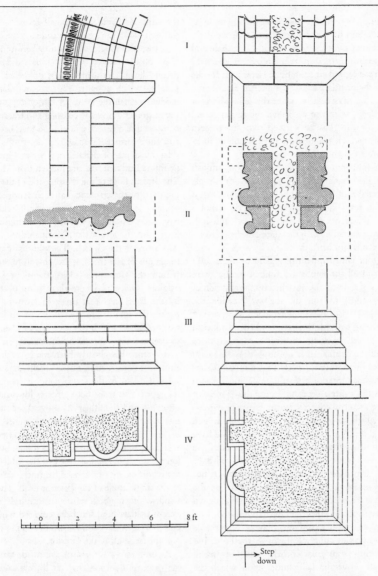

I

II

III

IV

0 1 2 4 6 8 ft

Step
down

FIG. 292. STOW, LINCOLNSHIRE

Details of the great arch from the nave to the tower. I, the western face and the soffit face of the northern springing of the arch, showing also the impost and the top of the jamb. Note the palmette ornament round the hood-moulding. Note also how the two pilaster-strips run into the impost; II, plans showing in full lines the outline of the mouldings of the arch and in broken lines the outline of the impost and the pilaster-strips; III, the western face and the soffit face of the lower part of the north jamb, showing the bases of the pilaster-strips and the great base of the jamb with its four chamfered orders and one square order; IV, plans of the bases. The east face of the wall is hidden behind the later medieval piers which carry the tower. It is, therefore, impossible to say with certainty whether the east face was plain as shown in the right-hand plan IV, or whether it had pilaster-strips like those of the west face.

by comparison of the mouldings with those at Bosham, and by contrasting them with the early Norman work in the west front of the Cathedral at Lincoln. Although the jambs are obscured within the central crossing by the later piers for the tower, the greater parts of the interior faces of the four arches may be seen, since the pointed arches of the later work rise up above the earlier round arches. It can thus be verified that the western face of the arch towards the nave is unique in its enrichment with palmette ornament.

The four remarkable arches rest on imposts which are rectangular in plan and of simple chamfered profile. The simplicity of the imposts is therefore remarkably at variance with the elaboration of the arches which they support; and it is equally at variation with the quite different character of the jambs beneath.

All four jambs are entirely plain on their soffit faces, indeed the jambs are fundamentally mere sections of the walling, enriched by the addition of pilaster-strips, to run up the wall beside the opening. Two of these pilasters flank each side of the opening towards the nave; and two flank each side of each opening towards the other three arms of the church. It is not now possible to say whether there were formerly two similar pilasters flanking each interior side of the openings, as seen within the central crossing; since those areas of walling are now covered by the heavy polygonal piers which carry the later tower. But it is a reasonable assumption that these faces would have been similarly treated. On all four visible faces, the pilaster-strips are of the same type; a bold half-round strip close to the opening, although not cut in the same stones as those which line the jambs; and a bold square strip, set at about its own distance from the other, and separated from it by a section of rubble walling. These remarkable pilasters do not continue down to the floor, but they spring from great corbels, which are set in the wall above the tall plinths upon which the jambs rest. It is an interesting fact that the several churches which have arches outlined by double patterns of pilasters and hood-mouldings all have

the same arrangement of a half-round shaft next the arch and a square one outside it.[1]

Before the nineteenth-century restoration, the floor of the church had been raised above its present level, and a great part of the impressive plinths, which support the crossing, had been hidden beneath the floor. Atkinson reported that the original floor of the crossing and transepts was composed of a sort of plaster; and that, between it and the Norman floor above, there was a considerable depth of charred debris, amongst which he found lead that had run molten from the roofs. The present floor of the crossing and of the adjoining parts of the transepts has been restored to the original level; and the present floor within the nave and chancel, one step above the Anglo-Saxon floor, is at the level of the Norman floor in those two arms of the church. The plinths supporting the jambs of the crossing are, therefore, best seen within the transepts; where the floor is at its original level, and where there is no obstruction by the later piers that carry the tower. In this region the plinths are seen to be of no less than five orders, of which the lowest is of plain square section and the upper four are chamfered.

Reference has already been made to the long-and-short construction of the salient angles of the splayed jambs of the south window in the south transept.[2] The space between this long-and-short quoining and the ashlar stone-work of the outer face is lined with rubble, and the arched surface of the round head is built of dressed-stone voussoirs, which are not through-stones, but are of long, thin shape, and are set in pairs which cover the whole extent of the head from its interior arris to the single stone of the exterior head. The north window of the north transept is similarly treated, except that its head has been covered with a flat lintel. The west window in this transept does not appear at all in the interior.

An interesting feature of the north transept is the original doorway, which leads through the west wall, into the modern vestry beside the north wall of the nave. The jambs of this doorway pass straight through the wall, and they are built

---

[1] At Skipwith, Yorkshire, the pilasters are separate as at Stow. At St Bene't's, Cambridge, the two pilasters are carved on single stones. By contrast with Stow, the hood-mouldings at Skipwith and Cambridge have the same

sections as the pilaster-strips. There are vestiges of pilasters, also, at Lusby, Lincolnshire, but in a very incomplete state.

[2] See Fig. 290, inner face of window.

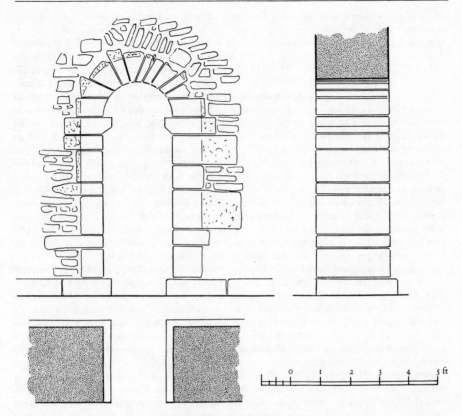

FIG. 293. STOW, LINCOLNSHIRE

The doorway leading westward from the north transept. Note how the jambs and arch are built wholly of through-stones. Note also the non-radial setting of stones in the arch, and the cutting back of the faces of the stones in a way which would give a smooth outline to the exposed faces of stone if the remainder were to be covered with plaster. Compare the treatment of the window in Fig. 290.

mainly of through-stones, laid alternately upright and flat in 'Escomb fashion'. They each rest on a simple square base, which is returned along the exterior wall, but not into the transept; and they support chamfered imposts which are not returned along either face of the wall. The round-arched head is of eleven through-stones, which are laid with somewhat non-radial joints and are of very varying length along the radius. The exposed surfaces of these voussoirs on the face of the wall have been marked with a semicircle, concentric with the arch; and the area outside this curve has been cut back slightly; so that, if the wall were

covered with plaster, the voussoirs would appear with a neat semicircular outline above and below, and their irregular extent beyond the outer curve would be concealed by the plaster. It is not at present certain what was the purpose of this door-way. Atkinson reported that during the restorations indications were found of outer walls beyond the present side walls of the nave. He suggested that these represented the outer walls of aisles; but they could equally well have belonged to *porticus*, in a way for which there seems to be an analogue at Britford, in Wiltshire. From outside the church there is some slight indication of a dis-

591

turbed area of walling in a corresponding position in the west wall of the south transept as if there might have been a similar doorway there.

THE DIFFICULT QUESTION OF THE DATE OF THE ORIGINAL CHURCH

Bede recorded how Queen Etheldreda preserved her virginity through two marriages; and how, after her release from her second husband, Egfrid, King of Northumbria, she founded the monastery at Ely and became its first abbess.[1] The twelfth-century *Liber Eliensis* gives more detail of her flight from Northumbria, and of how, after crossing the Humber with her two companions, she landed at Winteringham and on her southward journey rested awhile, placing her walking-stick in the ground at her head. When she awoke, her stick had become a stately ash-tree, which grew to be the largest tree in the province, thus suitably marking her resting-place, which to the time of the writer was known as Etheldreda-Stow.[2] Such a holy spot would clearly have been a suitable place for the foundation of a church; but even if it could be proved that it was the Danes in 870 who burnt the church at Stow and left the lower parts of the walls a ruin on which Eadnoth and others built their eleventh-century church, the evidence would still hardly be sufficient to establish Atkinson's claim that the church destroyed by the Danes in 870 was the original cathedral of the province of Lindsey, founded in 674 by King Egfrid. Indeed, it would be reasonable to assume that a cathedral founded by Egfrid would show more resemblance to Benedict Biscop's churches at Jarrow and Monkwearmouth, with the foundation of which Egfrid had been so closely connected. Since, however, the lists of bishops show that the diocese of Lindsey continued in being after 868, and was later merged with Leicester, and had its seat moved to Dorchester-on-Thames, it would be possible to assume that the church at Stow was a church built as the cathedral of the diocese of Lindsey at some time before 868; although this would seem to be a rash assumption to be based on no better evidence than the grand scale of the building and the special sanctity of the place.

Having said so much in caution against too ready acceptance of Atkinson's claim that the lower parts of the wall represent Egfrid's seventh-century church, we should recapitulate the reasons why we think they must be substantially earlier than Eadnoth's eleventh-century foundation. Our description of the church has set out fully the evidence that the walls show two distinct dates of building, separated by a disastrous fire. The palmette ornament over the south window and on the hood-moulding of the western arch fixes these as being of one single period, and they are also both in the upper part of the fabric, dating from after the fire. Leofric and Godiva's charter of about 1055 mentions no disaster, and it seems unlikely that a major disaster of this type, and the subsequent rebuilding could have been fitted into the period between that charter and the refoundation by Remigius. It therefore seems reasonable that the later parts of the Anglo-Saxon fabric should be accepted as the work of Eadnoth I and his immediate successors in the first half of the eleventh century, and that the lower parts of the building on which the new work was erected were ruins dating from events which were not fresh in mind at the time of the charter. In default of some unexpected further source of information or of the ability to determine the date of the fire by scientific means, it seems unlikely that an accurate dating of the original fabric can now be secured. Currently accepted ideas on the dating of plans of Anglo-Saxon churches would suggest that this developed transeptal plan should not be placed earlier than the tenth century, except on the basis of some very clear independent evidence for an earlier date.

THE VAULTING OF THE CHANCEL

Since Atkinson's early article is not now very generally accessible, it is perhaps worth while to put again on record the evidence which he gave about the vaulting of the chancel, and of the bearing which this had on the nature of a post-Conquest conflagration. Clapham recently questioned whether there had ever been a Norman stone vault over the chancel; although its walls had clearly been designed to carry such a vault,

---

[1] *H.E.* IV, 19.

[2] *Liber Eliensis*, ed. D. J. Stewart (London, 1848), 43–4.

because they had been provided with the appropriate vaulting-shafts.[1] Atkinson's evidence about the former existence of a Norman vault seems to us conclusive. He reported that, when the restoration was begun, it was regarded as an open question whether there had been a vault; but that, when the ceiling was taken down, the upper walls of the chancel were found to show rough areas where the stones of the vault had been torn away; the walls were found to be seriously calcined above the vaulting but not below; and the only reasonable explanation was that there had been a complete stone vault which had been destroyed by a disastrous fire in the main timbers of the roof above. Such a fire would therefore affect the upper parts of the walls of the chancel, while the parts below would be protected by the vault, although ultimately the vault must have been broken by the heat and by the falling timbers. Even more conclusive proof was found as the work proceeded, for the damaged areas in the upper parts of the walls were found to be patched with stones salvaged from the ruins of the vaulting. Atkinson described how stones with several different carved patterns were found built into the damaged walls, and how he and Mr Pearson satisfied themselves that these fixed the form of all the different vaulting-ribs that have been used in the existing vault.

DIMENSIONS

The church is one of the most impressive monuments which have survived from before the Conquest. The transepts are 23 ft wide internally from east to west, and their span from north to south is about 85 ft internally. Their side walls are only 2 ft 6 in. thick and about 33 ft tall.

The four arches of the crossing are on an unusually magnificent scale; about 14 ft wide and about 30 ft tall. The walls of the central crossing, through which these arches are cut, are 4 ft 6 in. thick.

The west doorway of the north transept is 2 ft 4 in. wide and 7 ft 2 in. tall.

The aperture of the south window of the south transept is 10 in. wide and about 6 ft 6 in. tall, with its sill about 13 ft 6 in. above the lowest order of the original plinth.

REFERENCES

G. ATKINSON, 'On the restorations in progress at Stow Church, Lincolnshire', *A.A.S.R.* 1 (1850–1), 315–26. An article of fundamental importance, since it gives first-hand accounts of what was seen during the work.

G. ATKINSON, 'Saxon churches: stone or wood', *Gents. Mag.* (1863, i), 755–62. Further accounts of the bearing of Stow on the argument advanced by Mr J. H. Parker that there were very few, if any, Saxon churches built in stone before A.D. 1000.

E. TROLLOPE, 'Notes on Gainsborough and other places', *A.A.S.R.* 8 (1865–6), 213–54. Stow, 245–51.

E. P. L. BROCK, 'Churches of the city of Lincoln', *J.B.A.A.* 46 (1890), 17–28. Transept windows at Stow compared with those at St Peter at Gowts, Lincoln; and dated before the Conquest, 23–4.

J. T. IRVINE, 'Barholm church, Lincolnshire', *ibid.* 47 (1891), 308–12. Palmette ornament at Barholm, Stow, and other places claimed as Norman.

E. M. SYMPSON, 'Where was Sidnacester', *A.A.S.R.* 28 (1905–6), 87–94. Suggested that Stow is perhaps more probable than any place except Lincoln; but that perhaps the supposed existence of such a place depends on a scribe's error in writing Syddensis Civitas in place of Lindensis Civitas, for the city of Lincoln.

V.C.H., Lincolnshire, 2 (London, 1906), 118. Brief historical account.

F. LIVINGSTONE-BLEVINS, *Stow, The Dowager Minster of Lincoln* (Lincoln, undated). An interesting historical account, with many references to early writers.

A. H. THOMPSON, 'Pre-Conquest church-towers in north Lincolnshire', *A.A.S.R.* 29 (1907–8), 43–70. Stow, 47.

A. W. CLAPHAM, 'Stow', *Arch. J.* 103 (1946), 168–70. Good plan, 169. Historical and architectural description, with the first reasoned claim for a pre-Conquest date for the arches of the crossing.

[1] A. W. Clapham, *Arch. J.* 103 (1946), 168–9. Clapham's argument was based on an eighteenth-century drawing preserved in the Banks' Collection in Lincoln. The drawing shows a flat ceiling at some height above the heads of those shafts, and there is no sign of any springing of a vault above the shafts. Both Clapham (*loc. cit.*) and Baldwin Brown (p. 355) wrongly cite Atkinson's article as *A.A.S.R.* 2 instead of *A.A.S.R.* 1 (1850–1), and there is therefore reason to doubt whether they had considered his evidence.

STOWE-NINE-CHURCHES

Northamptonshire

Map sheet 133, reference SP 638576

Figure 589

ST PETER AND ST PAUL

West tower and western part of walls of nave:
period C

The church of the small village of Stowe-nine-churches has a commanding position on a ridge of high land to the west of the Roman Watling Street, a little more than a mile to the south of Weedon, whence it has a fine view northward over the upper reaches of the valley of the River Nene. Of the original Anglo-Saxon church only the rather mutilated west tower has survived, with the possible exception of the adjoining sections of the walls of the nave.

The tower, built of rubble, is capped by a medieval parapet with battlements, and is wholly covered with plaster externally, except for a single carved stone, which was probably part of a cross-shaft, and which has now been built into the north-west quoin. The unbuttressed walls rise straight up without string-course or off-set, until they reach the belfry stage, which is separated from the much taller lower stage by a string-course. This is now much weathered but is probably original, since the later medieval windows are cut through it. On each of the east and west faces of the belfry stage, two vertical pilaster-strips, of plain square section, rise from the string-course and run up to the parapet, one on either side of the later window. Inside the tower it can be seen in the bell-chamber that the medieval windows are later insertions, and that in the east and west walls there were formerly simple round-headed windows, placed rather higher in the wall, no doubt so that their sills rested logically on the string-course. Within the bell-chamber it is also possible to see faint traces of earlier windows in the north and south walls, placed even higher and of an outline which suggests that they may have been double.

Still inside the tower, but at first-floor level, a round-headed doorway has survived in the east wall, where it no doubt formerly opened to a gallery; but it is now blocked and covered by plaster, so as to be invisible from the nave. This upper chamber is lit by a round-headed, double-splayed window which will also be noticed from outside.

In the west wall of the tower, externally, a blocked square-headed doorway has jambs of large stones laid alternately upright and flat in 'Escomb fashion'. Above the doorway, a wide,

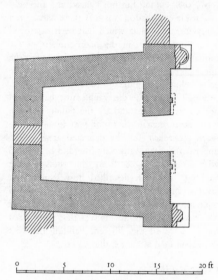

FIG. 294. STOWE-NINE-CHURCHES,
NORTHAMPTONSHIRE
Plan of the tower and west wall of the nave.

square-headed, late medieval hood-moulding indicates the former presence of a window of several lights, now replaced by a small round-headed opening of uncertain date. This serves to light the ground-floor chamber; and at some distance above it is the double-splayed, round-headed original window which lights the first-floor chamber. Between these two windows is a stone inscribed 1776, possibly the date of some restoration, perhaps even the strengthening of the tower by means of the two iron bands which run round it.

The north-west angle of the tower rests on a small section of chamfered plinth, from which a

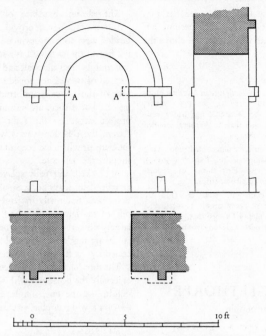

FIG. 295. STOWE-NINE-CHURCHES, NORTHAMPTONSHIRE

Detail of the west doorway from the nave to the tower. The walls are heavily plastered and it is not possible to see the jointing of the stonework. The broken lines at A indicate the conjectural original projection of the imposts.

plain square plinth runs as far as the blocked west doorway. Elsewhere there is no trace of plinth, but the ground may have risen sufficiently to obscure it. On either side of the tower the western quoins of the nave project slightly; and, within the nave, the western responds of the arcades seem to be parts of the walls of the original aisleless nave, through which the arches were later cut.

Access from the nave to the tower is by way of a small, original, round-headed doorway, with jambs which are cut straight through the wall but which slope inward slightly, so that the opening is narrower at the shoulders than at the sill. The doorway has originally been a feature of some elaboration, but has been rudely hacked about at some later date. On the face toward the nave it is outlined by pilaster-strips and a hood-moulding of plain square section; and its imposts, also of square section, are carried across the wall to meet the separate imposts, of rather greater projection,

which divide the pilasters from the hood-moulding. The soffit-face of the doorway seems to have suffered later modification, and the imposts have been cut back flush with the soffit. Towards the interior of the tower, the imposts project slightly, but there is no other ornament.

The tower is markedly irregular in plan, being more than a foot wider at the east than at the west.

DIMENSIONS

The nave is 13 ft 10 in. wide internally, with side walls 2 ft 5 in. thick and about 21 ft high. The tower is 9 ft 8 in. wide at the west and 10 ft 10 in. at the east; it is about 11 ft long from east to west; and its walls are about 3 ft thick and about 50 ft in height, excluding the later battlements.

The round-headed doorway on the ground floor is 3 ft 7 in. wide at floor-level and 7 ft 3 in. tall. The round-headed doorway on the first floor is 2 ft 2 in. wide and 6 ft tall, with its sill on the present floor at 21 above the floor of the nave. The double-splayed west window has an aperture 1 ft 1 in. wide and 2 ft 8 in. tall, splayed to become 2 ft 4 in. by 3 ft 6 in., with its sill 4 ft 5 in. above the first floor.

REFERENCES

J. R. ALLEN, 'Early Christian Sculpture in Northamptonshire', *A.A.S.R.* **19** (1887–8), 398–423. Stowe, 421–2. Stated that the Mercian kings had a residence near Weedon and that St Werburg founded a monastery there *c*. 680.

R. P. BRERETON, 'Notes on some unrecorded Saxon work in and near Northamptonshire', *ibid.* **27** (1903–4), 397–400. Stowe, 399. First notice of double-splayed window and of pilaster-strips.

Editorial 'Stowe-nine-churches', *ibid.* **28** (1905–6), xci–xciv. Account of very drastic restoration *c*. 1860. Note by Sir Henry Dryden that parts of the foundation of a very narrow Saxon church were then found.

STRAGGLETHORPE

Lincolnshire

Map sheet 113, reference SK 913524

ST MICHAEL

Nave: period C

About 7 miles east of Newark and 12 miles south of Lincoln, the tiny church of St Michael at Stragglethorpe stands beside a fine farmstead, whose open fields surround it on three sides, while the extensive farmyards on the south form the only entry to the church. The fabric is of roughly squared rubble, laid in courses, with larger stones in the quoins. The church now consists of an aisleless chancel, and a nave with north aisle, south porch, and bell-cote on the western gable. Of the side-alternate quoins of the original aisleless nave only that at the north-west has survived, for that at the south-west has been destroyed or concealed by later buttresses, while those at the east seem to have been swept away when a larger chancel was built, with its walls in the same alignment as those of the nave.

Internally, the north wall of the nave is pierced by a twelfth-century Transitional arcade of two round arches, but considerable sections of the original wall have been left at each end.

The clearest evidence of the Anglo-Saxon character of the nave is provided by the triangular-headed west doorway, which appears in the internal face of the west wall as a recess with its jambs cut straight into the wall and its triangular head formed of two stones sloped together. The structure of the jambs is unfortunately obscured by plaster; but if there are any imposts they do not project either on the soffit or into the nave. Externally, this doorway is wholly obscured by the buttress which has been added later, perhaps to support the bell-cote.

A blocked, internally splayed window of uncertain date may be seen above this blocked doorway. Externally its jambs appear on either side of the later buttress and its head, although largely obscured, appears to be flat. Internally its jambs are moderately splayed and its head is concealed by the flat plaster ceiling.

The interior fittings are of considerable interest, especially the box pews with simple brass candle-stands, and the fine, simple, cylindrical, arcaded font on a wide, double, circular plinth.

DIMENSIONS

The nave is 31 ft long internally and 16 ft 4 in. broad, with walls 2 ft 3 in. thick and about 13 ft high. The triangular-headed west doorway is 2 ft 1 in. wide and 5 ft 8 in. high. Its jambs are 4 ft 9 in. high, and the stones of its head are each 5½ in. thick and 1 ft 5 in. in length along their lower, sloping, faces.

REFERENCE

C. E. KEYSER, 'The church of St Michael and All Angels, Stragglethorpe', *A.A.S.R.* **36** (1921–2), 42–6.

STRETHALL

Essex

Map sheet 148, reference TL 484398

Figure 590

ST MARY THE VIRGIN

Nave and chancel-arch: period C3

This church is most attractively set in open rolling country about 3 miles west-north-west of Saffron

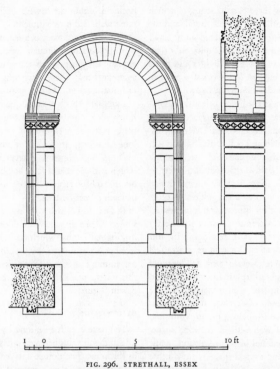

FIG. 296. STRETHALL, ESSEX

Details of the chancel-arch, showing particularly its through-stone jambs, its arch not of through-stones, its imposts with lozenge pattern and its pilaster-strips and hood-moulding of triple profile. On a subsequent visit to Strethall in 1961 we found that the arch and surrounding wall had been distempered or whitewashed and that the jointing of the stonework was no longer visible.

Walden, close beside a large farmstead, but otherwise remote from any dwellings. Its square west tower was added in the fifteenth century, and the north wall of the chancel was rebuilt about the same time, but the nave has retained the greater part of its pre-Conquest fabric, probably dating from about the middle of the eleventh-century. The fabric is of flint, with well-dressed limestone quoins.

By great good fortune the chancel-arch stands exactly as it was built, one of the finest examples of Anglo-Saxon workmanship in smaller parish churches. Its square jambs are wholly of through-stones laid in 'Escomb fashion', and its round arch of a single square order is of well-dressed stones laid with radial joints. The soffit of the arch used to be covered with plaster, so that it was impossible to tell whether or not the voussoirs were through-stones, but when we revisited the church in 1957 this plaster had been removed, and it was plain that none of the voussoirs passed through the full thickness of the wall. The east face of the wall towards the chancel is entirely plain, but towards the nave the chamfered ornamental impost is returned along the west wall and provided on either side of the arch with a separate capital for the pilaster-strip which is carried up each side of the opening and round its head as a hood-mould. Each of these strips also has a plain cubical base resting on, and serving as an outer stop for, the plain square plinths which project from the soffit face and west face of each jamb.

The strip-work round the opening is not the usual plain square Anglo-Saxon pilaster-strip; but it is carved to show three parallel strips, of which the inner is square, the central half-round, and the outer basically square, but chamfered on its inner face. The whole composition occupies only 6 in. in width and is of an altogether lighter and more imaginative character than the work at Lewes to which it is compared by Baldwin Brown.[1]

The imposts, also treated with unusual elaboration, are somewhat unkindly described by the Royal Commission on Historical Monuments[2] as being 'crude cable and roll-moulded imposts, chamfered beneath and enriched with rough saltire ornament'. Baldwin Brown also refers to the saltires on these imposts, and, having mentioned that saltires might involve a suggestion of Norman workmanship, then disposes of this suggestion by reference to the saltires on the arch of the early Saxon west doorway at Corbridge. In our opinion, the ornament on the imposts at Strethall should be described as carefully executed lozenges rather than as rough saltire ornament, and in no event can it be compared even remotely with the plain incised St Andrew's crosses at Corbridge. The chamfered face is about 4 in. in width and the lozenges are of well-defined diamond shape, framed in raised outlines of square section, while the interior diamond-shaped space is sunk more deeply at each side so as to leave a pronounced ridge along its vertical diagonal. Although the work is imaginative and elaborate it is, however, curiously imperfect both in the way the lozenges are deformed at the angle of the impost and also in the lack of attention to right angles and horizontal alignment. The vertical faces of the imposts, about 5 in. in height, are enriched with three parallel horizontal mouldings which consist of a square fillet along the upper edge, a cable-moulding in the centre, and a pair of rather ill-defined roll-mouldings at the angle.

At first sight it would appear that none of the original windows of the church has survived. It is indeed true that none has remained in use, but high up in the west wall of the nave a double-splayed round-headed window may be seen, now serving no useful purpose, since its outer face is enclosed within the tower. Still higher up in the same wall, and now visible only within the upper chamber of the tower, is a second early window, of double-splayed circular form. It is difficult to explain the purpose of these windows without assuming that there was originally an upper chamber over the western part of the nave.

Externally, both western quoins of the nave are in excellent condition, showing five or six complete pairs of well-dressed and closely jointed long-and-short stones set flush with the flint walling, and containing several stones each of which is more than 3 ft in height. The south-east quoin has been rebuilt and the north-east is hidden beneath a later buttress.

Both Baldwin Brown and the Royal Commissioners record that the south doorway has retained its original jambs, which have later been chamfered and surmounted by a pointed arch, but we see nothing in the present doorway to justify this statement. The chancel presents no Anglo-Saxon features.

DIMENSIONS

The nave is 26 ft 8 in. long by 16 ft wide, with side and end walls between 2 ft 3 in. and 2 ft 4 in. in thickness. The double-splayed windows in the west wall have their apertures about 8 in. from the west face of the wall, and the sill of the lower window is 19 ft above the floor. The aperture of the lower window is 8 in. wide and 2 ft tall, splayed to become 2 ft 2 in. by about 4 ft towards the nave, and 1 ft 3 in. by 3 ft towards the west. The aperture of the upper window is 8 in. in diameter, splayed to about 2 ft on the east face and about 1 ft 3 in. on the west. The centre of the upper window is 25 ft above the floor of the nave.

The chancel-arch is 5 ft 6 in. wide and 10 ft tall.

REFERENCES

J. H. SPERLING, 'On the churches of north-west Essex', T. Essex Arch. S. 2 (1863), 157–63. Fabric claimed as Anglo-Saxon but chancel-arch described as Norman, 159.

R.C.H.M. Essex, North-west, I (London, 1916), 295–6.

---

[1] G. Baldwin Brown (1925), 481. The work at Lewes consists simply of three identical mouldings in the form of flattish rolls, the whole strip being about 1 ft 4 in. across.

[2] R.C.H.M., Essex, I (London, 1916), 296. It seems to us, by contrast, that the work at Strethall is both imaginative and well executed.

SWAINSTHORPE

Norfolk

Map sheet 137, reference TG 219009

ST PETER

Blocked south window: period C

About 5 miles south of Norwich, the village of Swainsthorpe straddles the Roman road to Ipswich; and its small church stands on the higher land to the west. The aisleless chancel, the nave with north aisle and south porch, and the round west tower are mainly of flint, with dressed-stone facings; but in the nave there is also an appreciable admixture of Roman tiles; and the western quoins are of flint and tile, save where the lower part of the one on the south has been patched in modern brick.

The nave appears to be the earliest part of the church, and its pre-Conquest character is indicated by the flint and tile west quoins, and by the vestige of a round-headed, probably double-splayed, window, whose head is to be seen just to the east of the eastern slope of the roof of the south porch. The characteristic feature of this window is the way its head is arched in tiles which are set non-radially in the manner for which Baldwin Brown used the name 'Tredington fashion'.

No features have remained to justify a reliable dating of the tower; and the original eastern quoins of the nave have been destroyed or hidden in a relatively recent rebuilding of the junction between the nave and chancel.

DIMENSIONS

The nave is 34 ft 6 in. long internally, and 16 ft 6 in. wide. Its south wall is 3 ft 1 in. thick, and about 18 ft high.

SWALCLIFFE

Oxfordshire

Map sheet 145, reference SP 378379

ST PETER AND ST PAUL

Side walls of nave: period C 3

About 5 miles west-south-west of Banbury, the interesting church at Swalcliffe, standing high above the road to Shipston on Stour, now consists of a west tower, an aisled nave, and an aisleless chancel. It seems likely that the walls of the three western bays of its present nave, above their round arches, are the original side walls of a pre-Conquest church, while the eastern bay represents a later extension of the nave over the space originally occupied by the chancel.

This conjectural history is based on the nature of the arcades; which indicate clearly that an aisleless nave was first enlarged in Norman times by the building of a north aisle and the cutting of the three western arches of the north arcade through an existing wall, one of whose windows still survives above the second pier from the west; later, a south aisle was added, and the arcade of three Transitional arches opening to it was similarly cut through the south wall, where again an earlier window survives in part; finally, it will be seen that the eastern arch on each side of the nave is different from those already mentioned, and that there are indications of a change in the walling at the junction. It therefore seems probable that, soon after the completion of the three Transitional bays of the south arcade, preparations were made to extend the nave eastward, and the eastern arch of the north arcade was built in much the same style as the three western arches of the south arcade. The work perhaps took longer than was expected, and the subsequent eastward extension of the south arcade was completed in a more developed form of the Early English style. Throughout this period the Anglo-Saxon chancel probably continued in use, within the outer walls that were rising around it; and it may even have remained in use until the new chancel had been completed eastward of it in the fully developed Early English style.

It would perhaps be impossible to settle with certainty whether the account given above is the true story of the development of the present buildings; but we are certainly on firm ground in asserting that the three western bays of the nave represent the side walls of an earlier church, dating from before or about the Conquest; for the walls are only 2 ft 6 in. thick; and each of them contains, over the second pier from the west, the remains of a round-headed window, widely splayed internally. The southern window has

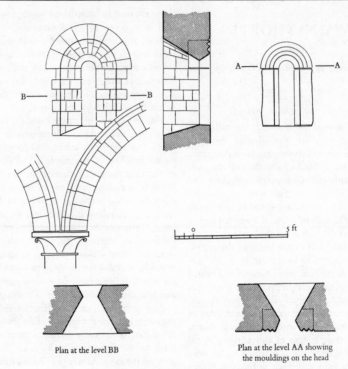

Plan at the level BB

Plan at the level AA showing
the mouldings on the head

FIG. 297. SWALCLIFFE, OXFORDSHIRE

Details of the window in the north wall of the nave, showing its relation to the Norman arches which cut part of it away. The exterior elevation, section, and plan show the triple moulding which surrounds the monolithic head. Baldwin Brown compares this to the mouldings at Somerford Keynes, but it more closely resembles the mouldings over the door at St Patrick's Chapel, Heysham.

lost its outer face and is little more than a fragment, but the northern one has the greater part of its jambs and head, both internal and external, showing that the actual aperture was about 6 in. from the outer face of the wall, and that the jambs and head were splayed both outward and inward from the aperture. The inner splayed jambs and arched head are formed of well-laid Norman-looking ashlar masonry; but the jambs of the outer face are plastered, and the head is cut from a single stone, which is enriched on its vertical face with three concentric roll-mouldings, reminiscent of work that appears from early Saxon times, as at Heysham or Somerford Keynes, and persists to the end of the Anglo-Saxon era, as at Great Hale. The windows, and the walls containing them, may therefore be accepted as Anglo-Saxon

on the evidence of the outward splay and the ornamented external head of the north window; and it may be assigned a late-Saxon date on the evidence of the nature of the interior splays of both windows.

A further indication of the persistence of Anglo-Saxon tradition in the district is given by the existence of a square-headed doorway placed high in the west wall of the nave and opening into the first-floor chamber of the Early English tower.

DIMENSIONS

If the history given above be correct, the original nave would have been about 45 ft long by 19 ft 6 in. wide, with side walls 2 ft 6 in. thick. The walls are now about 30 ft high; but it is probable that the upper 10 ft in height was added to carry the Perpendicular clear-storey windows. The aperture of the Anglo-Saxon north window is about 6 in. wide and 3 ft high and its sill is about 13 ft above the floor.

REFERENCE

C. E. KEYSER, 'An architectural account of Swalcliffe church', *Arch. J.* **61** (1904), 85-101. Good description, with plan, and many pictures.

SWALLOW
Lincolnshire
Map sheet 105, reference TA 176030

HOLY TRINITY
Lower stage of tower, and nave walls: period C3

About 8 miles south-west of Grimsby, on the way to Caistor, the church of the Holy Trinity, at Swallow, stands on high ground beside the main road, and now consists of an aisleless chancel, a nave with north aisle, and a west tower to which nineteenth-century restorers added a pseudo-Norman belfry stage. The lower stage of the tower and the side walls of the nave remain from before or shortly after the Conquest; while the north arcade and the chancel are of the Early English period.

The tall, plain, unbuttressed lower stage of the tower rises from a plinth of two chamfered orders, and ends above on a projecting string-course of square section. The nave has no similar plinth; but its west wall projects on either side of the tower like buttresses; and its quoins, like those of the tower, are of the well-defined side-alternate type in which larger stones are used than in the coursed rubble which forms the main fabric. The north, south, and east faces of the Anglo-Saxon tower are quite plain, without external openings; but the west face has both a door and a window.

The round-arched head of the doorway is of a single square order, without any hood-mould; and it is now blocked externally by a semicircular stone tympanum which is pierced with a circular window. The plinth of the tower is returned into the doorway to carry the square jambs, which in turn support square projecting imposts with a quirked chamfer on the west face but none on the soffit faces within the doorway.

Above the door, and about halfway up the lower stage of the tower, a small internally splayed window has each of its jambs formed of a single rectangular stone laid flat, and its round head formed in stilted fashion in the lower face of a roughly square stone.

Internally, the round-headed tower-arch of a single square order has plain chamfered imposts, plain square jambs, and a simple chamfered plinth; but neither the arch nor its jambs is of through-stones. Above the arch an off-set runs across the wall at the level of the tops of the side walls of the nave.

The nave has no surviving early windows to fix the date of its walls with certainty; but as they are aligned with the early quoining beside the tower, and in bond with it, they are probably original, particularly because they are also thin.

DIMENSIONS

The nave is 15 ft 7 in. wide internally by about 28 ft in length, with side walls about 14 ft high and only 2 ft 5 in. thick. The tower-arch is 7 ft 1 in. wide and about 11 ft high, in a wall 3 ft 8 in. thick. The tower is 10 ft 6 in. square internally, with side walls 3 ft 6 in. thick. Within the tower the west doorway appears as a simple round-headed opening 2 ft 11 in. wide by 8 ft 1 in. high, with a curiously downward-projecting keystone in the centre of its seven voussoirs.

REFERENCES

Editorial, 'Saxon churches', *Ecclesiologist*, **3** (1843-4), 138-9. Swallow noted as Anglo-Saxon, 139.

A. SUTTON, 'Churches visited from Grimsby', *A.A.S.R.* **29** (1907-8), 71-90. Swallow, 86-7. Note of very dilapidated condition before restoration.

A. H. THOMPSON, 'Pre-Conquest church-towers in north Lincolnshire', *ibid.* 43-70. Swallow, 69-70. Architectural description; with dimensions, some of which are inaccurate.

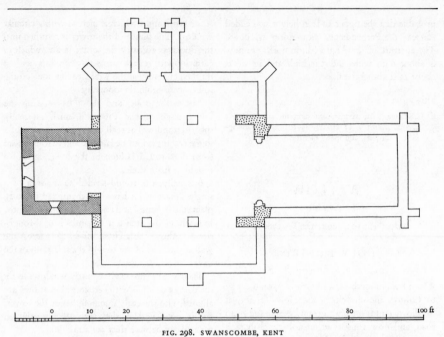

FIG. 298. SWANSCOMBE, KENT
Plan, showing the Anglo-Saxon tower and the Norman nave with side walls pierced by later arcades.

SWANSCOMBE

Kent

Map sheet 171, reference TQ 604740

Figure 591

ST PETER AND ST PAUL

Lower part of tower: period C

At one time Swanscombe must have been a beautiful village, situated as it is in rolling wooded country beside the Thames, about 3 miles west of Gravesend, and within a mile of the Roman Watling Street. The district has, unfortunately, been greatly spoiled by the extensive working of lime; and a rather dull modern part of the village is out of harmony with the pleasant older buildings around the church. In 1902 the church was seriously damaged by lightning and fire, but it is now in very good condition.

The Anglo-Saxon date of the lower part of the tower is fixed with certainty by the double-splayed round-headed window in its south wall.

Nothing now remains of the original tower-arch, but the nave has side walls only 2 ft 1 in. thick, in which Baldwin Brown recorded 'marks of old internally splayed windows...whose general appearance is more Norman than Saxon'. These windows have now been opened out and are clearly not Anglo-Saxon. They open from the nave into the aisles and have small pointed apertures in the outer face of the wall; they are widely splayed internally, with steeply sloping sills, so as to form large pointed recesses, which are outlined in the inner face of the wall with well-dressed ashlar facings. The general effect is of a period contemporary with the main arcades of the nave, transitional between Norman and Early English; and, although the openings are now below the level of the aisle roofs, it is reasonable to believe that the original twelfth-century aisles were narrower and that their roofs joined the nave walls below the sills of these windows.

The tower is built of flints, with dressed stone and tiles for the quoining, which is of a somewhat random and inconsequential character, quite in

602

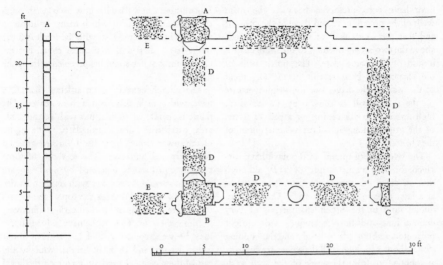

FIG. 299. SWAVESEY, CAMBRIDGESHIRE

The plan shows the surviving quoins A, B, C; and the relation of the small aisleless pre-Conquest church defined by them to the large aisled church of today. The elevations to the left show the extent to which two of the quoins still survive. A, fairly complete north-east quoin of the nave, visible only on the north face because the north wall of the chancel has been rebuilt against its east face; B, south-east quoin of the nave, much rebuilt but visible on both faces; C, two stones of the south-east quoin of the chancel, in clearly defined long-and-short formation; D, deduced position of the destroyed walls of the pre-Conquest chancel; E, deduced positions of the destroyed walls of the pre-Conquest nave.

keeping with Anglo-Saxon traditions. The jambs and head of the double-splayed window are formed mainly of tiles which are laid round the head, both internally and externally, in the curiously Anglo-Saxon fashion that makes no attempt at radial setting but has each side of the head formed of tiles laid at a fairly constant inclination.

DIMENSIONS

The aperture of the window is roughly in the middle of the wall, about 1 ft 4 in. wide and 3 ft tall. It is splayed to become about 3 ft wide and 5 ft tall in each of the faces of the wall.

The tower is 14 ft 6 in. from east to west internally and 15 ft 6 in. from north to south, with walls about 3 ft 3 in. thick.

REFERENCE

F. C. E. Erwood, 'Architectural notes on the church of Sts Peter and Paul at Swanscombe', *Arch. Cant.* **43** (1931), 241–6. Good description, with plan.

SWAVESEY

Cambridgeshire

Map sheet 135, reference TL 362693

ST ANDREW

Eastern quoins of nave, and south wall of chancel: period C

About 8 miles north-west of Cambridge, the village of Swavesey extends for some considerable distance between the Huntingdon Road and the railway from Cambridge to St Ives, with the church in the older part of the village, near the northern end.

The church is a pleasant and spacious building, now consisting of a west tower, an aisled nave with south porch, and a chancel partly flanked on the north by an organ-chamber and on the south by a chapel. From outside the church there is no immediate indication of workmanship earlier than the thirteenth century, but from within it is clear that the eastern quoins of a pre-Conquest nave have been preserved between the main walls of the present nave and those of the chancel; and that the south wall of the present chancel, above the two arches opening to the south chapel, is also of the same date. The north wall of the chancel has been rebuilt in the alignment of the wall of the nave, but the original nature of the south wall is shown by the survival, high up near the oak ceiling, of a pair of stones of the original long-and-short eastern quoin of the chancel.

The two eastern quoins of the nave have survived for their entire height of 23 ft, although that on the south appears to have been patched at a later date in a different style. The northern quoin, now in the organ chamber, is of very definite long-and-short technique, with upright pillar-stones about 3 ft in height and flat bonding stones about 8 in. high. All the stones are cut back at about 11 in. from the angle of the wall so as to form a stop for the plaster covering of the wall-face.

Externally, there may be seen on the eastern face of the eastern gable of the nave an older and more steeply pitched gable of rougher rubble fabric, perhaps the eastern gable of the original nave.

DIMENSIONS

The existing remains give no evidence for defining the length of the pre-Conquest nave, but they serve to fix its internal width as 18 ft, and to define a chancel internally 20 ft long by 15 ft 9 in. wide, with walls 2 ft 6 in. thick and 22 ft 9 in. high.

SYSTON
Lincolnshire

Map sheet 113, reference SK 930409

Figure 592

ST MARY
Probably post-Conquest

The church of St Mary at Syston used to stand in a quiet position within a wide bend in the main road, about 3 miles north of Grantham, on the way to Lincoln; but a new road has now been cut through the pleasant open fields which formerly adjoined the churchyard on the east, with the result that the traffic has a short and convenient route, but the church must suffer some inconvenience from the noise.

The church consists of an aisleless chancel, a nave with north aisle, and a west tower. The fabric is mainly of rubble, but with considerable areas patched in ashlar, particularly at the angles of the tower, which have also been strengthened with diagonal buttresses. The tower is of three roughly equal stages, separated by simple square string-courses, and provided with modern battlements and finials. Towards the top of the second stage there are signs of blocked earlier windows.

Along the south face of the nave, a base-course may be seen, constructed of large stones about 2 ft in length, and 18 in. in height; while at the east of the nave, and partly hidden by a medieval buttress, there are signs of quoining, formed of large stones laid on their faces, as in the chancel at Repton.

Baldwin Brown (p. 482) referred to the tower as having 'mid-wall work but with advanced details, such as angle shafts on the jambs of the double openings, and coupled mid-wall shafts under the through-stones to N and S'. He added that 'This work looks later than the lower part of the tower and represents only a survival. A similar overlap is in evidence in the chancel arch which has a soffit shaft with a thoroughly Norman volute cap with upright leaves below that carries a soffit roll...rather Late Saxon than Norman in tradition.'

This church presents many problems, for the belfry windows are far from being normal Anglo-Saxon double windows with mid-wall shafts. Instead, each window has a semicircular outer arched head which is supported by a semicircular tympanum made up of two quadrants. These tympana are supported by columns in the middle of the window, and the round heads of the two separate lights of each window are cut in the lower faces of the two quadrants which make up each tympanum. Altogether, the arrangement is much more like the construction of a Norman triforium than like any normal Anglo-Saxon belfry.

Internally, the north arcade is of two bays, of

simple Norman workmanship, cut through a wall that is only 2 ft 6 in. thick. The round-headed chancel-arch has two orders, of which the inner order, bearing the soffit roll referred to by Baldwin Brown, might possibly be early; but the very elaborate outer order facing the nave looks more like the work of modern restorers than of Normans. The round tower-arch of two recessed orders is thoroughly Norman in appearance, but the walls of the tower are only 2 ft 6 in. thick. There is therefore a conflict of evidence between the thin walls, which suggest an Anglo-Saxon fabric, and the elaborate details of the arches and windows, which indicate Norman or later work. The extent to which the original rough fabric has been patched in ashlar may suggest the solution, namely that the church represents a Norman rebuilding of an earlier fabric, whose walls were standing in a semi-ruined condition after the Conquest.

Perhaps the most interesting feature of the church is the head of the south doorway. This consists of a carved lintel which supports a semi-circular tympanum beneath a round-arched head. The arch is ornamented with a simple Norman diaper-pattern, and is outlined by a hood-moulding with billet-ornament. The tympanum, which seems originally to have been monolithic, is covered with the simplest of lozenge-patterns formed by two intersecting systems of lightly incised diagonal lines. The lintel is carved in quite high relief with an arcade of round arches, each of which encloses a standing figure. At some later date a considerable part of the lintel and the tympanum has been cut away, apparently to make way for a pointed doorway, whose outline is clearly to be seen in the repaired surface of the stone-work. The particular interest of these features is the simple and early character of the original part of the lintel. Whereas the restored part has something like cushion capitals and angular bases for its shafts, the original work has the simplest of rectangular capitals and bulbous bases. Moreover, on the left, the upper part of the lintel has been cut away to make room for the lowest voussoir of the arched head. Since the arched head is Norman, of an early type, it seems clear that the lintel is a pre-Norman stone, re-used in its present setting.

DIMENSIONS

The nave is about 33 ft long internally and 15 ft wide, with side walls 2 ft 6 in. thick. The tower is about 10 ft square with walls of the same thickness. The chancel-arch is 5 ft 2 in. wide and 11 ft tall.

REFERENCES

Editorial, 'Syston', *A.A.S.R.* **7** (1863–4), xvi. Note of recent restoration, which included replacement of part of the lintel of the south doorway, where it had been cut away for a pointed door.

E. TROLLOPE, 'Churches visited by the Society', *A.A.S.R.* **9** (1867–8), 1–37. Syston, 21–2. Earliest work dated as Norman. Note of recent restoration in which the chancel was 'rebuilt, but everything replaced as before except for a triplet in the east wall, in place of a Perpendicular window'.

TASBURGH
Norfolk

Map sheet 137, reference TM 201959

ST MARY

Round west tower, and parts of west wall of nave: period C3

Less than a mile west of the Roman road from Norwich to Ipswich the small village of Tasburgh lies within a loop of the River Tas about 8 miles south of Norwich, with its church on high land enclosed by the ditch and rampart of a large earthwork.

The round west tower, wholly built of flints, has no external openings of unmistakably pre-Conquest character; but the three narrow round-headed windows facing north, west, and south at about the level of the roof of the nave are more probably Anglo-Saxon than Norman, since their outer faces are formed wholly without the use of dressed stone. Their jambs are of flint like the rest of the walling and their heads are turned in roughly laid flattish pieces of stone rubble.

A feature of particular interest at this level is an arcade formed by seven tall round-headed recesses which surround the tower, with the western window in the centre of the western recess, and the north and south windows centrally placed in the pilaster-strips next to the most easterly recesses. Above this arcade yet a second arcade of generally similar form has been so placed that its recesses occupy the spaces above the pilasters of the lower arcade while its pilasters are above the lower recesses. The upper arcade, however, is incom-

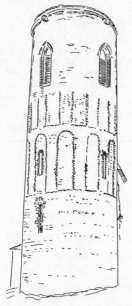

FIG. 300. TASBURGH, NORFOLK

A perspective drawing of the tower, from the south-west; based upon J. C. Buckler's drawing in *Archaeologia*, **23** (1831), pl. II.

plete at the top; as if the heads of its arches had been destroyed in a later medieval rebuilding, perhaps in the provision of the four large pointed openings in the belfry. The character and general effect of these arcades is similar to the sunken arcading on the side walls within the nave at Dunham Magna, in Norfolk; except that there the wall surface is plastered, and some of the pilasters have projecting capitals or imposts; whereas here the wall surface is bare, and the arches spring from the pilasters without any capitals. On the round towers at Haddiscoe Thorpe, also in Norfolk, and at Thorington, in Suffolk, somewhat similar pilaster-strips in flint are to be seen, again formed by recessing the intervening wall surface. The exterior of the tower at Tasburgh may therefore be

said to give a strong impression of Anglo-Saxon workmanship, without providing any feature to fix the matter beyond doubt.

From the churchyard, the north doorway leads into the church down a flight of several steps, and the west wall of the nave is then seen to contain a rather trivial medieval pointed doorway which has later been built into the original tower-arch. The tower itself is entered through the medieval doorway and up a steep flight of steps, within the original tower-arch, which is then seen to be of quite unusual proportions: 4 ft 7 in.

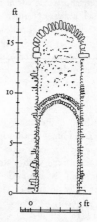

FIG. 301. TASBURGH, NORFOLK

The tower-arch, showing the exceptionally tall proportions of the original opening which is now partially blocked towards the nave by the later pointed arch.

wide and 16 ft 11 in. tall, if measured from the floor of the nave to the crown of the arch. The jambs, which pass square through the wall, are lightly plastered over the rubble structure; the imposts are plain, flat, roughly squared blocks of stone; and the round head of the arch, square in section, is roughly turned in flattish pieces of stone rubble, from which the plaster covering has largely flaked away. The whole impression is in favour of Anglo-Saxon workmanship, so that the tower may with confidence be placed in period C3. Above the tower-arch, with its sill about 20 ft from the floor, a round-headed doorway opens from the tower towards the nave. The details of its construction are, unfortunately, obscured by plaster.

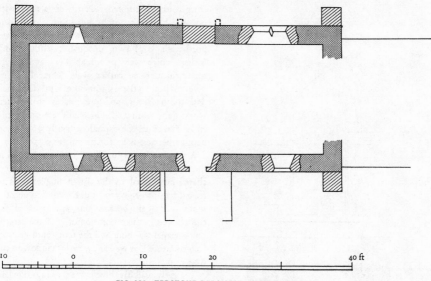

10   0   10   20   40 ft

FIG. 302. TEDSTONE DELAMERE, HEREFORDSHIRE

REFERENCE

J. GAGE, 'Observations on the ecclesiastical round towers of Norfolk and Suffolk'. *Arch.* **23** (1831), 10–16. We do not accept Gage's dating of the towers as Norman or later; but it is interesting to note that he regarded Tasburgh and Haddiscoe Thorpe as the earliest. There is a very good illustration of Tasburgh in plate II, with elevations of some of the details.

TEDSTONE DELAMERE

Herefordshire

Map sheet 130, reference SO 695585

ST JAMES

Nave: possibly Saxo-Norman

This little church is very pleasantly situated in a park, on high land west of the River Teme, about 3 miles north-east of Bromyard, with a fine view down the valley towards the Malvern Hills. The aisleless chancel and its north vestry seem to be of the nineteenth century, but the aisleless nave is Saxo-Norman in character. The two simple, round-headed, single-splayed windows high up in its side walls, towards the west, might be either Norman or late-Saxon, but the triangular-headed, blocked doorway in the middle of the north wall is of distinctly Anglo-Saxon type, even though the hood-moulding over its head has now been cut back flush with the walls. The south doorway which now serves as the entrance to the church is of pointed form, but it is still possible externally to see traces of the original, triangular-headed shape, and it is therefore clear that the church had two of these simple doorways, placed opposite each other, in the centre of its side walls. The doorways, the western windows, and the western quoins are all constructed of grey tufa, a stone which seems to have been much used for facings in this district in late-Saxon and early Norman times. (See Fig. 303, overleaf.)

DIMENSIONS

The nave is 42 ft long internally, and 15 ft 3 in. wide, with side walls 2 ft 6 in. thick and about 15 ft tall. The blocked north doorway is 4 ft 6 in. wide and about 11 ft tall, and the apertures of the windows are about 7 in. by 2 ft 10 in.

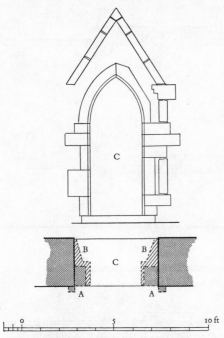

consists of a buttressed west tower; a nave with north aisle, south porch, and south chapel; and an aisleless chancel. The arcade opening to the north aisle is of two, unequal, twelfth-century arches, which were presumably cut at different times through an earlier wall. This, therefore, gives support to the assignment of a pre-Conquest date to the ruder, and presumably still earlier, work of the south wall, which is of ragstone, partly laid in flat courses, but predominantly set in well-defined herring-bone formation (Figs. 304, 305).

A wide arch was cut through this early wall in the fourteenth century, to open to a chantry-chapel established by Sir Brian Stapleton. This chapel fell into ruin after the Dissolution and the south wall again became the outer wall of the church; but in the restoration of 1868 the present south chapel was built and the fourteenth-century arch re-opened, as well as the early window to the west of it.

The early wall has three courses of ragstone laid horizontally at its base, then follow thirteen courses of herring-bone formation, above which the wall is again of horizontally coursed ragstone. The window is single-splayed, with the splay carried through the full thickness of the wall except for a very small external chamfer. Externally the jambs are built of roughly dressed stone; and the round head is cut in the lower face of a re-used stone, probably a grave-slab, on whose outer face it is still possible to see a pattern of four-strand plait-work. Internally the main body of the splayed jambs and round head is plastered, but the salient angles are formed in dressed stone (Fig. 305).

DIMENSIONS

The total surviving length of the early south wall, including 14 ft largely cut away by the fourteenth-century arch, is 27 ft. It is a wall 2 ft 4 in. thick and over 15 ft high; the three horizontally-laid courses occupy 1 ft in height, and the thirteen herring-bone courses occupy 8 ft 10 in.

The outer face of the window is 9 in. wide and 3 ft tall, with its sill 8 ft 3 in. above the floor of the chapel. Internally it is splayed to become 3 ft wide and 5 ft tall.

REFERENCES

J. E. MORRIS, *The North Riding of Yorkshire* (Methuen's Little Guides), 2nd ed. (London, 1920), 374. Morris

FIG. 303. TEDSTONE DELAMERE, HEREFORDSHIRE
Details of the blocked triangular-headed doorway, outlined by strip-work which is now cut back flush with the surface of the wall. A, the broken lines and shaded area projecting from the wall show the probable former projection of the pilaster-strips. The broken lines and shaded area within the doorway indicate the probable original form of the outer face of the doorway, now cut away by the masonry of the pointed medieval doorway; B, masonry of the pointed doorway, which also extends over the part of the area A which lies within the wall; C, later blocking of medieval doorway. Note the stepped profile of the surviving Anglo-Saxon impost.

TERRINGTON

Yorkshire, North Riding

Map sheet 92, reference SE 671707

ALL SAINTS

South wall of nave: possibly period C3

About 7 miles west of Malton, close to the west of the extensive estates of Castle Howard, the interesting church at Terrington is one of the considerable group of early churches which are a feature of the Vale of Pickering. The church now

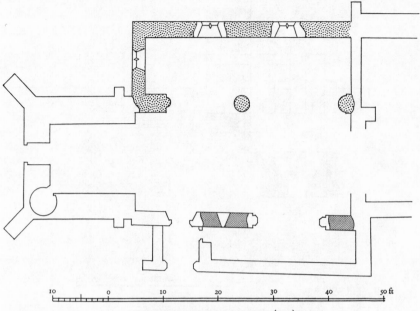

FIG. 304. TERRINGTON, YORKSHIRE (N.R.)

Plan showing the pre-Conquest or Saxo-Norman south wall and the Norman north aisle
which opens to the nave through two unequal arches.

refers to a triangular-headed doorway in the west of the tower as evidence of Anglo-Saxon or early Norman work, but we do not agree with this; it seems to us to be much later.

V.C.H., Yorkshire, North Riding, **2** (London, 1923), 205–6. Plan, 205. South wall dated to eleventh century, probably before the Conquest.

TEY, GREAT
Essex

Map sheet 149, reference TL 891258

ST BARNABAS
Lower part of tower: period C

The fine transeptal church of Great Tey, about 6 miles west of Colchester, is pleasantly placed in a well-kept churchyard, with a fine view over rolling country. Most of the nave was demolished

last century;[1] and the church now consists of a long, aisleless chancel; a large, square, central tower; and one bay of the nave, whose aisles are carried eastward to flank the tower and to form transepts.

Externally, the tower is of four stages. The belfry is Norman, with stone quoins and double windows of recessed Norman type. Both in style and in fabric it differs from the three lower stages, which may therefore with some certainty be accepted as earlier.

By contrast with the mixed stone and flint fabric of the belfry, the three lower stages of the tower are of plain, roughly dressed rubble fabric, with tile quoins; and these three stages are separated from each other by plain string-courses, each formed of two thicknesses of tiles. The uppermost of these stages has, in each face, two simple, round-headed windows, whose jambs and arched heads in the outer face of the wall are formed of

---

[1] Notes in the church record the demolition as having taken place in 1829.

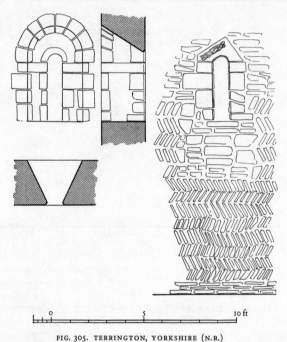

FIG. 305. TERRINGTON, YORKSHIRE (N.R.)

Details of the south wall, showing its thirteen courses of herring-bone masonry and the re-used grave-stone which forms the head of the single-splayed window. Five courses of herring-bone masonry have been interrupted for the insertion of the window in a way which suggests that it is of a later date than the main fabric.

tiles. Each window is recessed, and the inner order, containing the actual aperture, is also of plain square section, but of stone. Neither the inner nor the outer order has any imposts, and their round heads rise directly from the jambs.

Each face of the next stage contains six round-headed blind recesses, set in two groups of three, with a broad area of plain wall between the groups. Within each group, the adjoining recesses are separated only by a narrow pilaster which is formed of a single width of tiles; and the round head of each opening is formed of tiles, which spring from well-defined imposts of stepped pattern, formed by over-sailing tiles. Each face of the lowest stage contains two round-headed windows, with plain stone jambs and tile heads. On the south face, and only on it, a taller opening has been pierced between these windows, possibly a later insertion as a means of access to the roof-space of a former gable over the south transept.

Internally, the tower opens to the nave and the chancel through tall, wide, round-headed arches, which are of a single square order towards the east, but which are recessed to form two square orders on their western faces. The jambs are of the same section; and they are separated from the arches by imposts, which are of quirked and hollow-chamfered section, and are returned as string-courses along the east and west walls. An important feature has survived on the jambs of the eastern arch, where a vertical pilaster-strip of plain square section runs down the wall for a little more than 2 ft from the string-course and springs upward for about 6 in. like the vestige of a strip-work hood-moulding.

The north and south arches opening from the tower to the transepts are Perpendicular; and they are much lower than those to the east and west. There is, therefore, little doubt that the original arrangement was an axial tower without any

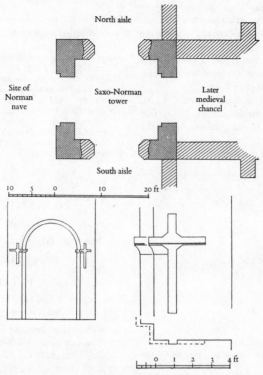

North aisle

Site of
Norman
nave

Saxo-Norman
tower

Later
medieval
chancel

South aisle

10   5   0   10   20 ft

0   1   2   3   4 ft

FIG. 306. GREAT TEY, ESSEX
Plan of the tower and elevation of the eastern arch, showing the vestiges of strip-work round the opening.
The larger scale inset at the right shows the strip-work in more detail.

openings in its side walls. The nave was probably also originally aisleless. A vestry now occupies the single remaining bay of the nave, and in its walls there are two interesting capitals which have survived from the demolished arcade. They are of a simple form which suggests early-Norman workmanship.

We accept the three lower stages of the tower as pre-Norman primarily because the belfry is Norman and the three stages below it are quite different in character; but the vestiges of strip-work round the eastern arch of the tower give strong confirmation to this dating.

DIMENSIONS

The tower is about 18 ft square internally, with walls 4 ft thick. The east and west arches are each about 10 ft wide and 18 ft tall, with their imposts 12 ft 6 in. above the floor. The strip-work round the eastern arch is 5 in. wide and 2½ in. in projection from the face of the wall.

THETFORD
Norfolk
Map sheet 136, reference TL 861831

DEDICATION UNKNOWN
Lower part of walls of chancel: probably period C

The public press contained accounts on 29 August 1957 of the discovery by officers of the Ministry of Works Ancient Monuments Division of the entire east end of an Anglo-Saxon church, with the remains of a stone altar, at a place west of Thetford, during excavations undertaken to locate the ancient town. A late-Saxon earthwork was also reported, of a kind not before known in this country, and near it between 50 and 60 skeletons, some with their heads cut off.

By the kindness of Group-Captain G. M. Knocker we were enabled to see his further excavation of these interesting remains during the summer of 1958. The complete plan of the chancel was established, with the south-east quoin of the

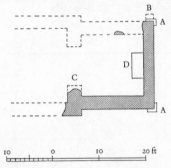

FIG. 307. THETFORD, NORFOLK

Plan of the ruined chapel excavated in 1957 by Group-Captain G. M. Knocker (to whom we are indebted for the information upon which this plan is based). A, large blocks of oolite used as bases for the eastern quoins of the chancel; B, vestiges of a pilaster-strip or buttress on the north face of the north-east quoin; C, flint foundation for the south jamb of the chancel-arch; D, rubble core for an altar, formed of clunch, and standing 1 ft 9 in. high. The south wall of the chancel stands to about 2 ft in height.

nave and the foundation of the south jamb of the chancel-arch. The walls were of mortared chalk-clunch, and the floor of the chancel was of chalk-cobbles. This floor had been largely cut away, and beneath it was dark soil containing middle-Saxon pottery and a *sceatta* bearing the name Wigraed. The eastern quoins each rested on large flat blocks of oolite.

DIMENSIONS

The chancel is about 13 ft 6 in. from east to west, internally, by about 12 ft 9 in., with walls about 2 ft 6 in. thick. The south-east quoin of the nave projects 1 ft 3 in. and thereby indicates a nave about 15 ft wide.

REFERENCES

The Times (29 August 1957), 4. Announcement of the discovery.

Medieval Archaeology, **2** (1958), 188. Brief account of the ruined church and its position within the earthwork. Sceatta dated *c.* 730. Suggestion that the church may be St Martin's 'which, with St Benet's are the only two hitherto unidentified early Thetford churches'. It should be noted on the other hand that T. Martin, *History of Thetford* (London, 1779), refers to the foundations of St John's which are visible close by the Brandon road on the left between the Canons' Barn and Red Castle.

THORINGTON

Suffolk

Map sheet 137, reference TM 424742

Figure 593

ST PETER

Round west tower, and possibly main fabric of nave: period Saxo-Norman

The small aisleless church at Thorington stands in isolation about 2 miles south-west of Blythburgh, on high land south of the River Blyth. The nave has a south vestry and north porch, and the round west tower has Norman belfry windows and an octagonal Tudor brick battlemented parapet.

The round tower is commonly regarded as early Norman, on the evidence of the belfry windows, the tower-arch, and the small, round-headed, ashlar-faced windows which light the stage below the belfry. We believe, however, that the tower should be dated at latest Saxo-Norman, by reason of its remarkable flint-work arcading, like that at Tasburgh and Haddiscoe Thorpe; and by reason also of the way in which the small windows at the level of this arcading appear to have been inserted in it without consideration of their relation to it.

The arcading consists of a series of eleven round-headed recesses, 2 ft 2 in. wide and about 9 ft high, which surround the middle height of the tower and are executed wholly in flints, without any use of dressed stone, in sharp contrast to the dressed-stone facings both of the Norman belfry windows and also of the small windows in the arcading.

There are three of these small windows, one in the panel facing west and one in each of the panels facing north and south. All three windows are of Norman appearance, with ashlar jambs and pseudo-arched heads; and, if they were part of the original composition, they would give strong support for a Norman date for the tower as a whole. But the small windows facing south and west are placed markedly out of centre in their panels, indeed so far from the centre that their ashlar facings impinge on the pilaster at the right of each of the panels. It is difficult to believe that the builder of

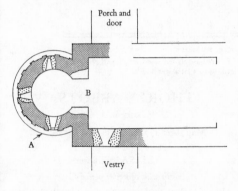

Porch and
door

B

A

Vestry

10   0   10   20 ft

FIG. 308. THORINGTON, SUFFOLK

Plan of the tower and nave, showing the blind arcading on the tower. Note how the Norman windows are erratically placed in relation to the bays of the blind arcade. The tower rests on a wide chamfered plinth, A; and the tower-arch, B, is a modern restoration of pseudo-Norman form.

the arcading would have had so little regard for his work as to have placed these windows so oddly in it. It is equally hard to believe that a mason who had stone available for facing simple openings like these little windows would have formed the decorative panelling in flints rather than in dressed stone. We therefore believe that the original tower is of Anglo-Saxon or Saxo-Norman workmanship, and that the Norman belfry windows and small, round-headed slit-windows are later additions or insertions. The tower-arch, and the pseudo-Norman west window both appear to be of nineteenth-century workmanship.

In the south wall of the nave, partially visible

outside and partially within the vestry, is a blocked early-Norman round-headed window; and in repairs to the church in 1958 two smaller round-headed windows were discovered in the side walls of the nave, high up and further to the east. These have unfortunately been covered again under modern plaster, but from the oral descriptions we have obtained locally, they would appear to have been of earlier character than the surviving Norman window.

DIMENSIONS

The nave is 27 ft 6 in. long internally, and 15 ft wide, with side walls 3 ft thick and about 16 ft high. The tower is 9 ft 9 in. in internal diameter, with walls about 4 ft thick and about 35 ft high, excluding the battlements.

THORNAGE
Norfolk
Map sheet 125, reference TG 049362

ALL SAINTS
Side walls of nave and chancel: period C3

About 3 miles south-west of Holt, the village of Thornage straggles for some way along the road to East Dereham, with its church close beside the road, near the south of the village. Although the church has suffered many alterations, the main substance of the original building has survived in the form of an aisleless nave and chancel, both of the same width and forming a structural unity. To this simple rectangular church there have been added a north porch and a small square west tower, while a blocked south arcade tells of the addition and later removal of a south aisle. The fabric is mainly of uncut flints with a few tiles here and there, while the surviving original north-west quoin is partly of dressed stone and partly of tiles.

The principal evidence of pre-Conquest workmanship is provided by two double-splayed, round-headed windows in the north wall, with vestiges of a third in the south. But the north-west quoin provides further supporting evidence, for its lower section of 8 ft in height is formed of five stones which are laid in well-defined long-

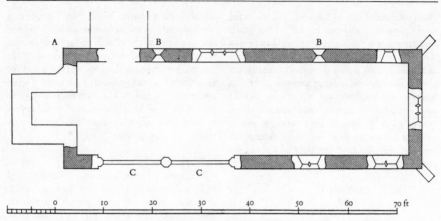

FIG. 309. THORNAGE, NORFOLK

A, original quoin, in long-and-short technique; B, double-splayed windows, much restored;
C, blocked arcade formerly leading to a later south aisle.

and-short technique, while the remainder is of tiles, now heavily patched in later ashlar.

Of the original windows in the north wall, one is in the nave and one in the chancel, thus serving to show that the present simple rectangular plan, without structural distinction between the nave and chancel, is original. Internally, their splays are heavily plastered, while outside they have been much restored, with ashlar stonework at the apertures. The treatment of the wall above the window-heads, and above the blocked window in the south wall of the chancel is, however, characteristically late-Saxon, with a few tiles laid in non-radial fashion to strengthen the flint arching of the heads.

DIMENSIONS

The church is 68 ft long internally and 18 ft 4 in. wide, with side walls 2 ft 9 in. thick and about 22 ft high. The windows have apertures 10 in. wide and 2 ft 6 in. high, splayed to about 3 ft by 5 ft 6 in. in the inner wall, where their sills are about 10 ft 6 in. above the floor.

REFERENCE

R. F. BRERETON, 'Notes on some unrecorded Saxon work', *A.A.S.R.* **27** (1903–4), 397–400. Thornage, 400. Note that the north windows had been opened out 'about four years ago'.

THORPE ABBOTS
Norfolk
Map sheet 137, reference TM 188789

ALL SAINTS
North wall of nave: period C

Although close to the main Bungay road, about 2 miles east of Scole, Thorpe Abbots church has a thoroughly rural setting, surrounded by open fields except for a fine group of farm buildings on the west. The village itself is some distance away to the north; and it appears to be more conveniently served by Brockdish church, which stands between the two villages.

Except for the brick south porch, the church is almost wholly built of flints, with stone dressings. It consists of a circular west tower with a Perpendicular octagonal belfry; an aisleless nave with a Tudor south porch; and an aisleless chancel, which shows clear signs of having been extended eastward about 4½ ft.

The tower stands on a chamfered brick plinth, which is presumably a later repair or improvement. The circular lower stage has no details to fix its date with certainty; and, although it is often said to be Saxo-Norman,[1] we are inclined to

[1] C. J. W. Messent, *The Round Towers to English Parish Churches* (Norwich, 1958), 212. H. M. Cautley, *Norfolk Churches* (Ipswich, 1949), 253.

regard it as part of a considerably later westward extension of a smaller Saxo-Norman church.

The nave has stone quoins at the west, and an ashlar south-east quoin; but this latter is clearly a recent rebuilding. By contrast, the north-east quoin is of plain flint construction without any use of stone; and it is reasonable to assume that this was also the original form of the rebuilt one at the south-east. The doorways in the north wall also give interesting evidence of date; towards the west is a simple Transitional Norman or Early English pointed doorway wholly faced in wrought freestone; while near the centre of the wall is a blocked earlier doorway, whose jambs and round-arched head are wholly formed of undressed flints. The north-east quoin and this round-headed doorway, both of which are formed wholly in flints, seem to us to be good evidence for assigning a late-Saxon or Saxo-Norman date to the part of the north wall in which they stand. The greater part of the north wall of the chancel appears to be of the same period, and the straight vertical joint between it and the later eastward extension probably represents an original plain flint quoin, like that of the nave. It also seems probable to us that the nave was extended westward at the time of building of the pointed Transitional north doorway, and that the lower stage of the west tower is an addition of that date.

DIMENSIONS

The church has been locked on each occasion when we have visited it, and the following dimensions are therefore *external*:

Nave   54 ft (east–west) by 24½ ft (north–south)

Chancel   20½ ft (east–west) by 21¼ ft (north–south)

Tower   20¼ ft in diameter.

The original length of the chancel appears to have been about 16 ft, later extended about 4½ ft.

THORPE-NEAR-HADDISCOE

see

HADDISCOE THORPE

THURLBY

Lincolnshire

Map sheet 123, reference TF 105167

Figure 594

ST FIRMIN

West tower, and parts of walls of nave: period C 3

About 2 miles south of Bourne, beside the main road from Lincoln to Peterborough, the interesting church of St Firmin at Thurlby has long provided material for controversy between architectural historians. No simple explanation has been given of the unusual dedication to St Firmin, bishop of Amiens, who was beheaded in 303 during the persecutions of Diocletian; and the dedication can be used to support either an early date of foundation or else a foundation soon after the Conquest. The situation of the church is also of some interest, with its west end immediately beside the bank of the Carr Dyke, which is now only a narrow ditch, but was in Roman times a wide channel connecting the Nene at Peterborough with the Witham at Lincoln.

The church now consists of a west tower wholly flanked by westward extensions of the aisles, an aisled nave with north and south transepts, and a chancel partly flanked by north and south chapels.

The early part of the church comprises the lower two stages of the tower and the walls of the nave above the arcades. One side of the controversy about the age of these buildings is given by Baldwin Brown (p. 482):

A fresh examination of this example has convinced the writer that the indications of l. and s. work on the quoins, especially the NW quoin of the tower, are not positive enough to be pronounced Saxon. Nor are the proportions of the interior, or the thin walls, 2 ft 4 in., or the plain ancient tower arch under-built with a later one, or even the triangular headed opening to the nave in the E wall of the tower.

But although there may be no single architectural feature that is quite conclusive proof of Anglo-Saxon workmanship, it will be evident even from Baldwin Brown's statement that there is an unusual body of facts each tending to that conclusion. In addition to the features noted by

Baldwin Brown one may note the simple string-courses of square section at the top of the first and second stages of the tower; the simple plinth of square section which may still be seen within the flanking aisles, under the two side walls of the tower; and the through-stone construction of the jambs of the triangular-headed opening above the tower-arch. On the whole, we are inclined to believe that the church has a better claim for inclusion in period C 3 than several others to which Baldwin Brown has given that privilege.

The two lower stages of the unbuttressed west tower are built of roughly coursed stone rubble with somewhat ill-defined long-and-short quoins at the two western angles of the lower stage and at all four angles of the upper. The string-course between the two stages is of perfectly plain square section; and a plain square plinth may be seen beneath the side walls of the tower within the later aisles, where the western quoins of the nave are also to be seen, of side-alternate construction, without any special characteristics which would determine their date. But the side walls of the nave above the Norman north arcade and later Transitional south arcade are only 2 ft 4 in. thick, which would be an unusual feature in Norman times.

The original round-headed tower-arch, of a single square order, is 9 ft 11 in. wide and about 14 ft 6 in. to the crown, with simple, square chamfered imposts. But although its proportions are Norman, it contains within it a Norman arch of two orders, whose presence it is difficult to explain without assigning an Anglo-Saxon or very early Norman date to the original arch.

About 19 ft above the floor, a plain off-set marks the second stage, in which a triangular-headed doorway gives access to the first floor. Both the head and the jambs of the doorway are in the main of through-stones, and the jambs have a distinct feeling of Escomb technique.

DIMENSIONS

The nave is long and narrow, about 48 ft by 16 ft 4 in., internally, with side walls only 2 ft 4 in. thick. The tower is 12 ft 6 in. square internally, with side walls 3 ft 3 in. thick, and east and west walls about 3 ft 8 in. and 3 ft 5 in. respectively. The two stages of the early tower have a combined height of about 30 ft.

REFERENCES

Editorial, 'Thurlby', *A.A.S.R.* 6 (1861), xx.

A. H. THOMPSON, 'Pre-Conquest church-towers in North Lincolnshire', *A.A.S.R.* 29 (1907–8), 43–70. Thurlby classed as pre-Conquest, 44.

THURSLEY

Surrey

Map sheet 169, reference SU 901395

Figures 595, 596

ST MICHAEL

Chancel and parts of nave: period C 3

The little church at Thursley, attractively situated on rolling heath, about 5 miles south-west of Godalming, was not suspected of containing fabric earlier than Norman until 1927, when the vicar noticed the outlines of two blocked windows in the otherwise blank north wall. These were carefully opened out; like others at the neighbouring parish of Witley, they were found to be round-headed, double-splayed windows, of late-Saxon date, with their original oak mid-wall window-boards still in place and in good condition. The church was originally of simple, aisleless, two-cell plan, and the nave was enlarged by the building of a north aisle and a western extension. Otherwise the plan has suffered little change; but many new windows have been inserted, and only the north wall of the chancel has escaped alteration.

In both side walls of the chancel, an off-set about 9 in. wide, at a height of about 10 ft 3 in. above the present floor, probably represents the seating for the floor of an upper chamber; and a rectangular recess in the north wall a little to the west of the east window has been interpreted as a charcoal-oven, possibly for baking wafers.[1]

Externally the north and east walls of the chancel rest on a plain square plinth, which is coated in stucco like the walls themselves. In the surviving

---

[1] *Surrey Arch. C.* 39 (1931), 109.

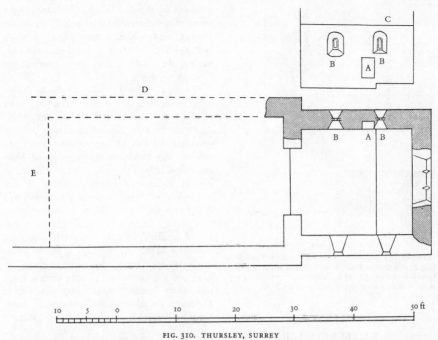

FIG. 310. THURSLEY, SURREY

The pre-Conquest features of the chancel. The broken lines in the plan show the shape of the nave before its enlargement in 1884-5. The elevation inset above the plan shows the interior face of the north wall of the chancel. A, rectangular recess, possibly for a charcoal oven; B, double-splayed windows with wooden frames for glazing; C, off-set in wall, possibly to support an upper floor; D, modern north aisle; E, modern western extension of nave.

original part of the north wall of the nave, above the arch which opens to the north aisle, is a round-headed, single-splayed window, on the evidence of which the nave was assigned a Norman date when this window was discovered last century. It is, however, of the simple type, with monolithic head, which is found both before and after the Conquest; and it alone gives no valid reason for doubting that the nave and chancel are contemporary, although it might be a later insertion in the wall.

DIMENSIONS

The chancel is 18 ft 6 in. long internally, by 17 ft 2 in. wide, with walls 3 ft 2 in. thick and about 15 ft high. The nave seems originally to have been about 39 ft long and is 21 ft 2 in. wide.

The actual apertures of the double-splayed windows are about 1 ft 9 in. tall and of tapering

shape, about 7 in. wide at the base, narrowing to 5 in. at the shoulders. The openings in the masonry are such as to show about 2 in. of the oak mid-wall slab all round the aperture; and the splays widen to yield openings about 2 ft 6 in. wide by 4 ft tall internally, and 2 ft by 3 ft externally. The mid-wall slabs are exactly in the centre of the thickness of the wall. (See Fig. 311 overleaf.)

REFERENCES

P. M. JOHNSTON, 'The church of Witley, and Thursley chapel-of-ease', *Surrey Arch. C.* **18** (1903), 81-95. Plan of Thursley, 94. North aisle and vestry added *c.* 1860; western extension of nave 1884. Church dated Norman.

P. M. JOHNSTON, 'Witley and Thursley churches', *ibid.* **39** (1931), 104-11. Account of discovery of double-splayed windows, plan, elevation, and photographs, 106-7.

V.C.H., Surrey, **3** (London, 1911), 59-61. Plan before 1860 enlargement. Early font compared with those at Tangmere, Walberton and Yapton.

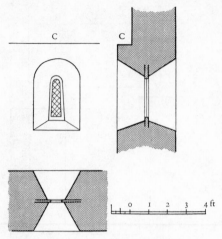

Details of the eastern double-splayed window. The off-set C is clearly shown 8 in. above the head of the window. Note how the aperture of the window narrows, from 7 in. at the base to 5 in. at the springing of the head.

TICHBORNE

Hampshire

Map sheet 168, reference SU 568302

Figure 597

ST ANDREW

Chancel, and possibly nave: Saxo–Norman

This church, pleasantly situated on high ground, overlooking the Itchen valley from the south, about 6 miles east of Winchester, consists of a brick west tower, an aisled nave, and an aisleless chancel. The latter is covered by a thin coat of plaster, but this does not obscure either its fabric of flint rubble or the series of features which serve to fix it in the period of the Saxo–Norman overlap, see Fig. 312.

The Anglo-Saxon side of the picture is presented by two double-splayed round-headed windows in the chancel, and by their having stone mid-wall slabs in which the actual apertures are cut. On the other hand, the Norman element is strongly evidenced by the thick walls, by the carefully dressed ashlar masonry of the outer faces of the windows, by the very broad pilaster-strips in the centre of each face, and by the angle-buttresses or clasping pilasters at each corner, none of which give any impression of Anglo-Saxon masonry, but on the contrary show every evidence of Norman technique.

The double-splayed window in the north face of the tower at Jarrow, almost certainly the work of Aldwine about 1075, has stonework which shows all the usual Anglo-Saxon irregularity of treatment and love of large upright stones. By contrast, the double-splayed windows at Tichborne are faced with carefully cut stones of regular size, in horizontal rectangular shape; and the Anglo-Saxon feeling survives only in the mid-wall slab for the glass, and in the double-splayed plan.

Similarly, although Sompting has many advanced details, the pilaster-strips on its tower can without hesitation be regarded as of the purest Anglo-Saxon technique by virtue of their thin form and the alternation of long upright strips with short bonding stones. By contrast, at Tichborne, the pilaster-strips have almost become Norman buttresses, with stonework directly comparable with that of the buttresses of the early Norman work at Stow in Lincolnshire. This is particularly true of the way in which some of the pilasters and corner-buttresses are built of courses which consist alternately of two headers and one stretcher.

On balance, we have no hesitation in placing the chancel at Tichborne after the Conquest, probably late in the second half of the eleventh century; but nevertheless it shows a survival of some Anglo-Saxon techniques in a building that is otherwise Norman. No original openings have survived to help in the dating of the nave, nor can any details of its construction be seen through the thick coat of plaster, but its walls are of roughly the same thickness as those of the chancel and there is no reason to doubt that the two are contemporary.

DIMENSIONS

The chancel is 16 ft 6 in. long internally, by 12 ft wide, with walls between 3 ft 3 in. and 3 ft 6 in. thick; and the nave is 28 ft by 17 ft 8 in. The two double-splayed windows have apertures 21 in. high by 6 in. wide, and their openings are splayed

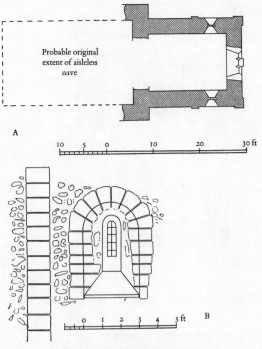

A

B

FIG. 312. TICHBORNE, HAMPSHIRE

Plan and details. A, plan showing the present chancel and the probable extent of the original aisleless nave; B, elevation showing the southern double-splayed window and the pilaster-strip beside it. Note the ashlar construction of both these features. Note also the stone window-frame which reduces the aperture from 3 ft by 1 ft to 1 ft 10 in. by 6 in.

to a height of about 5 ft and a width of about 3 ft in each of the inner and outer walls.

The clasping buttresses at the angles of the chancel are 2 ft in width, and the pilaster-strips in the middle of the north and south faces are each 1 ft 1 in. wide.

REFERENCES

D. H. HAIGH, 'Church notes taken near Winchester', *Trans. Brit. Arch. Ass.*, Winchester, *1845* (London, 1846), 407–14. Tichborne, 411; chancel noted as probably Anglo-Saxon because of double-splayed windows; pilasters noted as intermediate between Anglo-Saxon rib-work and Norman buttresses.

J. H. PARKER, 'Churches in the neighbourhood of Winchester', *Proc. Arch. Inst.*, Winchester, *1845* (London, 1846), 28. Early Norman chancel.

V.C.H., Hampshire and the I.o.W. 3 (London, 1908), 337–8. Chancel dated mid-eleventh century.

A. R. and P. M. GREEN, *Saxon Architecture and Sculpture in Hampshire* (Winchester, 1951), 28–9.

TITCHFIELD

Hampshire

Map sheet 180, reference SU 540057

Figure 598

ST PETER

West porch and west end of nave:
period B

About 8 miles east-south-east of Southampton, beside the road to Portsmouth, but now again restored to comparative seclusion by a by-pass which has been built to carry the main road, the church of St Peter at Titchfield has retained in its nave and west tower some parts of a church which Baldwin Brown, albeit somewhat tentatively, places in his period B on the ground that, while it is characteristically Anglo-Saxon, it

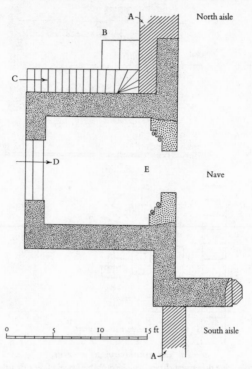

North aisle

B

C

D

E

Nave

0   5   10   15 ft

South aisle

A

FIG. 313. TITCHFIELD, HAMPSHIRE

Plan of the west porch, showing the external stairs to the later medieval upper chamber. A, later medieval west walls of aisles; B, buttress; C, external stairs leading up to north doorway of upper chamber; D, west portal, with two steps down from street to porch; E, Norman west doorway of nave. The whole of the south-west quoin of the original nave is visible. The north-west quoin is enclosed within the later medieval west wall of the north aisle, but a small part of the north side of the original west gable of the nave is visible above the top of the later wall, like a buttress on the north of the later tower (see K in Fig. 314).

possesses none of the special features which would justify its inclusion among the earlier churches of period A, nor yet any of the later characteristics which would require its placing in period C.

The Anglo-Saxon west porch, possibly originally of two storeys, was raised in the twelfth century to form a tower, which rises just higher than the ridge of the nave, and which is now capped by a shingled octagonal spire. The nave has been given aisles which are rather wider than the nave itself, and the medieval chancel shows no trace of its Anglo-Saxon predecessor. Of the original nave little now remains visible except its tall west wall on the south of the porch, with massive side-alternate quoining to separate it from the

later west wall of the aisle. The fabric of the porch and of the early west wall is of fairly small flat rubble, roughly coursed, and faced at the angles with side-alternate quoins of large blocks of Binstead stone. Above the west doorway, a bonding course is provided in the form of Roman tiles, laid three deep and continued round the side walls and across the west of the nave. The *Victoria County History* records that in the course of repairs it was found that this bonding course went right through the thickness of the wall.

Neither the early fabric of rubble nor the massive quoins continue upward on the tower to such a height as to suggest with any certainty that the original porch had a second storey. No

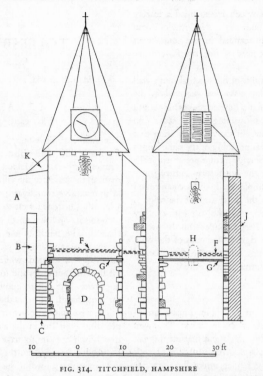

FIG. 314. TITCHFIELD, HAMPSHIRE

West and south elevations of the west tower. The original quoining is shown on the two western angles of the tower and on the south-west angle of the nave. The upper part of the tower, including the two small windows, is a later addition. The round-headed outline H is plainly visible and seems to be an original window, now blocked. A, later medieval west wall of north aisle; B, buttress; C, stairs up to later north doorway; D, original west portal; F, bonding course of Roman tiles; G, modern reinforcing iron band; H, blocked round-headed opening; J, section through later medieval west wall of south aisle; K, original west wall of nave, visible over the later west wall of the north aisle. The stones of the quoins and of the jambs and arch of the west portal are mainly of Binstead stone, of whitish texture; but others are of brown ironstone, and these are hatched in the figure.

original openings remain to settle the matter beyond doubt; although a gap in the tile bonding-course and an area of disturbed walling in the south face of the tower probably mark the former position of a round-headed window, at a height which indicates a porch of one storey rather than two. Access to the present upper chamber has been provided through a north door-way, which is approached by an external stone stair. About the level of the middle of this second storey, the fabric changes from the early walling of rubble to twelfth-century work, in roughly squared stone. The tile bonding course is about 2 ft above the level of the sill of the present north

doorway; and the massive early side-alternate quoining extends only a foot or two above this bonding course.

The outer west doorway is a very simple opening, whose round head of a single square order rests directly on square jambs, without any imposts. The through-stone voussoirs are formed of large blocks of Binstead stone and dark brown ironstone, laid in a rough alternating pattern, with fairly radial joints; although at the springing the lowest stones are curiously tilted, in a manner which is reminiscent of the arches at Brixworth, but less pronounced. The jambs are built of large stones laid upright and without the use of the flat bonding stones which are so usual a feature of Anglo-Saxon doorways. No Anglo-Saxon features have been retained in the inner west doorway, which is now of fine twelfth-century work.

Internally, about 6 ft of the original south wall of the early, aisleless nave has survived as the western respond of the nineteenth-century south arcade. A section of walling of the same thin character also remains at the east, indicating that the original nave was probably of the same length as its present successor. A picture preserved in the church shows that the nineteenth-century south arcade replaced a simple arcade of Norman round arches. No part of the north wall of the original nave has remained, for the fifteenth-century builders of the Perpendicular north arcade carried their arches right to the ends of the wall, without any responds, and supported the lateral thrust by adding buttresses externally.

DIMENSIONS

The tower is about 11 ft 4 in. square internally, with side walls 2 ft 5 in. thick. The west wall is only 2 ft 1 in. thick and that on the east 2 ft 10 in. The nave was originally about 23 ft wide and at least 52 ft long internally, with side walls 2 ft 6 in. thick.

The floor of the tower is now 1 ft below that of the ground outside, and the west doorway is 6 ft wide and 9 ft 8 in. tall, as measured from the ground, or 10 ft 8 in. from the floor.

The tile bonding course is about 14 ft above the ground, and the early fabric continues about 2 ft higher.

REFERENCES

J. H. PARKER, 'Churches in the neighbourhood of Winchester', *Proc. Arch. Inst., Winchester, 1845* (London, 1846), 28. Church noted as Norman.

V.C.H., Hampshire and the I.o.W. 3 (London, 1908), 230–2. Plan, 230. Good architectural description.

A. R. and P. M. GREEN, *Saxon Architecture and Sculpture in Hampshire* (Winchester, 1951), 22–4.

R. M. BUTLER, 'A Roman gateway at Portchester castle', *Ant. J.* 35 (1955), 219–22. Claim that the west arch at Titchfield is re-used Roman material from Portchester Castle.

TOLLESBURY
Essex
Map sheet 162, reference TL 956104

ST MARY
Nave: Saxo-Norman

The village of Tollesbury is a minor sea-port on the north side of the Blackwater Estuary, about 7 miles north-east of Maldon. Beside a crossing of roads in the centre of the village the church stands in an extensive churchyard; a large building with a heavily buttressed west tower, an aisleless nave with south porch and north vestry, and an aisleless chancel. The fabric of the nave and the lower storey of the tower is of yellowish boulder-clay, now much weathered; while brick has been used for the later buttresses and for the upper storey of the tower. The eastern quoins of the nave are of the same rough rubble as the main fabric.

The nave and the lower stage of the tower were probably built late in the eleventh century. The tower-arch appears to have been rebuilt in the fourteenth century, and the brick upper stage of the tower was added in the sixteenth century or soon thereafter. The church was heavily restored by E. P. L. Brock in 1872, when the chancel was rebuilt and the south porch added. The north vestry is dated 1955.

Before the restoration of 1872, the church was in a state of great neglect, the ground had risen 3 ft externally, the walls were covered with decaying cement, and the modern chancel of brick was in bad repair.[1] During the restoration, Brock found that the walls, high in proportion to the width of the church, were constructed of re-used Roman material and were of one thickness of uniform conglomerate, by contrast with the usual Norman method of ashlar facings and rubble infilling. Roman tiles were much in evidence, and also some flue-tiles such as were found at Westhampnett.

Brock's restoration brought to light the interesting tile-built rear-arch of the south doorway and the curious segmental arch of tiles over

[1] E. P. L. Brock, *J.B.A.A.* 32 (1876), 417–19.

the fourteenth-century pointed tower-arch of stone. Brock also discovered three blocked, single-splayed, round-headed windows, high up in the north wall near the eaves. He left all of these blocked, but the western one has subsequently been opened out and glazed. He also found a similar but slightly larger south window which he opened out and glazed.

A fifteenth-century pointed doorway of little merit has been built into the outer face of the early south doorway; but the tile-built jambs and round-arched head of the original opening may still be seen. The head is very irregularly laid, with a wide, wedge-shaped area at the top, very rudely filled in. The fifteenth-century ashlar facing extends through 16 in. of the thickness of the wall, after which the remainder has been opened up to show the original jambs of tile, cut straight through the wall. The arched head of this opening is curiously splayed upward so that the opening in the inner face of the wall is 11 ft 2 in. high by contrast with 10 ft 2 in. for the tile arch of the outer face.

The jambs and heads of the apertures of the early windows are all constructed of the same yellowish boulder-clay rubble as the walls themselves; and the heads are non-radially laid. The splays of the jambs and heads are carried straight through to the outer face of the wall, with no outer splay or rebate for glazing.

Baldwin Brown (p. 456) says that the brick arch of the south doorway is certainly not Anglo-Saxon; but we are nevertheless satisfied that the nave ought, on balance, to be regarded as Saxo-Norman. The positive indications of Anglo-Saxon workmanship are the non-radial setting of the stones in the heads of the windows, and of the tiles in the head of the doorway; the complete absence of dressed stone in the jambs and heads of the windows; the splays of the windows carried straight through to the outer face of the wall; and the rough rubble quoining of the nave.

The side walls of the western tower are aligned with those of the nave and it seems to us likely that the original building included this lower stage of the tower, which was probably then a western narthex or antechamber like that at South Elmham.

DIMENSIONS

The nave is about 41¾ ft long internally by 21½ ft wide, with walls 2 ft 10 in. thick and about 18 ft high. The nave and tower are markedly non-rectangular in plan. The apertures of the northern windows are 9 in. wide and about 3 ft high, with sills about 14 ft above the ground; internally they are splayed to a width of about 3 ft and a height of about 5 ft. The original south doorway is 4 ft 10 in. wide, both externally and internally, and its height is 10 ft 2 in. externally, rising to 11 ft 2 in. internally.

REFERENCES

E. P. L. Brock, 'Early Remains in Tollesbury church, Essex', *J.B.A.A.* **32** (1876), 417–19. Account of discoveries during restoration.

F. Chancellor and H. Laver, 'Tollesbury church', *T. Essex Arch. S.*, n.s., **9** (1904–5), 361–7. Good reasoned account of the age of the building.

R.C.H.M., *Essex, N.E.* (London, 1922), 216–17. Plan and brief architectural description.

TREDINGTON
Warwickshire (formerly Worcestershire)[1]

Map sheet 144, reference SP 259435

ST GREGORY
Side walls of nave, above later arcades: period C1

About 8 miles south-south-east of Stratford-on-Avon the small village of Tredington, on the main road to Woodstock and within half a mile of the Roman Fosse Way, has preserved within its later medieval fabric the side walls of an Anglo-Saxon nave of ample size and unusual interest. From outside, the church appears as a fine Gothic structure consisting of an aisleless chancel, aisled nave, and tall west tower with slender spire. But from within, the late Norman or Transitional arcades opening to the aisles are seen to carry walls

---

[1] This transfer of Tredington and certain other places was effected by the Gloucestershire and Worcestershire to Warwickshire Transfer Order 1931.

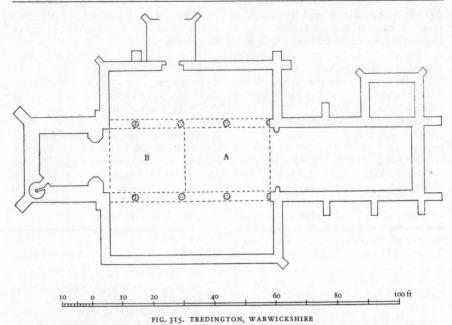

FIG. 315. TREDINGTON, WARWICKSHIRE

Plan showing the present church and the Anglo-Saxon nave whose walls still stand above the Transitional and later arcades of the present nave. The original nave occupied the areas A and B on the plan, and of this total space the western gallery seems to have covered the area B (see Fig. 316). For convenience the nave has been drawn as a rectangle; in fact it is somewhat askew, so that the diagonal from north-west to south-east is about 9 in. longer than the other.

which still contain not only eight windows but also two doorways, all of which belong to an earlier aisleless nave, of Anglo-Saxon date.

The walls themselves are 2 ft 6 in. thick and of flat pieces of rubble, while the remarkable remains of windows and doors preserved in them are the same on both sides of the nave and may be summarized as follows, see Fig. 316:

(a) The heads of three double-splayed, round-headed windows on each side, roughly level with the tops of the hood-moulds of the Transitional arches, at about 20 ft above the floor. These three windows occupy the extent of the two eastern bays of the nave; and, although they have been in large part cut away by the insertion of the later arcades, enough has remained to fix their nature beyond doubt, and to give considerable knowledge of the detail of their construction, as is mentioned below.

(b) A round-headed doorway on each side, close to the west of the third of the windows already mentioned, and with its head at about the same level. If the doorways were about 7 ft in height, their sills would therefore have been about 13 ft above the floor; and this can only mean that they were built to serve as entrances to a gallery over

the west of the nave, access to the doorways being given by wooden stairs or ladders from outside.

(c) A fourth window on each side, a little to the west of the doorway, round-headed and double-splayed like the others; but rather narrower, and placed appreciably higher, so that its sill would have been about the level of the heads of the others. These two windows at the west, must therefore have been built to light the western gallery.

The remains of the eight windows are equally visible on both sides of each of the walls. By contrast, the doorways are visible only within the aisles.

The first enlargement of the original aisleless Anglo-Saxon church seems to have been the building of narrow aisles on either side of the nave towards the close of the twelfth century. The evidence for these aisles is the arcade of three pointed Transitional Norman arches on each side of the nave. It should be noted that these aisles did not extend to the west of the nave, but that a section of the original side wall of the nave was

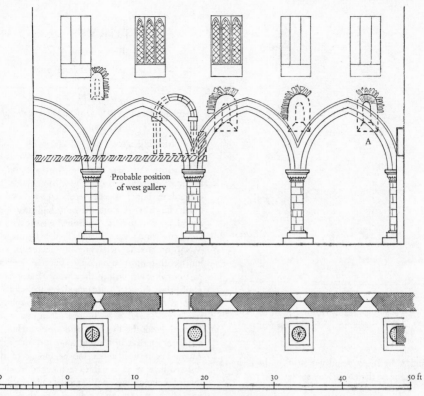

Probable position
of west gallery

A

10   0   10   20   30   40   50 ft

FIG. 316. TREDINGTON, WARWICKSHIRE

An elevation and plans of the north wall of the nave to show the Anglo-Saxon windows and doorways in relation to the present fabric. The full lines show surviving fabric, mostly as it is to be seen on the north wall but partly taken also from better preserved samples on the south. In particular, the detail of the mouldings of the doorway, and the inner face of the window A are based on their southern counterparts. The tracery of the clear-storey windows has for simplicity been shown in only two of the total of five.

left at the west in the region now occupied by the half arch which completes the western part of each arcade. Early in the fourteenth century the west tower was added and the present chancel was built in replacement of the small original chancel of which no trace is now visible. Later in the same century the aisles were widened, and still later they were extended westward to cover the full extent of the nave. It is easy to see how the western column in each arcade is made of two halves, with a straight vertical joint separating the

eastern twelfth-century half, which was originally a respond, from the western half which was added towards the close of the fourteenth century when the solid wall which it replaced was cut away. It is not now possible to say why the aisles were originally stopped short and were later extended, but it may be that this was associated with a retention for some time of some part of the western gallery of the Anglo-Saxon church.

It is recorded[1] that the parish was given to Worcester by Eanberht and his brothers Uhtred

---

[1] *A.A.S.R.* **24** (1898), xxviii. W. de G. Birch, *Cart. Sax.* no. 183.

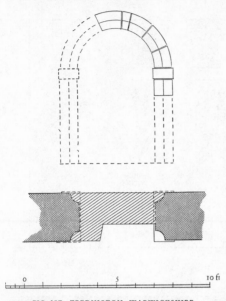

FIG. 317. TREDINGTON, WARWICKSHIRE

Details of the southern high doorway, showing the hollow moulding of its jambs and arch and the plain square shape of the imposts.

and Aldred in 757 and was held by the Bishop at the time of the Domesday survey.

DIMENSIONS

The nave is 54 ft long internally by 21 ft 3 in. wide, with walls 2 ft 6 in. thick and over 30 ft high. The original height of the walls is difficult to fix with certainty but the upper windows at the west show that the walls cannot have been less than about 26 ft in height.

REFERENCES

L. SHEPPARD, 'Tredington', A.A.S.R. 24 (1898), xxviii–xxxii. Historical and architectural description written before the discovery of the early fabric. Note on p. xxxii that, since the paper had been written, parts of the walls and windows of the Anglo-Saxon church had been discovered over the Norman arches.

V.C.H., Worcestershire, 3 (London, 1913), 547–9. Good architectural description and plan.

W. H. KNOWLES, 'Tredington church', T. Bristol Glos. A.S. 55 (1933), 39–40. Brief notice.

TURVEY

Bedfordshire

Map sheet 146, reference SP 940525

ALL SAINTS

South wall, and possibly north and west walls, of nave: period C3

This charming stone-built village, with a fine bridge over the River Ouse, about 7 miles west of Bedford on the main road to Northampton, is fortunate in having its church set back beside the grounds of Turvey House, separated by a loop of quiet village street from the busy highway. The church now comprises a buttressed west tower, an aisled nave, and a chancel partly flanked by chapels. Much of the fabric represents medieval and nineteenth-century rebuilding; but the western part of the south wall of the nave is clearly fixed as of pre-Conquest construction by the survival in it of the round heads of two double-splayed windows. These are to be seen close beside the pointed heads of the first and third arches of the Early English arcade that was cut through the Anglo-Saxon wall about the beginning of the thirteenth century. The third arch of the arcade is carried at the east by a heavy pier of solid masonry instead of an octagonal column like those that support the other arches; and this pier of masonry probably represents the eastern end of the original nave.

The north wall does not show any survivals of early windows, but it has the same arrangement of a solid pier of masonry at the east of the third arch, while both walls are of roughly the same thickness, between 2 ft 6 in. and 2 ft 9 in. It is therefore not unreasonable to accept both walls as part of the original pre-Conquest nave.

The west wall, now containing a medieval tower-arch and a three-light pointed window above, has to the north of the window the jambs of an apparently earlier blocked doorway. Above the window, the steeply pitched lines of an earlier gabled roof may be seen, suggesting that the west wall is probably contemporary with the two side walls, dating perhaps from the middle of the eleventh century.

DIMENSIONS

The original nave seems to have been about 38 ft long internally and 21 ft 3 in. wide, with side walls a little less than 2 ft 9 in. thick.

WAITHE

Lincolnshire

Map sheet 105, reference TA 284006

Figure 599

ST MARTIN

Axial tower: period C3

The tiny village of Waithe, about 6 miles south of Grimsby on the main road to Louth, now consists only of a few cottages beside the church of St Martin. Baldwin Brown records that the church was rebuilt in 1869, but the Lincolnshire Architectural Society's Report for 1861 describes in glowing terms how the church had recently been restored by Mr Fowler and the cost defrayed by Mr G. H. Haigh, thus serving 'as an example to the district around of what may be done in favour of a most dilapidated fabric when generosity, combined with taste and skill, unite to effect so good a work'.[1] It is perhaps unfair to criticize the complete destruction of the original nave and chancel without a full knowledge of how dilapidated the fabric really was before Mr Fowler's restoration in 1861, but one could wish that accurate records had been kept of the fabric that was swept away and replaced by the present apsidal chancel and aisled nave. All that remains of the original church is the axial tower, now provided with a south porch in the form of a pseudo-transept.

Externally, this unbuttressed tower is roughly square in plan, of two unequal stages, separated from each other and from the plain later parapet by projecting square string-courses. An unusual feature is that the fabric is of well-squared stones of fairly uniform size, almost like Norman ashlar, and with quoins and jambs of similar stones

bonded into the ordinary courses of the wall. This unusual form of fabric appears, however, to be the result of the nineteenth-century restoration, for a description of the tower in 1844, when its pre-Conquest character was first observed, records that the masonry was then of very rude ragstone, with large stone quoins.[2]

The lower stage, occupying about two-thirds of the total height, has no external openings, but the belfry stage has a double window in each of its four faces. All four windows have plain cylindrical mid-wall shafts, which rest on the square string-course as a sill, without any separate base, but with cushion capitals of Norman form. The rectangular through-stone slabs and imposts project slightly from the wall face, and carry the round window-heads, each of which is formed from a single stone, shaped to a semicircle below and above. The jambs are of plain square section, and of ashlar construction like the quoins, but the drawing made in 1844 shows the jambs of large stones and the walling of small, flattish rubble.

All constructional detail inside the church is hidden beneath plaster, and the arches of the tower now have no imposts to separate their square vertical jambs from their round heads of simple square section.

DIMENSIONS

The nave measures 26 ft by 15 ft 6 in. internally, with arcades cut through side walls which are only 2 ft 6 in. thick. The tower is about 10 ft 3 in. square, with walls 3 ft 9 in. thick. The tower-arches are 8 ft high to the crown and 8 ft 9 in. wide.

REFERENCES

Editorial, 'Saxon Churches', *Ecclesiologist*, **3** (1843–4), 138–9. The church was noted as pre-Conquest, and briefly described. Picture of belfry window facing p. 139.

Editorial, 'St Martin's, Waithe', *A.A.S.R.* **6** (1861), xxxv. Note of drastic restoration under the direction of Fowler.

A. H. THOMPSON, 'The pre-Conquest church-towers in north Lincolnshire', *A.A.S.R.* **29** (1907–8), 43–70. Waithe, 54 and 70. The ashlar masonry used as an argument in favour of a Norman date or of the adoption of Norman usage before the Conquest.

---

[1] *A.A.S.R.* **6** (1861), xxxv.
[2] *Ecclesiologist*, **3** (1843–4), 139. The drawing which

accompanies the text clearly shows the rubble fabric and the large stones of the jambs of the belfry window.

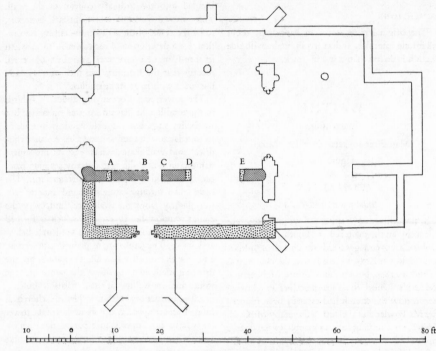

FIG. 318. WALKERN, HERTFORDSHIRE
The full lines in the plan show the two Norman arches AC and DE opening from the nave into the Norman south aisle. But the impost at C is of pre-Norman character, and Fig. 319 shows how we deduce that it is the impost, *in situ*, of an otherwise destroyed Anglo-Saxon doorway. The broken lines in the plan above show the resulting reconstruction of the south doorway BC of the aisleless Anglo-Saxon nave.

WALKERN

Hertfordshire

Map sheet 147, reference TL 293266

Figures 600, 601

ST MARY

Side walls of nave: period C

Situated in the heart of the country, about 4 miles north-east of Stevenage, the small Hertfordshire village of Walkern has a church of considerable interest. This now consists of a fourteenth-century west tower, a fifteenth-century two-storeyed south porch with priest's room on the first floor, and an aisled nave and chancel, the latter rather heavily restored towards the end of last century.

Baldwin Brown describes the church as follows (p. 483):

On the strength mainly of the thinness of its walls, 2 ft. 3 in., to which may be added faint reminiscences of Escomb technique in the jambs of its S arcade, the nave of this church, that has later aisles and chapels and W tower and chancel, is given pre-Conquest rank in the Herts Monument *Report*, and this we may accept. The nave measures 37 ft. 6 in. by 20 ft. 6 in. and built into the S face of the S wall near its W end are the remains of an apparently Saxon Rood carved in chalk, consisting of a mutilated figure 4 ft. high, doubtless of Christ, that seems to have worn a moustache, and has the knot of the belt round the loins arranged a good deal like that on the Daglingworth slab of St Peter.

This description presents certain difficulties; for, if the jambs of the south arcade are accepted as Anglo-Saxon on the evidence of 'Escomb technique' in their construction, then the church

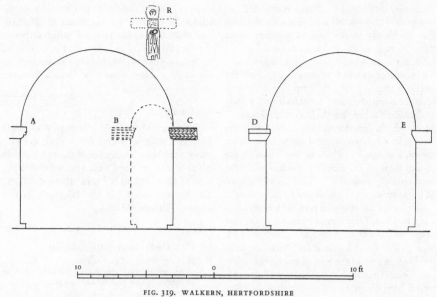

FIG. 319. WALKERN, HERTFORDSHIRE

Elevation of the south face of the south arcade. The elevation shows the four different imposts of the arcade. It also shows the defaced figure which is now oddly placed over the eastern slope of the western arch, but which would again be logically placed if the wall were to be restored so as to contain the doorway BC instead of the arch AC.

should be regarded as having possessed an aisle on the south side before the Conquest. But the Royal Commission certainly do not suggest this possibility, for they refer to the south aisle as having been added early in the twelfth century, and they mention the Rood as being placed over the former south doorway. We describe in more detail below our reasons for believing that the church was originally aisleless, and that the eastern jamb of its south doorway has survived as the eastern jamb of the western arch of the south arcade.

The interior of the church is unfortunately too heavily plastered to allow proper inspection of the south arcade, but this may be seen to be of two round arches, each of a single square order cut straight through the wall. The arcade is carried at the east and west on responds which are backed by considerable sections of the original wall, and a further section of the wall, more than 6 ft in length, forms the massive pier between the two arches. Neither the jambs nor the arches are of through-stones, and the indications of 'Escomb

technique' referred to by Baldwin Brown are indeed mere reminiscences; but there is a thoroughly Anglo-Saxon feature in the impost of the eastern jamb of the western arch. This is a through-stone, about 8 in. in height, returned along the south outer face of the wall and enriched on both faces with four parallel convex mouldings, which are marked with diagonal lines so as to give the effect of four parallel ropes or cables, twisted alternately in opposite directions. This impost alone is of this unusual character; the other impost of this arch being chamfered with a quirked roll moulding at the angle, while the two imposts of the eastern arch have simple chamfers.

The general effect of the arcade, both in detail and in proportions, is Norman rather than Anglo-Saxon, except for this one impost; and it seems to us that the correct interpretation of this rather peculiar arrangement is that this impost and its jamb originally formed the east side of the south doorway of the aisleless pre-Conquest nave and that they were retained in position and incorporated by the Normans into the later arcade

629

which they cut through the Anglo-Saxon wall. The top of the impost is 7 ft 2 in. above the floor, so that this theory would imply a doorway about 8 ft 6 in. high to the crown of its round arched head, not at all out of keeping with Anglo-Saxon forms and proportions. The way in which the impost is returned along the outer face of the wall and not along the inner would also be readily understood if it had been the impost of a doorway. Moreover, the carved figure described by Baldwin Brown in the passage quoted above occupies on the wall a position which is now close to the eastern curve of the arch but which would have been centrally situated a few feet above the head of the south doorway postulated by this theory.

The carved figure is well preserved, except that a section about 1 ft in height across the upper part of the body has been cut back to the surface of the wall, as if to form a seating for a beam or joist, no doubt as part of the roof of the narrow Norman aisle. The head is in high relief, with features well defined, including the moustache referred to by Baldwin Brown. The cutting back of the upper part of the body has entirely removed all trace of arms, so that it is not possible to say with certainty how the figure was portrayed; but the draped lower part of the body suggests the same general treatment as that of the large Rood at Langford. By contrast with the high relief of the head, the lower part of the figure is, however, quite differently treated; for the whole skirted form is shown quite flat, with only lightly incised lines to indicate the folds of the drapery and the knotted belt. In this respect the treatment is quite different from the Daglingworth slab referred to by Baldwin Brown or the Langford Rood mentioned above; but the long garment and the knotted belt should be compared with the similar treatment at Daglingworth and Langford. The two feet are shown below the skirt a few inches apart as was usual in Anglo-Saxon times, and in contrast to the crossed feet usually shown in later medieval representations of the Crucifixion. Above the head there appears to be some trace of incised lettering. That the figure is *in situ* seems to be shown with certainty by the way it has been cut across by the beam which supported the roof of the twelfth-century aisle at its junction with the main south wall of the nave. This callous cutting

away of part of the figure also provides strong independent support for assigning a pre-Norman date to the figure and to the wall which carries it, for it would be hard to believe that at the time of the building of a twelfth-century aisle the builders would have been allowed to treat a Norman sculpture in this fashion.

DIMENSIONS

The nave is 38 ft 4 in. long internally, and 21 ft 5 in. wide, with side walls 2 ft 4 in. thick and now about 30 ft high. The arches of the south arcade are 11 ft 9 in. wide and 13 ft 2 in. high, with the tops of their imposts 7 ft 2 in. above the floor. The Rood is about 4 ft 6 in. tall, with its feet about 12 ft above the floor.

REFERENCES

R.C.H.M., *Hertfordshire* (London, 1910), 224.

V.C.H., *Hertfordshire*, **3** (London, 1912), 155–7. Plan, 156. Good architectural description. Rood noted as probably marking position of south doorway.

WALSHAM, NORTH
Norfolk
Map sheet 126, reference TG 283302

DEDICATION UNKNOWN

Tall square building, probably formerly an axial tower: period C

A curious relic of earlier days has survived at North Walsham in the angle between the west wall of the wide north aisle of St Nicholas's church and the north wall of its ruined west tower. This interesting relic is a tall building about 18 ft square in external plan and set slightly skew to the axis of the present church. It is built mainly of large flints, regularly coursed; and its two western quoins may be seen, that on the north being of flint, tile, and reddish sandstone, while that on the south is of brown carstone.

The west face clearly shows the outline of a wide arch that formerly opened westward but is now blocked. Above this is a rectangular window of uncertain date; and still higher is an inverted V-shaped scar, which indicates the former line of junction of a steeply pitched roof.

The north face is crossed at a height of about 12 ft by a decorative band of brown carstone, below which is a blocked circular window. The lower curve of this window is formed of flints which are coursed with the walling; but the head is arched in long, thin blocks of brown carstone, which are set rather randomly in 'Tredington fashion', and which form part of the decorative band that runs across the face of the wall. The outer face of this window measures 2 ft 6 in. in diameter; and the window can, from its size and

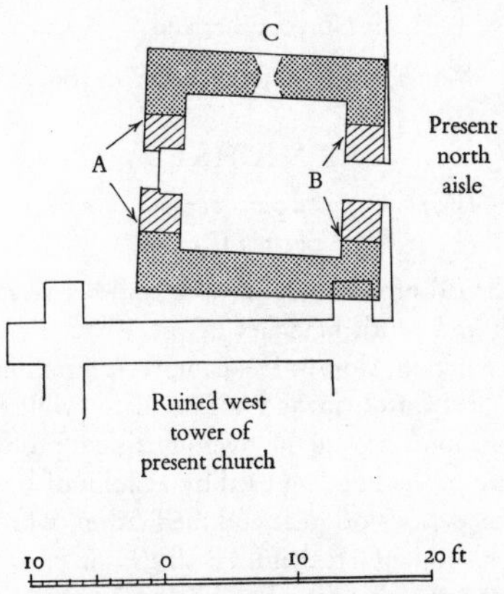

FIG. 320. NORTH WALSHAM, NORFOLK

Plan of the Anglo-Saxon axial tower. A, blocked western arch now containing a window, but presumably the original entry to and from the nave; B, blocked eastern arch now containing a doorway from the north aisle of the present church, but presumably the original chancel-arch; C, blocked circular window, most probably of double-splayed construction.

nature of construction, be assumed with reasonable confidence to be a double-splayed opening of the type so common in Norfolk.

Internally, the building now serves as a storeroom and heating chamber. Its inner walls are plastered, and no other distinctive features are to be seen.

There seems little doubt that this early building was originally an axial tower like that at Dunham Magna, opening westward to its nave through the arch that is now blocked, and with the roof of the nave joining the tower on the line that is now indicated by the scar to which reference has already been made. A pamphlet written by

the late C. H. W. Page and on sale in the church assumes that the surviving building was a west tower and refers to its nave as having run eastward as far as the third buttress of the present north aisle. If our theory of the axial nature of the tower is correct, the building to the east would, of course, have been the chancel.

There is clearly a need for excavation westward of this early tower to see if good evidence can be secured for the existence and size of the original nave.

REFERENCES

J. GUNN, 'Porch of the church of St Nicholas at North Walsham', *Norf. Arch.* 5 (1859), 341–7. Remnant of Anglo-Saxon church, 347.

C. H. W. PAGE, 'Recent work: North Walsham church', *ibid.* 27 (1938–40), 437–55. Remains of square tower dated to middle of eleventh century, 440.

WARBLINGTON
Hampshire
Map sheet 181, reference SU 729054

ST THOMAS OF CANTERBURY
Second storey of central tower (formerly western): period C

Except for the ruins of a medieval castle, the church of St Thomas at Warblington stands in complete isolation, about a mile south-east of Havant, with no trace of the houses which presumably must have been numerous in the thirteenth century to have necessitated the enlargement of the original church by the building of a large nave to the west of the Anglo-Saxon western tower and by the erection soon thereafter of a large new chancel in replacement of the whole of the Anglo-Saxon nave and chancel. The ground storey of the tower was completely swept away, leaving its upper storey supported on a wide Early English archway which serves to connect the medieval nave and chancel.

When seen from outside, the church is curiously divided in two by the early tower, which is only 9 ft square externally and therefore is much narrower from north to south than either the nave or the chancel. Access to its upper storey is, therefore, secured through two narrow troughs between the gabled end-walls of the nave and the chancel. Characteristically late-Saxon doorways open from the tower to north and south, with rubble-built jambs cut straight through the wall, and round heads of a single square order rather ineptly turned in rubble and tiles. These two openings appear to have been designed as doorways, since their jambs are cut straight through the wall; but they are very small, rather less than 2 ft in width and between 4 ft and 5 ft in height.

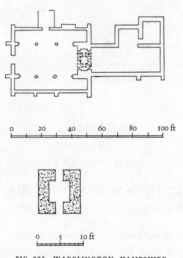

DIMENSIONS

The tower is only 9 ft square externally, with walls 2 ft 3 in. thick.

REFERENCE

V.C.H., *Hampshire and the I.o.W.* **3** (London, 1908), 137-9. Plan, 138.

0   20   40   60   80   100 ft

0   5   10 ft

FIG. 321. WARBLINGTON, HAMPSHIRE
The upper plan shows the relation of the small pre-Conquest tower to the much greater medieval church. The lower plan shows the simple form of the small tower.

Within the nave, a third opening of slightly greater size may be seen above the Early English archway; but it is now so heavily obscured by plaster that no details of its construction are visible.

The third stage of the tower is of the same, rough, rubble construction as the second, with small, narrow, round-headed windows faced in stone, of workmanship that suggests Norman rather than Anglo-Saxon technique; and the fourth stage, with double belfry openings, appears to be of Early English date.

The dedication in honour of St Thomas of Canterbury is clearly much later than the earliest fabric of the church.

WARDEN

Northumberland

Map sheet 77, reference NY 913664

ST MICHAEL

West tower, and parts of walls of nave:
period C3

The broad promontory of high land between the north and south branches of the River Tyne at their junction, close to Hexham, is rich in military remains of Roman and earlier date, while the level ground close to the river junction is probably the site of the building used by St John of Beverley for periods of quiet and meditation, while he was Bishop of Hexham. Bede (*H.E.* v, 2) describes how 'there is a building in a retired situation and enclosed by a sparse wood and a trench about a mile and a half from Hexham and on the opposite side of the River Tyne, with an oratory dedicated to St Michael the Archangel where the man of God used frequently, as occasion offered, particularly in Lent, to reside with a few companions'.

The present church shows nothing which could be ascribed to this early period, but the lower part of the tower and the western part of the nave appear to be of late pre-Conquest date. The main body of the church is largely of the thirteenth century, although it and the belfry stage of the tower were somewhat drastically rebuilt in 1765. The church is now a cruciform building with a west tower, an aisleless nave and chancel, and aisleless transepts.

Externally the tower is unusually plain even judged by Anglo-Saxon standards, for its unbuttressed walls rise unbroken by string-course or off-set, from the ground to the level where the eighteenth-century belfry replaces the earlier work. The fabric of the Anglo-Saxon tower is of roughly squared stone varying in colour from grey to brown and laid in courses averaging from 8 in. to 1 ft in height. The quoins are formed of much larger stones, laid in somewhat unusual fashion, partly in side-alternate technique and partly face-alternate, the two techniques alternating in random fashion up the whole height of the quoins.

On either side of the tower the original west wall of the nave projects about 2 ft 6 in.; but, unlike the tower, this wall stands on a rough plinth which is carried round the north-west quoin and some distance along the north wall. The nave has been widened southward, but the north-west quoin stands intact, of much the same character as those of the tower. It therefore seems reasonable to accept the west wall and part of the north wall as of about the same date as the tower, though perhaps somewhat earlier by reason of the rough stone plinth.

There are no openings in the north wall of the tower below the belfry, nor are any visible externally in the east face. About half-way up the west face a single-splayed round-headed window, about 1 ft 6 in. wide and 4 ft high, served originally to light a first-floor chamber. Its round head is cut in a single stone of irregular shape, roughly resembling a cross-head, and its jambs are built of massive stones, bonding sideways deeply into the wall. The south face has two single-splayed, round-headed windows; both are much smaller than that on the west; and one is placed higher and one lower, so that one lights the original second floor and the other lights the ground floor. The lower window is placed east of centre and has a monolithic head of irregular shape. Like the western window, its jambs are built of stones which are laid flat so as to bond deeply into the wall. The upper window is centrally placed, and has monolithic upright jamb-stones as well as a monolithic head. Each of these south windows is about 2 ft 6 in. tall and about 6 in. in average width, but tapering slightly towards the top.

By contrast with the warm irregular texture of the Anglo-Saxon part of the tower, the battlemented eighteenth-century belfry stage is a dreary structure of too carefully dressed ashlar, with a single wide pseudo-Gothic belfry window in each face.

Internally, the tower-arch forms an interesting feature, which is something of a problem. In proportions it is more Norman than Anglo-Saxon, about 5 ft 6 in. wide and only 8 ft high to the crown of the arch. But its plain square jambs are somewhat splayed, so that the opening is 5 ft 7 in. wide towards the nave and only 5 ft 4 in. towards the tower. Its imposts are moulded stones of apparently Roman origin, and its round arch is built of very rough voussoirs, which serve only to line the two wall-faces of the arch, leaving a large intervening area of the soffit faced only with rubble. Apart from the imposts, there are no through-stones either in the arch or its jambs, and no features that could be described as characteristically Anglo-Saxon; but it is equally hard to accept the crude workmanship of the arch as Norman.

The original upper floors of the tower have vanished, but their position is indicated by joist-holes. In place of three original floors below the belfry, there are now only two, so that the ground floor is lit by the south window and also by the higher window in the west wall. Within the ground-floor chamber there is also visible the original round-headed opening, which is now blocked, but which formerly led from the earlier first floor to the upper level of the nave.

The inner faces of all three windows of the Anglo-Saxon tower have their jambs built of ashlar masonry, with single stones for the inner faces of their round heads, separated by an area of rubble arching from the single stones which form the outer facing of their heads.

The belfry stage is the centre of some controversy. The internal fabric is of a rude character that contrasts sharply with the aggressively neat ashlar of the outer facing; and the window openings, about 3 ft wide and 5 ft high, are cut straight through the wall, with jambs built of five or six courses of roughly squared stones, and heads arched in roughly dressed stones laid in semi-circular or segmental arcs. Hodges, writing in 1893, said that 'economy seems to have stayed the hands of the [eighteenth century] beautifiers, and the wall surfaces are ancient'.[1] Baldwin Brown (p. 484) amplified this by saying 'The fact here attested is of much importance as it seems to present an exception to the almost universal rule in Saxon towers that the belfry openings are double. If Warden could be proved to be early it might show a form of belfry that preceded in time the double openings with the mid-wall work.' Gilbert has recently argued that the interior faces of these windows are not Anglo-Saxon, and he goes so far as to question whether any part of the tower dates from before the Conquest.[2] As will be seen from the description given above, we regard the lower part of the tower as reasonably firmly assured of a place in the late pre-Conquest group; but we agree with Gilbert in doubting whether the inner faces of the belfry windows, although older than the ashlar exteriors, are contemporary with the lower part of the tower. On the possible importance of this matter as bearing upon the question whether Anglo-Saxon belfry windows were ever single, we regard the question as being answered beyond doubt by the belfry at Bardsey, Yorkshire (West Riding), where the south windows of the two upper stages are of the usual double type, with mid-wall shafts supporting through-stone slabs, while the two east windows are single openings with monolithic round heads.[3]

DIMENSIONS

Externally, the tower is very roughly 16 ft square and 45 ft high to the top of the Anglo-Saxon lower stage. Internally it measures 9 ft 11 in. from east to west, by 10 ft 8 in., with walls 2 ft 10 in. thick. The tower-arch is 5 ft 4 in. wide on its west face, splayed to 5 ft 7 in. at the east face, and the jambs are 6 ft high to the top of the imposts. The arch is slightly less than a full semicircle and the full height from the floor to the crown of the arch is 8 ft.

The western walls of the nave project 2 ft 8 in. on either side of the tower, and the original

internal width of the nave appears to have been about 16 ft 6 in.

REFERENCES

C. C. HODGES, 'Pre-Conquest churches of Northumbria', *Reliquary*, n.s., **7** (1893), 65–85. Warden, 65–8. Plan of tower and west wall, 85.

E. GILBERT, 'New views on Warden, Bywell and Heddon-on-the-Wall churches', *Arch. Ael.*, 4th ser., **24** (1946), 157–76. Warden, 157–9.

WAREHAM
Dorset

Map sheet 178, reference SY 924872

Figures 602, 603

LADY ST MARY
Pre-Conquest fabric destroyed 1841–2: possibly period C

The church of Lady St Mary stands close to the north bank of the River Frome, a little to the east of the bridge that carries the main road from Wareham to the Isle of Purbeck. No pre-Conquest fabric now remains, but the following description is reconstructed from pictures and other records, including an account, based on letters now lost, of the deplorable history of the demolition in 1841–2 of what was almost certainly an unusually interesting pre-Conquest nave.[4]

Sir Stephen Glynne, who visited the church in 1825, described it as follows:[5]

The nave is broad and handsome, and is divided from the aisle by several semicircular arches of uncommonly narrow proportions with plain square piers. The whole is cased over and has a very recent appearance, but it seems that it is original Norman work. The clerestory windows are plain Norman with sloped sides. The clerestory is very high, but the upper portion is embattled and does not seem original, but the external appearance of it is unpleasing from the smallness of the windows and the quantity of bare wall. The aisles are particularly narrow and low. The north aisle has small windows of early Decorated character, as also has the south aisle, giving but

---

[1] *Reliquary*, n.s., **7** (1893), 65–8.
[2] *Arch. Ael.*, 4th ser., **24** (1946), 157–9.
[3] There are also many other examples, e.g. Wickham (Berkshire), Wooton Wawen (Warwickshire), and Barnack (Northamptonshire). Skipwith (Yorkshire, East Riding) is possibly a further example.

[4] A. Sturdy, 'Recollections of the contents of letters now lost referring to the rebuilding of the nave of Lady St Mary, Wareham, 1841–42', *P. Dorset N.H.A.S.* **62** (1940), 78–96.
[5] *P. Dorset N.H.A.S.* **44** (1923), 91.

little light from their small size. The chancel is divided from the nave by a semi-circular arch, but is of Decorated work and contains windows of very fine tracery.

The old paintings preserved in the church and reproduced in a descriptive pamphlet on sale there[1] give interior and exterior views of the original structure, conforming closely to Sir Stephen Glynne's description; and the appearance of the simple hood-mouldings over the plain round arches in the interior picture gives strong support to the belief that Glynne's 'Norman work' was really pre-Conquest. The exterior view shows what appears to have been a small, but tall, transept or *porticus* on the north, and it also indicates clearly the tall, bare walls described by Glynne. This exterior view from the north-west is confirmed by the engraving from the north-east in Hutchins's *History of Dorset* (London, 1774); the two taken in conjunction make it clear that the original nave had four clear-storey windows on the north, of which two were to the east and two to the west of the transept or *porticus*. Hutchins's brief description confirms that this was also true of the south side.

A plan of the church drawn in 1840 by Mr T. L. Donaldson, Architect, is preserved by the Rector, to whom we are indebted for permission to view it and to use it for checking the results which we had previously derived from the pictures and descriptions. The plan shows a nave 64 ft long by 25 ft 3 in. wide, with aisles 8 ft 6 in. wide; the outer walls were 2 ft 6 in. thick, and the main walls about 2 ft 9 in. Hutchins described the arcades as being of six arches; with five piers between; Donaldson's plan confirms this, except that it shows a seventh arch cut through on the south at a point where on the north there remained solid walling.

The plan shows the piers of the arcades as of plain rectangular section; and the interior painting preserved in the church shows plain round-headed arches of a single square order, as at Wing in Buckinghamshire. The plan shows the arches 5 ft 4 in. in span, separated by piers 4 ft 4 in. in width. *Antiquarius*, who described the church in a letter dated 3 September 1840,[2] said that the piers were

13½ ft high to the springing; and thus, if the arches were semicircular, they would have been about 16½ ft high to the crown.

The springing of the chancel-arch, as shown in the old painting, was a little lower than the heads of the arcades, perhaps 15 ft above the floor. In a nave 25 ft wide, the painting indicates the arch as about 15 ft wide and 22 ft high. By comparison, Mr Donaldson's plan shows the arch as 15 ft 3 in. wide; and if the springing was at 15 ft this would correspond to a total height of 22½ ft. The old painting clearly shows the head of the chancel-arch outlined by a semicircular hood-mould, apparently of plain square section.

With regard to the clear-storey windows, the old painting of the interior shows that in each of the north and south side walls a tall round-headed window was placed above each of the two easternmost arches of the aisle-arcade, while the wall above the third arch was quite plain. The windows were splayed internally; but the extent of the reveal shown in the picture suggests that the glass was not at the outer face of the wall and that the windows were probably, like those at Great Paxton, double-splayed. The glazed aperture appears to have been about 7 ft in height and perhaps 2 ft wide, with its sill about 20 ft above the floor. The side walls of the nave as seen within the church, appear from the picture to have been about 32 ft high, but the exterior view shows a much greater height of wall above the window-heads, thus giving support to the height of over 40 ft, as mentioned by *Antiquarius*.

The exterior view explains the absence of a window over the third arch from the east, because at this point the walls of the transept, and its gabled roof, covered the northern clear-storey wall to a height above the heads of the line of clear-storey windows. This exterior view shows one of the eastern clear-storey windows, the other being no doubt hidden behind the transept; it also shows two similar windows to the west of the transept. The aisle was, as mentioned by Sir Stephen Glynne, narrow and low; the transept, although tall and gabled, was no wider than the aisle.

[1] L. Howe, *The Churches of Wareham* (Gloucester, undated).

[2] *Dorset County Chronicle*. See Sturdy, *loc. cit.* p. 84.

We thus obtain a picture of a nave, with aisles to north and south, the central compartment of the north aisle (and no doubt of the south also) being raised to form a gabled transept with an outer doorway. All of this is confirmed by Mr Donaldson's plan, which shows the aisles as 8 ft 6 in. wide, with outer walls 2 ft 6 in. thick, by comparison with 2 ft 9 in. for the main walls. It also indicates responds for an arch across each aisle from the outer wall to each of the piers of

these stones were carved by members of a Romano-British Christian community; but there seems little substance in the reason which has been advanced for this view, namely that Cattug or Catocus was the name of a Breton who was one of a deputation sent by the Gaulish Bishops about 430 to visit the churches of this country to oppose the Pelagian heresy then prevalent. The advice which we have been able to collect about these inscriptions leads us to believe that they are much

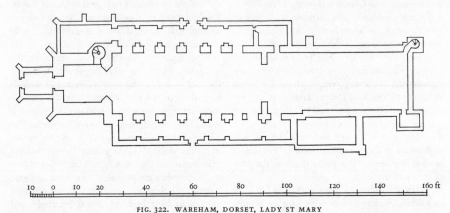

10   0   10   20   40   60   80   100   120   140   160 ft

FIG. 322. WAREHAM, DORSET, LADY ST MARY

This figure is a simplified copy of a plan drawn in 1840 by Thomas L. Donaldson, architect. It should be compared with Fig. 602, which shows a north view of the old church as published by J. Hutchins in 1774.

the main arcade. It is not possible to say whether these arches were original features or whether the 'aisles' were originally a series of independent side-chapels, separated by cross-walls, through which these arches were later cut.

Of this old nave, thus reconstructed in imagination from pictures and records, nothing now remains save some even earlier inscribed stones that were found during its destruction, built into the piers of the south arcade. They were described and illustrated in the second letter from *Antiquarius*.[1] The inscriptions seem to be in Latin; and they are incised in early characters of Celtic form, including names that have been read as Cattug, Gideo, and Gongorie. It has been suggested that

later than the fifth century but nevertheless pre-Conquest.

An important comparison of these inscriptions was made by Birch in 1885 with three crosses in Wales. He showed that the first of the names at Wareham should be read Catgugic, and he directed attention to the very close similarity between the gs on the Wareham stones and the gs on the cross at Carew, Pembrokeshire.[2] He directed attention also to the way in which in each case a very diminutive i follows one of the gs. By comparison with manuscripts, Birch and Romilly Allen were led to date the Welsh crosses and the stones at Wareham to the ninth century. A somewhat similar, but slightly later, conclusion about the

[1] See also *P. Dorset N.H.A.S.* **13** (1892), xxiv and xl. Compare also R. A. S. Macalister, *Corpus Inscriptionum Insularum Celticarum*, **2** (Dublin, 1949), 188 and pl. LXIII.

[2] W. de G. Birch, 'Notes on the inscription of the Carew Cross', *J.B.A.A.* **41** (1885), 405–11. For more

recent illustrations and interpretations of the inscription on the Carew cross see V. E. Nash-Williams, *The Early Christian Monuments of Wales* (Cardiff, 1950), 179–84, and C. A. R. Radford, *Archaeologia Cambrensis* (1949), 253–5.

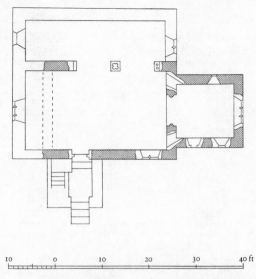

FIG. 323. WAREHAM, DORSET, ST MARTIN

Plan showing the original church and its later enlargements. The broken lines across the nave indicate the probable position of the original west wall.

date was reached in 1908 by Gasquet and Bishop,[1] who suggested that the names on the stones at Wareham are likely to be those of Bretons who came to England early in the tenth century, when the *Chronicle of Nantes* records that King Athelstan gave refuge to a great multitude who had fled from the Danes.[2]

REFERENCES AND DIMENSIONS

These have been given in the text and footnotes.

WAREHAM

Dorset

Map sheet 178, reference SY 923877

ST MARTIN

Main fabric: period C or earlier

Standing on the early ramparts of the town beside North Street, the church of St Martin is a prominent feature of the entry to Wareham by the road from Bournemouth. The church now consists of an aisleless chancel, a nave with north aisle, and a south porch of three storeys.

The architectural history of the church may be summarized as follows.[3] The original, tall, square chancel and rectangular nave were enlarged at the beginning of the thirteenth century by the addition of a north aisle, entered from the nave through an arcade of two Early English arches of semicircular form. In Tudor times the nave and aisle were extended a few feet westward, and finally in 1712 the tall south porch was added. It seems clear that the central pier of the north arcade was originally of four clustered Purbeck marble shafts, to correspond with the pairs of shafts in each respond; for its original capital and discarded base, now preserved in the aisle, are of the same form as those of the responds, but the shafts have been replaced by a solid square pier of fourteenth- or fifteenth-century date.

---

[1] F. A. Gasquet and E. Bishop, *The Bosworth Psalter* (London, 1908), 53 and 54. We are indebted to Dr E. A. Gee for drawing our attention to this and the previous reference.

[2] D. Whitelock, *E.H.D.* (1955), 317.

[3] C. Lynham, 'The church of St Martin, Wareham, Dorset', *Builder*, **74** (12 March 1898), 245.

Plan at jambs   Plan at capitals

0   5   10 ft

FIG. 324. WAREHAM, DORSET, ST MARTIN

Details of the chancel-arch. The mouldings of the arch are somewhat thickly covered with plaster or limewash, and are also rather damaged; but as far as we could see the stones pass through the full thickness of the wall as shown in this diagram.

From outside, the first impression is of unusual height; and this indication of pre-Conquest date is supported by the eastern quoins of the nave and chancel, all of which are of large stones laid with a distinct tendency towards long-and-short technique, which is particularly clearly shown in the north-east quoin of the chancel. The fabric is mainly of coursed rubble, with an admixture of larger, roughly dressed stones; and round the whole of the original structure there runs a double plinth of an upper chamfered order resting on a plain square lower course. In the north wall of the chancel, with its sill about 8 ft above the ground, there has survived a late-Saxon or early-Norman, round-headed, single-splayed window 10 in. wide and 35 in. tall, with monolithic pseudo-arched head, and jambs each formed of two large stones.

The south doorway of the nave has been much mutilated, and now shows no early features; but beside the western respond of the north arcade there may still be seen within the north aisle a small surviving fragment of the square-sectioned hood-moulding of a north doorway, which has otherwise vanished. A little higher up in the same wall may also be seen some vestiges of the outlining frame of a small north window.

The principal internal feature is, however, the chancel-arch, which has survived almost intact despite the cutting of squints through the walls on either side of it. The proportions of the round-headed arch are perhaps Norman; but its detail is distinctly Anglo-Saxon, with a half-round soffit-roll on the arch and jambs, and a hood-moulding of half-round section carried round the head of the arch. It is impossible now to say with certainty whether, as seems probable, this hood-moulding

638

was originally carried down in the form of pilaster-strips beside the jambs; for the wall on both sides has been savagely hacked away, no doubt in connexion with the formation of the squints. On the jambs, however, the soffit-roll is flanked on either side by a small rectangular moulding, 1½ in. square, which is carried down beside the shaft and copied in the plan of the imposts, which therefore show separate projections as capitals for each of these mouldings, as well as the semicircular capital for the soffit-shaft. The imposts are chamfered below, with a small quirk above the chamfer; they are also returned a short distance along the wall-face towards the nave but not towards the chancel. There is a step up into the chancel, and on this step the jambs have a raised square plinth, with separately formed chamfered bases for the soffit-shaft and for each of its flanking square mouldings.

DIMENSIONS

The internal dimensions of the original nave and the present chancel are, respectively, 24 ft 6 in. by 16 ft 6 in., and 12 ft by 11 ft 2 in. The walls are between 1 ft 9 in. and 2 ft in thickness, and their height is about 21 ft in the nave and 15 ft in the chancel. The chancel-arch is 5 ft 6 in. wide, in clear, and about 10 ft tall.

REFERENCES

WILLIAM OF MALMESBURY, *Gesta Pontificium*, ed. N.E.S.A. Hamilton (Rolls Series, 52) (London, 1870), 363–4. Aldhelm builds a church at a place near Wareham.

E. LEVIEN, 'Wareham and its religious houses', *J.B.A.A.* **28** (1872), 154–70 and 244–58.

C. LYNAM, 'The church of St Martin, Wareham, Dorset', *Builder*, **74** (12 March 1898), 245–9. Very valuable account, with excellent plans, elevations, and perspective drawings.

J. G. N. CLIFT, 'Wareham', *J.B.A.A.*, 2nd ser., **14** (1908), 19–44. Historical account.

G. S. WILLIAMS, 'The site of St Aldhelm's church, *juxta Werham*', *P. Dorset N.H.A.S.* **65** (1943), 60–7. The conclusion indicated is that Aldhelm's church was on this site.

WARNFORD
Hampshire

Map sheet 168, reference SU 622227

Figure 604

DEDICATION UNKNOWN
Part of west wall of nave: period uncertain

In the Meon Valley, about 12 miles north of Fareham, and a mile from West Meon, the small village of Warnford is served by a church which stands at some distance, across the river, in the private grounds of Warnford Park. The early village appears to have been beside the church until after the Conquest, when the lands were given to the de Porte family, of whom one, Adam, rebuilt the church between 1171 and 1213. His son, who took the name of St John, built the Norman house, whose great ruined hall, popularly known as King John's Lodge, probably derives its name from the family name of St John.

The church now consists of a massive Norman west tower, an aisleless nave and chancel, and a south porch. The eastern quoins of the tower run right down to the ground, and thus show that it was built against a narrower nave. Within the church there can be seen on the east wall of the tower the marks of the side walls and gabled roof of this earlier nave, against and on whose west wall the Norman east wall must therefore have been built. It thus seems reasonable to deduce that some of the substance of the east wall of the tower represents the west wall of the nave of a pre-Conquest church.

After the Conquest the church seems to have been enlarged in a series of operations, of which the first must have been the addition of the Norman west tower. Next must have followed the rebuilding of the nave by Adam de Porte as recorded on the inscriptions built into its north and south walls over the doorways.[1] Finally, the chancel was

---

[1] The inscription over the south doorway may be translated to read:

'Brethren bless in your prayers the founders both old and young of this temple. Wilfrid founded it, good Adam restored it.'

This is continued over the north doorway thus:

'May the whole race signed with the Cross bless Adam de Porte by whom I was thus restored.'

Adam de Porte held Warnford from 1171 to 1213 and so, although the inscriptions contain no date, they must relate to that period.

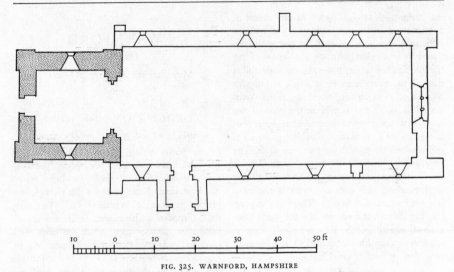

FIG. 325. WARNFORD, HAMPSHIRE

This plan shows the Norman west tower and the later nave and chancel. We explain in the text why we believe that the east wall of the tower incorporates the west wall of an earlier nave.

extended to the same width as the nave; and if this extension was made at an appreciably later date, it must have been done with much re-use of old material, since the details of the chancel are very like those of the nave.

There is no structural evidence of pre-Conquest date other than that already noticed in the west wall of the nave; but a feature of very great interest is a sundial, of a form almost identical with that at the neighbouring pre-Conquest church at Corhampton. This gives further support to the belief that there was a stone church at Warnford before the Conquest, for it is unlikely that such a sundial would be placed elsewhere than in the wall of a stone church. It is at present built into the south wall of Adam de Porte's nave, immediately above the first of his inscribed stones.

There is, unfortunately, no evidence now available to fix at what period before the Conquest the surviving part of the west wall of the early nave was built.

REFERENCES

H. P. WYNDHAM, 'Observations on an ancient building at Warnford', *Arch.* **5** (1779), 357–68. The neighbouring early thirteenth-century hall [quite unjustifiably]

claimed as a church, built by St Wilfrid. Inscription noted.

J. H. PARKER, 'Churches in the neighbourhood of Winchester', *Proc. Arch. Inst., Winchester, 1845* (London, 1846), 27. Church noted as mainly Norman.

B. BELCHER, 'Note on Warnford', *Arch. J.* **2** (1846), 190. Full transcription of the inscribed stones. Noted that no part of the church can reasonably be attributed to the time of St Wilfrid.

Editorial, *Arch. J.* **92** (1935), 402. Note of a visit by members of the Institute to the early thirteenth-century hall and to the church. Note of the text of the inscriptions.

WATERPERRY
Oxfordshire
Map sheet 158, reference SP 629063

ST MARY THE VIRGIN
Chancel-arch: period uncertain

In the small village of Waterperry, about 7 miles east of Oxford, the road ends at the manor, close beside the west bank of the Thame; and a foot-path leads to the church, which, although small, has many interesting features in addition to those described below as of pre-Conquest date.

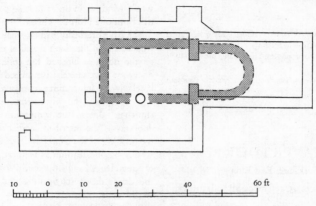

FIG. 326. WATERPERRY, OXFORDSHIRE

Plan of the present church and of the outline of the original church as established by the surviving chancel-arch and by the foundations excavated by the Rev. John Todd.

Until the removal of plaster in 1939, the church appeared to be a straightforward example of a twelfth-century nave with a slightly later south aisle and an aisleless thirteenth-century chancel. But the stripping of the wall above the pointed chancel-arch brought to light the tall, round-headed, upper arch of plain square section which gives Waterperry a good claim to a place in the list of pre-Conquest churches. The arch is of fourteen voussoirs, which are laid with reasonably radial joints, and are not through-stones, because the joints are differently spaced on the two sides of the wall. The imposts bond deeply into the wall and project on the soffit only, where their lower surfaces have a hollow chamfer. The jambs have some appearance of Escomb technique, with alternate stones bonding more deeply into the wall; but the stones are all of about the same height, whereas in the normal Escomb technique the flat bonding stones are appreciably less tall than the intervening vertical slabs.

The discovery of the chancel-arch was made by the Vicar, the Rev. J. Todd, who subsequently established by excavation the former existence of a small apsidal chancel. He also disclosed parts of the foundations of the original small nave, with its west wall about the position of the western pier of the present arcade, its south wall in the line of the arcade, and its north wall some feet south of the present north wall.

DIMENSIONS

In accordance with the plan based on Todd's excavations, the original nave was about 22 ft long internally by about 13 ft wide, and the apsidal chancel was about 12 ft in each direction. The surviving chancel-arch is 7 ft 1 in. wide and about 16 ft high to the crown, in a wall 2 ft 10 in. thick.

FIG. 327. WATERPERRY, OXFORDSHIRE

The chancel-arch as seen from the west, showing the pointed arch inserted in the blocking of the earlier round-headed arch. The lower parts of the jambs are obscured on the left by a reading-desk and on the right by box-pews.

REFERENCES

J. TODD, *Waterperry Church* (Oxford, 1955). A good account of all the interesting features of the church. Plan, p. 6; good photograph of the pre-Conquest arch, pl. III.

V.C.H., *Oxfordshire*, 5 (London, 1957), 306–7. Plan and photograph.

WEAVERTHORPE

Yorkshire, East Riding

Map sheet 93, reference SE 966710

ST ANDREW

West tower, nave, and chancel: early twelfth century, i.e. Norman; but with some surviving Anglo-Saxon traditions

The church of St Andrew has a striking position, on high land north of the village of Weaverthorpe, as though the builders had consciously sought an appropriate spot to display to advantage their tall west tower, and their aisleless nave and square-ended aisleless chancel.

By contrast with the tall, gaunt towers of the late-Saxon period, most Norman towers are short and ornate; but Weaverthorpe provides an exception, in that the tower, and indeed the whole church, can be dated with some certainty to the early part of the twelfth century and yet the tower presents many Anglo-Saxon characteristics of general form, while showing its Norman date in the details of its construction. The tower has all of the Anglo-Saxon tall, gaunt, unbuttressed simplicity; but its fabric is of ashlar, with the quoins in the same courses as the main body of the walling. The belfry windows are double, and have mid-wall shafts; but these shafts, instead of supporting Anglo-Saxon through-stone slabs, support a thin tympanum-wall on twin arches which are recessed beneath an outer arch that encloses the

whole window, in the fashion so common in the triforium of a Norman church.

The nave originally had two side doorways, of which that on the south is still in use, while that on the north is blocked but still visible. Both doorways have semicircular arched heads and flat lintels, with intervening tympana of masonry like many of the Gloucestershire late-Saxon churches. But in the tympanum of the south doorway is the inscribed sundial which records the building of the church by Herbert of Winton whom Bilson identifies as Herbert, Chamberlain of King Henry I and father of St William of York, thus dating the church to the second decade of the twelfth century.[1]

Internally, the Anglo-Saxon tradition is maintained in the very tall tower-arch and in the way this arch is cut straight through the wall. But the later date of Weaverthorpe is borne out by the building of the jambs and arch in ashlar without any evidence of through-stone technique.

The chancel-arch is of much more Norman proportions and is recessed in two square orders, which are matched by square recessed jambs and recessed chamfered imposts, the whole executed in well-dressed ashlar masonry.

The surviving original windows are typically Norman, single-splayed, round-headed openings, about 1 ft 6 in. wide and 6 ft high, with their sills about 9 ft above the floor and the glass set about 3 in. from the outer wall-face.

DIMENSIONS

The tower is about 18 ft square externally and 65 ft high; internally it is 10 ft 9 in. from east to west by 10 ft 11 in., with walls 3 ft 6 in. thick. The nave measures 42 ft 11 in. by 23 ft 2 in. internally, with walls 2 ft 4 in. thick and 21 ft high, while the chancel is 22 ft 10 in. long by 16 ft 11 in. wide, with walls also 2 ft 4 in. thick. It should be noted particularly that the walls are thin; and that thin walls cannot therefore, by themselves, be accepted as satisfactory evidence of pre-Norman date.

[1] J. Bilson, *Arch.* **72** (1922), 51–70.

WENDENS AMBO

Essex

Map sheet 148, reference TL 512363

Figure 605

ST MARY THE VIRGIN

West tower: Saxo-Norman

The small village of Wendens Ambo clusters round Audley End station; and the church is in an angle of the road to Royston, just to the west of the railway.

The church now consists of a west tower, a nave with aisles carried westward to flank the tower, a south porch, and an aisleless chancel. The originally aisleless nave and the lower part of the tower are of late eleventh-century workmanship; the south arcade and narrow south aisle are of the thirteenth century; the north arcade is of the fourteenth century, and the north aisle was rebuilt in the nineteenth century. The fabric of the early part of the church is of flint with some stone rubble and Roman tiles. The quoins of the tower are of small, well-dressed limestone, almost ashlar, laid in side-alternate fashion; the jambs of the west doorway are partly of limestone and partly of clunch, and the round-arched head is of Roman tiles.

The west tower is of two stages, of which the lower is of two storeys, both of the same late-eleventh-century style; while the upper stage, although later in style, is still not later than the twelfth century. Apart from an inserted fifteenth-century window of three lights, the only opening in the ground floor is the fine west doorway. The first floor, still in the earlier part of the tower, has three small lancet windows, one in each of the west, north, and south faces; but these appear to be later insertions in the blocking of earlier windows. The traces of the round-arched heads of the original windows, turned in tiles, are most clearly seen on the south, where, from the size of the arch, it would appear that the original windows were either double-splayed, or else simple belfry windows cut straight through the wall.

The fine west doorway is cut straight through the wall except for an outer facing, or door-stop, of which both jambs and round-arched head are of two square orders. The jambs are of stone, with plain rectangular bases, and chamfered imposts which project on the soffit only. Both orders of the arch are of tiles, of which the lowest few courses are laid horizontally rather than radially. The arch is set back an inch or two behind the line of the jambs, and the semicircular tympanum space is filled by a single stone slab.

Internally, the tower-arch is of Norman proportions; and it is heavily plastered, so that no constructional details are visible. The interior walling of the nave is only lightly lime-washed, and it may be seen to be rough rubble, in bond with the walling of the tower. In the west wall, over the tower-arch, is some indication of an original opening, now blocked, to lead from the nave to the upper floor of the tower.

DIMENSIONS

The nave is 32 ft long internally by $17\frac{1}{4}$ ft wide, with side walls between 2 ft and 2 ft 6 in. in thickness. The tower is 13 ft square internally, with walls about 3 ft 6 in. thick. The rectangular opening of the west doorway is 3 ft 2 in. wide by 6 ft 10 in. high, and the round-headed rear-arch is 3 ft 9 in. wide by 9 ft high.

REFERENCE

R.C.H.M., *Essex (North-West)* (London, 1916), 329–31. Plan, 330.

WENLOCK, MUCH

see

MUCH WENLOCK

WESTHAMPNETT

Sussex

Map sheet 181, reference SU 881061

Figure 606

ST PETER

South wall of chancel: period uncertain

Westhampnett is now almost a suburb of Chichester, about 2 miles north-east from the

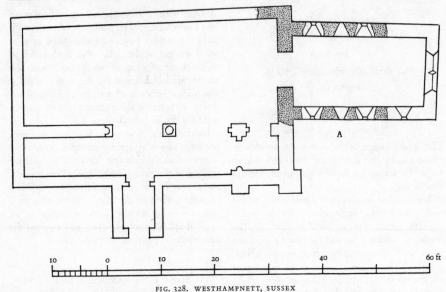

FIG. 328. WESTHAMPNETT, SUSSEX

Plan of the church before the alterations in 1868. The south wall of the chancel still survives,
with its early window A, but the chancel-arch was destroyed.

centre of the city, on the Roman Stane Street, which leads to London. The small church of St Peter is named by Baldwin Brown (p. 456) among a considerable class of south-coast churches which may be reckoned to date before 1100, but which have no clearly defined Anglo-Saxon features such as double-splayed windows, long-and-short quoins, or pilaster-strips. It is not, however, clear whether in reaching this conclusion Baldwin Brown took into account the evidence provided by a description and drawings of the church made before the destruction of its original chancel-arch in 1867.[1] On the basis of that evidence, which is given below, we have no hesitation in accepting part of the south wall of the chancel as of assured pre-Conquest construction, and possibly even of fairly early date in the Anglo-Saxon period. It is relevant to mention that Baldwin Brown (pp. 243 ff.) regarded herring-bone work as a distinctively Norman feature, and that there is much herring-bone work in the south wall at Westhampnett. But, for reasons that are set out

fully under Diddlebury, we regard herring-bone construction as giving no reliable evidence of date, and we accordingly think that the dating of Westhampnett must be based on the evidence of other features.

The church now consists of an aisleless chancel, lengthened eastward, and widened northward by a modern organ-chamber; a nave with a modern north aisle and a south aisle of the thirteenth century; and a low thirteenth-century tower at the east of the south aisle, with a shingled spire.

In the south wall of the chancel it is easy to see the junction between the thirteenth-century eastern extension and the original early walling. The latter is of stone and flint rubble, with a liberal admixture of Roman tiles laid in herring-bone fashion. This wall still contains its original south window, a round-headed, single-splayed opening, which narrows appreciably towards the top. The jambs are formed of tiles and pieces of stone rubble; these are laid right up to the external aperture, which is in the outer face of the wall,

[1] G. M. Hills, *Sussex A.C.* **21** (1869), 33–43.

with no rebate or groove for the fitting of a glass or shutter; and the head is formed of a single square stone cut to a pseudo-arch below, Fig. 606.

In the enlargement of the church in 1867 both this window and its companion on the north (now destroyed by the later addition of the organ-chamber) were discovered beneath the layers of plaster which had hidden them for many years. The chancel-arch, which had also been hidden beneath plaster, was uncovered and was found to be a simple, round-headed opening, of a single square order. The square jambs were of stone, but the arched head was wholly built of

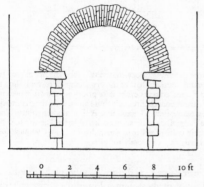

FIG. 329. WESTHAMPNETT, SUSSEX
A drawing of the east face of the chancel-arch before its destruction in 1868, based on the drawing by G. M. Hills.

Roman tiles, with the distinctively Anglo-Saxon feature that the lowest tiles on each side did not lie flat but were tilted up appreciably by a wedge of tiles under their outer edges. Roman tiles were also used liberally in the surrounding walling; all of which, with the arch itself, was torn out to make way for a wider opening to the chancel. But by great good fortune, a careful drawing of the arch is preserved in the article by Hills to which reference has been given.

There is nothing in the existing remains to give a clear indication of the date that should be assigned to this church within the pre-Conquest period. From the liberal use of Roman material in its walls, Hills argued that it was built early in the Anglo-Saxon era, and in this connexion he contrasted the much more sparing use of Roman material in the neighbouring church at Rumbolds-

whyke; which, he suggested, was probably built much later, when such materials were becoming scarcer. The narrow, single-splayed window with sloping jambs would be consistent with, and might be regarded as giving some support to, an early date, since most of the late-Saxon windows in Sussex seem to have been double-splayed.

DIMENSIONS

The original chancel was 13 ft 3 in. wide internally, and about 14 ft long, with walls 2 ft thick and now about 12 ft tall. The chancel-arch was about 6 ft wide and 9 ft tall, in a wall also only about 2 ft thick. The surviving south window has an aperture 2 ft 6 in. tall and 8 in. wide at the bottom, narrowing by about 1 in. towards the top.

REFERENCES

G. M. HILLS, 'The church of West-Hampnett', *Sussex A.C.* **21** (1869), 33–43. Drawing of chancel-arch and plan of church. Detailed description of Roman material found in the walls.

V.C.H., Sussex, **4** (London, 1953), 177–9. Plan, picture of church in 1782; south wall accepted as pre-Conquest; church mentioned in Domesday Book.

WESTMILL
Hertfordshire
Map sheet 148, reference TL 369272

ST MARY
South-east quoin and some parts of walls of nave: period C3

About a mile and a half south of Buntingford, and roughly midway between Royston and Ware, the small village of Westmill stands close beside the Roman road, but separated from it by a small stream and valley. The flint-built church, now comprising a west tower, a nave with north aisle, and a chancel, has been largely rebuilt in the middle ages and heavily restored in the nineteenth century; but the original Anglo-Saxon fabric remains in the south-east quoin of the nave, where five pairs of well-dressed and carefully jointed stones form a well-preserved long-and-short quoin extending up the whole of the height of the wall.

No early windows or doorways have survived

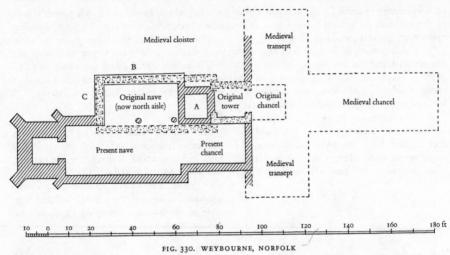

FIG. 330. WEYBOURNE, NORFOLK

Rough plan of the present parish church and of the ruins of the medieval priory, showing how these are related to the original pre-Conquest church and its axial tower. The surviving southern half of the pre-Conquest tower is shown in full lines. The vanished parts of the pre-Conquest church and the ruined parts of the later priory are shown in broken lines. We know of no visible evidence to determine the size of the original chancel, which is shown only diagrammatically on the plan. Its extent might perhaps be determinable by excavation. The building A is a modern vestry. The walls B and C of the present north aisle may incorporate some parts of the walls of the original nave. The full lines of these walls do not indicate their thickness; they are diagrammatic only, in order to show that the post-Conquest and pre-Conquest walls were on the same alignment. (This plan is only approximately to scale.)

to determine how much of the original side walls remain, but the nave measures 42 ft internally by 21 ft, with walls 2 ft 10 in. thick and about 20 ft high.

REFERENCES

R.C.H.M., *Hertfordshire* (London, 1910), 236–7. Nave accepted as substantially pre-Conquest.

V.C.H., *Hertfordshire* (London, 1912), 401–2. Plan accepted as pre-Conquest, but walls may be of thirteenth century. Church heavily restored 1875.

WEYBOURNE

Norfolk

Map sheet 125, reference TG 112430

Figure 607

ALL SAINTS

Axial tower: period C3

The ruined priory of Weybourne and its present parish church form an interesting and somewhat enigmatical group of buildings, about a mile from the sea-shore, and 3 miles west of Sheringham. They provide an unusual example of the survival of parts of a pre-Conquest parish church after its incorporation into and adaptation for use by a twelfth-century priory. During this adaptation, the original chancel was swept away in order to provide a larger successor, which in turn is now a ruin. The nave was enlarged westward and provided with a capacious south aisle, which now forms the greater part of the present parish church; and the only part of the original church which stands boldly forth to show its Anglo-Saxon origin is the tower. This was originally axially placed between nave and chancel, like those at Dunham Magna and Newton-by-Castleacre; but it now stands incongruously at the north-east of the present chancel. It seems likely that the south wall of the original nave stood south of the arcaded wall between the present parish church and its north aisle, while the north wall of that aisle was rebuilt in the nineteenth century, partly on the Anglo-Saxon foundations of the north wall of the original nave.

646

The surviving parts of the tower indicate that the original church was wholly built of uncut flints, without any use of dressed stone; they also provide a wonderful testimony to the quality of the mortar used by the builders; for, in spite of the fall of the northern half of the tower, the remainder stands to full belfry-height, with its flint-built quoins and decorative arcading all in perfect condition. Below the belfry, the walls apparently fell sheer to the ground without off-set or ornament; but the belfry is even now quite elaborate, with a simple, square, string-course of flints to separate it from a plain lower stage. The remains indicate that each face of the belfry had a double window, with twin triangular-headed openings; and that the wall-spaces flanking these windows were ornamented with raised flint strip-work, in the form of vertical shafts, which rise from the string-course and support two blind round arches on each side of the belfry window. The strip-work is also carried over the head of the belfry window in the form of an inverted W. All details of the window have vanished and its openings are blocked, but the outlining strip-work has survived intact.

Above the level of the belfry windows, each face of the tower must originally have had two circular double-splayed windows or sound-holes, of which both survive on the south face and one on each of the faces to east and west.

DIMENSIONS

The tower is about 19 ft square in external plan, and about 55 ft high to the top of the surviving belfry. It appears to have had walls about 3 ft thick. The nave seems to have been about 50 ft long and 20 ft broad internally, with walls also about 3 ft thick.

REFERENCES

J. GUNN, 'Notices of remains of ecclesiastical architecture in Norfolk supposed to be of the Saxon period', *Arch. J.* **6** (1849), 359–63. Picture of belfry, 362.

E. A. FREEMAN, 'Weybourne church, Norfolk', *Gent's Mag.* (July 1860), 66–73.

C. R. MANNING, 'Weybourne church and Priory', *Norf. Arch.* **10** (1888), 262–70. Important account, with plan.

F. H. FAIRWEATHER, 'The Augustinian priory of Weybourne', *ibid.* **24** (1930–2), 201–28. Large plan, detailed description of remains, account of excavations.

WHARRAM-LE-STREET
Yorkshire, East Riding

Map sheet 92, reference SE 863659

Figure 608

ST MARY
West tower, parts of nave, foundations of chancel: period C3 or earlier

The small village of Wharram, about 6 miles south-east of Malton, on the line of the Roman road to Beverley, is pleasantly situated at the foot of the Wolds that bound the Vale of Pickering on the south. The church, which is now somewhat neglected, stands near the cross-roads, beside the village school. Despite the addition of a fourteenth-century north aisle and the rebuilding of the chancel and south wall of the nave in the nineteenth century, the original plan of the church has been preserved, in the form of a square-ended chancel, an oblong nave, and a square west tower. The church was very fully described and illustrated by Bilson, who gave reasons for ascribing its original building to the beginning of the twelfth century.[1] We agree with Bilson's argument for dating the tower-arch and the west doorway in the early part of the twelfth century; but, for reasons set out below, we believe that these archways are later insertions in a main fabric which was built before the Conquest.

The unbuttressed tower, roughly 16 ft square externally, and 51 ft in total height, rises sheer from the ground to a plain, chamfered string-course below the belfry stage, and is built of roughly squared stones laid in courses, with side-alternate quoining of stones which are appreciably larger than those of the walling, but by no means megalithic. The west wall of the nave projects about 2 ft 6 in. on either side of the tower, and is of similar fabric.[2] The south wall of the nave has

---

[1] *Arch.* **73** (1923), 55–72.

[2] Bilson said the tower was bonded into the west wall of the nave. We are less certain of this, and think that it may be a later addition. But this does not affect our main argument.

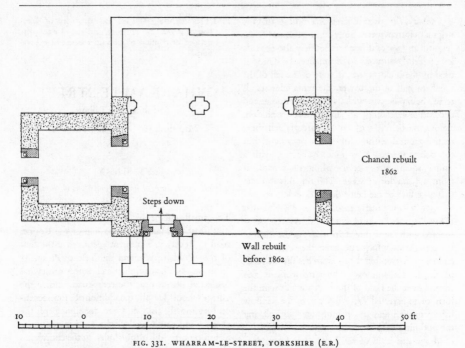

FIG. 331. WHARRAM-LE-STREET, YORKSHIRE (E.R.)
The plan shows how we regard the main fabric of the tower and nave as Anglo-Saxon while we regard the arches
as Saxo-Norman insertions, after the Conquest, probably in the time of Nigel Fossard, c. 1100.

been largely rebuilt, but its original south-west quoin remains; and much of the south doorway, which may be of about the same date as the tower-arch, but is more probably a little later. The north wall has been cut through to form an arcade of two unequal arches opening to the fourteenth-century north aisle; but both its original quoins remain, as well as a section of the wall itself, at the east, between the nave and the aisle.

The tower appears to have been lowered slightly at some period, when its original top was replaced by a simple parapet of four courses, slightly corbelled out from the main face of the belfry. This parapet forms an effective capping to the tower, but it appears to have cut away part of the original composition of the four belfry windows. These are of the style that is found only in Northumbria, with double openings outlined by square-sectioned pilaster-strips, which here, as at St Mary, Bishophill Junior, York, begin on corbels some feet below the sills of the windows.

Here, unfortunately, it is no longer possible to say with certainty how the windows were treated above the level of the heads, for at this point the later parapet begins; and, if there were originally semicircular strip-work hood-mouldings, these have been swept away, leaving the pilasters to end somewhat lamely on splayed imposts a little above those of the windows, see Fig. 334.

The four belfry windows themselves are of the usual late-Saxon form in which each double window consists of two narrow openings separated by a plain cylindrical mid-wall shaft. The shafts have no bases but support hollow-chamfered through-stone slabs. The jambs have similar hollow-chamfered imposts, and are formed of stones which are much larger than the average stones of the walling. The semicircular heads of the individual lights are each cut in a rectangular lintel-stone. As at York, the jambs show a straight joint which is carried down below the present level of the sills to the string-course, as

648

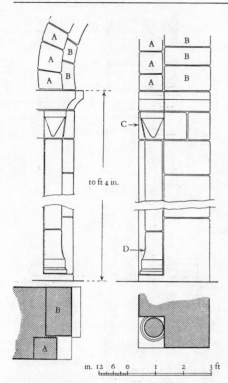

10 ft 4 in.

C→

D→

in. 12 6 0   1   2   3 ft

FIG. 332. WHARRAM-LE-STREET, YORKSHIRE (E.R.)
Details of the tower-arch. These elevations and plans
show the peculiar features of the tower-arch and its jambs.
Note particularly how the voussoirs A of the outer order do
not rest upon the voussoirs B of the inner order, but form
a separate arch. This appears particularly clearly in the
elevation of the soffit, where the straight joint may be
seen running up the wall between the two separate arches.
Note also the curious triangular treatment of the capitals
C and the bell-shaped treatment of the bases D.

if the windows had originally been deeper, or
alternatively had had sloping sills such as are shown
in an early illustration of the windows at York.[1]

Below the belfry stage, the north and east faces
of the tower have no external openings; but the
south and west faces each have a small window
close below the string-course, to light the second
floor of the tower, and a slightly larger window,
lower down, to light the first floor. All four of

these windows are narrow, internally splayed
lights with round heads cut in stone lintels and
with jambs formed of single upright stones. The
lower windows are about 6 in. wide externally,
and about 2 ft tall. Internally, all four are splayed
and have flat heads covered by stone lintels.

The west doorway of the tower, now blocked
and converted into a window, was tall and
narrow, about 2 ft 6 in. in width by nearly 10 ft
in total height. The jambs are slightly inclined so
that the doorway is about 2 in. narrower at the
top than at the bottom; but this indication of early
date is offset by the recessing of the western face,
with nook-shafts in the angles, and by the advanced
nature of the mouldings on the arch itself.[2] The
nook-shafts have tall bell-shaped bases, and simple
capitals in which the cubic upper portion is reduced to the circular shape of the shaft below by
the device of chamfering the faces and the angles
so as to form pendent triangles. The abaci have
deep hollow chamfers below their flat vertical
faces; and while the abacus above each nook-shaft
is logically returned from the opening along the
west face, that over the main jamb is not returned
either along the east or the west face. The arch
itself is of two orders to match the recessed jambs;
but the arrangement is unusual, because the two
orders are set side by side instead of the outer
order resting upon the inner. The inner order is of
plain square section save for a small V-moulding
which runs round the soffit near the west. The
outer order, however, has an advanced moulding
which Bilson regarded, with one exception, as
thoroughly Norman in profile. The moulding
consists of a bold angle-roll, outlined on the
archivolt by a hollow with a quirk on either side.
The only Anglo-Saxon feature is on the soffit,
where the lower face of the arch is set back by
about the radius of the angle-roll; whereas the
Norman practice would have been to set it flush
with the roll, and separated from it only by a quirk.

Internally, the tower is of well-dressed stonework, not plastered; and the tower-arch opening
to the nave is a larger-scale edition of the west
doorway which has already been described. The
stones of the jambs and of the soffit of the arch

[1] T. Rickman, *Styles of Architecture in England*, 5th ed.
(London, 1847), appendix, xxxix.

[2] See Fig. 333. Bilson cited Norman parallels at
Norwich, Lincoln, and Durham.

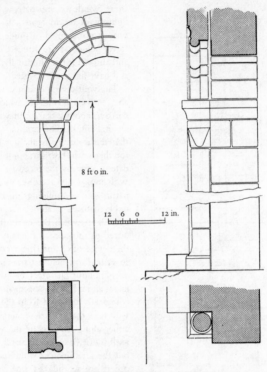

8 ft 0 in.

12 6 0   12 in.

FIG. 333. WHARRAM-LE-STREET, YORKSHIRE (E.R.)

Details of the west doorway of the tower. These elevations and plans show how closely the west doorway resembles the tower-arch in its construction. In particular the outer order again does not rest upon the inner but forms a separate arch. The doorway differs from the tower-arch by having a moulded outer order instead of one of plain square section. Notice particularly the way in which the base of the jamb does not stand upon the double plinth of the tower but stands only on the lower order of that plinth. This arrangement should be contrasted with the west doorway at Kirk Hammerton (Fig. 507). It suggests to us a confirmation of our theory that this west doorway at Wharram-le-Street is an insertion in an earlier wall.

pass through the full thickness of the wall that is supported by the inner order; and, as in the west doorway, the outer order of the arch does not rest on top of the inner order, but is a separate and independent arch standing in front of it. Above the tower-arch, and now visible only within the upper floor of the tower, is a blocked, round-headed doorway which originally opened towards the nave. Its jambs are coursed with the walling; and its round head, of a single square order, is arched with voussoirs which seem to be through-stones and which are of very erratic shape, and non-radial jointing. This doorway is 2 ft wide and 6 ft 4 in. tall.

The east and west walls of the nave have remained, and the original masonry of the north wall has survived at the east, and above the western arch. The south wall has been entirely rebuilt, apparently on the original foundation, but the south doorway was regarded by Bilson as being contemporary with the tower, although it is clearly of more advanced detail than the west doorway or tower-arch. Its outer face is recessed like the west doorway but has lost its nook-shafts. Its proportions are much less tall and narrow than those of the west doorway, and its capitals have angle volutes. The arch is of two orders, of which the inner is square, while the outer is similar to that of the west doorway, but with the addition of a flat roll outside the quirked hollow and without the sunk soffit. The arch has a shallow hood-moulding, which consists of an outer vertical face enriched by a lightly incised chevron ornament, and an inner roll-moulding cut to form billets.

The chancel-arch has been replaced by a pointed arch of two orders but the jambs appear to be earlier. They are recessed towards the nave, with detached nook-shafts which have bases and capitals of distinctly Norman type. The bases are in the form of a hollow above a series of rolls, and the capitals have angle volutes. We are inclined to regard both the chancel-arch and the south door-way as later than the tower-arch and west door-way; and, for reasons set out below, we regard all these arches as insertions in an earlier fabric.

THE DATING OF THE MAIN FABRIC

Bilson's argument for the dating of the church and tower in the early part of the twelfth century depends both on recorded history and also on the special character of the eastern and western arches of the tower. The manor of Wharram was re-corded in Domesday Book as of 12 carucates, lying in waste, and held under Robert of Mortain by Nigel Fossard. This Nigel's son Robert gave to Nostell Priory in Yorkshire a number of churches, including Wharram. Now it was from Nostell that King Alexander of Scotland, son of St Margaret and Malcolm Canmore, brought monks to St Andrews by way of Scone; and it was one of those monks who, shortly before Alexander's death in 1124, became Bishop Robert of St Andrews, one of that cathedral's great builders. Bilson pointed out that the eastern and western arches of St Regulus's chapel at St Andrews not only have mouldings of exactly the same unusual section as those of the arches of the tower at Wharram, but also have the same abnormal arrangement whereby the two orders of the arch are set side by side instead of one over the other.

Since both churches were connected with Nostell and both showed similar and unusual arrangements in their fabric, Bilson argued that masons from Nostell had been employed at both churches. He accordingly dated both churches about the end of the first quarter of the twelfth

century, when Bishop Robert might well have brought to St Andrews a master-mason who had recently built the church at Wharram that had just been given to Nostell.

But, while this argument gives good reason for regarding the arches at Wharram and the similar arches at St Andrews as having been built early in the twelfth century, we believe that a correct interpretation of the argument leads to earlier dates for the main fabric of the two churches. For if the two churches had been built by the same masons, there would surely be other similarities besides the arches. In fact, the two churches are remarkably unlike. Whereas Wharram is built of rough rubble of moderate size, with larger side-alternate quoins, St Regulus's is of ashlar, of very large stones, most carefully coursed, and with its side-alternate quoins forming part of the same courses. Whereas the tower at Wharram is relatively squat, that at St Regulus's is excep-tionally tall; and, while the belfry windows at Wharram are outlined by strip-work in the peculiar Northumbrian fashion, those at St Regu-lus's have no such treatment, but are recessed, and were perhaps originally provided with angle-shafts in the recesses, see Fig. 334.

These dissimilarities indicate to us that the two churches were originally built by different people, with quite different traditions. We accept Bilson's argument as showing that a single master-mason was responsible for the erection of the great arches in the two churches early in the twelfth century, but we think that 'in each case they are insertions in a main fabric that was built earlier. As Bilson himself pointed out, the district round Wharram was still lying waste at the time of the Domesday survey as a result of the Conqueror's devastation in 1069–70. It therefore seems to us that the main fabric of the church at Wharram is a pre-Conquest building, that was taken over in derelict condition by Nigel Fossard or his son Robert, and was brought back into use at the turn of the century. This would account for the insertion in the earlier fabric of the arches in the newer style which the same masons later used at St Regulus's chapel in St Andrews.

At Wharram it is not easy to see clear and direct evidence that the arches are indeed later insertions, since the surroundings of the tower-

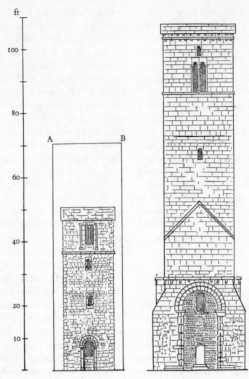

FIG. 334. WHARRAM-LE-STREET, YORKSHIRE (E.R.)

Comparative elevations of the tower at Wharram (left) and the tower of St Regulus's chapel at St Andrews. The drawing shows how the masonry at St Andrews is coursed ashlar throughout, even for the window-facings, whereas that at Wharram is only roughly coursed, with bigger stones for the quoins and for the facings of the windows. The proportions are also interesting: the outline AB is an enlargement of the Wharram tower so as to make its width equal to that of St Regulus's, and it will be noted that the resulting height is only 72 ft by comparison with St Regulus's 108.

arch are plastered. But two important pieces of evidence were recorded by Bilson himself. First, there is the fact that, while the joints of the fabric of the church as a whole are wide, the stones of the two arches are very closely jointed. This is not true of the original windows which have survived in the tower; and this marked difference in masonry argues in favour of the arches having been the work of different masons. Secondly, there is the evidence of the peculiar construction of each of the arches, in that its two orders are set side-by-side rather than one above the other. This side-by-side construction seems to us to be a trick which would lend itself particularly conveniently to the insertion of an arch into an existing wall, whereas it has no corresponding arguments in its favour if the arch and the wall are being built at the same time. A third indication that the west doorway is a later insertion is to be seen by careful inspection of the plinth of the tower, and by comparison of it with the treatment of the supports for the bases of the nookshafts. The tower stands on a double plinth which consists of two plain square orders of roughly dressed stones, each projecting about 1 ft from the fabric above it. The lower of these orders has been left intact at the time of the construction of the doorway, for which it now serves as the sill. But the upper order has been cut away flush with the jambs of the recesses that flank the outer face of the doorway; and the plinth which has been provided for the bases of the nook-shafts in these recesses is of smaller projection and is chamfered on its upper edges. The contrast between the chamfered plinth for the nook-shafts and the plain square plinth for the tower is sufficiently marked to suggest strongly that they are works of different times and of different craftsmen, see Fig. 333.

At St Regulus's there is clear evidence that the arches are later insertions in a pre-existing fabric, for the head of the western arch cuts away an elaborate ornamental string-course; and the jambs of both arches are very badly bonded into the adjoining wall. To us it is inconceivable that the masons who built the carefully-coursed ashlar fabric of the main building could have been so careless in the construction of the jambs of these great arches, where good bonding into the main fabric was clearly so important.

We therefore have no doubt in assigning the main fabric of both buildings to a date earlier than that hitherto accepted on the basis of Bilson's arguments.

DIMENSIONS

The tower measures 11 ft 5 in. from east to west internally, by 10 ft 7 in., with walls 2 ft 6 in. thick and now about 51 ft high. The nave is 29 ft by 15 ft 10 in., with walls originally 2 ft 7 in. thick and now 17 ft 2 in. high, on the north. The chancel appears to have been 16 ft in length by 12 ft in width. The west doorway is 2 ft 6 in. wide by 9 ft 6 in. high; the tower-arch is 6 ft 1 in. wide by 13 ft 10 in. high; and the chancel-arch is 7 ft 1 in. wide by 11 ft 4 in. high.

REFERENCES

Editorial, 'Wharram-le-Street', A.A.S.R. 6 (1861), cxvi. Tower noted as Anglo-Saxon. Chancel recently rebuilt by J. B. Atkinson at the cost of Lord Middleton, and nave restored.

W. G. COLLINGWOOD, 'Anglian and Anglo-Danish sculpture', Yorks. Arch. J. 23 (1915), 129–299. Sundial built into tower about 15 ft from ground, 3 ft long by 1 ft 3 in. broad, but scarcely visible from below, 260.

J. BILSON, 'Wharram-le-Street church, Yorkshire, and St Rule's church, St Andrews, Arch. 73 (1923), 55–72. Detailed description and history, with plans, many pictures, and architectural drawings. A most valuable survey.

A. R. GREEN, 'Anglo-Saxon sundials', Ant. J. 8 (1928), 489–516. Sundial described, 504.

WHEATHAMPSTEAD
Hertfordshire
Map sheets 147 and 160, reference
TL 176140

ST HELENA
South and west walls of south transept: possibly Saxo-Norman

The cruciform church at Wheathampstead, about 5 miles south of St Albans, is attractively situated on the south bank of the River Lea, about 4 miles west of Welwyn Garden City. It is built mainly of cut flints, with some tiles; and its facings are of dressed stone. It now consists of a central tower, with lead-covered spire, an aisleless chancel with north vestry, and an aisled nave with north and south porches.

The south and west walls of the south transept are marked as of different date from the remainder of the church by being of less carefully cut flints and by a complete absence of tile. In the south wall, under a much later four-light window, is a blocked, round-headed opening of very primitive character. The arched head of this opening is turned in very rough stone, of friable character, quite unwrought, and laid with no attention to radial setting of the voussoirs. A later, chamfered plinth, which surrounds the whole church, has been carried across this blocked doorway; and the ground has risen appreciably, so that the head of the doorway is now only 5 ft 3 in. above the ground, although it is 7 ft 2 in. above the floor of the transept.

In the interior, the rear-arch is somewhat elliptical in shape, taller than a semi-circle; and it is 3 ft 6 in. wide, by contrast with an external width of 3 ft.

There are no other clear indications of the character of the early building that was incorporated into the south transept; but in the west wall there are indications of a blocked western doorway. The walling is 3 ft thick. The indications of pre-Conquest date are far from conclusive, but the church is recorded here in order that it may be further investigated.

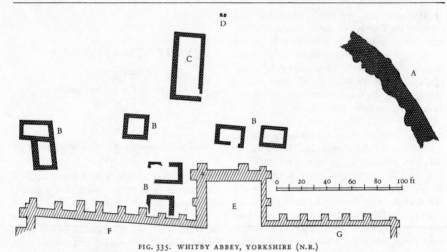

FIG. 335. WHITBY ABBEY, YORKSHIRE (N.R.)

Site plan, showing the early remains in relation to the great medieval abbey. A, foundations, probably of the wall surrounding the early monastery; B, small dwellings forming part of the nuns' quarters; C, larger building; possibly refectory, or school-house; D, bases of Anglo-Saxon crosses; E, F, G, north transept, nave, and chancel of later medieval abbey church.

REFERENCES

V.C.H., Hertfordshire, 2 (London, 1908), 309–12. Note that the church was restored 1865–6 by E. Browning.

R.C.H.M., Hertfordshire (London, 1910), 238–9. No reference to early work in the transept.

WHITBY

Yorkshire, North Riding

Map sheet 86, reference NZ 903112

DEDICATION UNKNOWN

Domestic buildings and wall of seventh-century abbey found by excavation at the north side of the medieval abbey ruins: period A2

The foundation of the abbey at Whitby by St Hilda in the year 657 is described by Bede (*H.E.* III, 24), who associates it with the vow made two years earlier by King Oswy of Northumbria that, if he should be victorious over the heathen King Penda of Mercia, he would give twelve pieces of land for abbeys and would devote his daughter Elfled to the monastic life. After the victory, Elfled was first placed in Hilda's monastery at Hartlepool, but two years later she moved with Hilda to the new monastery on the high land south of the harbour of Whitby, then known as *Streoneshalch*. The new abbey was organized, like many Anglo-Saxon religious establishments, as a double house for men and women, presided over by an Abbess. Bede records how it attained a high reputation for piety, and how many of the clergy were trained there, including St John of Beverley. But the early abbey of Whitby is perhaps best known for the Council which was held there in 663, when St Wilfrid so ably pleaded the cause of the Roman ritual that he carried the day against the supporters of the Celtic ritual under Colman, Bishop of Lindisfarne.[1]

The imposing ruins on the southern heights above Whitby are, of course, those of the post-Conquest abbey; and it was not until the site was excavated in the years 1924–5 that the remains of the seventh-century monastery were found.[2]

---

[1] For the autumn of 663 as the date of the Council of Whitby, see F. M. Stenton, *Anglo-Saxon England*, 2nd ed. (Oxford, 1947), 129.

[2] C. R. Peers and C. A. R. Radford, 'The Anglo-Saxon monastery at Whitby', *Arch.* 89 (1943), 27–88. Also *Whitby Abbey* (London, H.M. Stationery Office, 1952), 4–7.

These excavations exposed a substantial part of the domestic quarters of the early abbey, and part of its surrounding wall. The buildings whose foundations were discovered were, with one exception, small dwellings, consisting of one or two rooms each 15–20 ft long by 10–12 ft wide. The one exception was a larger rectangular building about 50 ft by 15 ft, which may have been a refectory, or school-house. From the loom-weights and other objects found within the dwellings, these were indicated as the nuns' quarters. Some of them retained evidence of having had open hearths; and there was also evidence of wells, and of a system of drainage in rough stone-built channels.

Nothing was found of the church or churches of the monastery; and it seems reasonable to suppose that the ruins of the medieval abbey overlie the whole of their seventh-century predecessors.

WHITFIELD
Kent
Map sheet 173, reference TR 311458

Figure 609

ST PETER
Main fabric: possibly period A with alterations of period C

The interesting church of St Peter, at Whitfield, is now reached by narrow by-roads, about 3 miles north of Dover, although originally the Roman road from Dover to Richborough passed less than half a mile away to the east. The name Whitfield apparently came into common use only in the seventeenth century, before which time it had been Beuesfeld, or other closely-related forms. The manor was given by Offa, King of Mercia, in the fifth year of his reign, to St Augustine's Abbey

at Canterbury, but there is no reference to the church in the deed of gift, which therefore does not help in the dating of the church.[1]

The church now consists of a nave, with north aisle and south porch, a small chancel, with north aisle and south vestry, and an aisleless sanctuary. A full acount of the church and of the various forms through which it passed, before taking its present shape under Ewan Christian's supervision in a restoration in 1894, was given in 1928 by Canon Livett,[2] but the claims of the church to pre-Conquest date were first advanced by Loftus Brock in 1895.[3] It can be accepted that the pre-Conquest date of the existing nave and chancel was established beyond doubt by these two writers; but we doubt the validity of Livett's argument for a pre-Conquest church of three-cell type, consisting of the present nave and chancel, and a small apsidal sanctuary lying wholly within the present east end. Our doubts arise not only because no other example of such a plan is known from before the Conquest, but also because all of Livett's arguments for such a form would equally well suit a history in which the original building had been a two-cell structure, consisting of the present nave and chancel, to which a small sanctuary (apsidal or square-ended) had been added in Norman times. This seems a more probable history, especially in view of the existence of several such three-cell Norman churches,[4] and of the known modification of the two-cell Anglo-Saxon church at Darenth into a three-cell form in Norman times.

The fabric of the early nave and chancel at Whitfield is almost wholly of flint, stone being used only in the west window and in a few other isolated places such as the large blocks in the south-west quoin. Apart from this, where the quoins survive, they are of flints. In the west wall of the nave there are indications of the former existence of a west doorway, with its head roughly turned in larger and flatter flints laid radially;

[1] E. Hasted, *History of Kent*, **1** (Canterbury, 1778), 14; and Thomas of Elmham, *History of St Augustine's Abbey*, ed. C. Hardwick (Rolls Series, 8) (London, 1858), 331–2. The charter is Birch, *Cart. Sax.* no. 207.
[2] G. M. Livett, 'Whitfield, *alias* Beuesfeld', *Arch. Cant.* **40** (1928), 141–58.

[3] E. P. L. Brock, 'The Saxon church at Whitfield', *ibid.* **21** (1895), 301–7.
[4] Livett named Norman three-cell churches at East Ham, Essex; Sutton by Dover, Kent; and the ruins of St James, Dunwich, Suffolk. To these might be added several others such as Kilpeck and Moccas, Herefordshire; Newhaven, Sussex; and Steetley, Derbyshire.

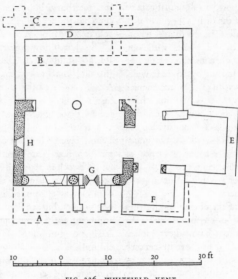

FIG. 336. WHITFIELD, KENT

A, destroyed Norman south aisle; B, destroyed Early English north aisle; C, destroyed Jacobean north chapel; D, Victorian north aisle; E, Victorian chancel; F, Victorian south chapel; G, double-splayed window over porch; H, single-splayed window high in west gable, above pointed window.

but it is not now possible to say whether there might also have been dressed-stone facings.

The original chancel-arch almost certainly survived until Christian's restoration in 1894, for Brock described the arch as 'lofty and narrow, very irregular and ugly in form', while Livett recounted how at the restoration it was faced with brick and plastered. So far as we know, there is, unfortunately, no record of the exact nature of the arch that was thus destroyed in 1894.

Two of the original windows have, however, survived; and they are of such markedly different forms as to give a strong indication that the church shows two separate periods of Anglo-Saxon workmanship. The west window, placed high up in the gable, with its sill about 18 ft above the floor, is of an early-Saxon form, single-splayed, with an external rebate for a shutter. Its head, jambs, and sill are formed of single large stones; the head is cut to a rough round shape below, and the jambs are sloped towards each other so that the opening narrows from 16 in. at the bottom to 13 in. at the top. By contrast, the window in the

south wall, over the modern porch, is of the late-Saxon double-splayed form. Its aperture, about 18 in. high and 9 in. wide, is in the middle of the wall and its inner and outer splays are plastered.

It seems natural, on the evidence of the windows and of the simple main structure, to ascribe the original building of the church, with its west window, to period A, perhaps to about the time of King Offa's gift of the manor to St Augustine's, and to regard the south window as a period C insertion.

DIMENSIONS

The original nave and chancel are both far from rectangular in plan; their internal dimensions are about 21 ft by 13 ft 3 in., and about 9 ft 6 in. square, respectively; their walls are between 2 ft and 2 ft 3 in. in thickness, and about 15 ft in height.

REFERENCES

These have been given in the footnotes. There are several good plans and pictures in Canon Livett's article.

WHITHORN

Wigtown (Galloway)

Map sheet 80, reference NX 444403

DEDICATION UNKNOWN

Possibly some foundations of the east end of the eighth-century church

The mission of St Ninian to Whithorn and his conversion of the southern Picts about the end of the fourth century lies far outside the scope of this book, but a Northumbrian bishopric was established at Whithorn not long before 731 with Pecthelm as its first bishop.[1] Some rectangular lines of stone foundations, faced with white plaster, to the east of the Norman and later priory church at Whithorn, may be the remains of the stone church of Pecthelm's time; but the chief interest of the district lies in its rich collection of inscribed stones, which seem to provide a link between Ninian's mission and the later Northumbrian see. The 'Latinus' stone in the museum at Whithorn is usually attributed to the early part of the fifth century, while there and at Kirkmadrine, across Luce Bay, are others of the sixth and seventh centuries.[2] A considerable group of carved stones at Whithorn can be assigned to the period of the Northumbrian bishopric in the eighth century, although none can compare in quality with the first rank of the great Northumbrian crosses.[3] The traditional site of St Ninian's church is about three miles away to the south-east.

WHITTINGHAM

Northumberland

Map sheet 71, reference NU 066119

Figures 610–13

ST BARTHOLOMEW

Lower part of west tower; quoins, west wall, and parts of side walls of nave: period C, with possibly some remains of an earlier period

The village of Whittingham, about 7 miles west of Alnwick, is about a mile upstream from the Bridge of Aln, where the Roman road known as the Devil's Causeway crosses the river. The church remains an important Northumbrian example of the Anglo-Saxon period, notwithstanding an unfortunate rebuilding in 1840, when many of its pre-Conquest features were replaced in the Gothic style then fashionable. By singular good fortune Rickman visited the church in 1834 and later published a description and drawing which, with the existing remains, give a fairly accurate picture of the church as it was before the nineteenth-century destruction.[4]

Symeon of Durham names Whittingham as the home of the widow who, on St Cuthbert's advice in a vision, bought a slave Guthred, son of Hardacnut, to *Oswiu's Down, c.* 883, where he was made king by Bishop Eardulf and the whole army. Symeon also records that Whittingham was one of the places which were given to St Cuthbert's church in 737 by King Ceolwulf when he resigned his kingdom and became a monk at Lindisfarne.[5] It has been suggested that Whittingham might be the place which Bede (*H.E.* IV, 26 (28)) referred to as *Ad Tuifyrdi*, on the River Aln, where in 684 a synod unanimously chose St Cuthbert to be Bishop of Lindisfarne; but this identification is uncertain and the place of the synod has also been identified as Alnmouth.[6]

The church now consists of a west tower, a nave, with north and south aisles, aisleless transepts, and an aisleless chancel with north vestry. Of Anglo-Saxon workmanship there remain only the four quoins of the originally aisleless nave with

---

[1] Bede (*H.E.* III, 4 and v, 23). This Northumbrian bishopric is our justification for including Whithorn, in spite of its lying outside the borders of England.
[2] A. W. Clapham (1930), 15 and 62; W. G. Collingwood, *Northumbrian Crosses* (London, 1927), 2–4.
[3] S. Cruden, *The Early Christian and Pictish Monuments of Scotland* (Edinburgh, H.M. Stationery Office, 1957), 7–8.
[4] T. Rickman, *Styles of Architecture in England*, 5th ed. (London, 1848), appendix, ix.
[5] Symeon of Durham, ed. T. Arnold, *Hist. Regum* (Rolls

Series, 75, II) (London, 1885), 114; and *Hist. Dunelm. Ecclesiae* (Rolls Series, 75, I) (London, 1882), 47, 68–9 and 203. At p. 202 note that the earlier *Hist de S. Cuthberti* records that the church was consecrated by Bishop Esdred (*recte* Ecgred) (Bishop of Lindisfarne, c. 830–45).
[6] W. Bright, *Early English Church History*, 3rd ed. (Oxford, 1897), 373. The second and third editions both associate Twyford with Whittingham, but the first edition (Oxford, 1878), 331, associates it with Alnmouth. Plummer refers to Bright's first identification.

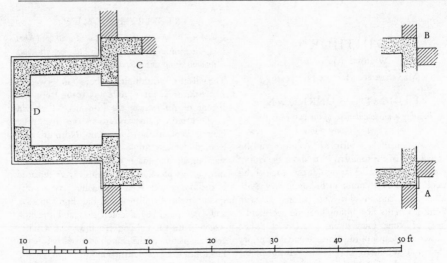

FIG. 337. WHITTINGHAM, NORTHUMBERLAND

This outline plan shows the surviving early fabric. The west tower and the west wall of the nave both rise from a simple plinth, which is also visible under the south-east quoin A of the nave, in the angle between the later south aisle and the chancel. The north-east quoin B is visible in the vestry. Vestiges of an early round arch C have recently been exposed by the removal of plaster from the north wall of the nave. At D the early wall of the tower has been broken for the insertion of a pointed window. The length of the nave is not shown to scale.

the western parts of its walls, and the lower parts of the walls of the tower, in which all the windows have been rebuilt in Gothic fashion.

The tower, about 15 ft square externally and now about 60 ft in height, stands on a chamfered plinth, which is also carried round the original nave. The fabric is of roughly squared stone laid in courses, and varying in colour from grey to brown, with some blocks of dark red. Both the tower and the nave have a most distinctive quoining, whose character shows a pronounced change at a height of about 6 ft from the ground, possibly indicating two separate building periods. In their lower part the quoins are formed of large blocks laid in side-alternate fashion; whereas the upper part is in long-and-short technique, of a type which is unusual except in the south of England but is common in Sussex. The special feature of this type of long-and-short quoining is that adjacent upright or pillar stones are separated, not by single flat square stones, but by pairs of stones which are rectangular in plan and which are laid so that one serves to bond the quoin deeply into one face of the wall while the other bonds into the adjoining

face. The west wall of the nave is of the same fabric as the tower and is bonded into it. On the north it projects 3 ft 3 in. and on the south 3 ft 7 in., the extent being clearly defined not only by the quoining, which is of the same general form as that of the tower, but also by the plinth.

As shown in Rickman's drawing, the tower had two small windows in the west face, in much the same positions as are now occupied by much larger nineteenth-century lancets. There appears never to have been any opening to the north; and the small ground-floor window in the south wall does not appear in Rickman's drawing, although it now looks as if it might be a nineteenth-century modification of an original window. Nothing at all now remains of the Anglo-Saxon belfry stage, which Rickman's drawing and description indicate as having had in the west face a late-Saxon double belfry window with its two lights separated by a rude baluster, whereas its south face had a single round-headed opening. It would be a mistake to assert on the evidence provided by Rickman's published engraving that Whittingham was originally, like Bardsey in Yorkshire, an

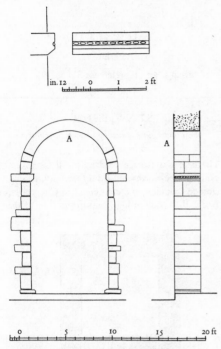

in. 12   0   1   2 ft

FIG. 338. WHITTINGHAM, NORTHUMBERLAND

Details of the tower-arch. The upper voussoirs in the part A of the arch have not been drawn since they are modern restorations. The surviving original voussoirs are not through-stones. The larger scale inset at the top of the figure shows one of the chamfered imposts, with its line of ovoid ornament.

example of the Anglo-Saxon use of both double and single windows in one and the same belfry chamber; for, although Rickman's picture clearly shows a round-headed single window in the south face, by contrast with the double window in the west face, this is not the case in the original pencil sketch by William Twopenny, upon which we believe Rickman's picture to have been based. The pencil sketch is preserved in the Print Room of the British Museum. On the west it clearly shows the same double window as in the published drawing. On the south, however, it shows the remains of a similar double window, of which the eastern light is shown complete, whereas the western light is shown blocked by masonry, but

with its round head still clearly marked by its stone lintel (cf. Figs. 612 and 613).

Internally, a most striking feature is provided by the fine tower-arch, which is illustrated and described by Baldwin Brown (p. 404). The perfectly plain square jambs are constructed of large through-stones[1] laid in something approximating to 'Escomb fashion'. The chamfered imposts, also of through-stones, project on the soffit only; and their tall vertical faces are enriched, just above the chamfer, by an unusual ornament consisting of a line of raised oval pellets in a narrow groove. The jambs rest on chamfered plinths which, like the imposts, project on the soffit only. The semicircular arch, of plain square section, is now largely a modern restoration; but the original arch appears to have differed from the jambs in not having been of through-stones, for none of the original stones which remain on either side at the springing passes through the thickness of the wall.

At the west of the arcades of the nave, a few feet of each of the original side walls still remain, to show the form of the early aisleless nave. In the north wall there has now been exposed to view the jamb and part of the arch which Rickman recorded in 1834 as probably being a pre-Conquest opening at the west of a Norman arcade. His description is of sufficient interest to quote in full:

One arch of what appears to me to be the original nave remains; it is very plain, has a large rude abacus or impost and a plain square pier; it is now stopped and forms part of the vestry. The next arch eastward on the same side is a common Norman one with the usual round pier and a capital with a sort of bell and a square abacus.

The greater part of the western arch and the whole of the Norman arcade were swept away in 1840, when the western jamb and three stones of the arch were built up in a section of solid wall to form a new respond for a pointed north arcade, copied from that on the south side of the nave. The remains of the jamb and arch agree precisely with Rickman's description, but it is difficult to give them a reliable date. From Rickman's description it seems clear that the arch was earlier than the Norman arcade, but the western quoins of the nave indicate that the nave was originally aisleless. The arch could, however, have been an original opening to a northern *porticus*. What now remains

---

[1] The top course on the south side is an exception, but it is a later insertion.

of this tantalizing opening does not serve to give any certain indication of date, although it does not suggest a date contemporary with the tower-arch. The jamb and impost consist of eleven stones totalling 8 ft 10 in. in height; and of the arch only three stones remain, showing that both jamb and arch were of plain square section. It is impossible to say whether the stones pass through the full thickness of the wall; and if the impost ever projected, either on the wall-face or the soffit, it has now been cut back.

The south-eastern quoin of the original nave may be seen externally in the angle between the chancel and the aisle, standing on a chamfered plinth like that at the west; and the vestiges of the north-eastern quoin may be seen in a similar position within the vestry. The full extent of the original nave may therefore be fixed with certainty.

DIMENSIONS

The nave is 53 ft long internally, and 17 ft 9 in. wide, with walls 2 ft 6 in. thick, and over 20 ft tall. The tower measures 11 ft 4 in. from east to west internally, while from north to south it is 10 ft 10 in. wide at the west and 11 ft 2 in. at the east. The east wall of the tower at the arch to the nave is 2 ft 9 in. thick while the other three walls are between 2 ft 3 in. and 2 ft 6 in. The floor of the tower is raised above that of the nave by a single step of 8 in. in height, flush with the east face of the east wall, and the tower-arch is 8 ft 2 in. wide and 17 ft 0 in. high, from the tower floor to the crown,[1] while the tops of the imposts are 12 ft 5 in. above the tower floor.

REFERENCES

C. C. Hodges, 'Pre-Conquest churches of Northumbria', *Reliquary*, n.s., **7** (1893), 65–85. Whittingham, 74–8. Copy of Rickman's drawing, 75; picture of tower after rebuilding, 76. Record of the destruction in 1839.

C. C. Hodges, 'The church of St Bartholomew, Whittingham', *Arch. Ael.*, 4th ser., **5** (1928), 81–6. Plan and good illustrations.

History of Northumberland, **14**, ed. M. H. Dodds (Newcastle, 1935), 482–527. Plan, 488.

H. L. Honeyman, 'Some early masonry in Northumberland', *Arch. Ael.*, 4th ser., **12** (1935), 158–86. Whittingham, 177–82.

WICKHAM
Berkshire

Map sheet 158, reference SU 394715

Figure 614

ST SWITHUN

West tower surmounted by nineteenth-century belfry: period C

The line of a Roman road may still be traced, running west-north-west from Newbury, passing close to Swindon, and continuing to Cirencester. Beside this road, on high land to the west of the

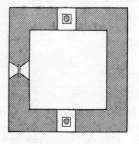

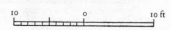

FIG. 339. WICKHAM, BERKSHIRE

Plan of the belfry stage of the tower, showing the double windows in the north and south faces and the double-splayed window to the west.

small village of Wickham, the church of St Swithun stands in the pleasant park of an extensive estate. The church was drastically rebuilt in 1845, and of the earlier structure nothing now remains except the tower, to which a tall belfry was then added.

The original tower, roughly 16 ft square externally and about 40 ft in height, is built of flints, with well-defined long-and-short quoins. In the south face, about 8 ft above the ground, is a blocked round-headed doorway with heavily restored square jambs and imposts. The *Victoria County History* suggests that this doorway was originally

[1] Baldwin Brown (p. 404) says 7 ft 4½ in. wide by 17 ft 10 in. high.

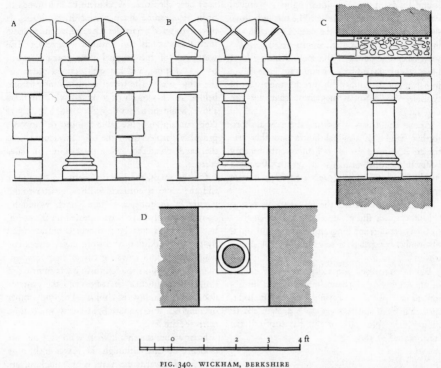

FIG. 340. WICKHAM, BERKSHIRE
Details of the double belfry windows, showing their turned baluster-shafts probably of Roman origin. A, elevation
of the south window, showing its restored jambs; B, elevation of the north window, showing its original megalithic
jambs and projecting imposts; C, section of the north window; D, plan of the north window showing the square
plinth and circular base of the turned baluster.

the sole means of entry and was placed high in the
wall for defensive purposes. The raised ground-
floor chamber to which it leads seems to have had
no other external openings except the doorway;
and the first-floor chamber above it has only a
small, round-headed, double-splayed window.

The second floor now has openings in all three
external faces: namely a late-Saxon, double belfry
window in each of the north and south faces, by
contrast with a single, round-headed, double-
splayed window in the west face, similar to that on
the floor below, but more widely splayed. The
eastern wall of the tower at this level is now below
the ridge of the modern roof of the nave, and it is

built up in brick, so that it is impossible to say
with certainty whether it originally contained a
second double-splayed window like that to the
the west. This unusual arrangement of double
belfry windows on one axis with single windows
on the other is also to be seen at Bardsey in
Yorkshire, where it occurs on two levels.

The double belfry windows at Wickham present
the usual Anglo-Saxon arrangement of mid-wall
shafts supporting through-stone slabs which project beyond the wall face. The mid-wall shafts
are, however, recorded by Baldwin Brown as
being re-used Roman shafts similar to many others
found on Roman sites throughout Britain.[1] The

[1] G. Baldwin Brown (1925), 60 and 486.

round heads of the individual lights are arched with roughly shaped voussoirs. The through-stone slabs project boldly from the face of the wall, and in the north window the imposts project on the soffit face. The jambs of the south window have been rebuilt in ashlar, without any projecting imposts; but the jambs of the north window are of typically Anglo-Saxon megalithic character (see Fig. 340).

Above the belfry windows there is a short, further height of original fabric and then the tower is capped by a tall nineteenth-century belfry in pseudo-Norman style, set back from the Anglo-Saxon tower, and separated from it by a string-course.

Baldwin Brown dates the tower to his period C1 or C2, on the ground that it has 'double-splayed openings and long-and-short quoins and is obviously earlier than the so-called "Lincolnshire" towers'.

Bloxam recorded the existence at Wickham of an Anglo-Saxon chancel-arch, which he described as 'plain, of a single sweep or soffit, springing from square piers, with a plain abacus or impost'.[1] No trace of this has survived the 'restoration' of 1845.

DIMENSIONS

The tower is about 10 ft 6 in. square internally, with walls about 3 ft thick and originally about 40 ft high.

REFERENCE

V.C.H., *Berkshire*, 4 (London, 1924), 123–4.

WICKMERE
Norfolk
Map sheet 126, reference TG 165337
Figure 615

ST ANDREW

Round west tower, and part of nave: Saxo-Norman

About 6 miles south of Sheringham, beside one of the small streams that flow south from the higher land near the coast, Wickmere church stands in open fields, some distance west of its village. It now consists of an aisleless chancel, an aisled nave with south porch, and a round west tower. The west wall of the original nave contains much brown carstone, and has well defined quoins of the same stone. The tower is mainly of carstone below, and has much of it mixed with the flints above, while the later aisle walls, though mainly of flint, contain an appreciable amount of carstone, probably derived from the original side walls of the nave when they were pierced by the later arcades.

On the south, the junction between the tower and the nave is enriched with a quarter-round pilaster in carstone, a feature which would no doubt originally have been repeated on the north, but which has now been obscured or destroyed by the later addition of a stone stair-turret. The windows of the tower give no help towards fixing its date, since the four belfry windows are of simple Perpendicular character, and the ground-floor west window is similar. The only other opening is a small square light facing south at an intermediate level.

Even within the church there is no very definite evidence of date, although the tower-arch, now chamfered towards the nave, is of a single square order without imposts. It is of the strange shape which is to be found elsewhere in Norfolk, and which suggests that it may have been formed by setting flints in mortar over a template formed by an upturned boat or by suitably shaped trees such as were used in the building of wooden 'cruck-houses'.

The north and south aisles open from the nave through arcades, each of three pointed arches, with appreciable sections of walling as responds at their east and west ends. These sections of walling appear to be aligned with the western carstone quoins and they may therefore be parts of the original side walls of the nave. They are under 2 ft 6 in. in thickness, and they define a nave about 46½ ft long internally by about 17½ ft wide.

It is difficult to be certain about the dating of this church, but we have tentatively accepted it as

---

[1] M. H. Bloxam, *Principles of Gothic Ecclesiastical Architecture*, 9th ed. (London, 1849); chancel-arch, 63; Bloxam had visited Wickham, 80.

Saxo-Norman on the evidence of the quarter-round pilasters, the carstone quoins and fabric, the cruck-shaped tower-arch, and the thin walls of the nave.

1100 by Ralph de Mortimer, and that the college lapsed when the abbey was founded about 1179 on a site a mile beyond Wigmore towards Shrewsbury.[1]

WIGMORE

Herefordshire

Map sheet 129, reference SO 412690

Figure 616

ST JAMES

North wall of nave: Saxo-Norman

A little to the west of the Roman road from Hereford to Shrewsbury, and about seven miles south-west of Ludlow, Wigmore church occupies a commanding position above its village, on a spur which juts eastward from the hills into the fertile plain beside the River Teme. Considerable sections of the solid side walls of the originally aisleless nave have survived at the west. The south wall is now wholly enclosed within the later south aisle, but a small Norman window high up in it serves to establish that it was originally an external wall. The north wall has also been pierced for a later aisle but only a small chapel now survives, and to the west of it the original wall may be seen to be of herring-bone construction externally for almost its whole height. Unfortunately no original openings have remained in this wall to give a reliable indication of its date, but this could perhaps be obtained if it were possible to strip the plaster from the south wall beside the Norman window. If this were found to be *in situ* in a herring-bone wall like that on the north, the date of both walls would be reliably established as post-Conquest; but if the window were found to be set in a wall of quite different character, or if it were obviously a later insertion in a herring-bone wall, then the herring-bone fabric would be given a reliable indication of pre-Conquest date. Tanner states that a small college of three prebendaries was founded in the parish church here in

WILLESBOROUGH

Kent

Map sheet 172, reference TR 029414

Figure 617

ST MARY

West and south walls of early nave, now forming south aisle: possibly pre-Conquest

This church stands between the road and the railway to Folkestone, about 2 miles south-east of Ashford, in what is now a thriving suburb. It is still beside open country, but will probably not remain so much longer. Its west tower has a somewhat squat shingled spire, its long aisleless chancel has a north vestry, and the principal interest of the church centres in the aisled nave, particularly the western part of the south aisle, which seems to have been the body of an earlier church. The fabric of this early church is of rough rubble, and the only quoin of which any part remains, that at the south-west, is of small stones, laid in a side-alternate fashion which gives no reliable indication of date.

The present south arcade of the later nave, replacing the north wall of the earlier church, is of Early English character; and therefore it does not serve to fix the date of the earlier church with more precision than to indicate that it was Norman or earlier. The only original opening which has survived is a small, blocked, round-headed window, high up in the west gable. It has a monolithic sill, jambs of small, roughly dressed stones, and head roughly arched in thin pieces of rubble, laid with very little attention to the principle of radial setting of voussoirs. The blocking of this opening is not flush with the outer face of the wall and the splaying of the

---

[1] T. Tanner, *Notitia Monastica*, ed. J. Nasmith (Cambridge, 1787), Herefordshire, xxi. Also D. Knowles and

R. N. Hadcock, *Medieval Religious Houses* (London, 1953), 159 and 344.

jambs and head may be seen to be quite slight but to be continued to the outer face of the wall.

Pending further investigation, we think the early part of the church can provisionally be regarded as pre-Conquest on the evidence of its tall, thin walls, and of the simple, single-splayed window with its non-radially laid head and its splays continued through the full thickness of the wall.

DIMENSIONS

The walls are 2 ft 7 in. thick, and the south wall was originally about 16 ft tall. The early nave was 18 ft 7 in. wide internally; and the window in the west gable is 1 ft 5 in. wide and 2 ft 9 in. tall, with its sill 17 ft 6 in. above the ground.

REFERENCE

H. R. P. BOORMAN and V. J. TOOR, *Kent Churches* (Maidstone, 1954), 81.

WILMINGTON
Kent

Map sheet 171, reference TQ 538724

ST MICHAEL
West wall and western parts of side walls of nave: possibly pre-Conquest

Although now in danger of being swallowed up as a suburb of Dartford, Wilmington is still a village set amid orchards and green fields on the western bank of the River Darent, about a mile south of the Roman Watling Street from London to Rochester. The church now consists of an aisled nave with western bell-cote, and an aisleless modern chancel which is partially flanked by side-chapels.

During the building of the south aisle, about 1881, a blocked window was discovered and opened out in the south wall of the nave, about 2 ft from its western angle. This is a narrow aperture, 7 in. wide and 1 ft 6 in. tall, splayed internally to 2 ft 4 in. by 3 ft 6 in. Its splays pass through the full thickness of the wall, except for a shallow chamfer which is carried round the outer face.

This window does not give any clear indication

of pre-Conquest date, and we have included the church provisionally in the pre-Conquest list principally because of its thin walls.

DIMENSIONS

The nave is 17 ft 3 in. wide internally, with side walls 2 ft 8 in. thick, of which about 7 ft remain as solid walls on each side of the nave, at the west of the later arcades. The inner sill of the small south window is about 7 ft above the floor.

REFERENCE

J. C. COX (revised P. M. JOHNSTON), *Kent* (Methuen's Little Guides), 6th ed. (London, 1935), 300. The window is wrongly described as double-splayed, and reference is made to a similar northern window which does not now exist.

WILSFORD
Lincolnshire

Map sheet 123, reference TF 006429

ST MARY
Eastern quoins of nave, with parts of adjoining walls: period C

About 8 miles north-east of Grantham, the busy road to Sleaford avoids the narrow streets of the small village of Wilsford and thereby leaves the village in peaceful seclusion, with its church pleasantly situated on higher ground to the south. The Roman Ermine Street from London to Lincoln passes about one and a half miles to the west of the village.

The church now consists of a west tower, with spire; an aisled nave, with south porch; and a chancel, with a short north aisle. The whole fabric is of pleasantly weathered grey stone. In the early, aisleless nave, the walls were of rough rubble laid in courses, with dressed stone for the long-and-short quoins. The later work was of dressed stone; and it is therefore fairly easy to see to what extent the side walls of the aisleless nave were retained or were replaced during the provision of the aisles.

The surviving pre-Conquest work that is visible externally on the south side of the church is confined to the south-east quoin of the nave; the adjoining section of south wall, which is now pierced by an Early English lancet; the adjoining section of east wall of the nave; and the western section, about 10 ft long, of the south wall of the chancel. On the north, no early work is visible externally; but the north-east quoin, which is now to be seen in the north aisle, is still largely original, although much modified. The adjoining sections of walling are also of the original rough rubble, but the greater part of the north wall of the nave, over the two tall, round arches which open to the north aisle, is of dressed stone and so is clearly a rebuilding. So also are the west wall, with its tall arch to the tower, and the south wall, except for the eastern part already noted from outside.

DIMENSIONS

The nave is about 30 ft long internally and about 18 ft wide, with walls 2 ft 5 in. thick and originally about 18 ft tall.

REFERENCE

Editorial, 'St Mary's, Wilsford', A.A.S.R. 6 (1861–2), xxxviii. Brief description and note of restoration.

WINCHESTER
Hampshire

Map sheet 168, reference SU 482293

THE OLD MINSTER

A detailed survey of the literary evidence for the character of the cathedral at Winchester in the form in which it was rebuilt by Bishop Ethelwold and his successor Alphege in the second half of the tenth century has recently been published. Excavations have been in progress since our text was written. An important interim report will be found in the third of the references cited below, and it is expected that further reports will appear in the Antiquaries Journal.

REFERENCES

R. N. QUIRK, 'Winchester cathedral in the tenth century', Arch. J. 114 (1957), 28–68.

R. N. QUIRK, 'Winchester New Minster and its tenth-century tower', J.B.A.A., 3rd ser., 24 (1961), 16–54.

M. BIDDLE and R. N. QUIRK, 'Excavations near Winchester Cathedral', Arch. J. 119 (1962), 150–94.

WING
Buckinghamshire

Map sheet 146, reference SP 880225

Figures 618–20

ALL SAINTS

Aisled nave; and apsidal chancel, with crypt beneath: period A, with alterations to the chancel and the crypt in period C

The important pre-Conquest church at Wing stands beside the road to Aylesbury, about 3 miles south-west of Leighton Buzzard, with a good view westward over pleasant green fields. The church now consists of a Perpendicular west tower, a pre-Conquest aisled nave with Perpendicular clear-storey, and a pre-Conquest aisleless apsidal chancel. The church is an unusually complete example of its type and period; for, of the small number of Anglo-Saxon aisled churches, Wing alone has retained an outer wall of one of its aisles. A complete pre-Conquest apse is also a rarity, and Wing is unique in possessing not only this but also an elaborate crypt beneath. The provision of Perpendicular clear-storey windows, the erection of the west tower, and the insertion of Perpendicular windows in the aisles and chancel have done much to make the church assume a late medieval appearance, but it is still fundamentally a pre-Conquest fabric. The arcaded nave has close resemblances to the nave at Brixworth, and it may well be of much the same date.

The church is built of rough limestone rubble, laid in small flattish pieces, with some attention to coursing; while the pilaster-strips with which the chancel is ornamented are of roughly dressed stone, in blocks of about the size of modern bricks. The early openings which have survived are faced with tiles, or thin rubble of similar shape; and their heads are arched in the same material.

Externally the Anglo-Saxon character of the church is apparent in the seven-sided apse, and in its elaborate system of vertical pilasters, which are connected by an arcade of round arches and by an upper row of straight-sided arches. The pilaster-strips run up each of the angles of the apse and serve to emphasize its seven faces. The arcade of

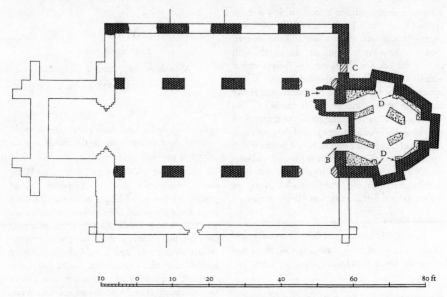

FIG. 341. WING, BUCKINGHAMSHIRE

Plan of the aisled nave and of the crypt beneath the apsidal chancel. This plan, based on information contained in Jackson and Fletcher's recent article, shows how the crypt was originally a large open chamber with a small reliquary chamber A, or *confessio*, at the west. Only later were the internal piers and vaults added, to produce the present plan with its central chamber surrounded by a narrow ambulatory. The evidence for these later additions is most easily seen in the straight vertical joints between the two sets of masonry at the points D in the recesses in the crypt. The plan also shows how narrow passages B gave access to the crypt from the east end of the nave. Note the surviving north and east walls of the north aisle, with an eastern doorway C, now blocked.

round arches rests on simple rectangular imposts, which are placed a little higher than the middle of the wall; and it serves to unite the faces, and to frame the windows. This lower stage of strip-work is in excellent preservation, except where it has been ruthlessly cut away for the insertion of hood-mouldings over the Perpendicular windows which now light the chancel. Unlike most other Anglo-Saxon strip-work (which usually consists either of a series of long, narrow stones, running in the direction of the strips or else of an alternation of long and short stones) the pilasters and arches at Wing are built of stones which are apparently set with their greater length running into the wall, so that their exposed faces are of a fairly uniform shape, like the ends of modern bricks. From between the springings of the round arches the pilaster-strips continue up to the top of the wall; but these upper strips are much less sharply defined, perhaps by original intent or

perhaps by more severe weathering. An upper arcade of straight-sided arches springs from about the middle of these upper pilasters, with the apex of each arch close beside the cornice which now surmounts the wall.

The chancel is now lit by three Perpendicular windows, one of which is in the east face, and one in the central face of each side. The large Perpendicular window that has been inserted in the east face has left no evidence to show whether there was originally an early east window; but by good fortune those in the north and south sides are smaller, so that a part of the head of an original window has remained above each of these two, arched in thin stones, and of a form which from its large radius indicates that it is most probably the outer face of a double-splayed window.

The upper arcade contains four round-headed openings, one in each of the panels intermediate between those that contain the Perpendicular

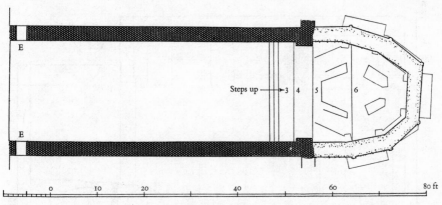

Steps up ──►3 | 4 | 5 | 6

| 0 | 10 | 20 | 40 | 60 | 80 ft |

FIG. 342. WING, BUCKINGHAMSHIRE

Plan of the chancel and of the upper part of the nave. The upper doorways E are shown at the west of the nave, and the remarkably wide chancel-arch at the east. The outline of the walls of the crypt is shown by faint lines in order to show the relation of these walls to the walls of the chancel above. A later pre-Conquest date is shown only for the external part of the walls of the chancel, in conformity with Jackson and Fletcher's deductions that the core of the wall is old and that the exterior facing, including the arcading of pilaster-strips, is a later modification.

windows. On the south side, these upper openings are well-formed, circular-headed recesses, or, blocked windows; while on the north there are vestiges of similar openings, though the openings and the upper range of strip-work are much less well preserved than on the south. The jambs of the openings are faced with rubble like that of the walling and the round-heads are turned in similar rubble, laid with reasonably radial joints. Within each opening the jambs and arches appear to be at right angles to the wall face, while the wall which blocks the opening appears to be of the same rubble fabric as the main walling. There therefore seems to be good reason for thinking that these upper openings were decorative recesses rather than an upper row of windows, but a careful examination of the interior of the wall might give better evidence for settling this question. In any event, the general arrangement of the apse has striking resemblances to that at Deerhurst.

As at Deerhurst, the general character of the exterior of the apse suggests a later date than that of the nave. This conclusion has recently been confirmed in detail by Jackson and Fletcher.[1]

Their conclusions may be summarized by saying that the main body of the church (including the arcaded walls of the nave, the outer walls of the crypt, and the core of the walls of the chancel) is of period A; while at a later date, probably in period C, a vaulted interior structure was built within the crypt, and the walls of the apsidal chancel were substantially modified so as to assume their present form.

In the lower parts of the faces of the apse, below its three main windows, a further group of three windows served to light the crypt. These openings, which appear to have been only slightly altered from their original form, have square jambs and round heads of a single square order, all built of rubble, and now visible a few feet above ground. That on the south has been adapted to form a doorway to the crypt by way of an external stone stairway. There is no evidence here, as at Repton, of the former existence of stone arches to cover recesses that led outward from these openings, and it may therefore be assumed that the openings were simply windows to light the crypt. The walls of the crypt appear to be thicker both

[1] E. D. C. Jackson and E. G. M. Fletcher, 'The apse and nave at Wing, Buckinghamshire', *J.B.B.A.*, 3rd ser., 25 (1962), 1–20. We are greatly indebted to Mr Jackson and Dr Fletcher for having been allowed to see the text of their article before publication.

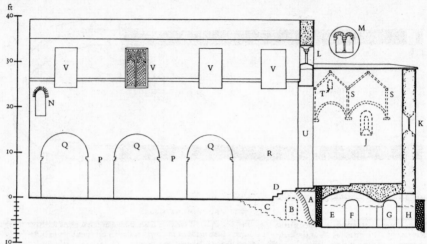

FIG. 343. WING, BUCKINGHAMSHIRE

Longitudinal section through the church, looking north, and showing the relative levels of the nave, the crypt and the chancel. On the upper area of the chancel we have shown in dotted outline the positions of certain features of the exterior of the chancel; and beneath the floor of the nave we have shown in dotted outline the positions of parts of the entrance passages of the crypt. A, the original *confessio* or reliquary, later partially blocked with earth as shown on its western side; B, the outline of the northern original entrance passage, where it turns south; C, the outline of the conjectural position of steps down from the nave to the northern original entrance passage; D, steps up from the nave to the chancel; E, the central chamber of the present crypt; F, the archway from the central chamber to the northern ambulatory; G, the eastern ambulatory; H, the eastern recess, under the east wall of the chancel; J, the outline of side windows (north and south) whose round heads have survived above later three-light windows; K, a conjectural reconstruction of a similar window in the east wall where the whole space is now occupied by a four-light Perpendicular window; L, the double window above the chancel-arch; M (inset), elevation of the double window as seen from the nave; N, the high doorway which must have served as the north entry to a western gallery; P, the piers of the north arcade, with double-stepped imposts; Q, the arches of the north arcade; R, solid walling through which a pointed arch has now been pierced; S, blind arcading on the outer wall of the chancel; T, one of four recesses on the outer wall of the chancel; U, the chancel-arch, 19 ft 10 in. wide and 22 ft 6 in. tall if measured from the step at the entrance to the chancel, or 25 ft if measured from the floor of the nave; V, the four Perpendicular clear-storey windows. (The wall between the chancel-arch, U, and the upper window, L, should have been shown with date shades: early below and later above.)

internally and externally than those of the chancel above; and externally there is an off-set about the modern ground-level.

The crypt itself consists of a roughly octagonal central chamber surrounded by an outer ambulatory, from which it is partly separated by four massive piers that carry the slightly domed barrel-vaults of the central chamber and of the four bays of the ambulatory. Three arched openings between the piers lead north, south, and east from the central chamber to the ambulatory; and these are continued outward, as wider arched openings, or recesses, whose upper parts contain the external windows. A fourth arched opening, or passage, leads westward towards the nave; from this passage Mr G. G. Scott, who supervised the clearing of the crypt in 1881, reported that a squint formerly led to the foot of the chancel steps.[1] Such a squint to allow a view of the sacred relics in the crypt was a not unusual arrangement in early churches, where the steps leading up to the chancel were then divided into two flights, with a narrow flight between them, leading down to allow the worshipper to look through the squint.

The ambulatory communicated with the body

[1] The recent excavations by Jackson and Fletcher confirm the former existence of a cavity in the place mentioned by Scott, but it seems clear that it was a small reliquary chamber leading westward from the main crypt (see A in Figs. 341 and 343).

of the church by passages which led westward and then turned north and south and again west, up steps, now blocked, into the aisles or the nave. The whole of the piers, quoins, walls, and vaulting of the crypt is constructed of roughly coursed large pieces of brown stone. It was first noted by Scott and has been subsequently recorded by several writers that the whole of the fabric of the crypt is a later insertion within an earlier open chamber that still retains the plaster inner facing of its original walls.[1]

It may well be the case that the crypt was originally intended to be a large hall of the same size as the present chancel, with a passage surrounding it externally as at Brixworth. The intention of providing access to such a passage is indicated by the doorway in the east end of the north aisle. If this was the original intention, it was later abandoned for some reason, perhaps because of the difficulty of vaulting so large a chamber. The present arrangement provides a central chamber about half the width of the chancel, together with an ambulatory surrounding it, all within the main walls of the chancel. It has been mentioned above how the passages that lead westward from the ambulatory turn to the north and south as though to lead up into the aisles. This would have been a very convenient arrangement, for it would have left the whole space between the side walls of the nave to be used for the steps up to the chancel and for the narrow flight down to the squint. All early references to the clearing of the crypt by Scott in 1881 refer explicitly to these passages as having 'led into the eastern ends of the aisles'.[2] Recent investigations seem, however, to show that the passages turned once again westward and led into the east of the nave, not into the aisles.[3]

Outside the church at the north-east, an original round-headed doorway, now blocked, may be seen in the east end of the north aisle. Its jambs are of roughly dressed large stones, and its arched head is turned in rubble, of which the lower courses on either side are appreciably tilted. This doorway is not in the centre of the wall, but close to the south angle, perhaps to leave room for an aisle-altar, or alternatively with the original intention of providing access to an external ambulatory, as at Brixworth. The east wall of the north aisle is fixed as of pre-Conquest date by this doorway; and the north wall may be similarly dated by virtue of its similarity of construction, its plinth, and its thickness of only 2 ft 6 in., by contrast with the west wall of this aisle and the walls of the south aisle, all of which are very close to 3 ft in thickness.

Within the church, the most important early features are the broad, round-headed chancel-arch; the double window above; and the two arcades, each of which is of three round-headed arches, cut straight through the wall. These arcades rest on plain rectangular piers with stepped imposts, of which those in the north arcade are formed of two oversailing courses of stone or tile, while those in the south arcade are similar but with three steps. The whole surface of the walls is plastered, so that no details of the construction are visible; but removal of a little of the plaster has shown that all the arches are turned in rough rubble, without the use of dressed stone.[4]

At the west of each of the side walls of the nave an entirely new feature was uncovered in 1954: namely, a narrow, round-headed doorway about 2 ft wide and 6 ft high, with its sill about 18 ft above the floor.[5] The heads of these two doorways are turned in thin stones, with reasonably radial joints; and the head of that on the south had previously been noticed from outside the church, but had been thought to belong to an early clear-storey window. The true character of the openings

---

[1] W. Niven, *R. Bucks.* **11** (1920–6), 49; also J. T. Micklethwaite, *Arch. J.* **53** (1896), 341–2.

[2] Editorial, *R. Bucks.* **5** (1878–86), 147; J. T. Micklethwaite, *Arch. J.* **53** (1896), 307 and 341; G. Baldwin Brown (1925), 322; W. Niven, *R. Bucks.* **11** (1920–6), 48.

[3] In a letter dated 3 February 1961 Mr Woodman told us that some years ago he had removed a large quantity of earth and stones from the north passage and had found that, instead of passing through the north wall of the nave into the aisle, it made a right-angled turn westward as

though to lead up into the nave; moreover, the north wall of the nave showed no trace of any opening. This conclusion has been confirmed by the recent work of Jackson and Fletcher.

[4] We were originally indebted to Mr Woodman for this information. It has been confirmed in detail by the recent investigations of Jackson and Fletcher.

[5] A. V. Woodman, *R. Bucks.* **16** (1953–60), 50 and 114. Also, A. V. Woodman, *Wing Church, Bucks.* (Aylesbury, 1958), 3 and 4.

as doorways is, however, settled beyond doubt by their being cut straight through the wall, without any splay. Prior to the discovery of these doorways, the remains of similar high doorways at Tredington were regarded as unique instances of such entries to a western gallery; but now, in addition to these well-established instances at Tredington and Wing, there are further examples at Jarrow and at Stoke d'Abernon. Access to the upper doorways at Wing may have been by way of a wooden stair, within a two-storeyed aisle; or else by an external stair, leading to a platform over the roof of a lower aisle.

Passing next to the eastern end of the nave, it should be noted that a pointed arch has later been cut through what was probably at first a length of solid walling at the east end of each of the Anglo-Saxon arcades. The present position of the flight of three steps leading to the chancel would be more easily understood if the solid wall at the east of the original arcades were imagined once more in place; for then the steps would run from wall to wall instead of ending lamely, as at present, under these later arches.

Between the nave and the chancel there is now almost no intervening wall, for the chancel-arch is of an unusually wide span, occupying almost the whole width of the chancel. The round arch and its jambs are of a single, plain, square order, and there are no imposts; but the western face of the arch is outlined by a shallow, concentric off-set of the wall-surface above. The arch is unusual, not only for its great span, but also for its absence of imposts. There seems to us justification for wondering whether the present wide arch may be the result of the removal of an inner order of a recessed opening, or whether an appreciably narrower arch and its adjoining wall were later cut away.[1] The Royal Commission on Historical Monuments describe the chancel-arch as original, but Clapham does not include it amongst his list of outstandingly large Anglo-Saxon chancel-

arches; and although Baldwin Brown makes fourteen separate references to Wing he does not mention this arch.[2] It would clearly be desirable that some plaster should be stripped from the arch so as to enable its character to be settled with certainty.

Above the chancel-arch, with its sill about 30 ft from the floor of the nave, a further interesting and unusual feature is provided by the double window which was discovered in 1892. It is of two round-headed lights, which are arched in tiles and are separated by a turned mid-wall baluster-shaft with a cubical capital and a primitive bulbous pyramidal base. The square jambs have stepped imposts of two oversailing orders, like those of the north arcade; and the arrangement for supporting the twin arches in the middle is unique, for the mid-wall shaft does not support a through-stone slab but, instead, the wall is thinned down by two pendentive surfaces to a square shape which rests on the abacus. Jackson and Fletcher suggest that the window originally had an ordinary through-stone, and that the present arrangement is a later modification.

The side walls of the nave show a pronounced off-set internally, about half-way up the sides of the Perpendicular clear-storey windows, at a height of about 26 ft above the floor of the nave; and it has been commonly suggested that this represents the original height of the Anglo-Saxon walls. There appear, however, to be three difficulties in the way of accepting this without question. In the first place, a similar but less pronounced off-set appears on the east wall at the same height, and well *below* the double window, in fact at just the height that would have been appropriate for the floor of a chamber lit by that window. Secondly, if the walls of the nave had ended at the height of the middle of the present clear-storey windows, the walls of the chancel would have been appreciably higher than those of the nave. Finally, but less conclusively, it may be remarked that there is

---

[1] C. C. Hodges (*Reliquary*, n.s., **8** (1894), 8–11) suggested that the arches at Norton had been enlarged by the removal of an inner order, and G. M. Livett (*Arch. Cant.* **42** (1930), 75) suggested that the present chancel-arch at Wing had resulted from the cutting away of a narrower arch.

[2] If Clapham believed that the chancel-arch at Wing

was original, it is odd that he did not include it in his list ((1930), 111) of the most notable chancel-arches. By comparison with those which he listed (Bosham, 11 ft 2 in.; Worth, 14 ft 1 in.; Great Paxton, 15 ft; and Wittering, 7 ft) the chancel-arch at Wing is 19 ft 10 in. wide; and it is complete, whereas that at Great Paxton has been replaced by a pointed arch.

no appreciable change in the fabric of the walls as seen from outside the church at any point corresponding to the position of the interior off-set. It therefore seems at least possible that the nave originally had a floor at the level of the off-set; and that this upper floor was lit by the double window at the east and by side windows in the positions of the tops of the present clear-storey windows, while the nave itself was lit by side windows in the positions of their lower parts. A careful study of the west end will show that there would still have been space for the western gallery below this upper floor.

As to the date of the church, the pilaster-strips and the double window with turned baluster shaft all suggest something in period C, and this is consistent with the theory advanced in Mr Woodman's booklet that the church was founded by the Lady Aelfgifu, who left Wing and other places to King Eadgar of England shortly before the year 975.[1] On the other hand, the arcaded nave closely resembles the surviving early fabric at Brixworth. Moreover, we have evidence for the former existence of similar arcaded naves, now destroyed, in the early buildings at Hexham and Jarrow. We therefore accept Jackson and Fletcher's suggestion that the main body of the church dates from period A and that the gifts of the Lady Aelfgifu are to be associated with a later modification of the church in period C. This later modification included the insertion of the vaulting within the main walls of the crypt, the substantial modification of the upper walls of the chancel, and the insertion of the double window in the east wall of the nave. All these deductions about the dating of the fabric are illustrated in Figs 341, 342 and 343.

DIMENSIONS

The nave is 61 ft long internally and 21 ft 2 in. wide, with side walls 3 ft thick and about 35 ft in total height, or 26 ft to the off-set. The chancel is 21 ft in width and about 20 ft in depth as measured from the eastern face of the chancel-arch. In the original arrangement, when the side walls of the nave were solid at the east, the effective area of the chancel would have extended to the top of the steps leading down into the nave, i.e. to a point about 28 ft from the east wall of the chancel.

The present chancel-arch is 19 ft 10 in. in width; and about 25 ft tall, if measured from the floor of the nave. The main arches of the arcades of the nave are 10 ft 4 in. in span and about 14 ft tall, with their imposts 9 ft above the stone floor of the nave. They rest on rectangular piers 3 ft thick and about 6 ft 4 in. in length.

The high side doorways recently discovered are about 2 ft wide and 6 ft tall, with their sills about 18 ft above the floor. The double window over the chancel-arch is about 4 ft wide and 4 ft tall, and its sill is about 30 ft above the floor of the nave.

The main walls of the church are 3 ft thick, but those of the north aisle are 2 ft 6 in. The doorway in the east wall of this aisle is 2 ft 6 in. wide and about 5 ft in height, as measured from the present external plinth.

REFERENCES ◆

Editorial, *Ecclesiologist*, 10 (1849–50), 230. Note of extensive restoration under the direction of Mr G. G. Scott, later Sir Gilbert Scott.

G. G. SCOTT, 'Anglo-Saxon remains at Iver and Wing in Bucks', *ibid*. 11 (1850–1), 58–9.

Editorial, 'Re-opening of a Roman basilica under the chancel at Wing', *R. Bucks*. 5 (1878–86), 147–8. Account of reopening of the crypt by Mr G. G. Scott (the younger) in 1880, it having been originally discovered by his father Sir Gilbert Scott, but not opened out.

G. G. SCOTT (the younger), *Essay on the History of English Church Architecture* (London, 1881), 44 and pl. X.

F. H. TATHAM, 'Wing Church', *R. Bucks*. 7 (1892–7), 153. Account of discoveries associated with removal of plaster in 1893, notably the pilaster-strips on the apse and the double window in the east of the nave.

F. H. TATHAM, 'The restoration of Wing church', *ibid*. 7 (1892–7), 328–31. Extracts from Mr T. O. Scott's report on the restoration. The arches of the main arcade claimed as Anglo-Saxon, as well as the apse and crypt; but some doubt cast on the chancel-arch because of its rough soffit and its lack of imposts.

W. NIVEN, 'Wing Church', *ibid*. 11 (1920–6), 48–9. Note of earlier references, and also that the vaulting and inner walling of the crypt is a later insertion within an earlier crypt that still has original plaster on its walls.

[1] A. V. Woodman, *Wing Church, Bucks*. (Aylesbury, 1958), 3 and 4. The will is no. VIII in D. Whitelock's *Anglo-Saxon Wills* (Cambridge, 1930), 21 and 119. It is possible that Aelfgifu was King Eadwig's widow, in which case the bequest would have been to her brother-in-law.

A. V. WOODMAN, 'Wing', *R. Bucks.* **16** (1953–60), 50 and 114. Details of discovery of the high side doorways like those at Tredington. Photograph facing p. 112.

J. T. MICKLETHWAITE, 'Something about Saxon church building', *Arch. J.* **53** (1896), 293–351. Wing, 307–8 and 341–4. Chancel-arch said to have been widened, 307.

R.C.H.M., *Buckinghamshire, North*, **2** (London, 1913), 331–5. Plan, 332. Photographs of exterior and interior. Chancel-arch said to be original.

E. D. C. JACKSON and E. G. M. FLETCHER, 'The apse and nave at Wing, Buckinghamshire', *J.B.A.A.*, 3rd ser., **25** (1962), 1–20. Important account of fresh excavations, with new deductions about the date of the fabric.

WINSTONE

Gloucestershire

Map sheet 157, reference SO 965093

Figures 621, 622

ST BARTHOLOMEW

Nave: period C3

Of the several late-Saxon or Saxo-Norman churches in the neighbourhood of Cirencester, Winstone is one of the most pleasantly situated, between the upper reaches of the Frome and the Churn, about 7 miles from Cirencester and within a mile of the Roman road to Gloucester. This church is a small, three-cell structure, consisting of a medieval west tower with saddle-back roof; an aisleless nave, marked as having been built about the time of the Conquest, by its north door and window; and a square-ended aisleless chancel, which might be contemporary with the nave, but which has no distinctive features other than its Early English side windows. The fabric is of small rubble with dressed-stone facings.

The medieval tower of two stages, with angle-buttresses at the west, is not bonded into the nave,

but is simply built against and over the west end, which has subsequently been strengthened with lateral buttresses.

The building of the nave by Anglo-Saxon workmen at a period not far removed from the Conquest is indicated by the early character of the north doorway and window, and by the more advanced character of the south doorway. The window closely resembles one at the neighbouring church of Coln Rogers; but whereas the evidence of the window is supported at Coln Rogers by pilaster-strips and by long-and-short quoining, there is no such definite confirmatory evidence at Winstone.

The north doorway is cited by Baldwin Brown as a typical example of Cotswold late-Saxon workmanship.[1] It has exceptionally large monolithic jambs, a massive flat lintel, chamfered on its upper edge, and a monolithic tympanum which is recessed 3 in. behind the round-arched head of the doorway. The doorway narrows appreciably towards the top, but its jambs are not built of through-stones; and they are rebated internally for the hanging of a door.

The north window, placed high in the wall, a few feet east of the doorway, is a small, narrow, round-headed opening, widely splayed internally. Its outer face is formed in a single rectangular stone slab, in which the aperture is outlined by a recessed rectangular area, within a raised outer frame about 4 in. in width.

The south doorway, by which the church is entered, is of the same general form as that on the north, with arched head, solid tympanum, and flat lintel; but more advanced Norman details are clearly in evidence side-by-side with Anglo-Saxon traditions. The latter show in the 'Escomb technique' of the jambs, and the simple bulbous bases of the nook-shafts; while the Norman influence appears in the recessing of the doorway, the cushion capitals of its nook-

[1] G. Baldwin Brown (1925), 395–6. It should be noted that the tympanum is monolithic, not of rubble masonry as shown in Baldwin Brown's fig. 182. Baldwin Brown (p. 396) says it would be difficult to date doorways of this type were it not that a doorway of similar type occurs on the north face of the tower at Wootton Wawen. But, as we mention under the latter place, we believe it is clear that the doorway at Wootton Wawen did not originally have its present chamfered lintel, which we believe to be an insertion of the same date as the blocking of the doorway. Nevertheless, we accept the doorway at Winstone as Anglo-Saxon on the cumulative evidence: first, of its rugged simplicity, particularly its monolithic jambs; secondly, of the adjacent window, so closely resembling that at Coln Rogers; and finally, of the small projecting stone *prokrossos* above the head of the arch. This *prokrossos* is not shown in Baldwin Brown's diagram.

shafts, the diaper pattern on the lintel, and the lozenge pattern cut on the tympanum. The archivolt-roll that is carried round the arched head of the doorway may be compared with that on the belfry windows at Langford, and it may therefore serve to confirm the fixing of this south doorway in the period of Saxo-Norman overlap.

The chancel-arch is of bold and simple character, of a single square order, of the full thickness of the wall, but not of through-stones. It is peculiar in possessing a second order of voussoirs, which form an outer arch, framing the inner, but neither projecting beyond it on the archivolt nor continuing to the imposts. Knowles states that the tooling on these outer voussoirs shows them to be an addition at the time of the restoration of 1876, when the upper part of this wall was rebuilt.[1] The square imposts are chamfered below and the square jambs are chamfered on the angle towards the nave; but these chamfers are perhaps a later 'improvement'. The north jamb is formed of a single huge stone, and that on the south is built of four through-stones in 'Escomb technique'.

If the chancel is contemporary with the nave, it now retains none of its original openings. There is no east window; the double window to the north is a later insertion, and of the two lancets to the south the western one at least appears to be original and therefore to fix the chancel as of Early English date. A well-defined square plinth runs round the whole of the nave and chancel and therefore seems to fix the plan as original even if the chancel has later been rebuilt.

DIMENSIONS

The nave measures 35 ft 8 in. by 17 ft internally, with walls 2 ft 5 in. thick and about 17 ft high. The chancel measures 16 ft 2 in. from east to west internally, by 13 ft 2 in., with walls also 2 ft 5 in. thick. The north doorway is 5 ft 11 in. high, by 2 ft 10 in. wide at the bottom, narrowing to 2 ft 8½ in. at the top; while the south doorway is 6 ft 7½ in. high by 3 ft ½ in. wide. The small north window, 6½ in. wide by 2 ft 6 in. high, has the sill of its aperture 8 ft above floor level. The chancel-arch is 4 ft 7½ in. wide by 7 ft 1 in. to the top of the imposts and about 9 ft 5 in. to the crown of the arch.

WINTERBORNE STEEPLETON

Dorset

Map sheet 178, reference SY 629898

Figure 623

ST MICHAEL AND ALL ANGELS

Main fabric of nave; with angel traditionally said to have stood over or beside the west door, but now built into south wall near west quoin: period uncertain, but probably C

About 4 miles west of Dorchester, the small church of Winterborne Steepleton stands close beside the seasonal stream which gives the village the first part of its name; while the second part is readily to be understood by reason of the western tower, with its stone steeple, which forms a prominent part of the small aisleless church.

The fabric is of roughly coursed small stone rubble, with large blocks of dressed stone for the quoins. The existence of a stone church on the site before the Conquest seems to follow with certainty from the survival of the carved stone angel, which is generally similar in form to the well-known pair at Bradford-on-Avon, but which is carved in higher relief and is seen full-face, with head upright, wings extended, body horizontal, and lower legs kicked up. That the present fabric is later than the carving itself also seems to follow from the way in which the angel-slab, about 30 in. long by 16 in. high, is now built inconsequentially into the south wall, immediately beside one of its quoin-stones, about 3 ft from the ground. The carving is dated by Talbot Rice to the first half of the tenth century, 'nearer 910 than 950', or possibly even to the reign of Alfred,[2] and it would therefore be possible for the present nave to be a

[1] W. H. Knowles, 'Winstone church, Gloucestershire', *Arch. J.* **85** (1928), 176–87. Detail of chancel-arch, 180. Plan facing p. 177. A very valuable account of the church.

[2] D. T. Rice, *English Art, 871–1100* (Oxford, 1952), 94.

later rebuilding of a tenth-century church which had been destroyed in the unsettled times of the tenth or early eleventh century.

Apart from the angel, which cannot reasonably be assumed to be *in situ*, the indications of pre-Conquest workmanship in the nave are the massive quoins, mainly of side-alternate technique; the stone-rubble walls, only 32 in. in thickness; and the tall, narrow, north and south doorways, whose heads are outlined by hood-moulds of half-round section. Both these doorways have plain semicircular solid stone tympana beneath their arched heads. These tympana rest on the jambs, without any imposts; and they leave rectangular doorway openings, both of which are about 7 ft high. Both doorways have their jambs rebated for the hanging of doors; and internally both doorways are of plain round-headed form without any imposts. The south doorway-opening is 47 in. wide and the north one only 36 in.

These indications are far from conclusive as to date; and it is a matter for great regret that no original windows have survived. There are some rather doubtful indications of a blocked window near the east of the south wall and others above the south doorway. The earliest surviving window is an Early English lancet in the west end, now opening to the tower; but there seems to be no doubt that the fabric of the nave is either of late-Saxon or early Norman date, and we think the former is the more probable.

DIMENSIONS

The nave is 39 ft long internally, by 16 ft 2 in. wide, with walls 2 ft 8 in. thick and about 15 ft high.

REFERENCES

Editorial, 'Saxon sculptured angel', *Wilts. A.N.H. Mag.* **46** (1932–4), 389. Brief notice of discovery.

Editorial, 'Carved angel from Dorset', *Ant. J.* **13** (1933), 315. May be dated to second half of tenth century.

WINTERTON
Lincolnshire

Map sheet 104, reference SE 928186

Figure 624

ALL SAINTS
Lower part of tower: period C3
Parts of walls of nave: earlier in period C

The Roman Ermine Street, running north from Lincoln to the Humber, passes within a mile of Winterton, about 3 miles before meeting the river at Winteringham Haven. At Winterton, and also at Roxby, nearby, considerable Roman remains have been found, including fine tesselated pavements.

The church of All Saints now consists of a long chancel, in the geometrical Decorated style; an Early English nave, with north and south aisles separated from the chancel by transepts; and a west tower, which is Anglo-Saxon to just above the level of the ridge of the roof of the nave. The aisles have been carried westward to flank both sides of the tower, so that much of its detail is only to be seen within the aisles. The fabric of the tower and of the original walls of the nave is of coursed rubble, with side-alternate quoins of relatively small stones.

The tower, which stands on a plinth of two square orders, is now of three stages, of which the lower two are Anglo-Saxon and the uppermost Early English. The only openings which now remain visible externally in the lowest stage are a west doorway and a debased lancet window above it. The doorway has been claimed as an original feature, modified in later times, but it shows no features which seem to us to justify this claim. Its jambs are built of rough ashlar and its head is formed of three parallel lintels whose lower faces appear to have been roughly cut away into a curve, perhaps to raise the level of the head when the level of the ground rose outside.

The second stage is separated from the lowest by a chamfered string-course on which stand double belfry windows in the three external faces to the north, south, and west. The through-stone slabs in these windows are supported by circular cylindrical mid-wall shafts. These shafts stand on square bases and have cushion capitals, of which that on the south face is enriched with chequer pattern. The square jambs, built of rough ashlar, support square imposts, which project slightly from the wall-face like the through-stones; and the round heads of the individual windows on the north and

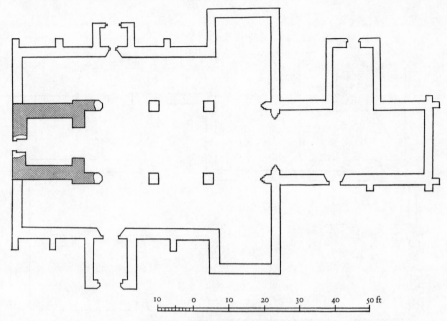

FIG. 344. WINTERTON, LINCOLNSHIRE

In this plan we have not distinguished in date between the earlier walls of the nave and the later side and west walls of the tower. On the site it is easy to see how the tower has been built against and over the earlier west wall of the nave.

west faces are cut in pairs of square lintels; while those on the south face are arched in well-laid voussoirs, as at the neighbouring church of Alkborough. Above the double windows, and separated from them by a further chamfered string-course, each face has a centrally-placed circular sound-hole, of which some are pierced through single square stone slabs, while others are made of two semicircles cut in rectangular slabs. A further string-course ends the Anglo-Saxon work, and separates it from the Early English belfry above.

Within the western ends of the aisles, almost the whole of the side faces of the lowest stage of the tower may be seen, with a tall, narrow, round-headed, internally splayed window high up in each face. The jambs are built of stones rather larger than the quoining, and the round heads are cut in the lower faces of square lintels. The east face of the tower towards the nave has a broad round arch of a single square order. This rests on square jambs with chamfered bases and quirked chamfered imposts, which are returned for short distances along both faces of the wall. Above the tower-arch, a narrow, flat-headed doorway with its sill about 16 ft from the floor opens to the upper chamber of the tower.

DIMENSIONS

The tower is 13 ft 6 in. square internally, with walls 3 ft 2 in. thick. The nave is 17 ft 2 in. wide; and sections of its side walls, 2 ft 9 in. thick and about 3 ft in length, remain at the west to serve as substantial responds for the arcades.

REFERENCES

J. T. FOWLER, 'Notes on All Saints, Winterton', *A.A.S.R.* **19** (1887–8), 363–75. Plan, history, and architectural description.

Editorial, 'All Saints Winterton', *ibid.* **27** (1903–4), lxvi–lxvii. Note of recent restoration, addition of clear-story and removal of plaster.

J. T. FOWLER, 'Discovery of a primitive nave at Winterton', *P. Soc. Ant.*, 2nd ser., **20** (1904), 20–4. Important evidence that the nave was built earlier than the tower.

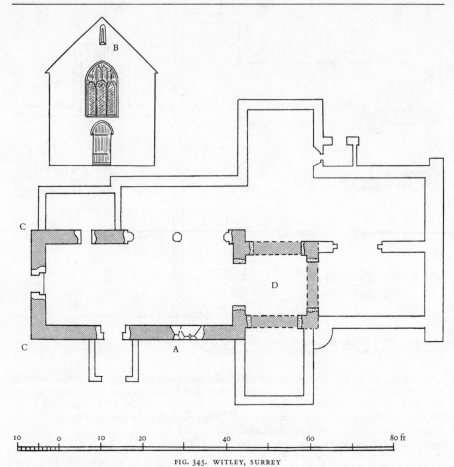

FIG. 345. WITLEY, SURREY

The plan shows the present-day church and the small two-cell pre-Conquest building from which it developed. A, the partially destroyed double-splayed south window discovered in 1916 (for details see Fig. 346); B, elevation of the west end, at the same scale, showing the complete double-splayed window high up in the gable; C, western quoins of plain rubble construction; D, the former pre-Conquest chancel, now cut through by Norman arches, and thus forming the base of the Norman tower.

WITLEY

Surrey

Map sheet 169, reference SU 946396

ALL SAINTS

South and west walls of nave: period C3

In pleasant rolling country, about 3 miles south-south-west of Godalming, the church at Witley stands close beside the road to Petworth. It now consists of a chancel with large northern Lady Chapel; a central tower with transepts; and a nave with north aisle. But there is reason to believe that the south and west walls of the nave are those of the original Anglo-Saxon aisleless nave, and that the tower stands on the site of the early chancel.

This dating of the nave is indicated by two tall, narrow, double-splayed, round-headed windows which have survived in the south and west walls.

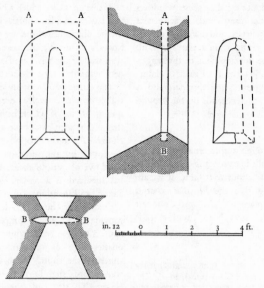

FIG. 346. WITLEY, SURREY

Details of the double-splayed south window. The interior face does not taper upward, whereas the actual aperture and the outer face both taper markedly, so that the aperture narrows from 9 in. at the sill to 6 in. at the springing of the head. The rectangular broken line in the interior elevation represents the outline of the oak frame for the window. Sufficient fragments of this were found in the wall to establish the rectangular shape of its head, and the wedge-like shape of its sides as shown at B in the plan. The sill is 10 ft above the floor of the nave.

The window in the south wall is close beside an inserted thirteenth-century window which nearly caused its destruction; and the other is in an unusual position, high up in the west gable, perhaps to light an upper chamber above the nave.[1]

The apertures of these windows are 3 ft 3 in. tall, and about 9 in. in width at the bottom, narrowing to 6 in. in width at the top, with the glass placed not in the middle of the wall but only 9 in. from its outer face. When the south window was first opened out, in 1918, it was found that a considerable part of the original oak framing had remained in place, where it had been built in during the erection of the wall. The inner and outer splays of the window and of its head were all found to be built of thin pieces of stone covered with plaster.

Repairs to the roof of the nave in 1927 gave an opportunity for opening out the second early

window, high up in the west gable. This window was also found to be of plastered rubble construction with its glazing slab still in position and in sound condition, cut from an oak plank 4½ in. thick. This slab was rebated externally, where clip-headed iron nails remained in position, no doubt to fasten a sheet of glass or horn. As in the south window, the glazing slab was not centrally placed; but in this window it was 11 in. from the outer face of the wall and 2 ft 6 in. from the interior.

The walls themselves are of plaster-covered brown stone rubble, with quoins and window-facings also built of rubble and faced with a thin coating of plaster. The walls vary between 3 ft 2 in. and 3 ft 6 in. in thickness, and for this reason Baldwin Brown regarded the windows as Anglo-Saxon survivals in an early Norman fabric; but the existence of a church here is recorded by Domesday Book and there seems no

[1] Compare Strethall, Essex.

good ground for doubting that these windows and the walls in which they stand are at least as old as the Domesday survey, and that the Norman south doorway is a later insertion in the early wall.

The history of the development of the neighbouring church of St Peter and St Paul at Godalming gives a strong presumption that here also at Witley the Norman tower stands on the ground plan of the Anglo-Saxon chancel.

DIMENSIONS

The nave is 44 ft 6 in. long internally by about 20 ft wide, with walls between 3 ft 2 in. and 3 ft 6 in. in thickness, and about 20 ft high. If we are correct in assuming that the Norman central tower takes the place of the pre-Conquest chancel, this would have been roughly 14 ft square in plan internally.

REFERENCES

P. M. JOHNSTON, 'The church of Witley, and Thursley chapel of ease', *Surrey A.C.* **18** (1903), 80–95. The church had not yet been recognized as having any pre-Norman features. Plan facing p. 80.

P. M. JOHNSTON, 'An early window and wall paintings in Witley church', *ibid.* **31** (1918), 28–44. Account of the discovery of the south window and its opening out. Dated plan, 29.

P. M. JOHNSTON, 'Witley and Thursley churches', *ibid.* **39** (1931), 104–11. Opening out of the west window.

V.C.H., *Surrey*, **3** (London, 1911), 67–9. Plan and brief architectural description before the discovery of the Anglo-Saxon features.

WITTERING
Northamptonshire
Map sheet 123, reference TF 056020

Figure 625

ALL SAINTS
Nave and Chancel: period C

An unusually complete example of a small parish church of the two-cell type has survived close beside the Great North Road about 3 miles southeast of Stamford on the outskirts of the busy modern development associated with the Royal Air Force aerodrome. To the originally aisleless

nave there has been added a Norman north aisle of two bays; and a later north chapel has been added to the chancel. At the west, an Early English tower with stone spire has been built against the west wall of the nave, without bonding into it or destroying its long-and-short quoins.

The fabric is of roughly coursed flattish stone rubble with carefully dressed long-and-short quoins, all six of which have survived, although that at the north-east of the nave is now inside the church. All traces of original windows have been destroyed by the insertion of larger medieval windows of various dates; but the chancel-arch has survived as a remarkable example of late-Saxon workmanship.

Outside the church, the long-and-short quoins provide an excellent example of the type which appears to have been designed to show as vertical pilaster-strips of uniform width, clasping the angles of the church, with the main expanse of wall set back slightly, and probably covered with plaster. To this end, the dressed faces of the quoining stand forward about 2 in. from the main face of the rubble wall, and the majority of the long upright stones have been chosen or worked to a uniform width of just under 1 ft; while the flat clasping stones and any of the uprights which are wider than normal have had the remainder of their faces cut back level with the main surface of the wall. A well-defined plinth of roughly dressed large stones runs along the whole of the south face of the nave, and square bases resting on it have been provided at each end as supports for the quoining and to emphasize its dignity.[1]

In the laying of the rubble walling there appears to have been some attempt at ornament, or at structural bonding, by the provision of larger stones to continue the horizontal line of certain of the flat bonding stones of the quoining, almost in the form of string-courses, but not now projecting beyond the main face of the wall. One of these courses runs along the south face of the nave just above the level of the eaves of the later south porch, and another is very evident at the top of the original south wall of the chancel, where it serves to separate the early work from later courses added above it. At the east end it is

---

[1] Compare Brigstock, and Cambridge.

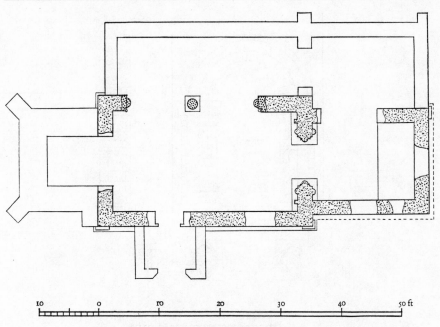

FIG. 347. WITTERING, NORTHAMPTONSHIRE

The plan shows how all six angles of the simple two-cell church have survived in spite of the addition of a Norman north aisle and a later west tower and north chapel. It also shows the plinth which supports the whole of the nave, and the massive bases upon which the long-and-short quoins rest. A corresponding plinth may be inferred round the chancel, and is shown by dotted lines; its existence cannot now be verified since a continuous skirting of stone flags runs along the base of the chancel wall. For details of the chancel-arch, see Fig. 348.

apparent that the gable has been raised at least twice to assume its present form.

The north-east quoin of the nave should be noticed within the north chapel, of the same form as the five quoins which still remain outside. The principal feature of the interior is, however, the chancel-arch, which is of a massive grandeur unequalled in any other of the smaller Anglo-Saxon churches. The heavy imposts are quite plain; but their faces, instead of being vertical, are sloped inward towards the jambs. The semi-circular arch and the jambs are both enriched with an unusual moulding, in the form of three rolls, of which one is on the soffit and one on each wall face. The nearest approach to this treatment is at Clayton in Sussex; but, whereas at Clayton a perfectly plain right-angled corner of wall projects to separate each pair of roll mouldings, here at Wittering a further enrichment has been provided

by cutting a hollow chamfer up each of the corners. The advanced character of the work might be taken to indicate a post-Conquest date were it not that the whole composition is outlined, on the western face towards the nave, by a characteristically simple Anglo-Saxon vertical pilaster-strip of square section, which is carried up beside each jamb and round the head of the arch as a concentric hood-mould. Finally, the jambs rest on perfectly plain square-edged plinths, and all the roll-mouldings have rudimentary bases and capitals in the form of slightly hollowed conical swellings; while the square strip-work is similarly provided with bases and capitals which, however, expand only sideways and not outward from the wall face.

DIMENSIONS

The nave is 30 ft long internally, by 16 ft broad, with walls about 2 ft 6 in. thick and about

FIG. 348. WITTERING, NORTHAMPTONSHIRE

Details of the chancel-arch. This arch should be compared with those at Bosham and Clayton (Sussex), and with the less sophisticated examples of square and half-round pilaster-strips at Stow (Lincolnshire), Skipwith (Yorkshire), and St Bene't, Cambridge.

25 ft high; while the chancel is 16 ft by 13 ft, with walls of the same thickness as those of the nave, and originally about 24 ft in height. The chancel-arch is 7 ft wide and about 14 ft in height.

REFERENCES

E. A. FREEMAN, *History of Architecture* (London, 1849), 209.

A. F. SUTTON, 'Churches visited from Stamford', *A.A.S.R.* **23** (1895-6), 81-101. Wittering, 85-7. Account of how it was proposed in 1869 to replace the church by a modern structure, but how the project was abandoned for lack of funds.

C. E. KEYSER, 'Notes on certain churches in Northamptonshire', *J.B.A.A.*, 2nd ser., **23** (1917), 1-22. Wittering, 20-2. Many pictures.

E. D. C. JACKSON and E. G. M. FLETCHER, 'Further notes on long-and-short quoins', *ibid.*, 3rd ser., **12** (1949), 1-18. Wittering, 12-14.

V.C.H., *Northamptonshire*, **2** (London, 1906), 540-1. Plan.

WITTON
Norfolk
Map sheet 126, reference TG 331315

ST MARGARET
West and north walls of nave, and possibly lower part of round west tower: period C3

From high land beside Witton Park, about 3 miles north-east of North Walsham, Witton church looks out across rolling country, with two or three other church-towers visible between itself and the sea.

The church has a sturdy round west tower; a nave with south aisle, south porch and north vestry; and an aisleless chancel, which is now of the same width as the nave but which clearly replaces an earlier, narrower, chancel, because its north wall is built with a straight joint against the original north-east quoin of the nave.

The fabric of the original north and west walls of the nave is mainly of uncut flints, but partly of carstone, with quoins of large blocks of the latter, about 7 in. in height and up to 2 ft in length along the wall. The original north wall of the nave, as defined by the quoins, is 44 ft 2 in. in length externally, and about 18 ft in height. Near to the top of this wall may be seen two circular, double-splayed windows, characteristic of the East Anglian late-Saxon period. The plaster coating on the external face of the wall is thin, and the splays of the windows may be seen to be built of the same uncut flints as the wall itself. The windows are not widely splayed, the openings in the wall-face being about 2 ft in diameter by comparison with mid-wall apertures of about 9 in. Their centres are about 15 ft above the ground and about 3 ft from the top of the original wall, which has subsequently been raised to form a clear-storey, with four Perpendicular windows.

The west tower has no features which would reliably define it as being contemporary with the original nave, for all its openings are of much later date; but it appears to be in bond with the nave, and an indication of pre-Conquest workmanship is given by the way in which a simple pilaster-strip is formed on the wall of the tower beside each of the junctions with the nave, as at Colney and Norwich, St Julian. These pilasters at Witton are 16 in. wide and 3 in. in projection.

There is little further detail to be seen internally, for the tower-arch is obscured by an organ; but a fragment of south wall remains to define the width of the nave, and the doorway opening to the north vestry may represent the remains of an early north doorway.

DIMENSIONS

The internal dimensions of the original nave were about 39 ft in length by 17 ft 6 in. in width, with walls 2 ft 9 in. thick and about 18 ft high.

REFERENCE

J. GUNN, 'Ecclesiastical architecture in Norfolk', *Arch. J.* **6** (1849), 359–63. Witton, 360, with picture from north-west.

WIVELSFIELD
Sussex

Map sheet 182, reference TQ 338208

ST JOHN THE BAPTIST
Saxo-Norman mouldings on north doorway

About 2 miles south-south-east of Hayward's Heath, the church at Wivelsfield has a pleasant outlook southward over open country. It now consists of a nave, with north and south aisles and south porch; a chancel, with south chantry; and a tower, which forms the western bay of the south aisle. The north aisle was added during a restoration and enlargement about 1869, and the only early feature surviving in the present church is the doorway which now stands in the outer wall of this aisle, whither it was moved, from the north wall of the nave, during those alterations.

This tall, narrow doorway has quite plain jambs, which are rebated for the hanging of the door. The imposts are chamfered, and the round head is of two orders, of which the inner is only slightly recessed, and both are carved with simple concentric mouldings on their vertical archivolt faces. On the inner order, the ornament consists of a half-round moulding between two of V-shape. The outer order has three concentric V-shaped mouldings, see Fig. 349.

On the strength of this doorway, we would not wish to claim a pre-Conquest date or Anglo-Saxon style. We would rather say that the date is uncertain and the style shows Anglo-Saxon affinities.

DIMENSIONS

The wall in which this doorway stands is 2 ft 6 in. thick, and the side walls of the original nave vary between this and 2 ft 9 in. Externally, the doorway is 2 ft 7 in. wide and 7 ft 2 in. tall; internally the rear-arch is 3 ft 3 in. wide and 10 ft tall.

REFERENCES

J. RUSH, 'St John the Baptist, Wivelsfield', *Sussex A.C.* **22** (1870), 50–6. Account of recent alterations, and plan prepared by the architects, Slater and Carpenter.

H. L. JESSEP, *Anglo-Saxon Church Architecture in Sussex* (Winchester, undated), 57.

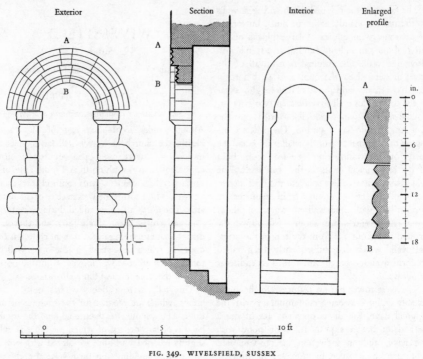

Exterior   Section   Interior   Enlarged
profile

FIG. 349. WIVELSFIELD, SUSSEX
Details of the north doorway.

WOODHORN
Northumberland

Map sheet 78, reference NZ 301888

ST MARY THE VIRGIN
Side walls of nave, over Norman arcades:
Saxo-Norman

Within a mile of the sea, by Newbiggin, Woodhorn church has a long aisleless chancel, an aisled
nave with south porch, and a square west tower
with double belfry windows of the Norman type
that may also be seen at Syston, Lincolnshire.
Woodhorn has sometimes been identified with
Wudecestre, one of the vills that were given to
St Cuthbert by King Ceolwulf when he resigned
the Northumbrian throne in 737 in order to
become a monk at Lindisfarne.

Within the aisled nave, the simple, round-
headed, single-splayed windows of an earlier,
aisleless nave may still be seen above the Norman
arcades which were later cut through the original
walls. The north and south arcades are both
Norman but of different dates, and the windows
which are cut into by the Norman arches must
therefore be of earlier Norman or pre-Norman
date. The latter seems more likely, since the walls
are only 2 ft 9 in. thick and about 20 ft high. The
windows are of a type which does not give any
reliable indication of date since it was used both
before and after the Conquest. The jambs are
built of stones that are larger than those of the
walling, but not megalithic; and the heads are
arched internally, but have monolithic pseudo-
arched external faces. On the whole, their character suggests a date early in the eleventh century,
particularly as their splays are carried through the
full thickness of the wall, without any external
rebate or chamfer.

682

Fragments of several pre-Conquest stones are set on the screen-wall between the nave and the tower; and some others are built into the walls of the south porch. These are all appreciably earlier in character than the fabric of the nave, and some may be as early as Ceolwulf's gift of vills to St Cuthbert.

DIMENSIONS

The nave is roughly 45 ft long internally and roughly 18 ft wide, with side walls 2 ft 9 in. thick and about 20 ft high. The north and south arcades are each of two Norman bays with an Early English bay at the east. It seems possible that the pre-Conquest nave was only as long as the two Norman bays, i.e. roughly 30 ft, and that the chancel was within the area now occupied by the eastern bay.

REFERENCES

F. R. WILSON, *Churches in the Archdeaconry of Lindisfarne* (Newcastle, 1870), 179–82. Description, south-west view, and plan.

Editorial, *T. Durham Northd. A.A.S.* 4 (1890–5), xxxi. Church dated as not earlier than twelfth century.

WOODSTON

Huntingdonshire

Map sheet 134, reference TL 186977

Figure 626

ST AUGUSTINE OF CANTERBURY

Small section of west wall: period C

Woodston is now a busy south-west suburb of Peterborough; and its ancient church, standing on the south side of the Oundle Road, has been rebuilt and enlarged no less than three times in the nineteenth century to provide space for the growing congregation. The fabric of the present aisled nave and aisleless chancel seems to be of the nineteenth century, with the exception of a small piece of Anglo-Saxon walling enclosed within the west tower, and a section of later medieval north wall in the western part of the chancel.

The pseudo-Norman west tower has been built partly within the church and partly over, rather than on, the ancient west wall; and the tower itself is supported on two large piers or buttresses within the church, and two which project as buttresses beyond the west front, so that the small piece of Anglo-Saxon walling is recessed behind and beneath the round west arch of the nineteenth-century tower, with a pointed west doorway of the same late date below it.

In this small fragment of rubble walling, about 2 ft thick, there survives a double-splayed, round-headed window, plastered within but bare without, so that the construction of its outer face is clearly to be seen. The jambs are built of the same thin pieces of rubble as the wall, and the head is turned with pieces of the same rubble laid in a characteristically Anglo-Saxon fashion, not radially, but with all the stones on one side of the arched head set roughly parallel, at an angle of about 45° to the horizontal. The wedge-shaped gap which is left at the crown of the arch is curiously filled by stones laid parallel to those in the north side of the arch.

The 'restoration' of 1845 was described at the time in the following words:[1]

The church of St Augustine, Woodstone, Hunts, well-known to ecclesiologists for its ante-Norman tower has recently been rebuilt and refitted throughout in a style and manner which deserve to be spoken of with high praise. The tower has been rebuilt exactly on the original plan with the exception of its now standing on four strong piers by which a portion of the original masonry of the lower part is preserved.

DIMENSIONS

The fragment of late-Saxon west wall which is visible externally is little more than 6 ft in width and rather less in height. It is about 2 ft in thickness. The double-splayed window has an aperture about 8 in. wide and 2 ft high, and its sill is about 9 ft above the floor of the church.

REFERENCES

R. P. BRERETON, 'Notes on some unrecorded Saxon work in and near Northamptonshire', *A.A.S.R.* **27** (1903–04), 397–400. Woodston, 398–9.

R.C.H.M., Huntingdonshire (London, 1926), 297.

---

[1] *Ecclesiologist*, **4** (1848), 138.

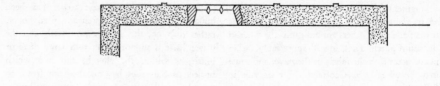

Tower

Chancel

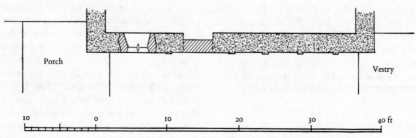

Porch

Vestry

10   0   10   20   30   40 ft

FIG. 350. WOOLBEDING, SUSSEX
Plan of the nave, showing its pilaster-strips. The later additions are shown diagrammatically.

WOOLBEDING

Sussex

Map sheet 181, reference SU 872226

Figure 627

ALL SAINTS

Nave: period C

About a mile north-west of Midhurst, in the valley of the Rother, the church of All Saints at Woolbeding has a most attractive setting, in the well-kept grounds of the manor, approached from the road by an avenue of yews, and with an extensive view to the south over open fields. The original church was presumably of the two-cell type, with a nave and chancel; but only the former has survived. The Domesday survey records the existence of a church at Woolbeding. There is a record of the building or repair of a chancel in the eighteenth century, when the present west tower was added; and the present chancel with its vestry and the south porch were added in 1870.[1]

The rectangular nave, now almost wholly covered by yellowish rough-cast, is clearly dated as a pre-Conquest building by the five vertical pilaster-strips on its south face and by three others, less well preserved, on the north. These vary between 6 in. and 8 in. in width, with a projection of about 2 in.; and, unlike most Anglo-Saxon pilasters, they are not of long-and-short construction, but of stones of fairly uniform vertical length between 1 ft and 2 ft. The pilasters are somewhat unevenly spaced along the wall faces, the eastern four on the south being at a spacing slightly greater than 4 ft with a gap of nearly 8 ft to the fifth, probably to allow space for a doorway, which is now blocked and visible only from inside. On the north face, the spacing is more difficult to understand, unless there was originally a fourth strip which has been destroyed by the insertion of the medieval window of three lights. If this were so, the four pilasters would have been at a more or less uniform spacing of about 7 ft. The pilasters run from the ground to the eaves, without any plinth or string-course to stop them at the ends.

Side-alternate quoining of large stones is

[1] V.C.H., Sussex, 4 (London, 1953), 86.

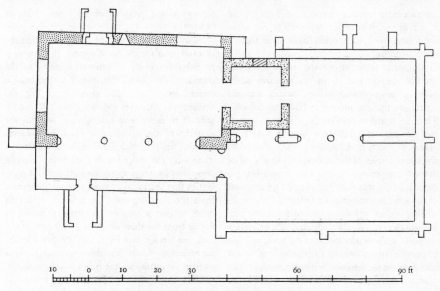

FIG. 351. WOOTTEN WAWEN, WARWICKSHIRE
The pre-Norman tower and the Norman nave, showing later additions in diagrammatic form.

visible at both the northern angles of the nave, that at the north-west being complete from the ground to the eaves. In the west wall of the nave, to the north of the tower, a vestige may still be seen of a plain, square string-course which must have run across the wall at the foot of the western gable, like those at Corhampton and Headbourne Worthy, in Hampshire.

No early windows have survived, nor are any Anglo-Saxon features visible internally, with the possible exception of the blocked south door, which at present shows no features that would serve to date it.

DIMENSIONS

The nave measures 34 ft 8 in. by 19 ft 3 in. internally, with walls varying between 2 ft 7 in. and 2 ft 10 in. in thickness.

REFERENCES

Sussex A.C. **7** (1854), appendix, 1–54. Lecture by Mr Sharpe on Anglo-Saxon Architecture in Sussex. Woolbeding noted, 14.

V.C.H., Sussex, **4** (London, 1953), 85–6. Plan, brief historical and architectural description.

WOOTTON WAWEN
Warwickshire
Map sheet 131, reference SP 153632
Figures 628–30

ST PETER

Central tower, below later Perpendicular belfry:
period C2

The attractive and interesting church of St Peter at Wootton Wawen stands beside open fields at a sharp corner of the busy main road, about 6 miles north-west of Stratford-on-Avon, on the way towards Birmingham. It now consists of a spacious nave with south aisle, a central tower, and a chancel with a large Lady Chapel along the whole of its south flank.

Only the lower part of the tower remains from the pre-Conquest church, the nave being fundamentally Norman, with Perpendicular windows, while its arcade and that of the Lady Chapel are both of simple Early English form. That the pre-Conquest church was cruciform in plan is shown by the four arches in the walls of the tower; but no trace now remains of that church except the tower, of which three arches are still in use, while the fourth has been partially blocked to form a north window.

All four of these tower-arches are of characteristically Anglo-Saxon form, with square jambs built of large through-stones, which are laid alternately upright and flat in 'Escomb fashion'. The plain, square imposts are also of through-stones; but the round arches each have a rubble or plastered section in the centre of the soffit; while the salient angles of the arches are constructed of dressed-stone voussoirs, whose lower members are remarkable in that they run round a great extent of the arch, in some cases up to thirty degrees. In all four arches, the voussoirs project about 2 in. beyond the faces of the wall, no doubt to form a support for the plaster facing of the wall, and also to provide an ornamental strip-moulding, which is stopped on the imposts. Where the walls are not plastered it is possible to see that, whereas the lower voussoirs are of thin stones of the shape of the projecting strip-moulding, the upper voussoirs are of considerable depth, bonding into the wall, with the strip-moulding worked on their exposed faces by cutting back the remainder.

The four tower-arches at Wootton Wawen are of particular interest, not only in their own right, but also for comparison with the two arches which have survived at Norton, in County Durham. The Norton arches are on a grander scale; but otherwise they present features closely similar to those at Wootton Wawen, namely a raised rib running round the wall-face at each arris, dressed-stone voussoirs on each arris, but rubble or plaster in the centre of the soffit, and a simple square soffit on simple square jambs. At Norton, all subsequent writers appear to have followed Hodges[1] in assuming that the arches were originally of two orders, of which the inner was at some later stage removed; but no such suggestion would appear to be tenable in the case of the arches at Wootton Wawen, because the imposts are intact, of simple square form appropriate to the jambs and the arches. We are therefore inclined to entertain some reservations about the accepted theory of the removal of an inner order at Norton.

Baldwin Brown recorded his opinion that the blocked north arch at Wootton Wawen was probably originally a doorway opening to the outside of the church; because its arched head is crossed by a horizontal stone lintel like the doorways at Miserden and Winstone.[2] We find it difficult to agree with this opinion or with the drawing of the doorway as given in Baldwin Brown's fig. 38, which shows the lintel as a piece of stone which is integral with the impost. Careful inspection on more than one occasion has satisfied us that the so-called lintel is entirely separate from the imposts, and of a different nature of stone, so that it must be an insertion, no doubt dating from the time when the lower part of the arch was blocked (see Fig. 352). We therefore see no reason to doubt that there was originally a transept or *porticus* on the north as on the south, and we think it would be of great interest if excavations could be made to verify this suggestion.

The fabric of the tower is of flat stone rubble, roughly coursed, with dressed stone for the long-and-short quoins, which are clearly visible on both eastern angles, where they run up from the later roof to the horizontal string-course, which separates the Anglo-Saxon tower from the Perpendicular belfry above. The western faces of the western quoins are visible within the nave, running from close above the medieval oak panelling to the full height of the roof-timbers. These western quoins end on corbels close above the oak panelling, thus seeming to indicate that up to that point the eastern wall of the Anglo-Saxon nave still remains, and that above this point the two short lateral sections of the later east wall were built upon the earlier wall and were abutted against the tower without bonding into it.

Externally, in the upper stage of the Anglo-Saxon tower, there are clear indications both to north and south of blocked round-headed openings, of which that to the north is sufficiently well defined to allow its size to be estimated at slightly less than 3 ft in width by about 4 ft in height. The *Victoria County History* records that similar

---

[1] *Reliquary*, n.s., 8 (1894), 8–11.

[2] G. Baldwin Brown (1925), 361. His fig. 38 is on his p. 68.

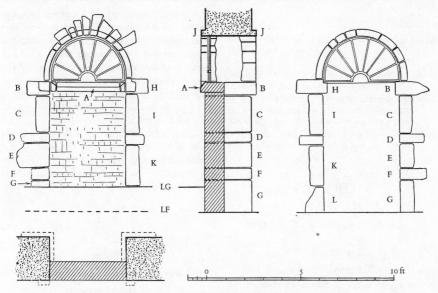

FIG. 352. WOOTTON WAWEN, WARWICKSHIRE

Details of the blocked northern arch of the tower. The proportions of the arch are not well seen externally because the level of the ground LG is now about 1 ft 3 in. above the level of the internal floor LF. The drawing shows clearly how the whole of the blocking masonry is a later insertion, including the 'lintel' A which Baldwin Brown mistakenly regarded as being integral with the imposts B and H. This 'lintel' abuts with straight joints at either end against the imposts, and it is made of stone of quite different texture from that of the imposts.

The broken lines in the section show how the jambs are constructed of through-stones. Note in the section and in the interior elevation how the imposts (which are also through-stones) project not only on the soffit but also into the church. By contrast, the external elevation shows how the soffit-faces of both imposts have been cut flush with the soffits of the jambs, no doubt when the opening was blocked. Note also how the projecting part of the impost H is 6 in. in height by comparison with the 9 in. total thickness of the impost itself, and note in the interior elevation how the excessive thickness has been cut away from the upper face of the impost.

The drawings show the unusual architectural composition whereby the strip-work hood-moulding J is placed on the arris of the arch. This shows particularly clearly in the section. It is true of all four arches at Wootton Wawen; and the same feature is also to be seen in the north and south arches at Norton (County Durham).

openings are to be seen inside the tower to east and west, and that they have rough, rubble, splayed jambs and heads.[1] It seems to us likely that this is the original belfry stage of the tower, and that these are original, single, belfry windows.

DIMENSIONS

The tower is 14 ft square internally, with walls about 2 ft 3 in. thick and roughly 40 ft high to the top of the Anglo-Saxon portion. The floor of the space beneath the tower is raised by two steps above the level of the floor of the nave, and the heights of the four arches recorded below are all measured from the internal floor-level:

	Width between jambs		Height to top of imposts		Height to crown of arch	
	ft	in.	ft	in.	ft	in.
West arch	6	10	9	8	13	1
East arch	4	8	8	1	10	6
North arch	4	1	6	9	8	10
South arch	4	2	6	9	8	10

The western quoining of the tower, as seen within the nave, extends downward to within about 16 ft of the floor; and if it is correct to assume that the corbels at the foot of the quoining rested on the original east wall of the nave, then the side walls cannot have been quite 16 ft tall.

---

[1] *V.C.H., Warwickshire*, **3** (London, 1945), 203.

REFERENCES

Editorial, 'Wootton Wawen', *A.A.S.R.* **16** (1881–2), xlvi. Note of recent restoration by Mr G. G. Scott.

Editorial, 'Wootton Wawen church', *Arch. J.* **83** (1926), 308–9. Brief description by the Vicar, with plan.

Editorial, 'Wootton Wawen', *J. Bristol Glos. A.S.* **55** (1933), 30–3. Architectural description by W. H. Knowles, and historical account by G. N. Rushforth.

V.C.H., Warwickshire, **3** (London, 1945), 201–5. Plan, pictures, and good architectural description.

WORLABY

Lincolnshire

Map sheet 104, reference TA 015140

ST CLEMENT

Tower-arch: period C

About 5 miles south of Barton-on-Humber, the village of Worlaby looks westward across the wide valley of the Trent from a sheltered position on the western slope of the ridge of high land that runs north from Lincoln to the Humber. The church of St Peter stands at the upper end of the village in extensive but rather neglected grounds. It has suffered so much at the hands of restorers that of its pre-Conquest fabric nothing now remains except the tower-arch, with the wall containing it, and the western ends of the side walls of the nave.

Records in the church relate that restorations were carried out in 1672 by Lord Belasyse; in 1837 by the Patron, John Webb; and in 1875 by Sir J. D. Astley. It is impossible now to know whether these works were really necessary, but their effect has been to produce a church with little character. The restorers spared the interesting tower-arch which, with the adjoining walling, may with reasonable certainty be regarded as original. The west wall in which it stands is of squared stone, laid in courses, with bigger stones

for the angles of the square jambs, and for the voussoirs of the round arch, which is of a single square order. The massive, square, chamfered imposts are single stones passing through the full thickness of the wall, and, although none of the other stones do so, the general impression is of massive Anglo-Saxon workmanship. The arch is 4 ft 3 in. wide and about 12 ft high, in a wall only 2 ft 6 in. thick.

Sections of what appear to be the original side walls of the nave remain to the west of the nineteenth-century arcades, serving to show that the original aisleless nave was 14 ft 9 in. in internal width, with side walls only 2 ft 6 in. in thickness.

WORTH

Sussex

Map sheet 182, reference TQ 302362

Figures 631–4

ST NICHOLAS

Complete cruciform church, which was very heavily restored in 1871:[1] period C3, or possibly earlier

The singularly complete church of St Nicholas, at Worth, 2 miles east of Crawley, is picturesquely situated on the outskirts of the Forest of Worth, which was formerly part of the great belt of ancient forest known as the *Andredswald*. A very complete account of the church before the restorations of 1871 was published in 1856, at which time the interesting double windows high up in the side walls of the nave had not been re-discovered.[2] Unfortunately, no record appears to have been kept of the nature of the fabric of the early walls of the apse when they were rebuilt in 1871, so that a unique opportunity was lost for settling once and for all whether pilaster-strips were a purely ornamental feature as is suggested by Baldwin Brown (pp. 239–43), or whether they were truly constructional features running

---

[1] G. Baldwin Brown (1925), 364, says 'The chancel... was rebuilt in our own time and has been, as the plan shows, disproportionately lengthened'. But his plan shows the internal length as 34 ft in complete agreement with the plan published by Walford in 1856 before the restoration. We believe that no change was made in the

ground-plan of the apse in the rebuilding of 1871. It is not clear to us that there is any evidence that the 're-building' of the chancel involved its demolition to ground-level as is implied in Baldwin Brown's statement.

[2] W. S. Walford, *Sussex A.C.* **8** (1856), 235–49.

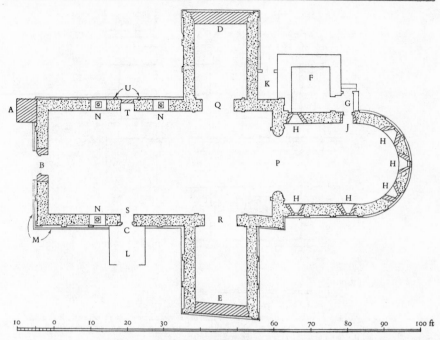

FIG. 353. WORTH, SUSSEX

General plan of the pre-Conquest church as it survives at present. The plan omits a number of later insertions of doors and windows which cannot easily be shown without hindering the clear representation of surviving pilaster-strips. The post-Conquest additions shown on the plan are: A, fifteenth-century buttress; B, thirteenth-century west doorway; C, fourteenth-century outer face to south doorway; D, E, thirteenth-century end walls to north and south transepts; F, G, modern tower and priests' doorway (1871); H, modern chancel windows (1871); J, modern doorway with window of type H above it; K, spiral stair to tower; L, modern porch (1886).

The principal distinctively Anglo-Saxon features of the church which appear on the plan are: the plinth which surrounds almost the whole church, particularly the double-stepped plinth M at the south and west; the many pilaster-strips, and the projecting long-and-short quoins; the double windows N on both sides of the nave; the great chancel-arch P; the two transeptal arches Q and R; the tall narrow doorways S and T. Outside the blocked north doorway T the broken lines U indicate pilaster-strips and a hood-moulding which formerly outlined the doorway but which have now been cut back to the face of the wall.

deeply into, or even right through, the wall, as has been suggested recently by Fletcher and Jackson.[1] We think it is almost certainly true that Anglo-Saxon pilaster-strips were primarily functional in derivation, even if they were also used for decorative purposes, but it would be most satis-

factory if a further opportunity should occur, as at Worth, for settling the matter with certainty.[2]

The church now consists of a nave with north and south transepts, an apsidal chancel slightly narrower than the nave, and a northern annexe which was added to the chancel in 1871, to provide

[1] E. D. C. Jackson and E. G. M. Fletcher, 'Long and short quoins and pilaster strips in Saxon churches', *J.B.A.A.*, 3rd ser., **9** (1944), 12–29, particularly p. 20 and fig. 9. Much the same suggestion was made as long ago as 1863 by Sir Gardner Wilkinson, who reported having seen buildings of similar technique in Tunisia, erected in the time of Justinian; in which the rubble fabric of the wall had wasted away, leaving the great upright pilasters

standing like columns, of the full thickness of the wall (*A.A.S.R.* **7** (1863–4), 41 ff.).

[2] Since this text was written, we have had the opportunity of examining the Anglo-Saxon pilaster-strip in the south wall of the nave of St Sampson's church at Cricklade (*Wilts. A.N.H. Mag.* **58** (1961), 16–17) and have been able to establish that it runs at least 11 in. deep into the wall.

FIG. 354. WORTH, SUSSEX

Detail of one of the double windows. The string-course which serves as a support for the windows is at a height of about 16 ft from the ground. The base for the mid-wall shaft has wrongly been shown square in plan. It should be rectangular, passing through the full thickness of the wall.

a vestry and to carry a small tower capped by a spire. Prior to the restorations, the north transept itself carried a wooden superstructure with a small shingled spire.

The outer walls of the church are of roughly coursed stone rubble; and they stand on a boldly projecting plinth which continues round the church as a support for the main walls, for the long-and-short quoins, and for the broad pilaster-strips which divide the walls into panels. Both the quoins and the pilaster-strips project about 3 in. from the face of the wall and, where any of their individual stones are wider than the standard width of the quoin or pilaster, the excess has been cut back so that the quoin or pilaster shows as a vertical strip of a uniform width of about 14 in. The decorative effect of this treatment would have been greatly enhanced if, as was probably the case, the whole surface of the wall was plastered.

The quoins run up the full height of the walls to the eaves, but the pilaster-strips are stopped on a bold horizontal string-course of about their own breadth, which runs round the whole church, but

which is placed at slightly different heights on its different parts. On the nave it is at a height of a little above 16 ft; on the chancel at a little below 15 ft; and on the transepts it serves as an eaves-course, at a level just below that of the string-course on the nave.

The string-course on the nave has the further purpose of serving as a base for the three remark-able double windows of which there appear originally to have been four; since two have sur-vived in the north wall and one in the south; while the space that would have been occupied by the second on the south is now taken by a much larger fifteenth-century window of three lights. These double windows have square jambs, which are cut straight through the wall and are each formed of two or three through-stone slabs set on edge. These jambs rest on bold, oblong, through-stone bases, and support similar imposts. All three windows have slightly bulging mid-wall shafts, which rest on bold, through-stone bases of rect-angular section, and which support rectangular through-stone slabs; while the round heads of the

FIG. 355. WORTH, SUSSEX

Details of the chancel-arch. The elevation shows the west face, as seen from the nave. The section shows how the arch is wholly built of through-stones. The left-hand plan is at the level of the jambs, thus showing the half-round section of the jamb and of the eastern pilaster-strip. The right-hand plan is at the level of the impost, thus showing the square section of the arch and of both its eastern and western hood-mouldings.

individual lights of each double window are arched in voussoirs which also seem to be through-stones.

Within the nave, the principal features are the three great arches which open to the chancel and transepts, the three double windows already described, and two very tall narrow doorways in the side walls of the nave. The doorway on the north is complete, but blocked; while the lower parts of the southern one have been cut away by the insertion of a wider but lower fourteenth-century doorway. These remarkable doorways are extreme examples of the Anglo-Saxon love of tall narrow openings, for their height is about four times their width. Their jambs are formed of large stones that are laid with something approximating to the alternating pattern of upright and flat stones that

is known as 'Escomb fashion'; and their arched heads rest on square imposts which project boldly on the soffit. In the southern doorway, most of the stones of the jambs and arch pass through from the inner face of the wall to the later medieval stonework of the outer face, a distance of about 2 ft 3 in. Rather less of the soffit of the northern doorway is visible, but the stones pass right across it. No trace of the southern doorway has survived externally; but in the outer face of the north wall it is possible to see the greater part of the arched head of the north doorway and parts of its jambs. A feature of particular interest is that the opening is outlined by strip-work which is carried up beside the jambs and round the head, and which, although now cut back flush with the face of the wall, is still clearly visible. The exterior face of the doorway is only 3 ft 3 in. wide, by comparison with 3 ft 9 in. internally, and it is therefore clear that the doorways were rebated internally for the hanging of doors. It should also be noted that, in contrast, to the rough rubble of the remainder of the exterior of the church, the walling in the neighbourhood of the north doorway is of squared stone.

The chancel-arch is one of the most impressive that survive from before the Conquest. The whole composition is thoroughly Anglo-Saxon in all its somewhat incongruous but nevertheless impressive components. The simple round arch, of a single square order, is wholly formed of through-stone voussoirs. The imposts themselves each consist of a massive, upper, square, flat slab which is separated by a quarter-round moulding from a smaller but thicker slab, whose lower edges have been rounded off to give a shallow cushion effect. Finally, the jambs or responds consist of half-round soffit shafts, only slightly less in diameter than the thickness of the wall. On both faces, the arch is outlined by strip-work, which is carried up beside the jambs and round the head as a concentric hood-moulding. On the west face towards the nave, the vertical pilasters are of plain square section, and the hood-moulding has apparently originally been of double, square-stepped, section; but, except for a small piece near the northern impost, the outer step has disappeared, leaving a broad flat moulding of plain square section. On the east face towards the chancel, the hood-moulding is of square section, like the moulding that remains on the greater part of the west face; while the pilaster-strips are of half-round section.

The two arches leading to the transepts are of generally similar form, but smaller and simpler. That on the south has been very heavily restored, and its jambs and imposts are now almost wholly restorations. Both arches are semicircular and of a single square order of through-stones; and both are outlined by a hood-moulding of simple square section, which is also carried down beside the jambs as pilaster-strips. The imposts are of two oversailing flat square slabs; and the jambs are of the same plain square section as the arches.

A peculiarity of the pilaster-strips and hood-mouldings of all three of these arches is that,

instead of the pilasters descending vertically from below the springing of the hood-mouldings, the pilasters are in all cases set a little further out from the soffit. This is particularly noticeable on the arches of the transepts and on the east face of the chancel-arch.

Apart from the three double windows of the nave there appear to be no others that can with certainty be said to be original. The narrow splayed window in the east wall of the north transept may be original, but it appears to have been modified later. High in the west wall of the south transept is a round-headed, blocked window, with built-up jambs and monolithic head, of a form which suggests that the window might be either a survival of the original fabric or an early Norman insertion.

In conclusion it should be noted that the plan of this cruciform church is characteristically pre-Norman in that the transepts and chancel are narrower than the central space against which their walls are built. The eastern quoins of the central space therefore stood free in the angles between the chancel and the transepts. The south-eastern quoin still stands free, but the north-eastern quoin has been obscured by the nineteenth-century vestry and tower. The plan should be compared with those of other late-Saxon transeptal churches, such as Dover and Breamore.

DIMENSIONS

Internally the nave is 59 ft 6 in. long by 26 ft 6 in. wide, with walls between 2 ft 7 in. and 3 ft thick, and about 30 ft high. The chancel is 34 ft 9 in. long (including the space of the chancel-arch) and 21 ft broad; while the transepts (excluding the space of their arches) are about 19 ft in length from north to south, by about 14 ft broad. The walls of the transepts are only about half the height of those of the nave, and their north and south end walls both appear to have been wholly rebuilt except at the quoins.

The chancel-arch is 14 ft 1 in. in width and 22 ft 6 in. in total height. The arches to the transepts are about 8 ft 8 in. wide and 14 ft 7 in. high. The remarkable north and south doorways are about 14 ft high, and in width they are 3 ft 9 in. internally, and only 3 ft 3 in. externally.

The double windows are about 4 ft 6 in. wide

and 5 ft 9 in. tall, with individual lights about
1 ft 6 in. wide. Their sills are about 17 ft above the
floor.

REFERENCES

W. S. WALFORD, 'On the church at Worth', *Sussex A.C.*
8 (1856), 235–49. Good architectural description, with
plan and many important sketches of details before
the restoration of 1871.

Editorial, 'Notices', *Arch. J.* **13** (1856), 197–8. Extracts
from Walford's paper.

G. G. SCOTT, *Lectures on the Rise and Development of
Medieval Architecture*, **2** (London, 1879), 44–6. Plan,
and sketches showing details after the restoration.

C. LYNAM, 'A Brighton congress note', *J.B.A.A.* **42**
(1886), 304.

J. T. MICKLETHWAITE, 'Something about Saxon church
building', *Arch. J.* **53** (1896), 293–351. Worth, 325.

V.C.H., Sussex, **7** (London, 1940), 197–9. Plan, and
pictures from old prints to show church before
restoration.

P. EDEN, 'Worth: church of St Nicholas', *Arch. J.* **116**
(1959), 240–1. Discussion of dating; some details of
the extent of the restoration in 1871; good plan;
interesting pre-restoration pictures.

WOULDHAM
Kent
Map sheets 171 and 172, reference TQ 712643

ALL SAINTS
*Main fabric of nave, pierced by later openings:
period C*

The small village of Wouldham stands on the east
bank of the Medway, about 3 miles upstream
from Rochester, with its interesting church close
beside the river. The church now consists of a long
aisled nave and aisleless chancel, with an organ-
chamber at the east of the north aisle and a square
tower oddly placed to the north of the same aisle
and near its western end. The present nave comprises both the nave and the chancel of the original
church, and the present Early English chancel is
wider than the eastern part of the nave. The church
has developed into its present form by a series of
additions which have left the architectural history
very plainly recorded, and for this reason the
church is of particular interest.

The original western quoins of the pre-Conquest

church may be seen externally at the west, built of
plain rubble, with occasional bonding courses of
tiles. It is interesting to note that the narrow,
early, north aisle was not continued quite to the
west, so that the north-west quoin still shows as
an angle; while the west wall of the later and
wider south aisle is built in line with the main
west wall, but with a straight vertical joint against
the original south-west quoin.

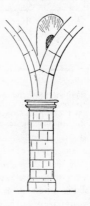

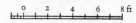

FIG. 356. WOULDHAM, KENT
The double-splayed window above the
later south arcade.

In the interior of the church it should be noted
at the east of the nave how the eastern bay, with
the organ-chamber on the north, is narrower than
the remainder and represents the original chancel.
The north wall, containing the opening to the
organ-chamber is original; but the south wall has
been rebuilt in line with the original south wall of
the nave.

The clearest evidence for the date of the original
fabric is provided by the double-splayed, round-
headed window which has survived in the south
wall of the nave, above the circular pier which
supports the two central arches of the south arcade.

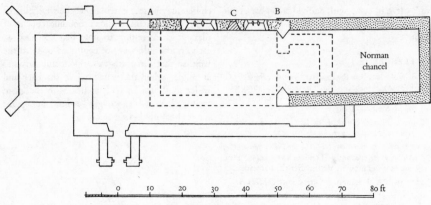

FIG. 357. WROXETER, SHROPSHIRE

Plan showing the surviving pre-Conquest north wall AB and the outline of the present church. The broken lines represent a somewhat conjectural reconstruction of the pre-Conquest ground-plan. The blocked window C has been shown as single-splayed. This is also conjectural but the shape could perhaps be settled with certainty if some plaster could be removed from the interior face of the wall.

The head and the eastern jamb of this window are practically complete, and they serve to fix the church with certainty in the late-Saxon period.

The history of the development of the aisles over a period of years is clearly to be seen from the differing character of their various arches and from the sections of solid wall which intervene between parts of the arcades which were developed separately. These, however, lie outside our province and we therefore do not describe them further, since they do not contribute to an understanding of the pre-Conquest fabric.

DIMENSIONS

The original nave is 14 ft 8 in. wide internally, and roughly 50 ft long, with side walls 2 ft 7 in. thick and about 17 ft high. The chancel seems to have been about 12 ft square.

The surviving double-splayed window was 2 ft 8 in. wide in the outer face of the wall, and at least 3 ft 8 in. tall, with its aperture placed not quite in the middle of the wall but a little nearer the outer face. Its head is 13 ft above the floor.

REFERENCE

J. C. Cox, *Kent* (Methuen's Little Guides), 6th ed., revised by P. M. Johnston (London, 1935), 303. Church restored by Christian in 1885. Double-splayed window noted, but incorrectly said to be near the west.

WROXETER

Shropshire

Map sheet 118, reference SJ 563082

Figure 635

ST ANDREW

North wall of nave: period doubtful but probably A

The ruins of the Roman town of Viroconium lie between the Severn and Watling Street, about 5 miles south-east of Shrewsbury. The present village of Wroxeter straddles the south part of the Roman town-wall, while the church of St Andrew lies just within the original enclosure. The fabric of the Anglo-Saxon north wall of the church is of large re-used Roman stones; and two Roman columns now serve somewhat incongruously as gateposts.

The church originally consisted of an aisleless nave and chancel, of which only the north wall of the nave now survives. A new chancel, slightly wider than the nave, but still aisleless, was added in the twelfth century; and it remains practically complete. The nave was extended westward in the thirteenth century, and was given a south aisle along part of its length in the fourteenth. The tower probably dates from the sixteenth century, although it contains much re-used earlier material. This brief account of the architectural history may be concluded by referring to the demolition of the south aisle and the widening of the nave southward over its whole length, in the eighteenth century.

The eastern 40 ft of the north wall of the nave represent the original north wall of the pre-Conquest nave; and, apart from the insertion of two later windows and the blocking of its original window, this section of walling has survived unchanged, with massive quoins at each end to mark its original extent. The wall is wholly of large, squared stones, laid in courses averaging about 20 in. in height; and the quoins are side-alternate in form, coursed with the walling. A square string-course, which runs along the top of the wall, is about 10 in. in height, with a projection of about 2 in.; and the fact that it is carried 2 in. beyond the west face of the quoining may be taken to show that the string-course was originally continued across the western gable of the nave.

The blocked window is unfortunately not visible internally; but its external face is of simple rectangular form. Its head consists of a large square stone, and its eastern jamb is also monolithic, while the western jamb is of two stones. The complete difference in type between this simple opening and the more developed, double-splayed, round-headed windows of well-wrought stone at the neighbouring churches of Barrow and Diddlebury seems to us to justify the assignment of an earlier date to Wroxeter. The existence of the horizontal string-course has, however, been commonly accepted as fixing a date in period C. It would probably be possible to get further evidence of date if the blocked window were to be opened out so as to allow the details of its construction to be seen.

High up in the eighteenth-century south wall of the nave there has been preserved, just below the corbel-table, a piece of cross-shaft about 4 ft long and 10 in. wide. It has a roll-moulding along its edges, and the visible face is ornamented with three roundels of vine-scroll, above a panel of interlace which springs from the tail of a creature like a giraffe. It is a fine piece of Mercian work, probably of the eighth or early ninth century.

Built into the base of the south jamb of the chancel-arch is another carved stone, about 2 ft long and 6 in. tall, with a band of carving which shows rather fat, fowl-like birds pecking at worms or snakes. The pattern is reminiscent of the Roman stone that is now built into the south wall of the nave at Hexham, but the execution is much less accomplished.

DIMENSIONS

The original internal dimensions of the nave seem to have been about 37 ft by 20 ft.

The blocked north window is 2 ft wide and 2 ft 6 in. tall, externally, with its sill 11 ft 6 in. above the ground.

REFERENCES

H. M. Scarth, 'The church and monuments of Wroxeter', *J.B.A.A.* 17 (1861), 85–99. Church described as Norman and later. Note of the fragments of carving. Note that church was mentioned in Domesday Book.

D. H. S. Cranage, *An Architectural Account of the Churches of Shropshire*, 2 (Wellington, 1912), 650–60. Good account of the architectural history.

C. A. R. Radford, 'Wroxeter Church', *Arch. J.* 113 (1956), 209–10. Good architectural history, with dated plan. Cross-shaft dated as good Mercian work of eighth century or early ninth.

YAXHAM

Norfolk

Map sheet 125, reference TG 007107

ST PETER

Round west tower, west and north walls of nave: Saxo-Norman

About 2 miles south-east of East Dereham, the small village of Yaxham has a church of considerable interest. Cox places the round west tower and the arch leading to the nave in the early Norman period, and he assigns the rest of the church to the fourteenth century, with some later insertions;[1]

---

[1] J. C. Cox, *County Churches, Norfolk*, II (London, 1911), 131.

Messent, on the other hand, cites the round tower as a good sturdy example of the Saxo-Norman period, with a high opening to the church on its east side;[1] while Cautley says that the lower storey of the round tower is undoubtedly pre-Conquest.[2]

The church now consists of the round west tower, a nave with south aisle and south porch, and an aisleless chancel with north vestry. The fabric is mainly of flint, but the walls of the nave also contain a proportion of brown carstone; but their western and north-eastern quoins are wholly of this stone, while three decorative bands of it are carried round the tower between the level of the top of the Perpendicular west window and the top of the roof of the nave.

The church is difficult to date with any certainty. Features which indicate a pre-Norman date are the use of carstone, particularly for quoins and to form decorative courses; the filling of the re-entrant angles between the nave and the tower with quarter-round pilasters; the tall, round-headed tower-arch with non-radial voussoirs; the tall round-headed upper doorway high above; and the very tall thin side walls of the nave. Against this and in favour of a Norman date are the tooling of the carstone quoins; and the construction of the tower-arch and the upper doorway wholly without the use of through-stones. On balance, we favour an Anglo-Saxon or Saxo-Norman dating for the reasons given above, particularly the use of quarter-round pilasters.

DIMENSIONS

The nave is 20 ft 9 in. wide internally, and about 51 ft long, with side walls 2 ft 7 in. thick and over 20 ft in height.

The tower-arch is 7 ft 7 in. wide and 15 ft 8 in. high, in a wall 4 ft 10 in. thick. The upper doorway, about 3 ft wide and over 6 ft tall, has its sill about 19 ft 6 in. above the floor.

The tower is 12 ft 6 in. in internal diameter, with walls 3 ft 6 in. thick and about 55 ft high.

YEAVERING
Northumberland

Map sheet 71, reference NT 925305

Buildings associated with King Edwin's
'villa regalis ad Gefrin': period A

A brief account must be given of the remarkable discoveries at Old Yeavering about 4 miles west of Wooler. The site was located by aerial photography in 1949[3] and was excavated between 1953 and 1958.[4]

Bede (*H.E.* II, 14) refers to *ad Gefrin* as the place to which Paulinus went with King Edwin and at which he baptized many of the Northumbrian people in the waters of the River Glen; but the excavations have established that the township was established well before Edwin's time and was occupied for many years afterwards, although twice destroyed by fire.

The earliest structure was a large fort, which was enclosed by a double palisade of timber and earth. It is thought to be a work of the second half of the sixth century, and is of a type hitherto unknown in Britain. The development of the township outside the fort began early in the seventh century, probably in the reign of Æthelfrith. The buildings associated with this period comprised a large and massive timber hall, a number of smaller halls, perhaps for retainers, one building of more primitive type, perhaps for servants, and one building that showed unusual features suggesting that it might have been a pagan temple, which was later converted to Christian use.

A remarkable feature of this township was a large timber grand-stand, which the excavations indicated as having been enlarged at a later date, and repaired after partial destruction by fire. It may reasonably be interpreted as the meeting-place of the moot.

The great hall was later replaced by another, of more ambitious design; and the grand-stand was

---

[1] C. J. W. Messent, *The Round Towers to English Parish Churches* (Norwich, 1958), 248.

[2] H. M. Cautley, *Norfolk Churches* (Ipswich, 1949), 272.

[3] D. Knowles and J. K. S. St Joseph, *Monastic Sites from the Air* (Cambridge, 1952), 270.

[4] A preliminary account of the results of the excavation, directed by B. Hope-Taylor, was given in *Medieval Archaeology*, I (1957), 148–9. The ground has been restored to agricultural use, and no trace of the early buildings can now be seen.

enlarged, as has been mentioned above. These developments are probably to be associated with Edwin's reign; for the next evidence was of a disastrous fire, which virtually destroyed the township, and which may be associated with the ravaging of Northumbria by Cadwallon after Edwin's defeat and death in 632.

The township was next rebuilt, but in a lighter construction; and the buildings were of a new plan, with a porch at the gable-ends. At this period an extensive cemetery developed round a church; and then the evidence indicated a second destruction of the village by fire, perhaps a result of Penda's ravaging of Northumbria in 651, when Bede (*H.E.* III, 16) records his attempt to reduce the fortress of Bamburgh by fire.

After this second destruction, the township was again rebuilt; and a coin found in the great hall indicates that it was occupied until 670 at least. Bede (*H.E.* II, 14) records that the township was later abandoned in favour of a place called *Melmin*. Further photographs suggest that this latter place is to be identified with Milfield, about 2 miles to the north, beside the River Till into which the Glen flows.[1]

YORK

Map sheet 97, reference SE 607520

ST CUTHBERT
East wall of chancel: period uncertain

The medieval walls of York form an almost complete enclosure round the city; but there is a gap at the north-east, where the waters of the River Foss and the marshes beside it were used in place of a wall and ditch. The northern part of the wall ends beside the Foss at the junction of Jew-bury and Peasholme Green, with St Cuthbert's church just inside the wall.

The east end of the chancel is of earlier fabric than the rest, and it is of interest to note that there is no east window. In the absence of any opening, or of distinctive quoining between the early wall

and its lateral extensions, it is difficult to give any reliable indication of date, or indeed even to say with certainty that the wall is of pre-Conquest workmanship. This church is, however, one of those mentioned in the Domesday Book.

YORK

Map sheet 97, reference SE 600514

Figures 636–8

ST MARY BISHOPHILL JUNIOR
West tower: period C3

Even in the complicated maze of York's ancient streets it is easy to find this church by entering the city through Micklegate, on the road from Tadcaster, and by turning first right into Priory Street, and then left, to where the church stands on the corner of Bishophill.

The church used to be closely hemmed in by buildings, but recently the area has been greatly cleared; the north side, however, is still inaccessible unless permission be obtained to enter a private garden. Internally the church is attractive, although rather dark. It is entered down steps from the street; and it now consists of a chancel with north chapel, an aisled nave, and a west tower.

The masonry of the tower is of very varied character: in part it is of quite large blocks of brown sandstone; in part of Roman tiles; and in part of limestone, which is sometimes in blocks, and sometimes in small flat pieces that are laid either horizontally or in slanting herring-bone formation. The quoins are mainly of the brown sandstone, laid in side-alternate fashion; and in the lower part of the tower they are of quite large blocks.

The tower is the most southerly of the interest-ing group in which each double belfry window is outlined by a surrounding frame of strip-work.[2] Of this group, St Mary's is unique in the mixed nature of its building material, all the others being of roughly squared blocks of stone of uniform character throughout the walls and quoins. This

---

[1] D. Knowles and J. K. S. St Joseph, *loc. cit.* 270.
[2] The surviving instances of belfry windows of this type

are at Billingham, Bywell, Monkwearmouth, Ovingham, Wharram-le-Street, and York.

may reflect the antiquity of the establishment of a church on this site and the re-use of material from an early predecessor in the building of the present fabric. Articles found in Roman coffins have given evidence of the existence of Christianity at York in Roman times; and Eusebius recorded the presence of a Bishop of York at the Council of Arles in 314. A church at York in those days would have been outside the walls; and it is known by finds in the surrounding district that Bishophill was then thickly populated.

The unbuttressed square tower rises sheer from the ground to the small off-set which separates the belfry from the plain lower stage. The ground floor is lit by windows on the south and the west; but both of these are later insertions that have left no trace of what may have been there before. Still in the plain lower stage, the first-floor chamber is lit by two narrow windows with rubble jambs and square lintel heads, one in each of the north and south walls.

The simplicity of the tall lower stage gives further emphasis to the richer belfry stage, with its four double windows. The window in the west face has been replaced by a round-headed, Gothic opening of two lights, but the strip-work at the sides has not been disturbed. The other three windows have survived intact. Their plain, circular, cylindrical, mid-wall shafts have no bases or capitals; and they support plain, chamfered, through-stone slabs. Their square jambs are faced in ashlar masonry, with chamfered through-stone imposts; and the round heads of the individual lights are arched with thin slabs of rubble, which are laid with reasonably radial joints. The outlining strip-work, of plain square section, rises in the form of vertical pilasters from square bases which rest on the off-set, some feet below the sills of the windows. These pilasters cross the main imposts, to support their own imposts just above; and a hood-moulding then runs round the whole head of each window in a semicircle, enclosing a plain tympanum of the same fabric as the rest of the surface of the wall.

As at Wharram-le-Street, the masonry of these belfry windows shows a straight joint which runs down the wall from the foot of each jamb, as if the windows had originally been much deeper, or had had steeply sloping sills which had later been built up into the present form. Baldwin Brown favoured the former of these alternatives, but Jewitt's drawing published by Rickman in 1847 appears to confirm the latter, for it shows windows with apertures of the present size, but with sills extending horizontally only through the inner thickness of the wall and then sloping steeply to the level of the off-set beside the bases of the surrounding strip-work.[1]

The original masonry of the tower extends for a few courses above the hood-mouldings of the belfry windows; and the tower then ends in a later medieval battlemented parapet with corner finials.

The ground-floor chamber of the tower is now almost wholly occupied by the organ, but this has fortunately not been allowed to block the tower-arch which Baldwin Brown regarded as perhaps the finest from before the Conquest, with the possible exception of those at Barnack and Cambridge. The arch is recessed, in two plain square orders; and so are its jambs and their imposts, each of which is constructed of two superimposed, over-sailing slabs of stone. The arch is outlined on both eastern and western faces by a plain square hood-moulding; but this is not now carried down beside the jambs in the form of pilaster-strips. There seems, however, to have been provision for pilasters beside each jamb, because a short section of pilaster runs from the upper section of each impost, across the face of the lower section, and then ends somewhat lamely. The two orders of the arch are logically constructed of separate sets of voussoirs; whereas in the jambs the two orders are sometimes of separate stones, but are sometimes formed by cutting the necessary outline on great single stones which run through the full thickness of the wall.[2] The jambs rest on plain cubical bases about 1 ft 4 in. tall, which also serve to support the sides of the single step which leads up from the nave to the tower.

---

[1] G. Baldwin Brown (1925), 403. T. Rickman, *Styles of English Architecture*, 5th ed. (London, 1848), appendix, xxxix.

[2] Baldwin Brown, 404, said 'The stones of the jambs are through-stones in which the recessing is cut'; in fact, as noted above, this is true of some courses, but not of others.

A puzzling feature in the wall above the tower-arch is provided by what appear to be two straight vertical joints in the masonry running vertically upward from the two imposts, as if the arch and the wall above it were later insertions in an earlier wall. Closer inspection shows, however, that these straight vertical lines are not joints in the wall but are shallow recesses cut in it. We are indebted to Dr E. A. Gee for the information that they formerly housed gas-pipes, which led to brackets on the imposts.

No distinctive openings have remained in the side walls of the nave to help with the assignment of a date; but as they are thin (2 ft 8 in. on the north and 2 ft 1 in. on the south) it is possible, although by no means certain, that they are early walls through which the later arcades have been cut.

In 1913 a fragment of a cross-shaft was discovered in the south wall of the chancel to the west of the priest's door, whence it was removed and placed in the church.[1] It is a piece about 34 in. high and 14½ in. by 8¼ in. below, tapering to 9½ in. by 7 in. above. Three sides bear basket plait, and a serpent with coiled tail. The fourth side has a debased scroll, with branches which are not all joined to the stem.

DIMENSIONS

The tower is roughly 26 ft square in external plan and about 73 ft in total height. Its walls are 3 ft 1 in. thick at the base, thinning to 2 ft 5 in. at the belfry. The tower-arch is 10 ft wide and 16 ft high from the floor of the nave to its crown. The nave is now 21 ft 8 in. wide internally.

REFERENCES

Anonymous, 'Anglo-Saxon church', Ecclesiologist, 1 (1842), 190–2. Claimed as Anglo-Saxon. Details of belfry and tower-arch.

C. C. HODGES, 'Pre-Conquest churches of Northumbria', Reliquary, n.s., 8 (1894), 202–5.

YORK

Map sheet 97, reference SE 601514

Figures 639, 640

ST MARY BISHOPHILL SENIOR

Lower parts of west and south walls of nave; and upper part of north wall of nave, above Transitional Norman arcade. Period uncertain, but perhaps as early as A

On the west side of the Ouse, Bishophill Senior runs roughly parallel to the river, and mid-way between it and the city wall. Bishophill Junior joins it on the north, and at the south Cromwell Road runs down to the Ouse at Skeldergate Bridge. When we first visited St Mary Bishophill Senior in 1961 it was a roofless ruin, scheduled for demolition, and clearly in a very dangerous condition.[2] It had not long been appreciated that any part of the fabric was earlier than Norman; and we are indebted to Dr E. A. Gee for directing our attention to the earlier fabric and for describing to us the Romano-British walling which he found beneath the Anglo-Saxon nave. As we saw it in 1961, the church consisted of a nave and a chancel without structural separation, a north aisle, a square tower over the western bay of the aisle, and a south porch of entry.

The chief indications of pre-Conquest fabric were to be seen in the south-west and north-east quoins of the nave, but the megalithic construction of the lower courses of the south wall was also significant. The lower part of the south-west quoin was of regularly laid side-alternate character, of big stones such as are to be seen in many of the early Northumbrian churches. On the exterior of the south wall, to the east of the porch, there was clear evidence of a straight vertical joint where the megalithic fabric of the original nave joined the much smaller rubble fabric of the later chancel. The same contrast of fabric could also be seen internally; where there was also the suggestion of the stub of a wall turning northward at the east of the original nave.

The best evidence was, however, to be seen over the late-Norman north arcade of three bays. These arches had clearly been cut through the pre-Conquest wall, for the outer face of the north-east quoin could clearly be seen in the aisle over the third column from the west. A straight vertical joint ran up the wall at the east side of this quoin,

[1] *Yorks. Arch. J.* 23 (1915), 360.   [2] The whole church has now (1964) been demolished.

where the later wall of the widened chancel abutted against the quoin, without any bonding. The earlier wall to the west was clearly distinguishable from the later wall to the east, not only by its different fabric, but also by the large areas of early plaster which still remained in place on the outer wall of the early nave. The south face of this wall within the nave, also gave clear indications of the architectural history, for not only was there the same straight vertical joint between old and new fabric, but it was also easy to see, at a distance of about 2 ft 6 in. to the west of that joint, another straight vertical line which clearly indicated the western edge of the original east wall that had been cut away when the chancel was widened in the Middle Ages.

ROMANO-BRITISH REMAINS

Dr Gee told us of the survival of the west and south walls of a Romano-British building roughly beneath the corresponding walls of the Anglo-Saxon nave but slightly differently oriented. On the site it was possible to see that the south-west angles of the two structures were practically coincident but that the west wall of the earlier fabric soon began to protrude westward like a plinth below the Anglo-Saxon wall. Inside the nave it was also possible to see the earlier wall protruding northward from the Anglo-Saxon south wall. The Romano-British structure consisted of a rectangular building divided by a cross-wall into two cells, respectively about 28 ft and 18 ft in internal length from east to west. The excavations had yielded no domestic remains; and it was therefore possible that the building was a church, although there was no positive evidence to prove this.

DATE OF THE ANGLO-SAXON FABRIC

In the absence of any surviving openings it is difficult to assign a reliable date to the Anglo-Saxon church, but the megalithic side-alternate quoining is consistent with an early date (period A) and this is also supported by the way in which the fabric is placed on top of a Romano-British building. It is tempting to believe that the use of the words Senior and Junior in the names of the two churches is an indication of their relative dates.

There is certainly good ground for believing that this church is earlier than any surviving part of St Mary Bishophill Junior.

DIMENSIONS

From the surviving fabric it was possible to say with certainty that the original nave had been 18 ft 6 in. wide internally, and about 35 ft long, with side walls 2 ft 6 in. thick and at least 20 ft high.

YORK

Map sheet 97, reference SE 603521

Figures 641, 642

Early work underlying the cathedral church
of St Peter

Extensive foundations of concrete rubble indicating an apsidal church with aisles or 'porticus' and with an eastern transept. Also parts of the main side walls: period uncertain, possibly A 3

At first sight the magnificent cathedral church at York does not seem to contain any fabric earlier than the thirteenth-century transepts in the Early English style, and one is tempted to believe that its history has been like that of so many other early cathedrals where the early fabric has been entirely swept away by later builders. In the crypt beneath the present choir there are indeed some Norman columns, but they support four-centred arches, and it is clear that the Norman materials have been re-used in a crypt which is roughly contemporary with the choir that now surrounds it.

But in the course of repairs after a disastrous fire in 1829, a local antiquary, John Browne, discovered a Norman shaft and capital *in situ*, just above the floor of the present choir, and not far from the organ-screen. With the co-operation of the Dean and Chapter, he was enabled to undertake an ambitious programme of excavation, as a result of which the greater part of a Norman crypt was exposed to view, at the west of the later crypt mentioned above. Browne's careful excavation of the crypt and his far-sighted interpretation of the material which he found were fortunately matched, not only by the care and accuracy with

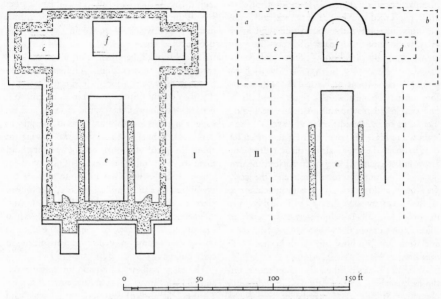

FIG. 358. YORK, THE CATHEDRAL CHURCH OF ST PETER

Plans showing the early foundations and contrasting the observations of John Browne in 1829–47 with those of C. R. Peers in 1931. In each plan the early foundation is denoted by the continuous thick outline. For ease of comparison Browne's larger rectangular outline is shown as a dotted overlay in plan II, where it will be seen that the observations by Peers differed not only by his discovery of the apse but also by his omission of the flanking areas (*a*) and (*b*) of transeptal shape. Although Peers did not comment on his reasons for this omission it should be noted that in Browne's original plates II and III (from which our plan I is derived) these transeptal areas are not very clearly distinguished from the foundations of Archbishop Roger's twelfth-century choir. We have therefore accepted the observations made by Peers in our attempts to interpret the early work.

In plan I we have shown Browne's conjectural reconstruction of the Anglo-Saxon chancel, as in his plate III, but we do not accept this as correct. The alternative reconstruction based on the observations made by Peers is shown in Fig. 362.

Peers and Browne agree in showing open areas *e* and *f* in the centre of the foundation. Browne also showed open areas *c* and *d* in his projecting transeptal areas *a* and *b*, but these areas lie wholly outside the foundations as drawn by Peers. Both Peers and Browne agreed in showing the reinforcement with wooden baulks only in the area within the foundation as drawn by Peers; this seems to us an additional confirmation for accepting the outline in our plan II.

which he recorded his observations, but also by his appreciation of the need of future antiquaries to have access to the crypt which he had discovered.[1] Many later writers have based their conclusions on Browne's work, but none has given plans and architectural drawings which approach in elegance those that were first published by Browne. He was given full access to documentary evidence belonging to the Chapter, particularly their fabric rolls, from which he attempted to build up a reliable and comprehensive account of the architectural history of the church. It is a matter for regret that Browne was later drawn into a controversy with James Raine about the interpretation of the fabric rolls, as a result of which he seems to have lost much of the credit that was due to him for his pioneering work.[2]

It was Browne who discovered beneath the

[1] A full record of the discoveries is given in Browne's *History of the Metropolitan Church of St Peter, York*, 2 vols. (London, 1847). The Norman crypt and the area west of it were covered over by a brick vault. The public do not normally have access to this area, and we are particularly grateful to the Cathedral authorities for permission to make detailed inspections on several occasions.

[2] J. Browne, *The Fabric Rolls of York Minster*, 2nd ed. (York, 1863), and J. Raine, *The Fabric Rolls of York Minster*, Surtees Society Publication no. 35 (Durham, 1859).

Norman crypt a remarkable foundation of concrete, reinforced with baulks of timber; and it was he who interpreted the foundation, and some early walls upon it, as parts of a pre-Conquest church built by Archbishop Albert and consecrated by him in 780. In 1931 Sir Charles Peers published an account of further investigation of this concrete foundation as a result of which he had established that it had an apsidal east end.[1] The shape of the foundation as observed by Peers is shown in Fig. 358, where there is also given for comparison at the same scale the shape as drawn by Browne last century. Peers summarized the evidence for dating the foundation and the early walls on it; and he came to the same conclusion as Browne, namely, that they were probably parts of Archbishop Albert's eighth-century church, in spite of the fact that the walls were 4 ft 8 in. thick and were faced on both sides with herring-bone masonry.

Professor Willis ascribed the foundations and the early walling to the Anglo-Saxon cathedral church of St Peter, and maintained that Archbishop Albert's church was on some totally different site.[2] Other writers between the times of Willis and Peers have, however, supported Browne's interpretation that the foundation and early herring-bone walling were parts of Archbishop Albert's church.[3] On the other hand, serious doubts have recently been cast on the attribution of the foundation and the herring-bone walling to any pre-Conquest date.[4]

The massive concrete rubble foundation is now covered by a modern paving, but through a manhole at the east the foundation can be seen to be 2 ft in thickness. In Browne's excavations, a length of about 130 ft of foundation was laid bare, running eastward from the base of the north-eastern pier of the great central tower. Moreover, Browne found that the concrete had been reinforced by bedding baulks of timber in it; these

had decayed and had left rectangular cavities within the foundation. By floating wooden rods in the water which he found in these cavities, Browne was able to discover that they extended far to the west of the present central tower; Peers repeated these observations and found that the foundations were at least 197 ft in total length, so that they continued westward for more than 60 ft beneath the floor of the central crossing and the nave. On these foundations, beneath the present floor, and running eastward from the crossing for about the space of 2½ bays of the present choir, there are two continuous sections of early walling. These walls lie wholly within the area of the present arcades of the choir, so that the present piers are not supported on them but on later independent masses of masonry which stand against the outer face of the early walls and incorporate many re-used fragments from an early building.

The early walls are of composite construction, and in places are as much as 10 ft in total height. Their core consists of continuous walls, which are 4 ft 8 in. thick, and are faced on either side with herring-bone masonry. These walls are encased on both sides with later masonry, of which that facing inward was quite roughly laid, while that facing outward was good Norman ashlar. This ashlar masonry formed the inner walls of passages which led, beneath the aisles of the Norman choir, from the central crossing into the Norman crypt. After having been thickened in this way the early walls were a little over 10 ft in total thickness; and they served to support the western bays of the Norman choir, of which the eastern bays were supported on massive columns that may still be seen in the crypt to the east of these walls.[5] Fig. 361 shows the plan of the early walls and the later Norman facings as they are to be seen at present in the crypt that was built after John Browne's excavations beneath the present choir.

[1] C. R. Peers, 'Recent discoveries in the minsters of Ripon and York', *Ant. J.* **11** (1931), 113–22.

[2] R. Willis, 'The architectural history of York cathedral', *Proc. Arch. Inst., York, 1846* (London, 1848).

[3] J. Raine, *The Fabric Rolls of York Minster*, vii–ix; A. Hamilton Thompson, in *V.C.H., Yorkshire*, **3** (London, 1913), 6.

[4] F. Harrison, *York Minster* (London, 1927), 1; and

K. Harrison, 'The Saxon cathedral at York', *Yorks. Arch. J.* **39** (1956–8), 442.

[5] It should here be noted that the Norman choir was narrower than the present late fourteenth-century choir, and that the main arcades of the latter are borne on separate piers erected *outside* the walls or piers that carried the Norman arcades.

In order to interpret these foundations and walls in the crypt, it is necessary first to review the early history of York Minster. The beginnings are recorded by Bede (*H.E.* II, 14), with King Edwin's erection of a wooden church dedicated to St Peter, for his baptism at York on Easter Day 627, and his later enclosing it within a stone church, which was built *per quadrum*, and which was incomplete at the time of his death. This stone church was later completed by Edwin's successor Oswald; and Edwin's head was buried in the *porticus* of St Gregory the Pope (*H.E.* II, 20). In 669, when St Wilfrid became bishop of York, he found the church in bad repair; he covered the roofs with lead, put glass in the windows, white-washed the walls, and provided new vessels for the altars.[1] Symeon of Durham records that in 741 the *monasterium in Eboraca civitate* was burnt,[2] and in the same year the *Anglo-Saxon Chronicle* records the burning of York itself. The church of St Peter cannot have been completely destroyed by this fire, or if destroyed was rebuilt, for Alcuin's poem on the Archbishops of York tells how Archbishop Albert (767–80) set up a new altar to St Paul in the church where Edwin was baptized, and how he presented to it many costly ornaments.[3] Alcuin's poem later describes how Albert began and completed the building of a new church, in honour of *Alma Sophia*, the Holy Wisdom, a church with round arches and solid piers, with many *porticus* and upper chambers, and with thirty altars. This great new church did not displace St Peter's as the cathedral church, for in 796 King Eardwulf of Northumbria was crowned in the church of St Peter, at the altar of St Paul given by Archbishop Albert.[4] Under 1069, the 'D' version of the *Anglo-Saxon Chronicle* records that the Normans laid waste and burnt down the sacred church of St Peter, and under 1075 it records that two hundred ships came from Denmark and that the Danes went to York, broke into St

Peter's church, carried off much booty, and went away.

After the Conquest, the work of the Norman bishops may be summarized as follows from the writings of Hugh the Cantor and Thomas Stubbs.[5] Archbishop Thomas of Bayeux (1069–1100) 'found the church despoiled by fire; he repaired and newly covered it so as to serve for a time; he also repaired the refectory and the dormitory; and afterwards he built the church that now is from its foundations'.[6] Archbishop Roger de Pont l'Eveque (1154–81) 'constructed anew the choir of the cathedral church of St Peter at York, together with its crypts, and the archiepiscopal palace at York'.[7] The piers of Thomas's Norman nave were seen by Browne in 1863 beneath the present floor, and it should be noted that, unlike the piers of the Norman choir, they were in the same alignment as the later piers that replaced them. It should also be noted that the present great central tower was not built afresh when the new transepts, nave, and choir were erected, but that parts of the Norman fabric still survive within the tower, and are simply encased behind a fresh outer surface, which was applied at different times to match the adjoining later fabric.[8]

The Early English transepts are works of the thirteenth century, probably of about fifty years after 1215. The nave, in the Decorated style, followed soon after, along with the chapter house and its vestibule, all of which were completed before 1350. When a new choir was begun in 1361, it was placed wholly to the east of its Norman predecessor which remained intact until the new work, namely the four bays next to the present east end, had been completed about 1370. Only then did work begin on the replacement of the Norman choir; the new fabric was erected outside the earlier alignment, and the church as it now stands was completed soon after the beginning

---

[1] Eddius Stephanus, *The Life of Bishop Wilfrid*, ed. B. Colgrave (Cambridge, 1927), 35.

[2] Symeon of Durham, *Hist. Regum*, ed. T. Arnold (Rolls Series, 75, II) (London, 1885), 38.

[3] Alcuin, 'De pontificibus Ebor.', in *Historians of the Church of York*, ed. J. Raine (Rolls Series, 71, I) (London, 1879), 393.

[4] Symeon, *loc. cit.* 57–8.

[5] In *Historians of the Church of York*, ed. J. Raine (Rolls Series, 71, II) (London, 1886).

[6] J. Raine, *loc. cit.* (1886), 108 and 362.

[7] J. Raine, *loc. cit.* (1886), 398.

[8] Norman ashlar and part of the shaft and base of a column of the Norman triforium may be seen on the north-west pier of the great central tower above the vault of the side aisle (F. Harrison, *York Minster* (London, 1927), 10).

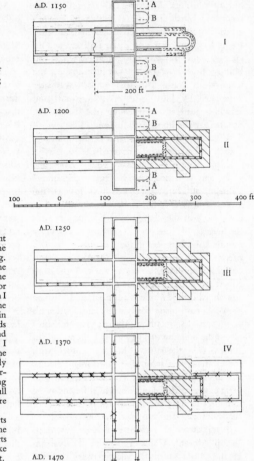

- Norman column

+ Early English column

× Decorated or Perpendicular column

⧱ Decorated column of the nave, on the site of one of the Norman columns, and probably incorporating some of its fabric

— Single storey wall of aisle

== Taller wall of the main body of the nave, transept, or chancel

▨ Norman crypt

▨ Perpendicular crypt

FIG. 359. YORK, THE CATHEDRAL CHURCH OF ST PETER

Plans illustrating the development of the present cathedral church, and showing the position of the early foundations in relation to the present building.

In plans I and II we have shown at A and B, the alternative possibilities of rectangular chapels on the east sides of the transepts (as postulated by Browne) or of apsidal chapels (as postulated by Willis). In plan I we have given the early concrete foundation the eastern apsidal shape that was discovered by Peers in 1931; we also show how the foundation extends about 200 ft westward, under the central tower and under part of the nave. Following Willis, plan I assumes that in 1150 the chancel incorporated the herring-bone walls which still survive on the early foundation. It shows in full outline the present surviving parts of the herring-bone walls; and, following Peers, it shows a chancel continuing to the full eastern extent of the concrete foundations and there flanked by rectangular chapels or *porticus*.

Plans II, III and IV show how the surviving parts of the herring-bone walls were encased within the passages of the Norman crypt, while the eastern parts of the herring-bone fabric were demolished to make way for the open eastern area of the Norman crypt.

Comparison of plan V with the earlier plans will show how it was not until 1470 that the main body of the chancel became the same width as the central tower. In plan I the main body of the chancel, defined by the herring-bone walls, is of an overall width of 37 ft, by comparison with 55 ft for the tower. In plans II to IV the main body of the chancel, defined by the surviving piers of the Norman crypt, is of an overall width of 45 ft, i.e. still 10 ft narrower than the tower.

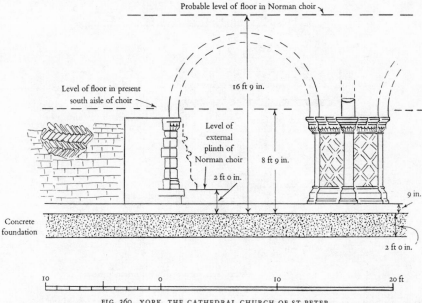

Probable level of floor in Norman choir

Level of floor in present
south aisle of choir

16 ft 9 in.

Level of
external
plinth of
Norman choir

8 ft 9 in.

2 ft 0 in.

9 in.

Concrete
foundation

2 ft 0 in.

10   0   10   20 ft

FIG. 360. YORK, THE CATHEDRAL CHURCH OF ST PETER

The level of the Norman choir. A section through the building to show how the floor of the Norman choir was at a
much higher level than the floor of the present choir. In addition to showing the levels of the Norman choir and
of the south aisle of the present choir, the diagram shows the position of the early concrete foundation, and (in dotted
outline) the profile of one of the external buttresses of the north wall of Archbishop Roger's Norman choir as now
visible within a side chamber of the crypt that was found after the fire of 1829. It will be noted that this Norman
ground-level is 2 ft above the level of the upper surface of the early concrete foundation.

of the fifteenth century.[1] This detailed but nevertheless very abbreviated account of the building
of the present church is illustrated pictorially
in Fig. 359.

It is next necessary to consider some questions
of levels. The floor of the Norman crypt was
about $3\frac{1}{2}$ ft below the level of the floor of the
Norman nave, and it can be seen from the piers
and from the springing of destroyed arches in the
crypt that the stone floor of the Norman choir
that was borne on the vaulting must have been
about 16 ft above the floor of the crypt, or about
$12\frac{1}{2}$ ft above the floor of the Norman nave.[2]
It accordingly follows that in Norman times a
great flight of steps must have led up from the
nave to the choir, in much the same way as is still
the case at Canterbury cathedral. Bearing in

mind the way in which the choir was narrower
than the central space beneath the tower, Willis
suggested that this flight of steps must have been
placed like those at Canterbury under the tower;
and that, under this flight of steps, there must have
been a transverse passage which led from one
transept to the other. He further suggested that
access was gained from this transverse passage to
the ambulatory of the crypt, by way of two
flights of steps beneath the aisles of the Norman
choir. These questions of levels are illustrated
pictorially in Fig. 360.

Fig. 361 shows the walls which were first
observed by Browne, and which may still be seen
beneath the present floor in chambers that were
specially built for the purpose. The records made
by Peers in 1931 agreed precisely with those made

[1] For a fuller account of the architectural history of the
cathedral, see R. Willis, loc. cit.: or F. Harrison, loc. cit.,
particularly chs. I–VII.

[2] R. Willis, loc. cit. 16.

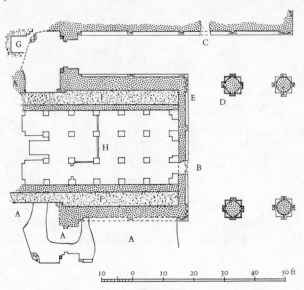

FIG. 361. YORK, THE CATHEDRAL CHURCH OF ST PETER

The herring-bone walls on the early foundations, showing how their western parts were refaced and incorporated within the Norman crypt. A, regions from which the post-Norman infilling of the crypt was not excavated during the repairs after the fire of 1829; B, part of the west wall of the Norman crypt now cut away to give access to the inner area H; C, part of the Norman north wall of the chancel cut away to allow access to the outer face of the wall; D, E, Norman pier and respond which appear in Fig. 360; F, the herring-bone walls; G, arched recess of somewhat doubtful date. It was thought by Browne to be of the same date as the herring-bone walls; and we have shown it so, without wishing to be committed. The dotted diagonal wall in front of this arch is of later date than the Norman facings on either side of the herring-bone walls; H, the area within the herring-bone walls. The rectangular array of square piers was built after Browne's excavations in 1829.

by Browne in 1830 about the dimensions and general character of these walls. Each has a central core, about 50 ft long, of earlier walling that is 4 ft 8 in. in thickness and is faced on both sides with herring-bone masonry. At the east, these early walls are roughly cut away and are roughly bonded to a transverse wall of Norman ashlar masonry, which links the two of them together and which forms the west wall of the main chamber of the Norman crypt. The Norman ashlar is also returned westward for a distance of about 40 ft along the outer faces of the early herring-bone walling in the form of a skin 3 ft 6 in. in thickness. These later Norman facings of the earlier walls not only served as the inner walls of the passages leading to the Norman crypt but also allowed the piers of the Norman arcade of the choir to be placed 7 ft wider apart from north to south than would have been possible

if the herring-bone walls alone had been used for the foundations of the Norman choir. The inner faces of the herring-bone walls are also coated with a later skin, but in this case of quite rough masonry which incorporates much re-used material, including wrought stones, and stones covered by a plaster coating on which lines have been drawn to represent the jointing of masonry. On the north wall, this inner coating of rough masonry is 2 ft thick and on the south wall 2 ft 4 in. The space (H) between the walls was filled with earth, upon which the paved floor of the choir rested before the excavations of 1830.

One further remarkable fact remains to be recorded about the foundations, before we pass to a discussion of the possible dates at which they and the herring-bone walls could have been built. Although the foundations extend westward at least 60 ft under the tower and the nave, and although Browne described them as extending laterally under the present eastern transept, yet both Browne and Peers were explicit that the foundations did not extend laterally beneath the main transept.[1]

All accounts of these early remains agree that, since the foundations extend westward beneath Thomas's tower, they cannot have been built later than by Thomas; moreover, the herring-bone walls must be earlier than the Norman facings which were added to them. It therefore follows that the foundations and the herring-bone walls must either be parts of the church which Thomas 'built from its foundations' or else must be parts of the Anglo-Saxon church which 'he found despoiled by fire, and repaired and newly covered so as to serve for a time'.

The arguments against attributing the foundations and the herring-bone walls to any part of the pre-Conquest era have recently been summarized as follows:[2]

(a) The upper surface of the foundations is at the same level as the floor of a Norman house in Stonegate, about 150 yards away.

(b) The apsidal east end of the foundation is 10 ft in width, which seems unreasonable for an Anglo-Saxon church, but which is closely matched by the 9 ft foundation of the central apse of St Mary's abbey, which stands close-by in York, and which is known to have been built in 1090.

(c) Anglo-Saxon walls are usually less than 3 ft in thickness, whereas the herring-bone walls are no less than 4 ft 8 in.

(d) Baldwin Brown rejected herring-bone fabric as an indication of pre-Conquest date and asserted that it was an indication to the contrary.

These appear to be formidable arguments in support of an assignment of the herring-bone walls and the concrete foundation to Archbishop Thomas. Moreover such an assignment would fit the historical records that while Thomas 'built the church that now is from the foundations', Roger 'constructed anew the choir of the cathedral church of St Peter at York, together with its crypts'. If the herring-bone walls can correctly be attributed to Thomas, the Norman ashlar facings fit conveniently as the work of Roger when he constructed the crypts anew.

On the other hand, Peers pointed out formidable difficulties in the way of assigning either the foundations or the herring-bone walls to Thomas:

(a) It seems inconceivable that if Thomas built the foundations he would not have extended them laterally under his transepts.

(b) The herring-bone fabric is quite at variance with the surviving fabric in the Norman part of the tower.

(c) If the herring-bone walls had been part of Thomas's church, even in their present state they define a choir at least 50 ft long, with solid side walls and a width of only 26 ft 6 in. The abnormal proportions would be much more striking if, as seems natural, the herring-bone walls originally continued to the apsidal east end of the foundation, thereby defining a choir about 120 ft long.

So far as we are aware, another powerful argument against attributing the herring-bone walls to any post-Conquest era has until now been overlooked, although the facts have been noted on many occasions. We refer to the unusual arrangement whereby the Norman choir was about 10 ft narrower than the central tower against which it stood. This unusual feature gives an important indication about the dating of the early fabric, for in Norman times it was the custom to make the four arms of the church of the same width as the central crossing, whereas in Anglo-Saxon churches the central tower was often appreciably wider than any of the four arms of the church, as may be seen at Dover, Norton, or Stow. Moreover, in order to achieve the present alignment of the choir, the Norman builders had to place thick ashlar walls against the outer faces of the herring-bone walls. If the latter had themselves carried the main walls of Thomas's choir it would have been about 17 ft narrower than his tower.[3]

On balance, therefore, we accept the foundations and the herring-bone walls as works belonging to a pre-Norman period, notwithstanding the arguments advanced by Harrison and Melmore. Against those arguments we think it can be said:

(a) That in a distance of 150 yards it would be possible for minor variations in ground-level to mask the differences that might be expected in a single place between

---

[1] J. Browne, loc. cit. 2 (1847), pl. III; C. R. Peers, loc. cit. 119.
[2] K. Harrison, Yorks. Arch. J. 39 (1956–8), 442; and S. Melmore, Notes on the Early Architectural History of York Minster (privately printed, York, 1954), 4 and 6.

[3] See also R.C.H.M., Dorset, West (London, 1952), xlix–l, where a corresponding relation between the tower and the nave at Sherborne is used as an argument for a pre-Conquest date.

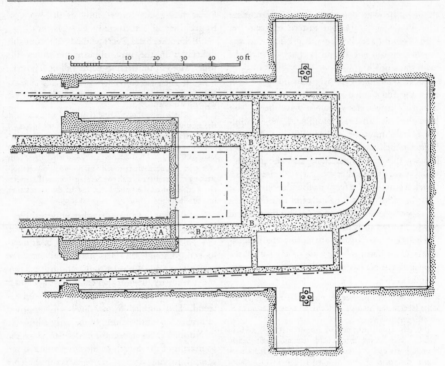

FIG. 362. YORK, THE CATHEDRAL CHURCH OF ST PETER

Tentative reconstruction of the early building of whose side walls parts are preserved beneath the Minster. This reconstruction follows closely the pattern given by Peers in 1931, but it differs by placing the outer walls nearer the edge of the early foundation and by showing the outer walls thinner than Peers suggested (i.e. 2 ft instead of his 3 ft). These changes allow the lateral chambers to be wider (11 ft 6 in. and 10 ft 6 in., instead of his 9 ft 6 in. and 8 ft 6 in.).

The outline of the early foundation is shown by a chain pattern of broken lines and dots. The complete outline of Archbishop Roger's crypt is shown as a means of giving a precise location of the early foundation; but in order to avoid undue complication we have omitted all Roger's columns except the two that are placed in the eastern transepts of his crypt.

The walls AA are the surviving herring-bone fabric. The walls BB are our tentative eastern termination of the building. It is this reconstruction which is shown at a very much smaller scale in plan I of Fig. 359.

Anglo-Saxon and Norman levels. If arguments about the date of the early foundation are to be based on its level in relation to the level of the ground in Norman times, these arguments should be related to the level of the ground in the vicinity of the cathedral. As is shown in Fig. 360 there is information on this matter, and it shows that the level of the external plinth of Archbishop Roger's twelfth-century choir was 2 ft above the level of the top of the early foundation.

(b) That, although the 10 ft width of the foundations of the apse is indeed abnormal for any ordinary Anglo-Saxon church, it is known that one church of unusual elaboration was built at York, namely that built by Archbishop Albert and consecrated in 780.

(c) That although thin walls are indeed usual in Anglo-Saxon churches, the main piers of the arcades at Brixworth are 4 ft in thickness, and Alcuin's description of Archbishop Albert's church indicates a church of such elaboration and with such abundance of upper galleries that thick lower walls would surely have been reasonable.

(d) That although Baldwin Brown claimed herringbone walling as an indication against Anglo-Saxon workmanship, we have given evidence to show that he was mistaken in this belief.[1]

In conclusion, it remains to say what indications can be given of the probable pre-Conquest date when these remarkable structures were built.

---

[1] See particularly under Diddlebury, which Baldwin Brown himself said was 'crucial' to his belief.

From their great scale they are unlikely to have belonged to the church begun by Edwin and finished by Oswald. Moreover, from documentary evidence Harrison was led to the conclusion that the site of Edwin's church was most probably in the area of the concrete paving outside the present west doors of the Minster. The great scale of the foundations would, however, be consistent with their being part of the elaborate church built by Albert and consecrated by him in 780 a few days before his death. This church dedicated in honour of *Alma Sophia* would therefore have been on the same axial alignment as the earlier church dedicated to St Peter, in conformity with an Anglo-Saxon practice of which there are other examples at Canterbury and Jarrow; and possibly also at Hexham.

It should at once be repeated that this attribution of the early fabric to Archbishop Albert is not new. It was made by Browne between 1830 and 1847 and has been repeated by others, including Sir Charles Peers in 1931. Browne assumed that the original church of St Peter had been destroyed in the fire of 741 and that Albert's new church replaced it. He went so far as to assign the area (*f*) (Fig. 358) within Albert's church as the site of the original wooden oratory built by Edwin. From what has been said above it will be clear that we disagree with Browne on this point and agree with Harrison (and Peers) in thinking that the site of Edwin's wooden oratory was further to the west.

In Fig. 362 we show a very tentative reconstruction of the form of Albert's church. This differs from the reconstruction shown by Peers in 1931 only in that we suggest that the flanking *porticus* were slightly wider than was suggested by Peers.

DIMENSIONS

According to Browne's plate III, the overall width of the foundation, measured across the eastern 'transept', was 136 ft; measured across the body of the church, the width of the foundations was 88 ft. Excluding parts which continued westward under the tower, Browne showed the length of the main foundation as 140 ft from east to west. Peers showed the extreme width of the foundation as 65 ft and its length as not less than 197 ft.

Measurements recorded by Melmore give the upper surface of the foundation as 5 ft below ground-level, or 9 ft below the floor of the south aisle of the present choir. According to Peers and Melmore, the foundations are 2 ft thick. The walls faced with herring-bone masonry stand 10 ft in height and about 50 ft in length. They are 4 ft 8 in. thick and they enclose a space 27 ft in width. If the eastern apse was in the position suggested by Peers, the chancel of the Norman cathedral as shown in Fig. 359, plan I, was 27 ft wide and about 120 ft long.

REFERENCES

P. F. Robertson, 'On the newly discovered crypt at York Minster', *T.R.I.B.A.* (later *J.R.I.B.A.*) I (1836), 105–8. Good drawings and brief description.

J. Browne, *The History of the Metropolitan Church of St Peter, York*, 2 vols. (London, 1847). Vol. I gives a detailed historical and architectural description. Vol. 2 contains a magnificent collection of plans and architectural drawings.

J. Browne, *The Fabric Rolls of York Minster*, 2nd ed. (York, 1863). Largely devoted to the argument with Raine; but gives a valuable account of further discoveries in the nave and transepts in 1863 in the course of the laying of gas-mains. The Norman nave had only six piers on each side, 177 B. Eastern aisles or series of square chapels on east side of main transept in Norman times (i.e. Norman transepts did not have apsidal chapels as shown by Willis), 177 C, D, and E.

R. Willis, 'The architectural history of York cathedral', *Proc. Arch. Inst., York, 1846* (London, 1848). Valuable plans showing the development of the church from Norman times to its present state. Good historical and architectural descriptions.

J. Raine, *The Fabric Rolls of York Minster*, Surtees Society Publication, **35** (Durham, 1859). Outline architectural history as a preface.

F. Harrison, *York Minster* (London, 1927). A very scholarly popular account of the history and fabric of the Minster. Plates showing details of much of the early work not normally accessible to the public.

C. R. Peers, 'Recent discoveries in the minsters of Ripon and York', *Ant. J.* **11** (1931), 113–22. Discovery of the apsidal east end.

K. Harrison, 'The Saxon cathedral at York', *Yorks. Arch. J.* **39** (1956–8), 436–44. Valuable account of the documentary evidence.

K. Harrison, 'The pre-Conquest churches of York', *Yorks. Arch. J.* **40** (1959–61), 232–49. Most valuable account of the history of the Minster, in the form of annals.

APPENDIX A

CHURCHES OF THE ANGLO-SAXON TOWER-NAVE TYPE
IN SCOTLAND

For comparison with the churches at Barton-on-Humber, Broughton, and Earls Barton, it seems important to record briefly the principal features of three similar churches in Scotland at Dunfermline, Restenneth, and St Andrews.

DUNFERMLINE
Fife

Map sheet 55, reference NT 090873

HOLY TRINITY

Foundations of two-cell church beneath Norman nave: probably period C

Malcolm Canmore, King of Scotland, married Margaret, sister of Edgar Atheling, and great-niece of Edward the Confessor, at Dunfermline about 1070. Shortly thereafter Margaret arranged for priests to be brought from Canterbury to set up regular services in the church, which she enlarged for the purpose. In 1128 her son David began the building of the present Norman nave, which he modelled closely on the work at Durham. Until excavations were carried out beneath the floor of the Norman nave in 1916,[1] it was not known that any part of the pre-Norman fabric had survived.

The excavations disclosed the foundations and lower courses of the walling of a small two-cell structure with a larger apsidal eastward extension. Since the whole is necessarily prior to King David's Norman nave, it seems clear that the small two-cell structure is to be regarded as the palace-chapel in which King Malcolm and St Margaret were married, and that the wider eastward extension is the apsidal chancel which she added for the priests from Canterbury.

The foundations of the western cell are square; and they extend about 1 ft 3 in. wider on each side

than those of the rectangular eastern cell. Moreover, the western foundations are of a uniform width of 6 ft while those of the eastern cell vary from 4 ft 6 in., under the east wall, to 5 ft under the side walls. It therefore seems clear that the chapel consisted of a square tower-nave and a rectangular chancel. If the walls of the tower were about 4 ft thick, the tower would have been about 12 ft square internally, and if the walls of the chancel had been about 3 ft thick it would have been about 19 ft long internally and about 12 ft wide.

RESTENNETH
Forfar

Map sheet 50, reference NO 482516

ST PETER

Tower: probably period C

The ruins of Restenneth abbey stand in an open area within a ring of woods about one and a half miles north-east of Forfar, and about 2 miles from the battlefield of *Nechtanesmere* (now Dunnichen) where King Egfrid of Northumbria was slain in 685.

The surviving fabric now consists of the square, unbuttressed, early tower; a much wider thirteenth-century chancel, displaced northward from the axis of the tower; and fragments of the south and west walls of the cloister. The later medieval

---

[1] G. Baldwin Brown (1925), 451–2.

nave has disappeared, but the marks of its roof on the west wall of the tower show that, like the chancel, it was set with its axis far to the north of the centre of the tower.

The original part of the tower, beneath the later medieval broach spire, is of two stages, separated by a plain square string-course. It is roughly square in plan and has thin walls built of large blocks of roughly squared brown stone. Its round-headed eastern arch is original, of a single square order formed wholly of dressed stones, none of which extends through the full thickness of the wall.[1] Its plain square jambs are largely, but not wholly, of through-stones. They rest on plain square plinths, and have through-stone imposts of quirked and hollow-chamfered section.

The round-headed south doorway is a fine example of early workmanship. It is outlined by a plain square pilaster-strip and hood-moulding, which are formed immediately beside the arris and are cut on the stones of the jambs and head. The jambs, like those of the east arch, are mainly but not all of through-stones, and the round head is cut in three massive lintel-stones each of which covers about one-third of the thickness of the wall. The doorway has a 4 in. by 4 in. internal rebate, for the hanging of a door.

The round-headed western arch in the tower is clearly a later insertion. It is not centrally placed, and there is a rough infilling of small stones beside its jambs and voussoirs.

Two very small, simple windows in the west and south faces of the lower stage of the tower served to light an upper chamber. A further chamber in the upper stage of the tower was lit by four triangular-headed windows, one in each wall.

Without excavation it is not now possible to say with certainty what was the nature of the original chancel; but, if the south wall of the surviving thirteenth-century chancel marks the original alignment, the chancel would have been about 3 ft wider than the tower-nave.

DIMENSIONS

The original part of the tower is roughly 10 ft 4 in. square internally, with walls 2 ft 8 in.

thick and about 50 ft high. The eastern arch is 8 ft 4 in. wide and about 14 ft high. The south doorway is 2 ft 4 in. wide and about 8 ft tall.

REFERENCES

D. MACGIBBON, and T. ROSS, *Ecclesiastical Architecture in Scotland*, 1 (Edinburgh, 1896), 178–85. Good description, with plan, and several drawings.

W. D. SIMPSON, *Restenneth Priory* (Edinburgh, H.M.S.O., 1952). Good description and plan.

W. D. SIMPSON, 'The Early Romanesque Tower at Restenneth Priory, Angus', *Ant. J.* 43 (1963), 269–83. Exhaustive description, plan, and many excellent photographs.

ST ANDREWS
Fife

Map sheet 56, reference NO 514166

ST REGULUS OR ST RULE
Tower and chancel: probably period C

The ruined cathedral at St Andrews is picturesquely placed at the top of cliffs which overlook the harbour and have an uninterrupted view east and north across the sea. Within the walled enclosure, and only a short distance to the southeast of the cathedral, is St Regulus's chapel, the earliest surviving fabric on the site, and also its most imposing land-mark.

St Regulus's chapel now consists of an exceptionally tall square west tower and a rectangular eastern chamber, or chancel, slightly wider than the tower and clearly contemporary with it since both are properly bonded together. These two units probably represent the whole of the original fabric, but they were later extended by the addition of a nave to the west of the tower and a chancel to the east of the present eastern compartment. No part of the fabric of these twelfth-century additions now remains above-ground, but their date is fixed by the character of the great arches which were cut through the original walls to open into the new chambers. It is tempting to think that the survival of the earlier fabric and the disappearance of the twelfth-century additions

---

[1] The illustration on p. 181 of Macgibbon and Ross's *Ecclesiastical Architecture in Scotland* wrongly shows all the voussoirs as through-stones.

are to be explained by the more durable construction of the earlier work. However this may be, it is certainly true that the surviving fabric is of exceptionally fine, well-dressed, ashlar masonry.[1] Except for certain areas associated with later alterations, the uniform coursing of the masonry is maintained round the whole fabric, including the side-alternate quoins and the jambs of the windows.

The square, unbuttressed plan of the tower is broken at the west, where the west wall continues a foot or so on either side, but it is likely that this abnormality is associated with the later addition of the nave, since the splayed plinth at the base of the tower passes through and behind these buttresses and then across the west face of the tower.

The plain rectangular eastern compartment or chancel has two round-headed, double-splayed windows high up in each of its side walls. It is not now possible to say whether the east end had any windows, since almost all of it is cut away by the large arch which opened to the later chancel. The four surviving windows are all of similar construction; externally, their round heads are cut in large monolithic lintels, and internally each head is formed by a system of corbelling in two courses of the walling. The lower course forms the greater part of the round head, while the upper course is corbelled out still further and the remaining small section at the head of the window is completed by a wedge-shaped keystone. An elaborate eaves-course along the tops of the side walls of the chancel is continued round the three walls of the tower as a decorative string-course.

The walls of the tower rise sheer throughout their height, but are divided into three stages by the elaborate decorative string-course and by an upper string-course of plain square section. The lowest stage occupies about a third of the total height, the second stage is much taller, and the belfry is comparatively short, occupying about a sixth of the height.

In the lowest stage, the great arch which occupies the western face is clearly a later insertion, not only because its head cuts away part of the decorative string-course but also because its jambs are not properly in bond with the walls. Moreover, the simple, chamfered plinth of the tower is returned along the western face, thus showing that a western annexe was no part of the original design. A tall, round-headed arch, now blocked, formerly opened between the ground-floor chambers of the chancel and the tower. The arch is now of two plain square orders, of which the outer order and its jambs seem to be contemporary with the main fabric, since the jambs are, throughout their height, coursed with the walling in which they stand. The inner order is almost certainly a later addition, because its jambs are not bonded into the main fabric and are quite differently coursed. It should be noted that the orders of this arch are of plain square section, by contrast with the elaborately moulded orders of the eastern arch of the chancel and the western arch of the tower, both of which we believe to be twelfth-century insertions in the eleventh-century fabric.

The tall second stage, which occupies about half the total height of the tower, has a number of single-splayed, round-headed windows to light the interior. These are all of a uniform pattern, with simple monolithic heads, and jambs each of two stones that form ordinary courses of the main wall. The interior splays of these windows are grooved about the centre of the wall for a wooden shutter or window-frame. The east face of the tower has no less than three separate gabled grooves for successive positions of the roof of the chancel; and, below these there is a round-headed doorway for communication between the tower and a gallery or chamber within the roof of the chancel. The west face of the tower shows a groove at a higher level for the gabled roof of the later nave.

The short uppermost stage has a double belfry window in each of its four faces, and close above each of these is a round-headed window like those of the stage below. The double belfry windows are generally similar to those of the Anglo-Saxon towers but have certain fundamental differences. In the first place, their jambs are recessed as though for angle-shafts, although it is

---

[1] The only Anglo-Saxon fabric in England of comparable excellence is the chapel of St Lawrence at Bradford-on-Avon, Wiltshire.

not clear whether angle-shafts were ever provided. Secondly, although the heads of the individual lights are supported on a through-stone slab, this is not supported by a shaft placed in the middle of the thickness of the wall but by a shaft which is illogically placed almost in the outer face of the wall.

A decorative eaves-course like that on the chancel marks the top of the original tower, and above this there has been added in the sixteenth century a projecting corbel-table and a tall, plain parapet.

For reasons which are set out fully under Wharram-le-Street, we accept Bilson's arguments for dating the great eastern and western arches about the beginning of the twelfth century, but, as has been stated above, we regard them as later insertions in an earlier fabric. By analogy with Wharram-le-Street, we believe that the original fabric consisting of the tower and chancel was probably erected about the first half of the eleventh century; but this dating should be regarded as much less reliable than the dating of churches in England.

DIMENSIONS

The tower is about 11 ft square internally, with walls 5 ft 3 in. thick and about 110 ft high to the top of the original work. The chancel is 26 ft long internally and 19 ft 9 in. wide, with walls 2 ft 9 in. thick and about 34 ft tall. The dimensions of the three arches are as follows:

	Width in clear		Height in clear	
	ft	in.	ft	in.
East arch of chancel	9	0	25	6
East arch of tower	9	10	27	0
West arch of tower	10	4	28	0

REFERENCES

D. MACGIBBON and T. ROSS, *Ecclesiastical Architecture in Scotland*, **1** (Edinburgh, 1896), 185–90. Good description, with plan and several drawings.

J. BILSON, 'Wharram-le-Street church, Yorkshire, and St Rule's church, St Andrews', *Arch.* **73** (1923), 55–72. St Rule, 66–72. Very full description, with many detailed drawings. For reasons stated under Wharram-le-Street, we reject Bilson's dating of the main fabric to the twelfth century while accepting his arguments for assigning that date to the east arch of the chancel and west arch of the tower.

S. CRUDEN, *The Cathedral of St Andrews and St Regulus Church* (Edinburgh, H.M.S.O., 1950), 1–10. Good historical and architectural description. Cruden accepts Bilson's dating which we reject. The important carved shrine is illustrated, described, and assigned to the eighth or to the tenth century, 23. There is a good representation, on the cover, of the thirteenth-century seal of the Chapter, showing what seems to be St Regulus's church as it was at that time, with the nave at the west of the tower, flanked by two western turrets that seem to be of circular plan.

C. A. R. RADFORD, 'Two Scottish shrines: Jedburgh and St Andrews', *Arch. J.* **112** (1955), 43–60. Shrine at St Andrews assigned to the tenth century.

APPENDIX B

CHURCHES WITH FEATURES WHICH HAVE BEEN CLAIMED AS ANGLO-SAXON BUT WHICH WE DO NOT REGARD AS SUFFICIENTLY DEFINITE TO JUSTIFY THEIR INCLUSION IN THE MAIN TEXT

In addition to the churches described in the body of the main text we have visted many others that were said to show Anglo-Saxon features. In many of these we found nothing which we regarded as being characteristically Anglo-Saxon, but in others there were features which were on the border-line, and which it seemed a pity not to record for further study. The list given in this Appendix is not exhaustive; we have not mentioned churches which seemed to us clearly to lie outside our province unless they have been firmly claimed as Anglo-Saxon and therefore a brief word of rejection seemed necessary. We have not shown any of these churches on our maps.

ALDINGBOURNE
Sussex

Map sheet 181, reference SU 923054

ST MARY
The north wall of the nave is only 2 ft 6 in. thick, and is pierced by three round arches, which formerly led to an aisle, but are now blocked.

ALNHAM
Northumberland

Map sheet 71, reference NT 991110

ST MICHAEL
The church looks early, but is probably Norman rather than pre-Norman.

ALVESTON
Gloucestershire

Map sheet 156, reference ST 632865

(Disused)

There is a plain, round-headed north doorway, whose arched head is enriched with wheat-ear and diaper ornament. It is probably Norman rather than Anglo-Saxon.

ANTINGHAM
Norfolk

Map sheet 126, reference TG 252328

ST MARGARET
Two churches stand side by side in one churchyard. St Margaret's is a ruin; the walls of its nave are only 2 ft 9 in. thick, and they have massive quoins of carstone.

ASHTEAD
Surrey

Map sheet 170, reference TQ 193580

ST GILES
The walls of the nave are between 2 ft 6 in. and 2 ft 10 in. thick, and are built of tile and flint, with quoins of clunch. The church is in an ancient earthwork.

ASTON-ON-TRENT
Derbyshire

Map sheet 121, reference SK 414294

ALL SAINTS
The west tower is Norman, and is built with a straight joint against the earlier wall of the nave. The north-west quoin of the originally aisleless

714

nave is visible externally, of massive side-alternate fabric, on a plain plinth. The lower few courses of a similar side-alternate north-east quoin on a similar simple plinth are visible internally, within the north-east aisle. Built into the north-west quoin, and thereby giving evidence of its lateness in the Anglo-Saxon era, or of its later rebuilding, is a section of Anglo-Saxon cross-shaft.

BAGENDON
Gloucestershire

Map sheet 157, reference SP 012067

ST MARGARET OF ANTIOCH

The walls of the nave are only 2 ft 1 in. thick, and the north wall is pierced by a Norman arcade of three round arches.

BAMBURGH
Northumberland

Map sheet 71, reference NU 178349

ST AIDAN

There is no doubt about the antiquity of the site. Hodges thought it was possible to see pre-Conquest masonry in the church, but we have been unable to find any.

BAWSEY
Norfolk

Map sheet 124, reference TF 663207

ST JAMES

The ruins of this three-cell church, with a square axial tower, stand on high land about 2 miles east of King's Lynn. The details are mainly Norman, but a triangular-headed doorway opens eastward from the first floor of the tower.

BIGNOR
Sussex

Map sheet 181, reference SU 983146

ST PETER

The aisled nave has thin walls and a simple round-headed chancel-arch, but there are no distinctive features to fix a pre-Conquest date.

BRATTLEBY
Lincolnshire

Map sheet 104, reference SK 947807

ST CUTHBERT

The church was almost entirely rebuilt in the nineteenth century, but the west and north walls of the nave were left, and they are only 2 ft 6 in. thick. The west doorway is a simple round-headed opening which is cut straight through the wall. The antiquity of the site is proved by a pre-Conquest carved stone in the churchyard.

BRAXTED, GREAT
Essex

Map sheet 149, reference TL 851154

ALL SAINTS

The walls of the nave and chancel are tall, and are only 2 ft 9 in. thick. The quoins of the nave are of tile, or of tile mixed with rubble. A single-splayed round-headed window in the north of the chancel has its splays continued through the full thickness of the wall.

BROCKDISH
Norfolk

Map sheet 137, reference TM 205795

ST PETER AND ST PAUL

A round-headed, single-splayed window in the north of the nave has been almost covered by a later buttress. It is more probably Norman than Anglo-Saxon.

BROMYARD

Herefordshire

Map sheet 143, reference SO 655548

ST PETER

There is an interesting carving of St Peter over the south doorway, and a cross carved in relief in a sunken circular background. These seem to be pre-Conquest, but they are not *in situ*.

BROOMFIELD

Essex

Map sheet 162, reference TL 705104

ST MARY

The round west tower is perhaps as late as the sixteenth century, but the quoins of the nave are of tiles. The chancel has been lengthened eastward and a tile quoin has survived about the middle of its south wall.

BURNHAM NORTON

Norfolk

Map sheet 125, reference TF 834427

ST MARGARET

The round west tower has many windows, all of which are constructed of flint, without any dressed stone; but the recessed belfry windows suggest Norman influence. A definite indication of date might be obtained if some of the blocked circular windows above the belfry could be opened out. The nave is long and tall, and its western quoins are of plain flint construction. The tower-arch is tall, and it is built of rough rubble.

BYLAND, OLD

Yorkshire, North Riding

Map sheet 92, reference SE 551859

DEDICATION UNKNOWN

Domesday Book records at *Begeland* "*presbyter et ecclesia lignea*" (*V.C.H.*, Yorkshire, **3** (London, 1913), 12). Thus it seems difficult to doubt a post-Conquest date for the present stone church, in spite of its Anglo-Saxon sundial (not *in situ*) and other early features.

BYTHAM, CASTLE

Lincolnshire

Map sheet 123, reference SK 988183

ST JAMES

The Norman north arcade has been cut through an earlier wall, whose side-alternate western quoin still survives, with the west wall of the later aisle built straight against it. The antiquity of the site is attested by three sections of pre-Conquest cross-shaft preserved in the porch.

CHESTER-LE-STREET

County Durham

Map sheet 78, reference NZ 276513

ST MARY AND ST CUTHBERT

The western part of the south wall of the chancel is of quite different fabric from the rest of the church, with very big stones which would be out of character except in the Anglo-Saxon period. There are pre-Conquest carved stones in the church, and the history of the site goes back to its occupation by the monks of Lindisfarne before they finally settled at Durham.

CHILCOMB

Hampshire

Map sheet 168, reference SU 507279

ST ANDREW

This small two-cell church has single-splayed windows, whose splays are continued through the full thickness of the wall, and whose glass is affixed to the outer face of the wall. The north and south doorways are tall, but have no definite Anglo-Saxon features. The round-headed chancel-arch is of a single square order, but its arch and jambs have no through-stones. The walls are 2 ft 10 in. thick.

CHOLSEY
Berkshire
Map sheet 158, reference SU 583870

ST MARY
Baldwin Brown (pp. 426 and 448) refers to this church as having a Norman tower with well-constructed normal long-and-short quoins. The tower and the church are certainly Norman, but we do not regard the quoining as a good instance of normal long-and-short technique. The north-west angle has a very irregular arrangement of pillar stones, clasping stones, and stones that are set on their sides. Only the north-east quoin approximates to true long-and-short construction.

CLIFTON REYNES
Buckinghamshire
Map sheet 146, reference SP 899513

ST MARY THE VIRGIN
The nave is long and narrow, with tall, thin walls; and the unbuttressed square west tower has a plain square plinth. No early doorways or windows have survived.

COPFORD
Essex
Map sheet 149, reference TL 934226

ST MICHAEL
All its features proclaim this as a Norman church. It is important to note that it has quoins that are built wholly of tiles, thus proving that plain tile quoins are not by themselves a valid criterion of Anglo-Saxon work. But the regularly laid tiles

at Copford are very different from the much rougher workmanship at the near-by church of Great Tey; and this contrast seems to us to support the other evidence for accepting Great Tey as pre-Conquest, or Saxo-Norman.

DUXFORD
Cambridgeshire
Map sheet 148, reference TL 477462

ST JOHN
In a recent appeal for funds for the restoration of this church a claim was made for a pre-Conquest date; but the church seems to us a straightforward example of the Norman three-cell type, with a late tower erected on the central cell. The south doorway has a tympanum carved with a cross which has a stepped pattern on the arms and the centre; but the tympanum is three-centred and seems to us to be post-Norman.

EASTERGATE
Sussex
Map sheet 181, reference SU 945050

ST GEORGE
This church has walls only 2 ft 6 in. thick, and the splays of its small round-headed north window are carried right through the wall; but we could see no conclusive evidence of Anglo-Saxon date.

EDLINGHAM
Northumberland
Map sheet 71, reference NU 114091

ST JOHN THE BAPTIST
The nave of this interesting church has a Norman south doorway and a narrow Norman north aisle. The western quoins of the nave are exceptionally massive, with stones up to 7 ft in length.

The antiquity of the site as a place of Christian worship is attested by the survival of part of an Anglian cross-shaft of which two faces have vine-scroll ornament and one face has vine-scroll with animals.

EDVIN LOACH
Herefordshire

Map sheet 130, reference SO 661584

ST MARY THE VIRGIN

The present church is Victorian; but its ruined predecessor, standing close by in open fields, is Norman or earlier. Its simple nave and chancel are built in a single rectangle; but they seem to be of two different periods, for the nave is mainly in herring-bone fabric, while the chancel is of coursed rubble, with a widely splayed Norman east window. The nave has a tall, square-headed, south doorway, beneath an exceptionally massive lintel, above which is a tympanum of coursed masonry and a round arch.

ELLERBURN
Yorkshire, North Riding

Map sheet 92, reference SE 841842

ST HILDA

This simple two-cell church has been heavily restored, but is basically Norman or earlier. Some Anglo-Saxon carved stones are preserved in the church.

FAIRSTEAD
Essex

Map sheet 162, reference TL 767166

ST MARY

This is one of the many Essex churches which have tile quoins and tile arches but which are, nevertheless, difficult to date with certainty. The heads and jambs of the two round-headed single-splayed windows are wholly formed of tiles, and a Gothic south doorway has been inserted within a taller, round-headed, blocked doorway with jambs and arch of tiles.

FISHLEY
Norfolk

Map sheet 126, reference TG 398114

ST MARY

The lower part of the round west tower has three large, blocked, plain, round-headed windows which might have been the original belfry windows of an eleventh-century church. The nave has a simple Norman south doorway, but an indication of pre-Norman date is given by the north-west quoin which is of plain flint construction, with the west wall of the narrow north aisle built straight against it.

FORD
Sussex

Map sheet 181, reference TQ 002037

ST ANDREW

This church was claimed as basically Anglo-Saxon by P. M. Johnston (*Sussex Arch. C.* **43** (1900), 105–55), but the claim was rejected by Baldwin Brown (p. 456). We have been able to visit Ford only once, and then, unfortunately, with too little time for careful investigation. Although the church has no feature which would by itself be conclusive, we are inclined to accept Johnston's argument.

HASKETON
Suffolk

Map sheet 150, reference TM 250504

ST ANDREW

The only early feature here is a blocked, round-headed window in the south wall of the nave. It has a monolithic head and tall monolithic jambs, with a shallow rebate, perhaps to house a wooden shutter. A series of small holes which are drilled in the jambs and head, within the rebate, possibly served for fixings for the shutter.

HATFIELD

Herefordshire

Map sheet 129, reference SO 595596

ST LEONARD

The eastern part of the nave is of earlier work-manship than the western part. Its north wall stands on a plain square plinth, and it has an eastern quoin of tufa. The square-headed north doorway has a semicircular tympanum of diagonally set masonry. Its remarkable lintel rests on a wooden beam, and is constructed of three stones with stepped joints.

HAUGHTON-LE-SKERNE

County Durham

Map sheet 85, reference NZ 307158

ST ANDREW

The round-headed windows in the side walls of the chancel look Norman, but have monolithic heads which are reminiscent of the early pre-Conquest churches of Northumbria. We are inclined to think of them as Norman re-use of earlier material. There is a vertical joint in the masonry of the chancel between an earlier western section and a later extension. Since the Norman windows occur in both sections, it seems to follow that the later eastern section is Norman and the earlier western section is pre-Norman. The church has a considerable collection of fragments of pre-Norman carved cross-shafts.

HINTON-IN-THE-HEDGES

Northamptonshire

Map sheet 145, reference SP 557369

HOLY TRINITY

The church consists of a square unbuttressed west tower, a nave with a Transitional Norman north arcade, and an aisleless chancel. The tower is probably of more than one date, and the belfry is Norman. The round-headed tower-arch is of Norman proportions, but is constructed of rubble, without any dressed stone. The imposts are large flat stones, almost unworked, but passing through the full thickness of the wall.

ILAM

Staffordshire

Map sheet 111, reference SK 133507

HOLY CROSS

The jambs and half of the round head of a tall, narrow, blocked doorway are visible in the south wall of the nave. The wall itself is 2 ft 9 in. thick and about 18 ft tall. It is built of rough rubble, and it stands on a simple, square plinth. The door-way is faced with large, very rough stones, which are very widely pointed. Its exceptionally tall and narrow proportions (8 ft 9 in. by 2 ft 9 in.) suggest Anglo-Saxon workmanship.

KIPPAX

Yorkshire, West Riding

Map sheet 97, reference SE 417303

ST MARY

The aisleless nave has walls that are 28 ft tall and 3 ft thick, very largely of herring-bone masonry. The earliest surviving openings are the round-headed single-splayed windows and the blocked round-headed Norman north doorway. The herring-bone masonry of the nave and the tower is, however, remarkably like that of the Anglo-Saxon tower at Carlton-in-Lindrick. A late pre-Conquest cross-shaft which was found in the masonry of the tower in 1875 was removed and placed in the chancel; but when we visited the church in 1960 it was not to be seen.

MALDON
Essex
Map sheet 162, reference TL 843063

ST GILES

Double apsidal foundations overlaid by the crossing of a ruined transeptal church deserve further study. The church is mainly Early English in date, but round-headed arches in the east and west walls of the south transept seem to be Norman. They therefore also suggest a pre-Norman date for the apsidal foundations.

MINSTER-IN-THANET
Kent
Map sheet 173, reference TR 312643

REMAINS OF ABBEY

Notes were published in 1930 by Canon Livett (*Arch. Cant.* 42 (1930), 225) about the remains of a three-cell church whose foundations had been discovered in the grounds of the manor house known as Minster Abbey, a few hundred yards north-east of the parish church. Although the site is traditionally associated with an eighth-century abbey, the foundations seem to be those of a Norman church.

MERTON
Norfolk
Map sheet 136, reference TL 912980

ST PETER

The round Norman west tower is later than the nave, for it blocks a single-splayed, round-headed window in the gable. The walls of the nave are now exceptionally tall (34 ft), and, although they seem to have been raised, the marks of an earlier gable in the west wall of the nave indicates that their original height was about 27 ft. The side walls and the west wall of the nave are only 2 ft 8 in. thick, and there is a plain flint quoin at the north-west angle of the nave.

SEDGEFORD
Norfolk
Map sheet 124, reference TF 706364

ST MARY

The round west tower of this church has been flanked by later aisles; but their west wall still leaves visible a little of the western part of the tower, including a small triangular-headed first-floor window. This is the only evidence of date, and we regard it as inconclusive. Anglo-Saxon occupation nearby is proved by the discovery of an extensive cemetery about 500 yd. east of the church (*Med. Arch.* 3 (1959), 298).

SEETHING
Norfolk
Map sheet 137, reference TM 319979

ST MARGARET OF ANTIOCH AND ST REMIGIUS

The tall narrow nave now has diagonal buttresses; but it seems to have been widened, and vestiges of quoins of plain flint mark the original narrow west wall. The circular west tower is joined to the early west wall by quarter-round pilasters of plain flint.

METTINGHAM
Suffolk
Map sheet 137, reference TM 363899

ALL SAINTS

The only evidence to indicate pre-Conquest date is the plain flint north-west quoin of the nave, and the plain square plinth, also of flints, on which the north wall rests.

SNAILWELL

Cambridgeshire

Map sheet 135, reference TL 642675

ST PETER

The walls of the nave were exceptionally tall even before the addition of the Perpendicular clerestorey. The round west tower seems to have been added later to a pre-existing nave, part of whose straight west wall is visible within the tower. The round-headed windows in the lower part of the tower have indications of Anglo-Saxon influence in the tall stones which are used in their jambs. The belfry looks like a later addition; and, although its double windows are not of the Anglo-Saxon type, yet they are not normal Norman belfry windows, particularly because they have no recessing.

SOBERTON

Hampshire

Map sheet 180, reference SU 609168

ST PETER

The *Victoria County History* (*Hampshire*, **3** (1908), 264) suggests that there is evidence that a pre-Conquest church has been incorporated into the fabric of the present church. We could see nothing to justify this opinion.

STODY

Norfolk

Map sheet 125, reference TG 056350

ST MARY

The church consists of a round west tower; an aisleless nave with south porch; north and south transepts; and an aisleless chancel. The inconclusive indications of pre-Conquest workmanship are a cruck-shaped tower-arch and a rectangular pilaster-strip of plain flint construction in the northern re-entrant angle between the tower and the west wall of the nave.

SUSTEAD

Norfolk

Map sheet 126, reference TG 182370

ST PETER AND ST PAUL

The round west tower is entered by a pointed south doorway, and it has no entry to the nave. The side walls of the nave are only 2 ft 7 in. thick, and the south-west quoin is of side-alternate construction, in blocks of carstone.

TANGMERE

Sussex

Map sheet 181, reference SU 901062

ST ANDREW

This is one of the several Sussex two-cell churches which are so difficult to date with certainty. Its walls are about 2 ft 8 in. thick and its single-splayed round-headed windows have their splays carried right through the wall, without any exterior chamfer or rebate. Their jambs are built of moderate-sized flat stones, and their heads are cut in large rectangular stones of which one is carved with a pattern which we failed to interpret.

TIBBERTON

Gloucestershire

Map sheet 143, reference SO 756219

DEDICATION UNKNOWN

The setting out of the nave and of the chancel-arch of this church is remarkable for its disregard of the right angle. This irregularity of treatment extends also to the hollow-chamfered imposts of the chancel-arch, neither of which is laid horizontally. The imposts are through-stones, but this is not so for any other stones of the arch or of the jambs; although many of the stones in the jambs are very large. A blocked round-headed south doorway is arched with very non-radial voussoirs.

TUFTON

Hampshire

Map sheet 168, reference SU 458468

ST MARY

This simple two-cell church can with some confidence be dated not later than the first quarter of the twelfth century, but some of its features suggest that it might be much earlier. The simple round-headed single-splayed windows narrow appreciably towards the top, and their splays are carried through the full 2 ft 9 in. thickness of the walls.

TUGBY

Leicestershire

Map sheet 122, reference SK 760010

ST THOMAS À BECKET

The square west tower of this church was claimed as pre-Norman as long ago as 1882 by M. H. Bloxam (*Principles of Gothic Architecture*, 11th ed. (London, 1882), 55), on the evidence of a 'double-splayed window in the west wall of the tower'. But the aperture is within 3 in. of the west face of the wall; and the window is more correctly to be described as of single-splayed construction, with a small external chamfer. We regard the whole tower as Norman.

WATER NEWTON

Huntingdonshire

Map sheet 134, reference TL 109973

ST REMIGIUS

The only indication of pre-Conquest date is the triangular head of a blocked doorway in the west wall of the nave. The jambs have disappeared, and a pointed doorway has been inserted into the wall.

WICKHAM BISHOPS

Essex

Map sheet 162, reference TL 824112

Old church of
ST PETER

This church was in a far-advanced state of ruin when we first saw it in 1960. The north-east quoin of the nave has some tiles in its fabric; but a stronger indication of pre-Norman date is given by the east jamb and the round-arched head of the south doorway. The west jamb has been cut away by a much later doorway, but the early opening seems to have been cut straight through the wall, without any rebate; and the eastern side of the arch springs from the jamb without any decorative imposts.

APPENDIX C

LIST OF CHURCHES WHICH GIVE
PRIMARY EVIDENCE FOR THE DATING OF ANGLO-SAXON
ARCHITECTURAL FEATURES

AVEBURY, WILTS. Single-splayed window cut away by Norman arcade.

BARHOLM, LINCS. Norman south doorway immediately beside blocked earlier doorway.

BARROW, SALOP. Early Norman tower obscures elaborate west door of nave, but nave is earlier than chancel.

BARTON-ON-HUMBER, LINCS. Upper belfry of a form approaching Norman, but probably earlier; remainder of tower below quite different in form.

BIBURY, GLOS. Norman north arcade cuts away pilaster-strip on exterior of original nave.

BILLINGHAM, CO. DURHAM. Pre-Norman tower built against and over west wall of nave.

BISHOPSTONE, SUSSEX. Norman west tower blocks west windows of earlier nave. Norman doorway inserted into earlier south *porticus*.

BRANSTON, LINCS. Norman arcading added later to an earlier tower. Tower is later than nave against and over whose west wall it is built.

BRIGSTOCK, NORTHANTS. Norman arcade cuts away single-splayed window. Tower has double-splayed upper windows and single-splayed lower windows. Character of walling and quoining is different below and above.

BRIXWORTH, NORTHANTS. Norman doorway in south arcade. Four separate building periods discernible in surviving pre-Norman fabric.

CANTERBURY, ST AUGUSTINE'S ABBEY. Literary evidence gives precise dates for church of St Peter and St Paul and church of St Mary, and for Wulfric's rotunda connecting them.

CANTERBURY, ST MARTIN. Literary evidence for a church on this site before the coming of Augustine. Architectural and archaeological evidence for dating western part of present chancel prior to present nave, and for placing present nave in early Saxon period.

CARLTON-IN-LINDRICK, NOTTS. Tower is of the Lincolnshire Anglo-Saxon type. It is butted against and built over the west wall of the nave.

CLAPHAM, BEDS. Upper belfry stage of tower is Norman. Lower part of tower is quite different.

COLSTERWORTH, LINCS. Herring-bone north wall only 1 ft 10 in. thick, cut through by two early Norman arches to the east of a later Norman arch.

CORBRIDGE, NORTHUMBERLAND. West tower of very simple form raised on west porch. Therefore porch and nave are earlier.

CORRINGHAM, LINCS. Simple Norman arcade cut through north wall of pre-existing church.

DEERHURST, ST MARY, GLOS. Several pre-Norman building styles. Evidence for later addition of west porch and later raising of it to form west tower. Evidence for addition of side-chapels or *porticus*, of two storeys to nave, and for their extension westward in stages. Evidence that present ruined apsidal chancel is later than nave.

DEERHURST, HOLY TRINITY, GLOS. Dated precisely by inscription.

DIDDLEBURY, SALOP. Triple plinth of original nave overlaid by early Norman enlarged chancel.

FRAMINGHAM EARL, NORFOLK. North and south doorways of plain round-headed form, cut straight through the wall and formed in the flint walling without any dressed-stone facings. Norman stone door-frames inserted in these openings.

GEDDINGTON, NORTHANTS. Norman arcade cuts away round-headed single-splayed window which itself cuts away decorative blind arcading.

GODALMING, SURREY. Norman tower raised on earlier square chancel. West wall of tower, formerly east gable of nave, still contains two circular double-splayed windows.

HACKNESS, YORKS, N.R. Norman south arcade cuts away earlier south window.

HART, CO. DURHAM. Norman chancel-arch cuts away taller and narrower earlier chancel-arch.

HOUGH-ON-THE-HILL, LINCS. Independent newel of stairway renders pre-Norman dating likely. Tower is built against and over west wall of nave.

IVER, BUCKS. Double-splayed north window of nave cut away by Norman arcade.

JARROW, CO. DURHAM. Chancel (formerly an independent church) precedes tower because it had its own west wall which was cut away after the building of the tower. Belfry stage of tower is Norman, but lower belfry is earlier in form, and lateral doorways at ground level are even earlier in form. Wide east and west archways of tower seem to be later (Norman) adaptations of earlier archways.

KILPECK, HEREFORDSHIRE. Church is Norman, but north-east quoin of nave belongs to some earlier structure.

KIRKDALE, YORKS, N.R. Precise dating of sundial by inscription.

LAUGHTON-EN-LE-MORTHEN, YORKS, W.R. Norman chancel built on top of plinth of same character as plinth of early north-west *porticus*.

LAVENDON, BUCKS. North window of nave cut away by Transitional Norman arcade.

LEDSHAM, YORKS, W.R. Norman belfry on tower of quite different character. Norman tower-arch cut through wall, partially obstructing original window. Tower built on earlier porch.

LEICESTER, ST NICHOLAS. Double-splayed round-headed windows in north wall which has later been pierced by Norman arcade.

LINCOLN, ST MARY-LE-WIGFORD. Tower built against and over west wall of nave. Inscribed stone recording building of church by Eirtig.

LINCOLN, ST PETER-AT-GOWTS. Tower built against and over west wall of nave.

LYMINSTER, SUSSEX. Tall narrow south door-way, cut straight through wall, has been partially cut away by later doorway of Norman form.

MIDDLETON-BY-PICKERING, YORKS, N.R. Tower of pre-Norman character is built against and over west wall of an earlier and narrower nave. Nave later widened, with quoins like those of tower.

MILBORNE PORT, SOMERSET. Norman upper stage of tower distinctly different from lower stage. Norman stair turret added later. Norman south doorway added to earlier nave.

MONKWEARMOUTH, CO. DURHAM. Upper stage of tower pre-Norman in form. Porch below tower earlier still, but this porch is built against nave and is not in bond, therefore nave is even earlier.

MUCH WENLOCK, SALOP. Foundations of small, single-cell fabric, wholly overlaid by Norman abbey.

NORTON, CO. DURHAM. Norman arches cutting away east and west walls of tower.

PETERBOROUGH, NORTHANTS. Foundations of early church beneath floor of Norman cathedral.

ROTHWELL, LINCS. Norman arcade cut through walls of a previously aisleless nave.

ST ALBANS, ST STEPHEN, HERTS. South window cut away by Norman arch.

SEAHAM, CO. DURHAM. Norman chancel of quite early character. Nave is quite different and certainly not later, therefore earlier.

SOMPTING, SUSSEX. Norman nave and chancel, but tower of quite different character.

STAINDROP, CO. DURHAM. Originally aisleless nave extended westward and later cut through by late-Norman arcades.

STOW, LINCS. Quoins of crossing and side walls and quoins of transepts are clearly of two separate building dates, the lower parts having been damaged by fire. Both are clearly earlier than the Norman nave and chancel. The arches of the crossing are unrelated to the piers which are themselves of two dates like the exterior walls. There therefore appear to be three pre-Norman building dates.

WALKERN, HERTS. Rood cut away for roof-plate of Norman aisle. Doorway adapted so as to use east jamb for Norman nave arcade.

WARNFORD, HANTS. Norman tower built over west wall of narrower nave. Twelfth-century wider nave built out from tower, leaving earlier west wall *in situ*.

WHITFIELD, KENT. Norman sanctuary added to an earlier two-cell nave and chancel.

WITTERING, NORTHANTS. Norman arcade cut through north wall.

WOULDHAM, KENT. Double-splayed window cut away by Norman south arcade.

WROXETER, SALOP. Early Norman chancel added to earlier nave.

APPENDIX D

ALPHABETICAL LIST OF ANGLO-SAXON CHURCHES BY COUNTIES

The following lists contain the names of all the churches which are listed in the body of the book and also those in Appendix B. The latter are given separately at the end of the list for each county, and they are enclosed in square brackets to indicate that they are not necessarily to be accepted as Anglo-Saxon. One or two churches which are described in the body of the book are there noted as having no features which we accept as Anglo-Saxon; they have been included in the body of the book because they were accepted as Anglo-Saxon by Baldwin Brown; the names of these churches are also enclosed in square brackets in the following lists, and the churches are not counted in the numbers of accepted Anglo-Saxon churches which are shown for each county in the summary at the end of this Appendix, but are included in the numbers shown as doubtful.

PART 1. ENGLAND

BEDFORDSHIRE

Bedford:
St Mary
St Peter
Clapham
Stevington
Turvey

BERKSHIRE

Wickham
[Cholsey]

BUCKINGHAMSHIRE

Hardwick
Iver
Lavendon
Wing
[Clifton Reynes]

CAMBRIDGESHIRE

Abington, Little
Cambridge:
St Bene't
St Giles
Ickleton
Shelford, Little
Swavesey
[Caxton]

[Duxford]
[Snailwell]

DERBYSHIRE

Bakewell
Repton
Stanton-by-Bridge
[Aston-on-Trent]

DEVONSHIRE

Sidbury

DORSET

Sherborne
Wareham:
Lady St Mary
St Martin
Winterborne Steepleton

DURHAM

Aycliffe
Billingham
Escomb
Hart
Jarrow
Monkwearmouth
Norton
Pittington
Seaham

Sockburn
Staindrop
[Chester-le-Street]
[Haughton-le-Skerne]

ESSEX

Bardfield, Little
Birchanger
Boreham
Bradwell-on-Sea
Chickney
Colchester
Greensted
Hadstock
Hallingbury, Great
Hallingbury, Little
Inworth
Mersea, West
Notley, White
Pentlow
Prittlewell
Springfield
Strethall
Tey, Great
Tollesbury
Wendens Ambo
[Braxted, Great]
[Broomfield]

[Copford]
[Fairstead]
[Maldon]
[Wickham Bishops]

GLOUCESTERSHIRE
Ampney:
    Crucis
    St Peter
Bibury
Bitton
Coln Rogers
Daglingworth
Deerhurst:
    Holy Trinity (Odda's Chapel)
    St Mary
Duntisbourne Rouse
Dymock
Edgeworth
Miserden
Somerford Keynes
Stanley St Leonard
Winstone
[Alveston (Old church)]
[Bagendon]
[Tibberton]

HAMPSHIRE
(see also Isle of Wight under W)
Boarhunt
Breamore
Corhampton
Fareham
Hambledon
Hannington
Headbourne Worthy
Hinton Ampner
Laverstoke (destroyed)
Quarley
Romsey
Somborne, Little
Tichborne
Titchfield
Warblington
Warnford
Winchester (no visible remains)
[Chilcomb]
[Soberton]
[Tufton]

HEREFORDSHIRE
Bredwardine
Castle Frome
Hereford:
    Chapel of St Katherine and
        St Mary Magdalene
Kilpeck
Peterstow
Tedstone Delamere
Wigmore
[Bromyard]
[Edvin Loach]
[Hatfield]

HERTFORDSHIRE
Northchurch
Reed
St Albans:
    Cathedral church of St Alban
    St Michael
    St Stephen
Walkern
Westmill
Wheathampstead

HUNTINGDONSHIRE
Paxton, Great
Woodston
[Water Newton]

KENT
Aldington
Canterbury
    Cathedral church of Christ
    St Martin
    St Mary
    St Mildred
    St Pancras
    St Peter and St Paul
Cheriton
Coldred
Darenth
Dover
Halstow, Lower
Kingsdown
Kingston
Langdon, East
Leeds

Lullingstone
Lydd
Lyminge
Milton-on-Swale
Minster-in-Sheppey
Northfleet
Orpington
Paddlesworth
Peckham, West
Reculver
Rochester
St Margaret's-at-Cliffe
Shorne
Stone-by-Faversham
Stourmouth, West
Swanscombe
Whitfield
Willesborough
Wilmington
Wouldham
[Minster-in-Thanet]

LANCASHIRE
Heysham:
    St Patrick
    St Peter

LEICESTERSHIRE
Aylestone
Birstall
Breedon-on-the-Hill
Foston
Leicester, St Nicholas
[Tugby]

LINCOLNSHIRE
Alkborough
Barholm
Barnetby-le-Wold
Barton-on-Humber
Bracebridge
Branston
Broughton
Bytham, Little
Cabourn
Caistor
Clee
Coleby
Colsterworth
Corringham

LINCOLNSHIRE (*cont.*)

Cranwell
Cuxwold
Edenham
Glentworth
Greetwell
Hainton
Hale, Great
Harmston
Harpswell
Heapham
Holton-le-Clay
Hough-on-the-Hill
Kyme, South
Lincoln:
  St Benedict
  St Mary-le-Wigford
  St Peter-at-Gowts
Lusby
Marton
Nettleton
Ropsley
Rothwell
Scartho
Skillington
Springthorpe
Stow
Stragglethorpe
Swallow
Syston
Thurlby
Waithe
Wilsford
Winterton
Worlaby
[Brattleby]
[Bytham, Castle]

LONDON

All Hallows by the Tower
Westminster Abbey

MIDDLESEX

[Kingsbury]

NORFOLK

Aslacton
Barsham, West
Beechamwell
Beeston
Bessingham
Burnham Deepdale
Colney
Coltishall
Cranwich
Cringleford
Dunham Magna
Elmham (North)
Forncett St Peter
Framingham Earl
Framingham Pigot
Gayton Thorpe
Gissing
Guestwick
Haddiscoe
Haddiscoe Thorpe
Hales
Heigham
Houghton-on-the-Hill
Howe
Kirby Cane
Letheringsett
Lexham, East
Lopham, South
Melton Magna
Morningthorpe
Morton-on-the-Hill
Newton-by-Castleacre
Norwich:
  Cathedral church of the Holy
    Trinity
  St John de Sepulchre
  St John Timberhill
  St Julian
  St Martin-at-Palace
  St Mary-at-Coslany
Quidenham
Rockland All Saints
Roughton
Ryburgh
[Scole]
Shereford
Snoring, Little
Swainsthorpe
Tasburgh
Thetford
Thornage
Thorpe Abbots
Walsham, North
Weybourne
Wickmere
Witton
Yaxham
[Antingham]
[Bawsey]
[Brockdish]
[Burnham Norton]
[Fishley]
[Merton]
[Sedgeford]
[Seething]
[Stody]
[Sustead]

NORTHAMPTONSHIRE

Barnack
Brigstock
Brixworth
Earls Barton
Geddington
Green's Norton
Nassington
Pattishall
Peakirk
Peterborough
Stowe-nine-Churches
Wittering
[Hinton-in-the-Hedges]

NORTHUMBERLAND

Bolam
Bywell:
  St Andrew
  St Peter
Corbridge
Ebb's Nook
Heddon-on-the-Wall
Hexham
Houghton, Long
Ingram
Lindisfarne
Norham
Ovingham
Warden
Whittingham
Woodhorn
Yeavering

[Alnham]
[Bamburgh]
[Edlingham]

NOTTINGHAMSHIRE
Bridgford, East
Carlton-in-Lindrick

OXFORDSHIRE
Caversfield
Langford
North Leigh
Oxford:
   [Cathedral church of Christ]
   St Michael
Swalcliffe
Waterperry

RUTLAND
Egleton
Market Overton

SHROPSHIRE
Atcham
Barrow
Diddlebury
Much Wenlock
Rushbury
Shrewsbury:
   St Mary
   [Destroyed early churches of
   St Alkmund, St Chad, and
   St Julian]
Stanton Lacy
Stottesdon
Wroxeter

SOMERSET
Cheddar
Glastonbury
Milborne Port
Muchelney

STAFFORDSHIRE
Stafford, St Bertelin
[Ilam]

SUFFOLK
[Barham]
Bradley, Little

Burgh Castle
Claydon
Debenham
Elmham (South)
Fakenham Magna
Flixton
Gosbeck
Hemingstone
Herringfleet
Thorington
[Hasketon]
[Mettingham]

SURREY
Albury
Cheam
Compton
Fetcham
Godalming
Guildford
Kingston-upon-Thames
Stoke d'Abernon
Thursley
Witley
[Ashtead]

SUSSEX
Arlington
Bishopstone
Bolney
Bosham
Botolphs
Chichester
Chithurst
Clayton
Elsted
Hardham
Jevington
Lewes
Lyminster
Nyetimber (domestic)
Poling
Rumboldswhyke
Selham
Shoreham, Old
Singleton
Sompting
Stopham
Stoughton
Westhampnett

Wivelsfield
Woolbeding
Worth
[Aldingbourne]
[Bignor]
[Eastergate]
[Ford]
[Tangmere]

WARWICKSHIRE
Tredington
Wootton Wawen

WESTMORLAND
Appleby
Crosby Garrett
Marton, Long
Morland

WIGHT, ISLE OF
Arreton
Freshwater

WILTSHIRE
Alton Barnes
Avebury
Bradford-on-Avon
Bremhill
Britford
Burcombe
Cricklade
Inglesham
Knook
Limpley Stoke
Netheravon
Potterne
Ramsbury

YORKSHIRE
(a) City of York
Cathedral church of St Peter
St Cuthbert
St Mary Bishophill Junior
St Mary Bishophill Senior

(b) East Riding
Aldbrough
Beverley

YORKSHIRE (cont.)

Kirby Underdale
Skipwith
[Weaverthorpe]
Wharram-le-Street

(c) North Riding

Appleton-le-Street
Bedale
Bulmer
Hackness

Hornby
Hovingham
Kirby Hill
Kirkdale
Lastingham
Masham
Middleton-by-Pickering
Stonegrave
Terrington
Whitby
[Byland, Old]
[Ellerburn]

(d) West Riding

Bardsey
Burghwallis
Collingham
Kirk Hammerton
Laughton-en-le-Morthen
Ledsham
Monk Fryston
Ripon
Ryther
[Kippax]

PART 2. CHURCHES NOTED IN SCOTLAND AND WALES

WALES

Presteigne (Radnorshire)

SCOTLAND*

Dunfermline (Fife)
Restenneth (Forfar)

St Andrews (Fife)
Whithorn (Wigtown, Galloway)

SUMMARY

	Accepted	Doubtful		Accepted	Doubtful
Bedfordshire	5	—		278	[44]
Berkshire	1	1	Nottinghamshire	2	—
Buckinghamshire	4	1	Oxfordshire	6	1
Cambridgeshire	6	3	Rutland	2	—
Derbyshire	3	1	Shropshire	9	—
Devonshire	1	—	Somerset	4	—
Dorset	4	—	Staffordshire	1	1
Durham	11	2	Suffolk	11	3
Essex	20	6	Surrey	10	1
Gloucestershire	15	3	Sussex	26	5
Hampshire	17	3	Warwickshire	2	—
Herefordshire	7	3	Westmorland	4	—
Hertfordshire	8	—	Wight, Isle of	2	—
Huntingdonshire	2	1	Wiltshire	13	—
Kent	36	1	Yorkshire:		
Lancashire	2	—	City	4	—
Leicestershire	5	1	East Riding	5	1
Lincolnshire	47	2	North Riding	14	2
London	2	—	West Riding	9	1
Middlesex	—	1		402	[59]
Norfolk	54	11	Wales	1	—
Northamptonshire	12	1			
Northumberland	16	3	Total England and Wales	403	[59]
	278	[44]	Scotland*	4	—

* Three of these are listed in Appendix A (Dunfermline, Restenneth, and St Andrews), and the fourth (Whithorn) is listed in the body of the book.

APPENDIX E

ABBREVIATIONS

Detailed references to those journals and books which give useful information about any church are given in the text immediately after the description of the church concerned. Footnotes are also used in the text to give authority for statements which would otherwise be left unsupported. The purpose of this list is, therefore, not to give any general bibliography but simply to specify a standard list of abbreviated references to those journals and books whose titles occur often in the footnotes and detailed references. Even at the expense of a certain loss of brevity we have used abbreviations which are more or less self-explanatory, in order that readers need not make frequent reference to this list.

The list is divided into three parts, which are concerned respectively with journals, other serial publications, and books. The lists of journals and books need no further explanation. Under the heading of other serial publications we have included not only the *Victoria County Histories* and the *Inventories* of the Royal Commissions on Ancient and Historical Monuments, but also the separately published accounts of the earliest annual meetings of the Archaeological Institute and of the British Archaeological Association. The records of later annual meetings form part of the *Journals* which are published annually by the two societies, but the important records of their first few annual meetings, from 1845 onwards, were published separately under the following titles (followed in each case by the place-name and year of the meeting):

> *Proceedings of the Archaeological Institute*
> *Transactions of the Archaeological Association*

In giving references to all the 'other serial publications' we have regarded them as books and have given the place-name and year of publication in brackets after the title. Thus, the reference to the record of the meeting of the Archaeological Institute in Winchester in 1845 (which was published in London in 1846) reads as follows:

> *Proc. Arch. Inst., Winchester, 1845* (London, 1846).

A. JOURNALS

Ant. J.   *Antiquaries Journal.*
Ant.   *Antiquity.*
Arch.   *Archaeologia.*
Arch. Ael.   *Archaeologia Aeliana.*
Arch. Cant.   *Archaeologia Cantiana.*
Arch. J.   *Archaeological Journal.*
Architec. R.   *Architectural Review.*
A.A.S.R.   *Associated Architectural Societies Reports.*
Burl. Mag.   *Burlington Magazine*
Berks. A.J.   *Berkshire Archaeological Journal.*

Essex R.   *Essex Review.*
Gent's Mag.   *Gentleman's Magazine.*
J.B.A.A.   *Journal of the British Archaeological Association.*
J.R.I.B.A.   *Journal of the Royal Institute of British Architects.*
J. Derby. A.N.H.S.   *Journal of the Derbyshire Archaeological and Natural History Society.*
Med. Arch.   *Medieval Archaeology.*
Norf. Arch.   *Norfolk Archaeology.*

731

N.Q. Som. Dorset.   Notes and Queries for Somerset and Dorset.

P. Camb. A.S.   Proceedings of the Cambridge Antiquarian Society.

P. Dorset N.H.A.S.   Proceedings of the Dorset Natural History and Archaeological Society.

P. Hants. F.C.   Proceedings of the Hampshire Field Club.

P. Soc. Ant.   Proceedings of the Society of Antiquaries of London.

P. Soc. Ant. Newcastle   Proceedings of the Society of Antiquaries of Newcastle.

P. Somerset A.N.H.S.   Proceedings of the Somersetshire Archaeological and Natural History Society.

P. Suff. Inst. Arch.   Proceedings of the Suffolk Institute of Archaeology.

R. Bucks.   Records of Buckinghamshire.

R.P. Lincs. A.A.S.   Reports and Papers of the Lincolnshire Architectural and Archaeological Society.

R.P. Northants. A.A.S.   Reports and Papers of the Northamptonshire Architectural and Archaeological Society.

Surrey Arch. C.   Surrey Archaeological Collections.

Sussex Arch. C.   Sussex Archaeological Collections.

Sussex N.Q.   Sussex Notes and Queries.

T. Bristol Glos. Arch. S.   Transactions of the Bristol and Gloucestershire Archaeological Society.

T. Cumb. West. A.A.S.   Transactions of the Cumberland and Westmorland Antiquarian and Archaeological Society.

T. Durham Northd. A.A.S.   Transactions of the Architectural and Archaeological Society of Durham and Northumberland.

T. E.Herts. Arch. S.   Transactions of the East Hertfordshire Archaeological Society.

T. E.Riding Ant. S.   Transactions of the East Riding Antiquarian Society.

T. Essex Arch. S.   Transactions of the Essex Archaeological Society.

T. Lancs. Ches. Ant. S.   Transactions of the Lancashire and Cheshire Antiquarian Society.

T. St Albans Herts. A.A.S.   Transactions of the St Albans and Hertfordshire Architectural and Archaeological Society.

T. Shropshire A.N.H.S.   Transactions of the Shropshire Archaeological and Natural History Society.

T. Worcs. Arch. S.   Transactions of the Worcestershire Archaeological Society.

Wilts. A.N.H. Mag.   Wiltshire Archaeological and Natural History Magazine.

Yorks. Arch. J.   Yorkshire Archaeological Journal.

B. OTHER SERIAL PUBLICATIONS

Proc. Arch. Inst.   Proceedings of the Archaeological Institute (at one of their early annual meetings).

R.C.H.M. [followed by the name of the county concerned]   Survey and Inventory by the Royal Commission on Historical Monuments.

Trans. Brit. Arch. Ass.   Transactions of the British Archaeological Association (at one of their early annual meetings).

V.C.H. [followed by the name of the county concerned]   Victoria County History.

C. BOOKS

Bede, H.A.   Bede, Historia Abbatum. The reference is generally extended to give a page-reference to C. Plummer's edition (Oxford, 1896).

Bede, H.E.   Bede, Historia Ecclesiastica Gentis Anglorum. References in the form H.E. v, 13 denote Book v, chapter 13. Since there is a uniform system of numbering books and chapters, we have not thought it necessary to give page-references to any named edition, except for references to notes in Plummer's edition. Such references are given in the form: Bede, H.E. ed. C. Plummer, 2 (Oxford, 1896),

G. Baldwin Brown (1925)   G. Baldwin Brown. The Arts in Early England, 2, Anglo-Saxon Architecture (London, 1925). References to any other volume of The Arts in Early England or to other books by Professor Baldwin Brown are given in full. Our indebtedness to Anglo-Saxon Architecture is shown by the frequency of references to it. References in footnotes are given in the form here specified, but in the body of the text we have used the expression 'Baldwin Brown (p. 247) says...' as implying that the statement will be found on p. 247 of *Anglo-Saxon Architecture*.

A. W. Clapham (1930)   A. W. Clapham, *English Romanesque Architecture before the Conquest* (Oxford, 1930). References to other books by Sir Alfred Clapham are given in full.

D. Whitelock, *E.H.D.* (1955)   D. Whitelock, *English Historical Documents*, I, *c.* 500–1042, gen. ed. D. C. Douglas (London, 1955). References to other books by Professor Whitelock are given in full.

ADDENDA

MASHAM

Yorkshire, North Riding

Map sheet 91, reference SE 226806

ST MARY

*West, north, and east walls of nave, above later
openings: period uncertain but perhaps A*

Masham stands on high land on the south bank
of the Ure, about 8 miles north-west of Ripon. It
is indicated as an important Anglian site by the
surviving lower part of a round-shafted cross
beside the south porch of the nave, and by the
fragments of a cross-head and a rectangular-
shafted cross preserved within the church.

The west tower of the church is Norman, and
can clearly be seen to have been built against the
west wall of an earlier and originally aisleless nave.
The two western quoins of this wide nave are of
good side-alternate construction, of large stones
such as were often used in the early Anglian period;
and so also is the south-eastern quoin. Even more
positive evidence of early pre-Conquest fabric is
to be seen within the church, where a square-
sectioned string-course runs along the greater part
of the originally external face of the north wall of
the nave, now within the much later north aisle,
at a height of about 16 ft above the floor.

A particularly important feature is to be noted
near the west of this wall where two separate
stones of this string-course *in situ* can still clearly
be seen to be decorated with simple interlaced
ornament such as is to be seen (but no longer *in
situ*) at Ripon.

The early parts of the west, north and east walls
are built of large stones that are roughly square in
shape, whereas the rebuilt lower parts and the
whole of the rebuilt south wall are of smaller stones
that are of much more elongated rectangular shape.

DIMENSIONS

The nave is 61 ft long internally and 25 ft 6 in.
wide. Its north wall is 2 ft 3 in. thick and over
16 ft tall.

POTTERNE

Wiltshire

Map sheet 167, reference ST 995585

DEDICATION UNKNOWN

*Evidence for wooden nave, chancel, side-chapels,
and south-eastern baptistry: pre-Conquest*

We are indebted to Dr Norman Davey for in-
forming us during the correction of our page-
proofs of his discovery of the ground-plan of a
wooden pre-Conquest chapel 100 yards south of
St Mary's church, Potterne. None of the timber
fabric has survived, but the plan is clearly defined
by slots cut in the greensand for the wall-plates
of the chapel.

Full details are to be published in the *Wiltshire
Archaeological and Natural History Magazine*, but
we have Dr Davey's permission to record here that
the original building seems to have comprised a
nave about 15 ft square and a chancel about 9 ft
square; to this there was later added a baptistry in
the south-east angle; still later the nave was extended westward to give it a total length of about
25 ft, and at the same time side-chapels were added
on the north and south, each about 9 ft square,
and a small porch at the west.

It has long been known that the font, with its
interesting inscription, in St Mary's church is a
survival from an earlier Anglo-Saxon fabric
(*Victoria County History, Wiltshire*, vol. VII
(London, 1953), 212), and the local tradition is
that it came from a nearby site. This has received
striking confirmation from Dr Davey's discoveries, because within the baptistry there is a
recess cut in the greensand of the same dimensions
as the base of the tub font.

This note forms an exception to our general rule
of including only material that we have visited.

DIMENSIONS

The nave was originally about 15 ft square, later
extended westward to about 25 ft. The chancel
and side-chapels were each about 9 ft square.

PLATES

ARRANGEMENT OF
THE PLATES

The plates are arranged in alphabetical order of places, in the same sequence as the corresponding churches in the body of the text. In order to avoid wasteful use of space on the plates, the descriptive text for each figure has been given in Volume I, on pp. xii–xix, immediately after the title of each figure in the List of Illustrations.

363. ALDBROUGH, YORKSHIRE (E.R.)

364. ALTON BARNES, WILTSHIRE

365. APPLETON-LE-STREET,
YORKSHIRE (N.R.)

366. ARRETON, ISLE OF WIGHT

367. ASLACTON, NORFOLK

368. BARDFIELD (LITTLE), ESSEX

369. BARDSEY, YORKSHIRE (W.R.)

370. BARHOLM, LINCOLNSHIRE

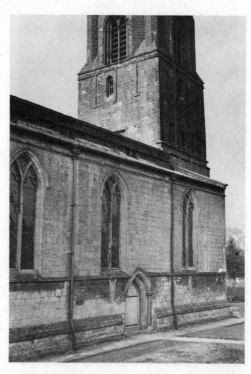

371. BARNACK, NORTHAMPTONSHIRE

372. BARNACK, NORTHAMPTONSHIRE

373. BARNACK, NORTHAMPTONSHIRE

374. BARROW, SHROPSHIRE

375. BARROW, SHROPSHIRE

376. BARROW, SHROPSHIRE

377. BARSHAM (WEST), NORFOLK

378. BARSHAM (WEST), NORFOLK

379. BARTON-ON-HUMBER, LINCOLNSHIRE

380. BARTON-ON-HUMBER, LINCOLNSHIRE

381. BARTON-ON-HUMBER, LINCOLNSHIRE

382. BARTON-ON-HUMBER, LINCOLNSHIRE

383. BEDFORD, ST PETER

384. BEDFORD, ST PETER

385. BESSINGHAM, NORFOLK

386. BIBURY, GLOUCESTERSHIRE

387. BIBURY, GLOUCESTERSHIRE

388. BIBURY, GLOUCESTERSHIRE

389. BILLINGHAM, COUNTY DURHAM

390. BILLINGHAM, COUNTY DURHAM

391. BITTON, GLOUCESTERSHIRE

392. BITTON, GLOUCESTERSHIRE

393. BOARHUNT, HAMPSHIRE

394. BOARHUNT, HAMPSHIRE

395. BOLAM, NORTHUMBERLAND

396. BOREHAM, ESSEX

397. BOSHAM, SUSSEX

398. BOSHAM, SUSSEX

399. BOSHAM, SUSSEX

400. BRACEBRIDGE, LINCOLNSHIRE

401. BRADFORD-ON-AVON, WILTSHIRE

402. BRADFORD-ON-AVON, WILTSHIRE

403. BRADWELL-ON-SEA, ESSEX

404. BRANSTON, LINCOLNSHIRE

405. BREAMORE, HAMPSHIRE

406. BREAMORE, HAMPSHIRE 407. BREEDON-ON-THE-HILL, LEICESTERSHIRE

408. BRIGSTOCK, NORTHAMPTONSHIRE

409. BRIGSTOCK, NORTHAMPTONSHIRE

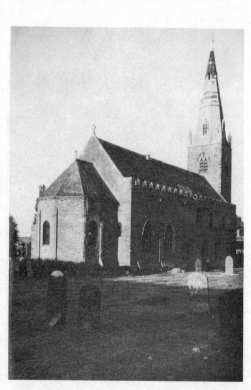

410. BRIXWORTH, NORTHAMPTONSHIRE

411. BRIXWORTH, NORTHAMPTONSHIRE

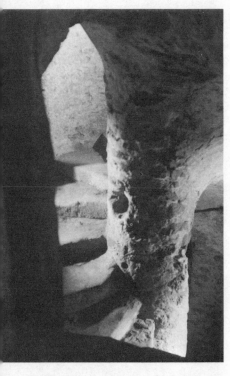

412. BRIXWORTH, NORTHAMPTONSHIRE   414. BYWELL ST ANDREW, NORTHUMBERLAND

413. BURGHWALLIS, YORKSHIRE (W.R.)

415. BYWELL ST PETER, NORTHUMBERLAND

416. BYWELL ST PETER, NORTHUMBERLA

417. CAMBRIDGE, ST BENE'T

418. CAMBRIDGE, ST BENE'T

19. CANTERBURY, KENT, ST MILDRED   420. CANTERBURY, KENT, ST PANCRAS

421. CARLTON-IN-LINDRICK,
NOTTINGHAMSHIRE   422. CARLTON-IN-LINDRICK,
NOTTINGHAMSHIRE

423. CARLTON-IN-LINDRICK, NOTTINGHAMSHIRE

424. CAVERSFIELD, OXFORDSHIRE

425. CHICKNEY, ESSEX

426. CLAYTON, SUSSEX

427. CLAYTON, SUSSEX

428. CLEE, LINCOLNSHIRE

429. CLEE, LINCOLNSHIRE

430. COLCHESTER, ESSEX

431. COLCHESTER, ESSEX

432. COLEBY, LINCOLNSHIRE

433. COLEBY, LINCOLNSHIRE

434. COLNEY, NORFOLK

435. COLNEY, NORFOLK

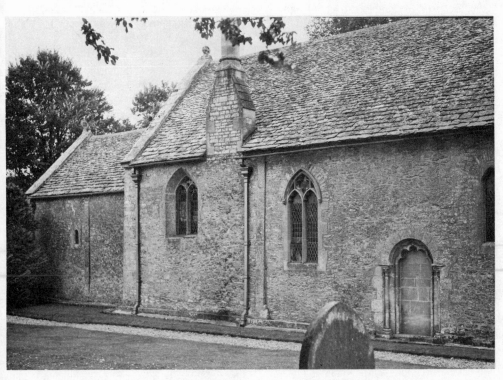

436. COLN ROGERS, GLOUCESTERSHIRE

437. COLTISHALL, NORFOLK

438. CORBRIDGE, NORTHUMBERLAND

439. CORBRIDGE, NORTHUMBERLAND

440. CORHAMPTON, HAMPSHIRE

441. CRANWICH, NORFOLK

442. DARENTH, KENT

443. DEERHURST, GLOUCESTERSHIRE

444. DEERHURST, GLOUCESTERSHIRE

445. DEERHURST, GLOUCESTERSHIRE

446. DEERHURST, GLOUCESTERSHIRE

447. DEERHURST, GLOUCESTERSHIRE

448. DEERHURST, GLOUCESTERSHIRE

449. DIDDLEBURY, SHROPSHIRE

450. DIDDLEBURY, SHROPSHIRE

451. DOVER, KENT

452. DOVER, KENT

453. DUNHAM MAGNA, NORFOLK

454. DUNHAM MAGNA, NORFOLK

455. DUNHAM MAGNA, NORFOLK

456. DUNHAM MAGNA, NORFOLK

457. EARLS BARTON, NORTHAMPTONSHIRE

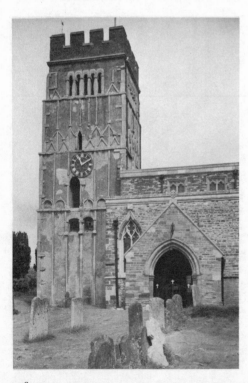

458. EARLS BARTON, NORTHAMPTONSHIRE

459. EDENHAM, LINCOLNSHIRE

460. EDENHAM, LINCOLNSHIRE

461. ELMHAM (NORTH), NORFOLK

462. ELSTED, SUSSEX

463. ESCOMB, COUNTY DURHAM

464. ESCOMB, COUNTY DURHAM

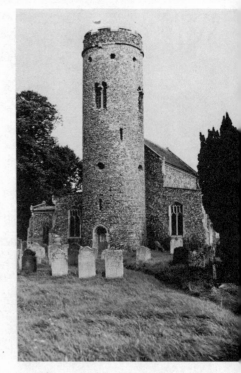

465. FORNCETT ST PETER, NORFOLK

466. FRAMINGHAM EARL, NORFOLK

467. GAYTON THORPE, NORFOLK

468. GEDDINGTON, NORTHAMPTONSHIRE

469. GLENTWORTH, LINCOLNSHIRE

471. GREEN'S NORTON, NORTHAMPTONS}

470. GODALMING, SURREY

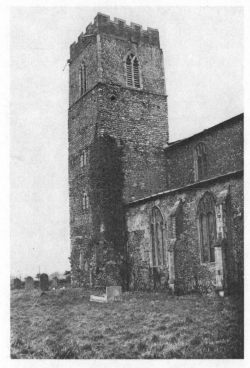

472. GREEN'S NORTON, NORTHAMPTONSHIRE

473. GUESTWICK, NORFOLK

474. GUESTWICK, NORFOLK

475. GUILDFORD, SURREY

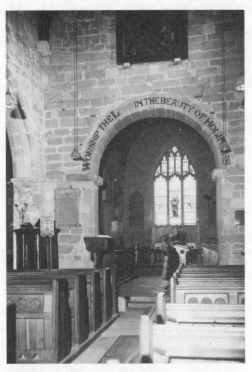

476. HACKNESS, YORKSHIRE (N.R.)

477. HADDISCOE THORPE, NORFOLK

478. HADDISCOE THORPE, NORFOLK

479. HADSTOCK, ESSEX

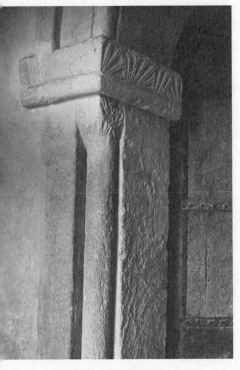

480. HADSTOCK, ESSEX

481. HADSTOCK, ESSEX

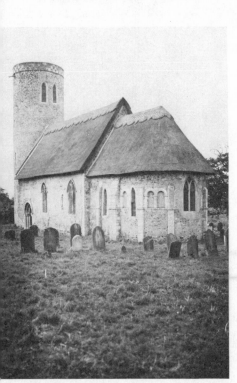

482. HALES, NORFOLK

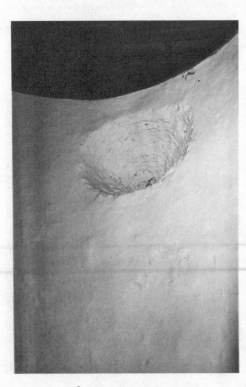

483. HALES, NORFOLK

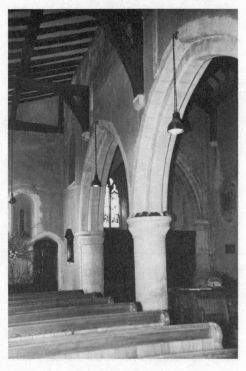

484. HAMBLEDON, HAMPSHIRE

485. HART, COUNTY DURHAM

486. HEAPHAM, LINCOLNSHIRE

487. HEYSHAM, LANCASHIRE

488. HEYSHAM, LANCASHIRE

489. HEYSHAM, LANCASHIRE

490. HOLTON-LE-CLAY, LINCOLNSHIRE

491. HORNBY, YORKSHIRE (N.R.)

492. HOUGH-ON-THE-HILL, LINCOLNSHIRE

493. HOUGHTON (LONG), NORTHUMBERLA

494. HOVINGHAM, YORKSHIRE (N.R.)

495. ICKLETON, CAMBRIDGESHIRE

496. INWORTH, ESSEX

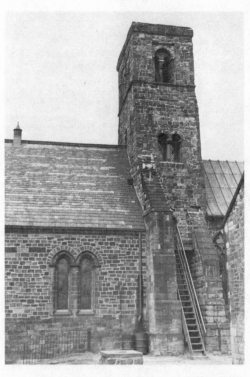

497. JARROW, COUNTY DURHAM

498. JARROW, COUNTY DURHAM

499. JARROW, COUNTY DURHAM

500. JARROW, COUNTY DURHAM

501. KILPECK, HEREFORDSHIRE

502. KINGSDOWN, KENT

503. KIRBY CANE, NORFOLK

504. KIRKDALE, YORKSHIRE (N.R.)

505. KIRKDALE, YORKSHIRE (N.R.)

506. KIRKDALE, YORKSHIRE (N.R.)

507. KIRK HAMMERTON, YORKSHIRE (W.

508. KIRK HAMMERTON, YORKSHIRE (W.R.)

509. KIRK HAMMERTON, YORKSHIRE (W.R.)

510. KIRK HAMMERTON, YORKSHIRE (W.R.)

511. LANGFORD, OXFORDSHIRE

512. LANGFORD, OXFORDSHIRE

513. LANGFORD, OXFORDSHIRE

514. LAUGHTON-EN-LE-MORTHEN,
YORKSHIRE (W.R.)

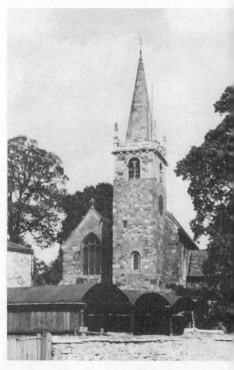

515. LEDSHAM, YORKSHIRE (W.R.)

516. LEDSHAM, YORKSHIRE (W.R.)

517. LEDSHAM, YORKSHIRE (W.R.)

518. LEDSHAM, YORKSHIRE (W.R.)

519. LEICESTER, ST NICHOLAS

520. LEICESTER, ST NICHOLAS

521. LIMPLEY STOKE, WILTSHIRE

522. LINCOLN, ST MARY-LE-WIGFORD

523. LINCOLN, ST PETER-AT-GOWTS

524. LOPHAM (SOUTH), NORFOLK

525. MARKET OVERTON, RUTLAND

526. MARTON, LINCOLNSHIRE

527. MELTON MAGNA, NORFOLK

528. MILBORNE PORT, SOMERSET

529. MISERDEN, GLOUCESTERSHIRE

530. MISERDEN, GLOUCESTERSHIRE

531. MONKWEARMOUTH, COUNTY DURHAM

532. MORLAND, WESTMORLAND

533. NETHERAVON, WILTSHIRE

534. NEWTON-BY-CASTLEACRE, NORFOLK

535. NEWTON-BY-CASTLEACRE, NORFOLK

536. NEWTON-BY-CASTLEACRE, NORFOL

537. NORTH LEIGH, OXFORDSHIRE

538. NORTON, COUNTY DURHAM

539. NORTON, COUNTY DURHAM

540. NORTON, COUNTY DURHAM

541. NORTON, COUNTY DURHAM

542. NORWICH, NORFOLK, ST JULIAN

543. NORWICH, NORFOLK, ST MARTIN-AT-P

544. NOTLEY (WHITE), ESSEX

545. OXFORD, CATHEDRAL CHURCH OF CI

546. OXFORD, ST MICHAEL

547. PAXTON (GREAT), HUNTINGDONSHIRE

548. PAXTON (GREAT), HUNTINGDONSHIRE

549. PAXTON (GREAT), HUNTINGDONSHIRE

550. PENTLOW, ESSEX

551. QUARLEY, HAMPSHIRE

552. QUARLEY, HAMPSHIRE

553. REED, HERTFORDSHIRE

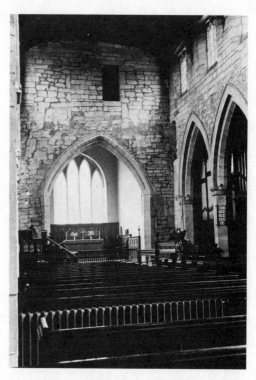

554. REPTON, DERBYSHIRE

555. REPTON, DERBYSHIRE

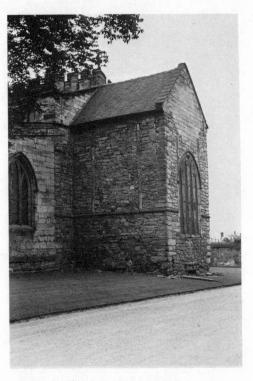

556. REPTON, DERBYSHIRE

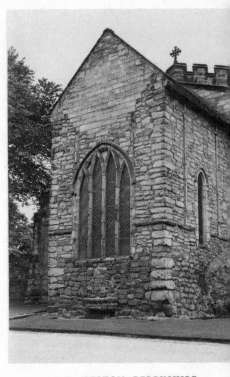

557. REPTON, DERBYSHIRE

558. REPTON, DERBYSHIRE

559. ROCKLAND ALL SAINTS, NORFOLK

560. ROTHWELL, LINCOLNSHIRE

561. ROTHWELL, LINCOLNSHIRE

562. RUSHBURY, SHROPSHIRE

563. RYTHER, YORKSHIRE (W.R.)

564. ST ALBANS, HERTFORDSHIRE, ST STEPHEN

565. ST ALBANS, HERTFORDSHIRE, ST STEPHE

566. SEAHAM, COUNTY DURHAM

567. SELHAM, SUSSEX

568. SELHAM, SUSSEX

569. SELHAM, SUSSEX

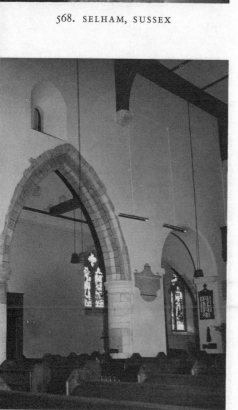

570. SHORNE, KENT

571. SKIPWITH, YORKSHIRE (E.R.)

572. SKIPWITH, YORKSHIRE (E.R.)

573. SKIPWITH, YORKSHIRE (E.R.)

574. SOMERFORD KEYNES, GLOUCESTERSHI

575. STAINDROP, COUNTY DURHAM

576. STAINDROP, COUNTY DURHAM

577. STAINDROP, COUNTY DURHAM

578. STANLEY ST LEONARD, GLOUCESTERSHIRE

579. STANTON-BY-BRIDGE, DERBYSHIRE

580. STANTON LACY, SHROPSHIRE

581. STOPHAM, SUSSEX

582. STOUGHTON, SUSSEX

583. STOUGHTON, SUSSEX

584. STOUGHTON, SUSSEX

585. STOW, LINCOLNSHIRE

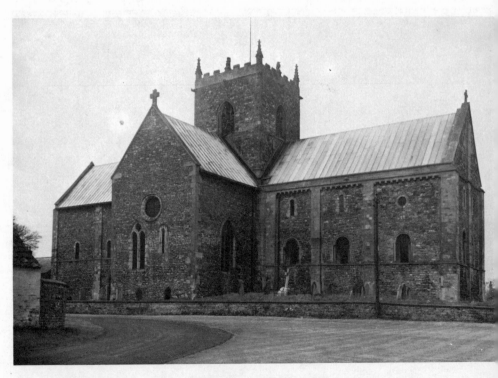

586. STOW, LINCOLNSHIRE

587. STOW, LINCOLNSHIRE

588. STOW, LINCOLNSHIRE

589. STOWE-NINE-CHURCHES,
NORTHAMPTONSHIRE

590. STRETHALL, ESSEX

591. SWANSCOMBE, KENT

593. THORINGTON, SUFFOLK

592. SYSTON, LINCOLNSHIRE

594. THURLBY, LINCOLNSHIRE

595. THURSLEY, SURREY

596. THURSLEY, SURREY

597. TICHBORNE, HAMPSHIRE

598. TITCHFIELD, HAMPSHIRE

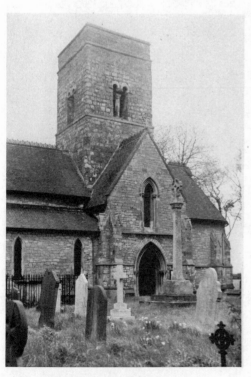

599. WAITHE, LINCOLNSHIRE

600. WALKERN, HERTFORDSHIRE

601. WALKERN, HERTFORDSHIRE

602. WAREHAM, DORSET

604. WARNFORD, HAMPSHIRE

603. (a) WAREHAM, DORSET
(b) and (c) CAREW, PEMBROKESHIRE

606. WESTHAMPNETT, SUSSEX

605. WENDENS AMBO, ESSEX

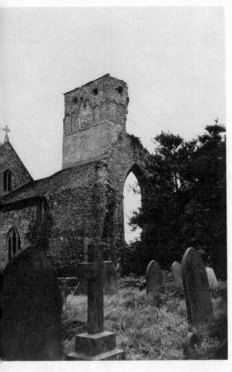

607. WEYBOURNE, NORFOLK

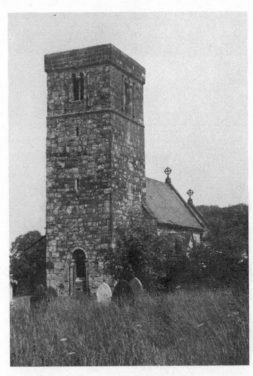

608. WHARRAM-LE-STREET, YORKSHIRE (E.R.)

609. WHITFIELD, KENT

610. WHITTINGHAM, NORTHUMBERLAND

611. WHITTINGHAM, NORTHUMBERLAND

612. WHITTINGHAM, NORTHUMBERLAN

613. WHITTINGHAM, NORTHUMBERLAND

614. WICKHAM, BERKSHIRE

615. WICKMERE, NORFOLK

616. WIGMORE, SHROPSHIRE

617. WILLESBOROUGH, KENT

618. WING, BUCKINGHAMSHIRE

619. WING, BUCKINGHAMSHIRE

620. WING, BUCKINGHAMSHIRE

621. WINSTONE, GLOUCESTERSHIRE

622. WINSTONE, GLOUCESTERSHIRE

623. WINTERBORNE STEEPLETON, DORSET

624. WINTERTON, LINCOLNSHIRE

625. WITTERING, NORTHAMPTONSHIRE

626. WOODSTON, HUNTINGDONSHIRE

627. WOOLBEDING, SUSSEX

628. WOOTTON WAWEN, WARWICKSHIRE

629. WOOTTON WAWEN, WARWICKSHIRE

630. WOOTTON WAWEN, WARWICKSHIRE

631. WORTH, SUSSEX

632. WORTH, SUSSEX

633. WORTH, SUSSEX

634. WORTH, SUSSEX

635. WROXETER, SHROPSHIRE

636. YORK, ST MARY BISHOPHILL JUNIOR

637. YORK, ST MARY BISHOPHILL JUNIOR

638. YORK, ST MARY BISHOPHILL JUNIOR

639. YORK, ST MARY BISHOPHILL SENIOR

640. YORK, ST MARY BISHOPHILL SENIOR

641. YORK, CATHEDRAL CHURCH OF ST PETER

642. YORK, CATHEDRAL CHURCH OF ST PETER

Anglo-Saxon Architecture Volume III

H. M. TAYLOR

In Volume III Dr Taylor discusses and illustrates the individual architectural features of 267 Anglo-Saxon churches, and provides a comprehensive index to all three volumes.

'It must at once be said that this complete presentation of a pre-Romanesque architectural landscape is a remarkable book which has no parallel in the whole literature of Romanesque building-technique in the western world.'   *Kunstchronik* (Munich)

'Unquestionably this is a masterpiece of scholarship, an immense contribution to its subject. Enduring it surely must be, not only as a source book, but equally as an inspiring model of vision and integrity of research.'   *Antiquity*

'The publication of [Taylor's] Vol III is a landmark in Christian Anglo-Saxon studies...a giant step has been taken towards the writing of ecclesiastical architectural history of the Anglo-Saxons. The completion of this fine and indispensable trilogy assures the enduring gratitude and remembrance of all Anglo-Saxonists.'
Archaeological Journal

'Among my most treasured possessions are the two volumes on Anglo-Saxon architecture that Dr and Mrs Taylor published in 1965... I feared mistakenly that my fund of pleasure was exhausted. Not at all. Though Mrs Taylor died in 1965, Dr Taylor has continued his labour of love and now provides a third volume...He has achieved more than one revolution in our understanding of Anglo-Saxon England... I express my gratitude for his incomparable work of scholarship.'
Observer

First published in May 1978   *Available in hard covers only*